THE TRAGEDY OF MARIAM, THE FAIR QUEEN OF JEWRY

*The publisher gratefully acknowledges the
contribution provided by the General Endowment Fund of
the Associates of the University of California Press.*

Elizabeth Cary, Lady Falkland

———

THE TRAGEDY OF MARIAM
THE FAIR QUEEN OF JEWRY

WITH

The Lady Falkland: Her Life
BY ONE OF HER DAUGHTERS

EDITED BY
Barry Weller
AND
Margaret W. Ferguson

UNIVERSITY OF CALIFORNIA PRESS   BERKELEY   LOS ANGELES   LONDON

University of California Press
Berkeley and Los Angeles, California

University of California Press, Ltd.
London, England

1994 by
The Regents of the University of California

Library of Congress Cataloging-in-Publication Data

Cary, Elizabeth, Lady, 1585 or 6–1639
The tragedy of Mariam, the fair queen of Jewry /
Elizabeth Cary, Lady Falkland. With, The Lady
Falkland : her life / by one of her daughters ;
edited by Barry Weller and Margaret W. Ferguson.
    p.   cm.
Includes bibliographical references.
ISBN 0-520-07967-1 (alk. paper).—ISBN 0-520-
07969-8 (pbk. : alk. paper)
1. Mariamne, consort of Herod I, King of Judea, ca.
57–ca. 29 B.C.—Drama.   2. Herod I, King of Judea,
73–4 B.C.—Drama.   3. Cary, Elizabeth, Lady, 1585 or
6–1639—Biography.   4. Dramatists, English—Early
modern, 1500–1700—Biography.   5. Women and
literature—England—History—17th century.
I. Weller, Barry, 1945–.   II. Ferguson, Margaret W.,
1948– .   III. Title.   IV. Title: Lady Falkland.
PR2499.F3T7   1994
822 PR' .3—dc20

92-36294
CIP

Printed in the United States of America
9 8 7 6 5 4 3 2 1

To our mothers, Mollie Weller and Mary Anne Ferguson

CONTENTS

PREFACE

Nurtured in many classrooms and jointly edited by colleagues who have been reading—and arguing—about Renaissance drama since their undergraduate years at Cornell University and their graduate years in Yale's Comparative Literature Department, this volume is most definitely a collective production. The editors of course take all responsibility for mistakes, but there are far fewer of those than there might have been had we not over the years had help with the project from so many colleagues and students—and had we not been trained in interpretation and argumentation by a series of fine teachers, among whom two deserve special thanks: Neil Hertz and Thomas Greene. For conversations that enriched and challenged our thinking about Renaissance women's writing and many other matters, we are grateful to Janet Adelman, Geoffrey Aggeler, Jean and Stephen Carr, Robert L. Caserio, Norman Council, Carla Freccero, Suzanne Gossett, Stephen Greenblatt, John Guillory, Richard Halpern, Jean Howard, Ann Jones, Rachel Jacoff, David Kastan, Karen Lawrence, Karen Newman, Mary Nyquist, Stephen Orgel, Jacqueline Osherow, Barbara Packer, Patricia Parker, Mary Poovey, Maureen Quilligan, Peter Stallybrass, Tom Stillinger, Lucy and Phil Tenenbaum, Nancy Vickers, Valerie Wayne, and Jennifer Wicke.

The idea for this volume arose in 1985, when one of the editors was reading madly in Yale's Beinecke Library in search of materials for a new undergraduate course she was planning on Renaissance women writers.

She discovered *The Tragedie of Mariam* in its original 1613 edition—a beautiful red-leather bound quarto—and found the play itself mesmerizing. So, in due course, did her students, who read the text in photocopies of the 1914 Malone Society reprint of the 1613 edition. A number of those students have since gone on to do graduate work in Renaissance literature, and it seems appropriate that this new edition of *Mariam*, fostered in its early stages by that extraordinary Yale seminar's discussion of textual and interpretive questions pertaining to the (then little-read) play, should be appearing in print in time for some members of that class to use it in teaching their own courses on Renaissance women writers, on biographical narratives, and on Renaissance drama. Such courses are increasingly being reconfigured by the new scholarship on women, to which this volume seeks to contribute. Three members of that Yale senior seminar, Bianca Calabresi, Molly Whalen, and Pam Erens, gave especially important early inspiration to this volume. Warm thanks also go to those graduate and undergraduate students at Columbia University, the University of California at Berkeley, the University of Utah, and the University of Colorado at Boulder who read *Mariam* with the editors and taught them much of what they know about Elizabeth Cary and her play. In the spring of 1990, graduate students in a class at the University of Colorado taught by R L Widmann read an early draft of this edition's annotations on *Mariam*; we thank that class for its help and, in particular, Laura Wilson, Amy Dilworth, and R L Widmann for their lucid written comments.

Like Cary's play, this book appears in print only after circulating in manuscript for several years; and we owe a debt even greater than our notes suggest to numerous scholars whose own writing about Cary is still circulating in manuscript as we go to press. Among those whose ideas we have most benefited from are Martha Slowe, Marta Straznicky, Betty Travitsky, Donald Foster, Elaine Beilin, Margaret Arnold, and Skiles Howard, all of whom wrote provocative papers on *Mariam* or closely related topics for a special session of the 1990 meeting of the Shakespeare Society of America, a session on Renaissance women writers and readers chaired by Margaret Ferguson and Ann Rosalind Jones. Writing on topics less closely related to this edition, other members of that SAA seminar also contributed substantially to the thinking behind this edition's notes and introduction: we thank them warmly. We also thank Emily

Detmer for writing to us about her thoughts on the play about Edward II possibly by Cary; she is currently working on a critical edition of that text. Unpublished papers on aspects of *Mariam* by James Fitzmaurice, Boyd Berry, Kristina Brooks, and Jonas Barish have also enriched our thinking and are listed in our bibliography for those readers who work, as many feminist scholars do perforce, in the border territory between oral discussion and (often long-delayed) printing of texts.

We owe a special debt to Carol Neely, Leah Marcus, Jonathan Goldberg, and Michael Rudick for reading drafts of the entire text of our volume and responding with generous critiques. Although we have not been able to incorporate all of their suggestions (which sometimes ran counter to each other), we have benefited immensely from their meticulous attention both to details of our work and to its general conception. We received valuable commentary on various drafts of the introduction from David Kastan, Mary Poovey, David Simpson, Jenny Hill, and R L Widmann. Jenny Hill served in addition as an excellent research assistant for both Margaret Ferguson and Barry Weller. Charles Wilcox, Yumna Siddiqi, and Pam Erens did an equally fine job for Margaret Ferguson. Donald Foster shared his extensive knowledge of Cary's life and work with us in a series of witty and informative letters. Elaine Beilin, Joseph Loewenstein, David Kastan, Mary Nyquist, Colin MacCabe, Mary Poovey, and David Simpson commented incisively on an essay on Cary by Margaret Ferguson that was published in *Tradition and the Talents of Women* (ed. Florence Howe, University of Illinois Press, 1991). Many of the ideas worked out in that essay have been incorporated into the introduction to the present volume, and we thank the colleagues and students who commented not only on written versions of that essay but also on those presented in lecture form at the Universities of Toronto, Pittsburgh, and Utah; at Bryn Mawr College; and at Yale, Princeton, McGill, Stanford, and the Johns Hopkins Universities.

We are also grateful to Mary Anne Ferguson, David Kastan, Mary Beth Rose, Michael Rudick, Thomas Tanselle, Elizabeth Welles, and Molly Whalen for generous help with aspects of our editorial work. M. Pierre Coustillas and Abbé G. Mathon responded swiftly to inquiries pertaining to the manuscript of the *Life* of Cary; and M. Henri Guy facilitated our work on that manuscript both by sending us a photocopy of it and by welcoming Barry Weller to study the original MS in the Archives of the Département du Nord in Lille, France. In Lille Mme. Isabelle Aristide and M. René Labins were particularly helpful, enabling access to the Archives even though they were officially closed for repairs. Mr. Paul R. Quarrie of the Eton College Library and Mrs. Lesley Le Claire of the Worcester College Library in Oxford not only made their libraries' copies of the 1613 *Mariam* available but also provided their bibliographical and historical expertise. We are also grateful to the staffs of the Houghton Rare Book Library (Harvard University); the Boston Public Library; the New York Public Library; Butler Library at Columbia University; Yale University's Beinecke Library and Elizabethan Club; the British Library; the National Art Library at the Victoria and Albert Museum; the National Library of Scotland; the Newberry Library; and the Folger Shakespeare Library.

Generous fellowship support from the National Endowment for the Humanities and the Guggenheim Memorial Foundation gave Margaret Ferguson time to work on this project; and research support from the University of Utah Research Committee and Charles Middleton, Dean of Arts and Sciences at the University of Colorado, helped defray many of the costs of our labor. Anne Lyons of the University of Colorado English Department provided much tactical and moral support for Margaret Ferguson, as did Mary Looser and Toula Leventis of the University of Utah English Department for Barry Weller. David Simpson did more than his share of cooking, childcare, and thinking during the years that Margaret Ferguson worked on this book: she thanks him warmly for everything. Barry Weller thanks Kris Jacobson and Julio Caserio for allowing him to pursue research in France and Great Britain without anxiety about obligations he had left behind.

We're extremely grateful for the expert and patient advice of our editors at the University of California Press: Margaret Denney, Doris Kretschmer, Scott Norton, and Rose Vekony.

Finally, but also, of course, from the start, we want to thank our mothers, Mollie Weller and Mary Anne Ferguson; to them we dedicate this book by and about an extraordinary seventeenth-century writer and mother.

Boulder, Colorado, and Salt Lake City, Utah
July 1992

INTRODUCTION

Elizabeth Tanfield Cary wrote *The Tragedy of Mariam* (1613), the first original play by a woman to be published in England.[1] She was also the first English woman writer to be memorialized in a biography, *The Lady Falkland: Her Life*, written by one of her daughters (probably between 1643 and 1650) and included, along with *Mariam*, in the present volume. The manuscript of the *Life*, which is preserved in the Archives of the Département du Nord in Lille, France [MS. A.D.N.xx.(ca. 1655)], remained unpublished until 1861, when a heavily and not always reliably edited version was printed in London.

The author of the *Life* went to some trouble to shroud her identity; she was certainly one of the four of Elizabeth Cary's daughters—Anne, Elizabeth, Lucy, and Mary—who became nuns in the Benedictine Convent at Cambray. Georgiana Fullerton's 1883 biography of Lady Falkland first identified the author of the *Life* as Anne, Elizabeth Cary's fourth child, who was born in 1615 and received into the convent in 1639 under the name of Clementia. Fullerton's biography, however, is often unreliable and offers no grounds for this attribution. Donald Foster nonetheless makes a resourceful case for Anne's authorship on internal grounds, and his research has recently led him to other manuscripts arguably in Anne's hand, including "the most authoritative extant MS of the *Revelation* of Julian of Norwich."[2] Our reading of the available evidence brings us to less certain conclusions: while Anne indeed seems a likely author, so does her younger sister Lucy, born in 1619 and received into the same convent in 1638 under the name of Magdalena.[3]

Thanks largely to this remarkable biography, which is discussed in more detail in the final section of this introduction, we know more about Elizabeth Cary's life than we do about Shakespeare's. Yet many facts remain obscure, and some aspects of Cary's literary career are simply not mentioned in the *Life*. Even the information it does present cannot always be taken at face value, for the author has both filial and theological investments in the representation of her mother.[4] Clearly designed to stress Cary's trials and triumphs as an "exemplary" subject of Catholic conversion, the *Life* nonetheless presents a rhetorically subtle and sometimes critical account not only of its prime subject but also of her Protestant husband, the author's difficult but by no means wholly unsympathetic father, Sir Henry Cary, viscount of Falkland. The tone of the *Life* is frequently surprising, as when the biographer comments that her mother "always much esteemed and loved order ⟨when she remembered there was such a thing⟩." The acid terminal phrase is marked for deletion, but its irony is by no means uncharacteristic of the narrative. And the author herself becomes a character, albeit a teasingly self-effacing one, in various parts of her narrative, including those episodes that outline the battle between Elizabeth and Henry Cary—and subsequently between Elizabeth and her eldest son, Lucius—for the love and religious faith of several of the younger Cary children.[5] Displaying a "dry intelligence" that leads Donald Stauffer to praise her work as "distinctive and original," the biographer warrants attention as an author in her own right.[6] Our primary focus, however, is on Elizabeth Cary as the author of *The Tragedy of Mariam*, a work not mentioned in the biography.

Our introduction, which begins by summarizing parts of the complex story told by the *Life*, supplements that text by drawing on material from later biographies of Elizabeth Cary and her son Lucius (notably by Kenneth Murdock and Kurt Weber, respectively), on references to Cary and to members of her family in letters[7] and other contemporary documents, and on writings by a number of modern scholars who have, in recent years, begun to notice Cary's texts and reevaluate her place in literary history.

ELIZABETH CARY'S LIFE AND WORKS

She was born, according to the *Life*, in "1585 or 6," the only child of Lawrence Tanfield, a wealthy Oxfordshire lawyer, and his wife, Elizabeth Symondes. Exhibiting a precocious intelligence, Elizabeth Tanfield not only learned to read "very soon and loved it much," but also mastered "without a teacher" French, Spanish, Italian, Latin, and Hebrew; as a girl she translated Seneca's *Epistles*. The *Life* also reports that she adroitly proved the innocence of an old woman being tried for witchcraft before Tanfield, who had become a judge. Elizabeth is also said to have read and disputed Calvin's *Institutes* at age twelve, a detail arguably designed to recall Christ's disputations in the temple at the same age.

Her mother was evidently strict: the *Life* describes Elizabeth kneeling to address Lady Tanfield and adds that she was "never kind" to her daughter. Forbidden to read at night, Elizabeth bribed the servants for candles (her debts to the servants were paid at the time of her marriage). The *Dictionary of National Biography* entry on Tanfield says that his wife was accused of taking bribes to influence her husband's cases and cites the complaints of her neighbors in Great Tew that "she saith that we are more worthy to be ground to powder than to have any favour shewed to us" (*DNB* 19:357). It seems likely that she considered herself of higher social standing than her neighbors and her husband; he, as the son of a "younger brother," received nothing when his father died except the means for a legal education, whereas she was the daughter of Giles Symondes, of Clay, Norfolk, by Catherine, daughter of Sir Anthony Lee, Knight of the Garter. The *Life* also indicates social tensions within the Tanfield household: Elizabeth Symondes objected, for instance, to her husband's decision "to provide for himself by following his profession," relying on his "own industry." Tensions stemming from differences in social status were present not only in the marriage of Cary's parents but also in her own, and they may well be refracted in Cary's dramatic representation of Mariam's conflicts with in-laws she considers "lower" than herself.

Although her mother might not have approved of Elizabeth's devotion to books, it was evidently admired—or considered a possible source of patronage—by others. In 1597, Michael Drayton dedicated two of the poems in his *Englands Heroicall Epistles* to Elizabeth and praised her wisdom, reading, and skill in languages. Later, in 1624, Richard Belling would dedicate to her the sixth book of his continuation of Sidney's *Arcadia*. She herself apparently thought that her great-uncle, Sir Henry Lee, could appreciate her talents, since she dedicated to him, as a "humble presente, the fruites and endeavours" of her "younge and tender yeares," her translation of Abraham Ortelius's *Le Miroir du Monde*.[8] In translating that book about geography (which includes descriptions of China, India, "Turkie," and America), she anticipates the fascination with "other worlds" displayed by such later English women writers as Margaret Cavendish, duchess of Newcastle, who published her *Description of a New World, Called the Blazing World*, in 1666, and Aphra Behn, who translated Fontenelle's *Discovery of New Worlds* in 1688, the same year she published her novella *Oroonoko*, based on her youthful visit to South America.

In the fall of 1602, at the age of about seventeen, Elizabeth was married to Sir Henry Cary, who became viscount of Falkland in 1620.[9] Nancy Cotton Pearse underscores the importance of marriage as an avenue of social mobility in the Tudor-Stuart era by remarking that Elizabeth's marriage to Henry "raised Tanfield from the upper middle class into the gentry [he was knighted in 1604 and became Chief Baron of the Exchequer in 1607], and the Tanfield fortune raised Henry Cary from the gentry into the peerage."[10] Thus, through the industry his wife seems to have scorned, Tanfield acquired the fortune that attracted a noble husband for his daughter. The author of the *Life* says that Sir Henry married his wife "only for [her] being an heir, for he had no acquaintance with her (she scarce ever having spoken to him) and she was nothing handsome." Hardly a romantic beginning to a union that was to prove stormy. Possibly unconsummated during its early years, when Henry was often abroad or at court, the marriage eventually produced eleven children "born alive," nine of whom survived to adulthood. It also produced serious conflicts: Elizabeth and Henry lived apart after 1626, fighting bitterly and publicly over religion and money.

Though Elizabeth evidently tried for years to bend her will to her husband's—he being "very absolute," according to the *Life*—she had also, since the early years of her marriage, been following her own will by pursuing her interest in Roman Catholicism. Soon after her marriage, she read Hooker's *Ecclesiastical Polity*, a "classic defense" of the Anglican Church; but "just as Calvin's logic had failed to convince, so Hooker's sweet reasonableness did not persuade."[11] She read the early church fathers and was evidently impressed by the favorable remarks of her husband's brother about Catholicism when he returned from a visit to Italy; she refused to attend Anglican services "for weeks at a time."[12] She sought theological advice from Richard Neale, dean of Westminster, and the *Life* reports that at his house she met "many of the learnedest . . . divines." While she was exploring her doubts and seeking to reconcile her "lawful" duty to the Church of England and her Protestant husband with her conviction that "to be in the Roman Church were infinitely better and securer" than to remain an Anglican, her husband was pursuing a courtier's career. Eventually, he became a protégé of the earl of Buckingham, King James's notorious favorite.

During her first year as Sir Henry's wife, Elizabeth apparently lived at home while her husband lived at court and at his parents' home in Hertfordshire. By 1604 he had left England for Holland, where he served as a soldier in the Protestant wars against Spain; in 1605 he was captured and imprisoned for three years while his father was raising ransom money. Though Henry did not, according to the *Life*, "care for his wife," he was sufficiently concerned with her welfare to want her to stay with her own family rather than with his evidently irascible mother, Dame Katherine, Lady Paget. That lady's wishes, however, soon prevailed, and Elizabeth moved to the house of one who "loved much to be humored." Failing to please Lady Paget, Elizabeth was locked in her room and subsequently, when her mother-in-law saw she enjoyed reading, denied books.

Kurt Weber, Lucius Cary's biographer, doubts that Elizabeth was as "caged" as her daughter's narrative suggests; he argues, indeed, that it was during these years of Sir Henry's absence that the still-childless Elizabeth was most likely to have participated in the countess of Pembroke's literary circle and there to have acquired an interest in Senecan drama. Barring the discovery of new evidence, we cannot ascertain the details of Elizabeth's life at this period, but it is clear that sometime between 1603 and 1610 she wrote several literary works. The *Life* mentions a verse life of Tamburlaine, now lost, as a work composed for her "private recreation." The *Life*, however, nowhere mentions *The Tragedy of Mariam*, the play that Cary surely wrote after her marriage and probably before the birth of her first child, Catherine, in 1609.[13] Although *Mariam* was published in 1613 in a single edition and was never performed onstage, the play had evidently circulated for some years in manuscript: it might have been known to Shakespeare when he wrote *Othello* (1607) and was very likely known to the anonymous author of *The Second Maiden's Tragedy*, licensed by the Stationers' Register on 31 October 1611. The former play's tragic hero resembles Cary's Herod at several key moments, as we shall argue later, and the latter play's tyrannical king not only resembles Cary's portrait of the passionately obsessed King Herod but also alludes explicitly to a literary source for the sentiment: "I once read of a Herod whose affection / pursued a virgin's love, as I did thine," says the king (lines 1856–57).[14]

Cary's play was definitely known to Sir John Davies before 1612.[15] In the dedicatory letter to *The Muses Sacrifice* (1612) Davies, who evidently served as one of Cary's childhood tutors, refers proudly to his erstwhile "Pupill's" plays—specifically, a drama set in Palestine (*Mariam*) and another play set "in Syracuse," now lost. (The dedicatory verses to *Mariam* also refer to this earlier play.) Davies urges not only Cary but also two other noblewomen of letters, Lucy, countess of Bedford, and Mary, countess of Pembroke, to publish their writings so posterity will believe that members of "the weaker Sexe" can write with strength.

Whether or not Davies's poem encouraged Cary to permit the publication of her play, she no doubt shared to some extent a view articulated by Davies and held by many prominent persons in Tudor-Stuart England that the emerging institution of publishing was an unsuitable arena for aristocrats in general and for noble ladies in particular. The "Presse," remarks Davies in the very poem ostensibly urging Cary to publish her plays, is frequented by "abject Rimers" and other "base" types.[16] The *Life* includes a cryptic mention of some early work by Cary being "stolen" for publication but "called in" by the author. Whatever this text was—Elaine Beilin has suggested identifying it with the dedicatory sonnet to *Mariam* that appears in only two known copies of the play—this passage in the biography testifies to the psychological and cultural obstacles that stood between women like Cary and the role of "public" author. English Renaissance women were to be "chaste, silent, and obedient," according to a formula repeated in numerous sermons, conduct books, and treatises on female education. Although *Mariam* explicitly interrogates, even challenges, this image of normative womanhood, Cary's life story dramatizes the many impediments that even a socially privileged Renaissance wife encountered when she attempted to assume the role of author.

In 1622, through Buckingham's good offices, Falkland received the viceregency of Ireland, a post in which it must have been particularly difficult to have a wife with Catholic sympathies, since a large part of his official duties consisted of enforcing conformity to Anglican ecclesiastical authority. Although he could not have assumed this post without her help—she mortgaged a jointure settled on her by her father so her husband could move to Dublin—he later complained that she had cost him more than he had ever gotten from her.[17] Her charitable expenditures might have particularly irritated him. While her son Patrick was still nursing, she undertook a large project for training Irish children in trades. The project met with various disasters, including fire and water spoilage in her workhouse. She later interpreted these setbacks as punishments from God for her children's attendance at Anglican services, but others "thought it rather that she was better at contriving than executing" (*Life*, 198). In any event, her husband decided that she should return to England in 1625, ostensibly to attend the birth of their first grandchild and possibly to persuade those at court "to give him more than he had been able to get by his letters."[18] The grandchild died, and so did the mother, Lady Home, the latter, according to the *Life*, in Elizabeth Cary's arms.

In April of 1626, within a year of his wife's departure for England, Lord Falkland wrote to a friend, Lord Conway, about her inadequacies as a diplomat: "I conceive women to be no fit solicitors of state affairs."[19] By December of the same year, he was outraged at the news that she had publicly converted to Catholicism (although the conversion became public more through the offices of one of Elizabeth Cary's so-called friends, Lady Denbigh, than through her own decision). Insisting that she must be sent back to her mother, who might yet save her from apostasy, he retrospectively pronounced the marriage a bad one, distancing himself from the politically embarrassing mate, "whom now I may say I have long unhappily called wife."[20] In letters written after the separation, he complained to the king and members of the Privy Council about her many faults (among them a refusal to live "quietly"); she complained, equally bitterly, of the poverty she suffered through Henry's failure to send her money. The *Life* presents Elizabeth Cary as more patient and long-suffering during this period than do other contemporary documents, including her own letters. The *Life* also suggests a partial reconciliation at the time of Falkland's death in 1633 (Elizabeth attended his sickbed, and their daughter hopefully but probably inaccurately surmises that Elizabeth led him back to Catholicism); but there is no doubt, even for the daughter-biographer, that the Cary-Tanfield union was not a marriage of true minds.

According to Henry, Elizabeth was disinherited by her father because of her conversion, but both her daughter's and Murdock's biographies suggest that Tanfield was perhaps even more irritated by her mortgaging of her jointure for her profligate husband than by her turn to Rome.[21] Edward Hyde, earl of Clarendon, writes that Sir Henry eventually "wasted a full fortune" in Ireland and at court, where his Irish services were little appreciated.[22] Clarendon also reports that both Sir Henry and his wife were discontented at being passed over in Tanfield's will, which left his money and lands in trust to Lady Tanfield for his eldest grandson, Lucius Cary, who was Clarendon's dear friend and, until recently, much better known than his mother.

Lucius evidently inherited some of her skill at languages (he taught himself Greek as an adult) and her deep interest in theological questions. His two houses near Oxford, stocked with books, became centers for relatively liberal discussions of religion. Among the many regular guests were the Protestant writer William Chillingworth and a number of Catholic divines introduced to Lucius by his mother. An eloquent defender of religious toleration, Lucius leaned toward conversion for some time but eventually resisted his mother's pressure. After Lady Falkland in 1636 boldly executed a plot to kidnap her two youngest sons, Patrick and Henry, from Lucius's house and what she felt to be Chillingworth's noxious influence, Lucius and his mother maintained only distant relations. Clarendon even suggests a causal connection between Elizabeth Cary's "rescue" of her youngest sons and Lucius's composition of treatises arguing, among other things, against the infallibility of the Roman Church. Although the main arguments of these tracts had probably been in Lucius's mind for some time, Clarendon, followed by Lucius's modern biographer, Weber, sees the "theft" of the boys as catalyzing a distinct turn in Lucius's tolerationist views: his "charity" toward Roman Catholics,

Clarendon writes, "was much lessened, and any correspondence with them quite declined, when, by sinister arts, they had corrupted his two younger brothers . . . and transported them beyond seas, and perverted his sisters: upon which occasion he writ two large discourses against the principal positions of that religion."[23] To Clarendon's regret, the two "discourses" in question, *A Discourse of Infallibility* and *The Lord Falklands Reply*, were not published during Lucius's lifetime; but the former, which was printed in five editions during the twenty years after his death, was certainly read in manuscript by Catholics and was answered by one of them, according to Weber, "through the Dowager Lady Falkland's mediation."[24] In his young manhood, Lucius was an avid admirer of Ben Jonson and was immortalized by that poet in his ode *To the Immortal Memory and Friendship of That Noble Pair, Sir Lucius Cary and Sir H. Morison.* He later became secretary of state for Charles I and died at the age of thirty-four in one of the first battles of the Civil War.[25]

After he came into his handsome fortune upon his grandmother's death in 1629, Lucius attempted to help both of his parents, but his mother took little and lived on less than two hundred pounds a year until her death in 1639. According to her daughter, she gave away much of what she had. Sir Henry too died poor, refusing to take any gifts from a son who had crossed his will as boldly, it turned out, as Elizabeth had: in 1630, Lucius married Lettice, the dowerless sister of his friend Henry Morison. The marriage, virtually an elopement, destroyed Lord Falkland's hope of recouping his fortunes—once again—through the marriage market.[26] Lucius remained a "good son," according to the *Life*, but that sisterly judgment is somewhat qualified by the *Life's* lengthy demonstration of how and why Lucius's friendship with Chillingworth soured his relations with his mother. Nonetheless, he again attempted to help her when in 1635 she requested that he remove his three youngest sisters from her care because she was too ill and poor to provide for them. The author of the *Life* (almost certainly one of these daughters, quite possibly Anne, who is described in this part of the biography as willfully loving to "go much abroad and to court") evinces considerable chagrin at her mother's having fallen into such a sorry state without her children's knowledge: "having used all means possible for the maintaining of her family" (that is, her household, which was "daily increasing" through

Elizabeth's habit of charity), "she was brought to the last extremity." Her state, however, was "so concealed from her children that they were the last to know it."

Recovering from this illness, with her household "discharged by her son," she proceeded to give "over clean all those entangling businesses in which she had dealt and by which she had always been a loser." The author of the *Life* presents this period as one of gradual withdrawal from "worldly distractions" and implies a parallel between the mother and the four daughters who will soon relinquish the world for a convent in France. Before Elizabeth died, she had seen six of her children safely converted to Catholicism and living in France, "out of the danger living amongst their Protestant friends might have put them into." Among these converts was the author of the *Life*, who was absent from her mother's deathbed but who clearly took comfort from the attending priest's report that she "died without any agony quietly as a child, being wholly spent by her disease ['a cough of the lungs'], the   day of October, the year of our Lord 1639, being three- or four-and-fifty year old." During her last months, Elizabeth was working, at a priest's suggestion, on a translation of a "part of Blosius" (the Flemish mystic Louis de Blois) that allowed her to renew "somewhat her Hebrew, and her Latin."

This translation, until recently considered lost, evidently exists in a manuscript (Colwich Abbey MS 36) which Donald Foster has examined and believes to be a copy of Elizabeth's translation in Anne Cary's hand. Foster has also recently discovered a funeral elegy on the duke of Buckingham that seems to have been written by Elizabeth Cary; the first six lines of the fifty-line poem "were widely circulated in seventeenth-century manuscripts," according to Foster, "the least corrupt of which is British Library MS Egerton 2725, fol. 60r ('An Epitaph upon the death of the Duke of Buckingham by the Countesse of Faulkland')."[27] Perhaps the elegy was among the "innumerable slight things in verse" that Elizabeth's Catholic biographer simultaneously points to and effaces. The *Life* also mentions Elizabeth Cary's writing—at an unspecified period—numerous verse biographies of female saints and hymns to the Virgin which are now lost (but which may, of course, resurface through modern scholarly work on women authors).

Many of these devotional works—and some secular ones, too—probably date from the years after Elizabeth's separation from her husband, when she apparently had more opportunity to write, even though during the early part of this period she was preoccupied with efforts to win financial support from her husband and to resist his order that she be "restrained unto the custody of her mother."[28] Refusing to go to her mother's house in the country (and elaborately petitioning the king for support in her rebellious course)[29] she lived in a cottage in London, attended only by one servant, Bessie Poulter, who had converted to Catholicism with her mistress.

In 1630, Elizabeth published a translation of the French Catholic Jacques Davy du Perron's *Réplique à la response du sérénissime roy de la Grand Bretagne* (1620), a polemical response to an attack on his work by King James I. Her translation, *The Reply of the Most Illustrious Cardinall of Perron*, which was printed at Douay and smuggled into England, was suppressed by Archbishop Abbot; only a few copies of the impression escaped burning. Ironically, this translation of a reply to James's attack on Catholic doctrine is dedicated to Henrietta Maria, the troublesomely Catholic wife of James's son Charles. Cary thus characteristically places religious truth (as she sees it) above tactful respect for marital harmony. She praises the queen for being "a woeman, though farr above other woemen, therefore fittest to protect a woeman's worke"; and, in her Epistle to the Reader, she identifies herself "as a Catholic and a Woman: the first serves for mine honor, and the second, for my excuse." Despite the stereotypical apology for the intellectual weakness of her sex ("if the worke be but meanely done, it is noe wonder, for my Sexe can raise noe great expectation of anye thing that shall come from me"), Cary offers readers a remarkably atypical deflation of another convention about normative femininity, and indeed about publication in general: "I will not," she insists, "make use of that worne-out forme of saying I printed it against my will, mooved by the importunitie of Friends; I was mooved to it by my beleefe that it might make those English that understand not French, whereof there are many even in our universities, reade Perron."[30]

With this sly glance at the pretensions of English university education (reserved, of course, for men), Cary comes closer than she does in any other extant text to staking a claim for female intellectual labor. But the boldness of her claim may well be licensed by the fact that she is appearing here not as an original author but rather as a humble translator serving a male theological authority. Translation itself had been personified as a "female" phenomenon by John Florio in the preface to his English version of Montaigne's *Essays*.

She certainly chose to hide her identity if she wrote or substantially revised either of two texts about Edward II that are now often ascribed to her, albeit by critics who hold widely varying views about the relation between the two quite different versions of the work, both published many years after her death. It remains, in our view, an open question whether she wrote the biographical narrative that is described as follows on the title page of its first edition, published in folio (in London, by J.C. for C. Harper, S. Crouch, and T. Fox) in 1680: *The History of the Life, Reign, and Death of Edward II. King of England, and Lord of Ireland. With the Rise and Fall of his Great Favourites, Gaveston and the Spencers. Written by E. F. in the year 1627, and printed verbatim from the Original.*[31] It is equally difficult to know whether she wrote a substantially shorter version of the narrative published in octavo (London: Playford, 1680)—a version which is often simply conflated with the folio text by modern critics who refer to Cary's authorship of *Edward II.* The title page of the shorter version lacks the initials "E.F.," a prime piece of evidence for those who think Cary wrote the folio version; but the shorter text offers instead a printer's claim, accepted uncritically by many modern scholars, that this text was found among *Henry* Falkland's papers and might therefore have been written by him: *The History of the Most Unfortunate Prince King Edward II. With Choice Political Observations on Him and his Unhappy Favourites, Gaveston & Spencer. Containing some rare passages of those Times, not found in other historians. Found among the papers of, and (supposed to be) Writ by, the Right Honourable Henry Viscount Faulkland, Sometime Lord Deputy of Ireland.*[32]

In 1935, Donald Stauffer argued that Elizabeth Cary was the true author of the folio *Edward*, which had generally been ascribed to Henry Falkland, evidently on the basis of its relation to the octavo version said by its printer to have been found among Falkland's papers; but the folio had also been ascribed (by a nineteenth-century cataloguer at the British Museum) to one "Edward Fannant," of whom no trace exists. Stauffer compares a passage from the folio with its octavo counterpart and concludes that the latter, in prose, reads like a "compression of the [former's] longer scene,"[33] an abridgment probably made by the printer in 1680. Though there exists "no proof positive" that the octavo is not the original text of which the folio is an elaboration, Stauffer thinks this "unlikely";[34] some modern critics have disagreed with this latter opinion. His basic view that Elizabeth Cary wrote the folio version is shared by a number of recent critics, among them Donald Foster, Tina Krontiris, Barbara Lewalski, and Isobel Grundy. These critics, however, hold substantially different views on the relation between the two versions, differences that testify to unresolved problems in the evidence for Elizabeth Cary's authorship of one or both versions of *Edward II.*

Krontiris's feminist reading of *Edward* assumes that Stauffer has "proved" Cary's authorship of the text(s) and follows his view that the octavo "condenses" (and hence presumably postdates) the folio.[35] She refers mainly to the latter text to illustrate her argument that the work displays Cary's sympathies for Edward's Queen Isabel.[36] Krontiris also assumes that there was a single "original manuscript" from which the printers of both the folio and octavo worked—and which neither of the printers read very carefully.[37] Lewalski also follows Stauffer in reading the octavo as an "abridgment" of the folio, but she differs from both Stauffer and Krontiris in seeing the abridgment—the only text directly linked to any of the Falklands—as wholly or partly written long after the Falklands' death with a topical allegory "clearly devised to comment on the Exclusion Crisis (1679–81)," which occurred when critics of King Charles II's Catholic sympathies wished him to set aside his definitively Catholic son, James, from the succession in favor of his illegitimate son, the duke of Monmouth. Lewalski also notes that the preface by the printer, John Playford, underscores the text's "relevance to present occasions."[38] As for the printer's attribution of the octavo to Henry Falkland, Lewalski speculates that it "is probably based on the discovery of the longer version among Falkland's papers."[39] There is, however, no corroborating evidence that the longer version was actually found among Falkland's papers.

Betty Travitsky, in contrast to Stauffer, Krontiris, and Lewalski, believes that the octavo is Cary's original text and the folio is her later poetic elaboration of it.[40] Donald Foster shares Travitsky's view that the octavo is the earlier text but, unlike Travitsky, he thinks that "the two texts are clearly the work of two individuals, each with a distinctive lexicon and with a unique set of stylistic fingerprints—and the *Unfortunate Prince* was written first."[41]

Although Foster does not spell out his evidence for this conclusion, he usefully complicates critics' assumptions about the precise nature of Cary's "authorship," even of the folio text, by maintaining that she should be considered a "plagiarist"—or, more neutrally, a "redactor"—of a previous text. The continuum from plagiarist to translator to imitator to "original" author was of course tricky to chart in Renaissance literary theory and practice (indeed, it remains so today); and Foster challenges any simple notion of authorship by suggesting that we are dealing here not with two texts but really with three: "First there is the narrative source [the *Unfortunate Prince*], about ninety percent of which resurfaces in Cary's redaction, much of it copied verbatim. Second is Cary's completed text, which is considerably longer." And third, there is an interesting "basket of fragments" consisting of the "*difference* between . . . [the] completed text and the original *Unfortunate Prince.*" It is in this "difference," Foster suggests, that the reader should look for traces of Cary's own interpretation of the story of Edward; his wife, Isabel; and his favorite, Gaveston.

Without mentioning Stauffer's article or subsequent work, mostly by feminist critics, on the *Edward II* texts, D. R. Woolf has argued that neither version of the text was written in the late 1620s and hence neither was written by Henry Falkland. Since he regards the folio text as merely derivative from the octavo and connection of the octavo with any papers of the Falkland family as spurious, Woolf does not consider the possibility that "E.F." might refer to Falkland's wife. But Woolf does make some interesting arguments for his view that the attribution of the octavo to Falkland was an instance of a common ploy, on the part of an editor or publisher, to "provide the book with an illustrious [i.e., aristocratic] father."[42]

Woolf bases his argument for a 1680 date of composition mainly on the diction of the folio and that text's undeniable relevance—as an oblique "warning" to a monarch about the dangers of relying on "evil favorites"—to English politics at the time of the Popish Plot and the subsequent Exclusion Crisis. Woolf's argument is weakened by assumptions about univocal reference: why must a phrase like "in the wars of late years" refer only to the era of the Civil War?[43] His arguments are also impaired by his dogmatic rhetoric (the ideology of the *History* "unquestionably" dates from 1680) and by his unargued assertion that the octavo is "simply an abridged and revised rendering" of the folio.[44] We also query his view that the *only* evidence linking the text to the Falklands is from the "revised" (that is, later, and hence less authoritative) octavo. Had he considered the possibility that the folio's title-page "E.F." might refer to Elizabeth Falkland, Woolf would have found it less easy to debunk an early date and a genuine "Falkland connection" for the texts.

Nonetheless, his argument against simply believing printers' claims is surely well taken, especially when we recall that the press in 1680, according to a contemporary observer, "was open for all such books that could make any thing against the then government."[45] Moreover, one of Woolf's arguments against the likelihood of Falkland's authorship seems equally relevant to—though by no means definitively against—the case for Elizabeth Cary's authorship, namely, that both versions of the *Edward* narrative, if they were indeed written in the late 1620s, would have been read as highly critical of the king's favorite, Buckingham. Falkland, as we have noted, was Buckingham's protégé; and Elizabeth Cary was a close friend of Buckingham's duchess. According to Foster, we recall, Elizabeth Cary wrote an elegy on Buckingham, a poem that contains no hint of the critical attitude the *Edward II* texts evince toward Gaveston. Either Henry or Elizabeth might, of course, have harbored critical views of Buckingham that they expressed in a "private" manuscript but did not wish to publish. Indeed, Woolf notes that Sir Francis Hubert had written "a long narrative poem on Edward II and his wicked minions" in 1628 and was dismayed when the poem was published without his permission; he rushed a watered-down version to the press, denying any topical intent.[46]

Woolf doesn't recognize that the Hubert example could support an argument for dating the *Edward* texts from the last years of Buckingham's career, but Woolf's opponents on the critical battlefield have done little to explain Cary's possible motives for criticizing Buckingham. Nor is a consensus emerging, even among the advocates of Cary's authorship, about the historical and bibliographical problems surrounding the fact that the only versions of the text we have were both published—and perhaps heavily revised, if not written—in 1680.

Perplexed by the multiplicity of inferences we find in the critical literature and lacking an opportunity to study the primary texts in detail, we have chosen to remain agnostic on the question of who wrote either the *History of the Life* or *The Unfortunate Prince*. The initials on the title page of the folio remain, in our view, the best evidence for the attribution and offer a suggestive parallel to the "E.C." on the title page of *Mariam;* as Foster remarks, after 1620 Elizabeth Cary regularly signed herself Elizabeth Falkland. Her husband regularly signed his letters "H. Falkland." Another suggestive piece of evidence in favor of Elizabeth Cary's authorship is "E.F."'s prefatory statement (in the folio version only) that she strives to please "the Truth, not Time; nor fear I censure, since at the worst, 'twas but one Month mis-spended."[47] In the address "To the Reader" prefacing her translation of Perron, Elizabeth Cary writes that she dares "avouch" that the copier spent "fower times as long in transcribing, as it was in translating," and a commendatory poem printed with the translation expresses wonder that "one woman in one Month" should write "so large a Book."[48] Lewalski considers "the analogous claim to have written the work in a month's time" an "incredible coincidence."[49] The coincidence is indeed fascinating, though the specific claim to a month's time for translation of Perron's book is made only in the commendatory poem.

If Cary did write the folio text, there is a fine irony in the publisher's advertisement of this version as a text "printed verbatim from the Original" in "so Masculine a stile" (A2r). The irony increases when one recalls that Edward Clarendon described Elizabeth Cary as "a lady of a most masculine understanding, allayed with the passions and infirmities of her own sex."[50] Reading D. R. Woolf's essay of 1988 encourages the suspicion that ideologies of gender still cloud the question of the authorship of this *History.*

According to the "Author's Preface to the Reader" in the folio version, the text was written when the writer took up a "melancholy Pen" to "out-run those weary hours of a deep and sad Passion" by writing about the "unfortunate" King Edward and his equally unfortunate wife, Isabel. Although critical efforts to read this "passion" in reference to Elizabeth Cary's biographical situation in 1627 should be pursued with caution (claims of writing for self-consolatory purposes were after all conventional: Samuel Daniel, for instance, in the preface to his *Cleopatra* [1594, discussed below] says he writes to relieve his passion), it is nonetheless tempting to consider "E.F." 's preface in connection with Cary's traumatic separation from her husband in 1626, a separation occasioned, as we have seen, by a conversion to Catholicism that became public (albeit more through Lady Denbigh's officiousness than by her own will). A biographical reading of the preface and the text of *Edward* is further encouraged by the obvious autobiographical dimensions of Cary's *Mariam*. If Cary twice relied on her pen to console herself for troubles engendered by her marriage, in both cases she turned to history for her material or, rather, to a historical narrative that other writers had already worked into various shapes and meanings. Thus she teases us to find her literary "identity" in the shadowy terrain between authorship, translation, and revision.

SUBTEXTS AND CONTEXTS FOR *MARIAM*

JOSEPHUS AND JEWISH MATERIALS

The major source for *Mariam* is the Jewish historian Josephus's account of Herod the Great's troubled marriage to the royal-blooded Jewish woman Mariam, or Mariamne. The marriage, which took place in about 42 B.C. following Herod's divorce from his first wife, Doris, strengthened his political alliances among the Jews. Josephus describes this marriage, with different and sometimes conflicting details, both in his *Jewish War* (A.D. 69–79) and in his *Antiquities of the Jews* (ca. A.D. 93). Cary seems to have relied chiefly on the version of the story in book 15 of the *Antiquities*, which describes Herod's slaying of Mariam and Sohemus, the man with whom she had been accused of committing adultery, after Herod's return from a visit to Caesar Augustus in 29 B.C. (In *The Jewish War*, Herod is said to have killed Mariam and a different alleged adulterer, Josephus, in 34 or 35 B.C., after returning from a visit to Mark Antony.) Cary compresses, amplifies, and transposes material from the *Antiquities* in order to observe the dramatic unities, and she alters the characterization of the heroine and other figures in ways that merit study. Among her most significant revisions of the source is her emphasis on different styles of female speech and on the critical reactions of male characters to Mariam's speech in particular. Cary even creates, as a foil for Mariam's problematic tendency to speak her mind, a more verbally "obedient" character named Graphina, not present in Josephus. For comparative purposes we include selections from Josephus's narrative in Appendix A.

Cary might have read Josephus's text in the original Greek, though that is not one of the long list of languages the *Life* credits her with mastering in childhood. She definitely could have read it in one or several Renaissance translations, for as Maurice Valency notes, "Josephus was among the first authors printed in the Renaissance."[51] A Latin translation appeared in 1470, in Augsburg, and numerous vernacular translations, French, German, and Italian, were subsequently published. The first English translation, by Thomas Lodge, was printed in 1602. Dunstan and Greg present considerable evidence for Cary's having relied heavily, if not exclusively, on Lodge's translation, which, having been licensed in 1598, might have circulated in manuscript before it was printed. There are a number of close verbal parallels between Cary's play and Lodge's translation, and there is the additional fact, not mentioned by Dunstan and Greg, that Lodge had publicly alluded to his conversion to Catholicism in his poem *Prosopopeia, Containing the Teares of the Holy, Blessed, and Sanctified Mother of God* (1596). It seems possible that Cary knew, or knew of, Lodge through Catholic channels and that both authors were drawn to Josephus's work because his accounts of Jewish oppression under the Romans offered rich allegorical resources for representing problems experienced by Catholics in Elizabethan England. However, Dympna Callaghan argues that Cary might also have known an earlier version of the Herod-Mariam story in Joseph ben Gorion's *Compendious and Most Marveilous History of the Latter Tymes of the Jewes Commune Weale*, translated by Peter Morwyn.[52] (The first of numerous editions was printed in London, 1558, by J. Daye for R. Jugge. The *Short-Title Catalogue* [Pollard and Redgrave et al.] notes that the author's name is a pseudonym and the narrative is derived from Abraham ben David's abstract in book 3 of *Sefer ha-Kabalah*.)

Although Jews had been officially banned from England since 1290 and would not be readmitted until 1656, there was evidently considerable interest in Jewish laws and customs during the Tudor-Stuart era, enough to lead one modern scholar to speak of "Philo-semitism" as a characteristic of the latter period.[53] Protestants were interested for theological and polemical reasons in a "return" to the Hebrew scriptures, but Catholics angered by Henry VIII's divorce from Catherine of Aragon, and by his and his ministers' attempts to justify the divorce on scriptural grounds, had also begun to scrutinize the Old Testament with new attention. Arguably as a result of the interest in Hebrew studies sparked by disputes about Henry VIII's divorce, the first Regius Professorship of Hebrew had been established at Oxford in 1540, and the first Hebrew grammar in English was printed in 1598, in Leiden. During this same period, there were evidently communities of Christianized Jews (the so-called Marranos) in London and some other English cities.[54] Rumors that Jewish religious observances were secretly practiced in such communities may or may not have reached someone like Elizabeth Cary. It seems likely that most of her knowledge of Jewish festivals and observances derived simply from a close reading of the Bible and Josephus's texts, though her extensive theological readings might have included some rabbinical commentaries on the Hebrew scriptures.

Herod, the major male character of Cary's play, is richly villainous in both Jewish and Christian traditions. Josephus portrays Herod through a complex filter of admiration and bitterness; an upstart "Idumean," or half-Jew, who succeeded in becoming Mark Antony's protégé, Herod was elevated by the Romans to the position of tetrarch, and subsequently king, of Judea. In two lengthy and often contradictory accounts of Herod's life (ca. 73–74 B.C.), Josephus portrays him as both a skillful politician and a ruthless murderer who killed his second wife, Mariam, as well as her brother, grandfather, and eventually the two sons she had borne him. Although Herod usually observed Jewish law in public, many observers clearly regarded him as a monster, as suggested by an Augustan epigram: "It was better to be Herod's swine than a son of Herod." Josephus, however, details not only Herod's villainy but also his acts as a brilliant general, a brave soldier, a sometimes generous ruler, and a passionate lover of women: he had ten wives. It is not surprising that Josephus's Herod should be a complicated and sometimes confusing character, since Josephus's main sources were "distinctly partisan" to the king.[55] Josephus himself remarks that "there are some who stand amazed at the diversity of Herod's nature and purposes."[56] Josephus's Mariam is likewise a morally complex figure: though virtuous and, at the end, brave, she is also criticized as stubborn, proud, and too outspoken. Josephus's sympathies often swing toward Herod as a beleaguered husband who "was accustomed to bear patiently" his wife's habitual insolence, but in general he renders the relationship between wife and husband with a nuanced recognition of their conflicting motives and perceptions. Although Herod clearly marries the Maccabean princess Mariam to cement his own claim to the Jewish throne, he becomes passionately attached to her and laments her death with considerable force and pathos.

Biblical and historical Herods

Besides Josephus's narrative, Cary's other major source is the Bible, specifically the various (and somewhat enigmatic) passages mentioning Herod in the Synoptic Gospels and Acts. At least three historical Herods are simply called "Herod" in the Bible and were consequently often conflated in later literary traditions. First, there is Herod the Great, presumably the figure referred to in Luke 1:5, which states that the events in the gospel began "in the days of Herod, King of Judea."[57] In the Gospel of Matthew (2:1), Jesus is also said to have been born "in the days of Herod the King," and Matthew goes on to describe Herod's summoning and questioning of three magi about their desire to worship a newborn king of the Jews. There follows the story of the Holy Family's flight to Egypt to save the Christ child from the "Slaughter of the Innocents." Enraged by the magi's failure to obey his hypocritical command to tell him of the Christ child's whereabouts "so I may come and worship him also," Herod orders all Jewish boys under the age of two to be killed. Matthew subsequently mentions Herod's own death, laconically suggesting that it is a punishment for the attempted persecution of Christ. "Go into the land of Israel," an angel says to Joseph, "for they are dead which sought the young child's life" (2:20). None of this material is present in Josephus, and many biblical scholars are skeptical about its historicity, partly because it seems a well-crafted parallel to the Old Testament story (which is also included in Josephus) about the birth of Moses and the Egyptian king who ordered the death of all male Israelite children because of a prediction that a Jewish child would humble the

Egyptians.[58] There is, moreover, an obvious chronological difficulty in dating Jesus' birth to the last year of the reign of a king who died in 4 B.C.! Nonetheless, Herod as "Slaughterer of the Innocents" became a major character in later religious drama, and this identification of Herod may contribute, associatively, to the definition of the character who bears his name in Cary's *Mariam*, especially in the play's final act, in which the dying Mariam acquires symbolic features of Christ and his precursors, the Slaughtered Innocents and the beheaded John the Baptist.

The second historical Herod mentioned by the Gospels is indeed best known as the king who was spurred by his wife Herodias and her daughter Salome to kill John the Baptist. Historically, this is the tetrarch Herod Antipas, who was Herod the Great's son by his fourth wife, Malthace. Herodias's daughter, who is not named in the Bible but who corresponds to a historical and later legendary Salome (of "the seven veils"), was readily conflated with Herod the Great's sister Salome, the villainess of Cary's tragedy. John the Baptist's death is related in Matthew 14:1–2, Mark 6:17–18, and, somewhat obliquely, in Luke 3:19–20 and 9:7–9.[59] Herod [Antipas] also appears in a brief passage, Luke 13:31–33, describing Jesus' reply to being told that Herod wanted to kill him: "Go and tell that fox, 'Behold I cast out demons.'"

In a third appearance, related only by Luke (23:6–12) and probably legendary (though Acts 4:25–26 also alludes to the episode), Herod [Antipas] questions Jesus, who has been brought before Herod by Pilate, and treats him "with contempt," clothing him in mock-gorgeous garments before sending him back to Pilate. Biblical scholars have suggested that the passage may reflect a desire to blame the local tetrarch, rather than the Roman Pilate, for Jesus' fate (in the apocryphal Gospel of Peter, Antipas's "responsibility for the condemnation of Jesus" is magnified over Pilate's).[60]

Finally, the Bible mentions a Herod who is evidently Agrippa I, grandson of Herod the Great and Mariam (through their son Aristobulus, whom Herod the Great killed). Herod Agrippa, who reigned as king from A.D. 41–44, is the Herod described in Acts 12:1–23 as persecuting the early Christian Church, arresting Peter and slaying James, son of Zebedee. Peter was miraculously freed by an angel, and Herod, in a parallel miracle, was smitten by an angel "because he did not give God the glory; and he was eaten by worms and died."[61]

MYSTERY PLAY HERODS

These three historical Herods, "all unpleasant people" and "easily confused with one another," as Valency remarks,[62] were represented as one tyrant in the main tradition of popular Christian drama that Cary would have known, the so-called mystery plays that developed from the medieval liturgical drama based on biblical stories. Herod figures most prominently in dramatizations of the Slaughter of the Innocents, though in one of the York mysteries, *Trial of Jesus*, Herod plays Antipas's part of bullying clown, and in one of the Coventry plays, *The Death of Herod*, the villain derives from the Herod Agrippa of Acts 12:23. It was as Slaughterer of the Innocents, however, that Herod assumed his most famous characteristics of ranting tyrant.[63] This was evidently the part played by Chaucer's clerk Absolon "on a scaffold hye" in the days "when the acting of the religious plays was still in the hands of the clergy,"[64] and by the fourteenth century this part had become a favorite for the bourgeois guild actors in the Corpus Christi plays in England. These immensely popular cycles sometimes included as many as forty-eight plays, unfolding Biblical history from Creation to Doomsday. The episode of Herod's Slaughter of the Innocents became "a powerful focal point" in the cycles, a moment of symbolic transition from Old to New Testament time when, as Cynthia Bourgeault observes, the death of the Jewish boys provided an ironic "counterpoint to the birth of Christ" and also a "foreshadowing of Christ's own innocent death."[65]

Hamlet famously scorns the Herod of the popular cycle plays—still being acted in the early seventeenth century—as a type of ranting tyrant ideal for an overblown style of acting aimed at pleasing the "groundlings": "It out-Herods Herod," Hamlet says of a performance that "offends" him; "a robustious, periwig-pated fellow tear[s] a passion to totters, to very rags, to spleet the ears of the groundlings. . . . Pray you avoid it," Hamlet advises the players who visit Elsinore.[66] Clearly Herod, as represented in Cary's tragedy, does not escape the rhetorical and gestural excess against which Hamlet advises, and indeed few Renaissance playwrights or actors could "avoid" the powerful model of the Corpus Christi play Herod. Among the reasons to see connections between the Corpus Christi pageants representing Herod and Cary's *Mariam* is the latter play's suggestion that when Mariam meets her death, she is herself a figurative Innocent. And Herod's raving expressions of regret for having ordered Mariam's death recall the ironic turn of plot in the Chester play of the *Innocents* in which Herod desperately laments the death of a child he has learned, too late, was his own son. Herod berates the child's foster-mother, as Cary's Herod berates Salome, for failing to prevent him from doing what he had once wanted to do: "fye, hore, fye! god geve thee pyne! / why didst thou not say that Child was myne?"[67]

CONTINENTAL CLASSICIZING DRAMAS ABOUT HEROD AND MARIAM

A somewhat later but overlapping tradition of drama—in this case, elite rather than popular—also provides important precedents for Cary's play. The most striking general characteristic of this tradition is its blending of Christian and classical forms and sometimes subject matters. With the rediscovery of classical manuscripts in the Renaissance, dramatists became increasingly interested in modeling their heroes and villains on figures from Greek and Latin texts, chief among them plays by Euripides and Seneca. Among the classicizing plays Cary could have read are Ludovico Dolce's *Marianna* (ca. 1565) and Hans Sachs's *Tragedia . . . der Wütrich König Herodes . . .* (1552); in addition, she might have known of Alexandre Hardy's *Mariamne* (written and performed in 1600 but not published until 1625). Dunstan and Greg conclude that there are no close verbal parallels between Cary's *Mariam* and these continental dramas; nevertheless, their similarities in plot, characterization, and above all, methods of transforming Josephus's narrative material into dramas with both classical and Christian elements warrant further study. Dolce's *Marianna*, for example, has some formal similarities to Cary's *Mariam*. In its first scene Marianna rehearses her conflicting feelings toward Herod (although with a confidante, her nurse, rather than in soliloquy); each act is punctuated with a choric commentary (although in the later acts the Chorus, composed of Marianna's waiting women, also addresses the other characters directly); and the final act represents Herod's mental and emotional collapse after the execution of his victims. On the other hand, between the opening and closing scenes, the tragedy focuses less on Mari-anna's situation than on the progress of Herod's jealous and destructive rage, which consumes not only Marianna but also Soemo (Sohemus), his mother-in-law Alessandra (Alexandra), and Alessandro and Aristo-bolo (Alexander and Aristobulus), his two children by Marianna, not to mention the cupbearer suborned by Salome who eventually renounces his perjury. Despite its terrible consequences, the grotesque petulance of Herod's tyranny falls short of tragic stature and evokes Leontes rather than Othello.

In contrast, Hans Sachs's *Tragedia . . . der Wütrich König Herodes, wie der sein drey sön and sein gmahel umbbracht,* observes neoclassical form, including the unities, far less closely; the play begins *before* Herod visits Caesar, and it is during the first act that Marianne extracts from Seemus (Sohemus) the secret that Herod's jealousy has prompted him to order her death in case of his own. On his return she first shuns and then reviles him, declaring he values her only "des schnöden wollust wegen" ("for the sake of his vile pleasure," act 2, line 22). As in Cary's tragedy, Herod infers an adulterous intimacy between Marianne and Seemus, and Salome bribes Herod's wine steward to accuse Marianne of trying to poison the king. Again as in Cary, Salome urges Marianne's execution with manic urgency, and Herod finally orders the queen's decapitation. Her parting words are "Nun bin ich fro von hertzen grundt, / Das ich nur von dir, du bluthundt, / Durch den todt wie sol ledig wern. / Ich wil sterben willig und gern" ("I'm glad from the bottom of my heart, you bloodhound, that I will be free of you through death. I shall die willingly and gladly," act 2, lines 119–22). Mo-ments after he has ordered the execution Herod summons Marianne to feast with him, and confronted with the consequence of his rash com-mand, castigates himself for his "grosse untrew an dir, / Die du warst so holdtselig mir / Für alle weibsbilder auff erdt[.] / Hymlisch war dein schön and geberdt" ("great disloyalty to you, who were loveliest [or most gracious] to me of all women on earth; heavenly were your beauty and your bearing," act 2, lines 149–51).

Some parallels with Cary's *Tragedy of Mariam* are apparent, but Sachs's Marianne dies by the end of the second of five acts. The succeeding acts illustrate the relentless rhythm of dynastic struggle as Alexander and Aristobulus, seeking revenge for their mother's death, are undone by a conspiracy of Salome, Pheroras, and Antipater; and Antipater, the new heir, seeking to hasten Herod's death, is in turn betrayed by Salome and sentenced to execution. The play ends with Herod's death in great physical pain. The rapid succession of incident, represented in sturdy rhymed tetrameter couplets, makes Sachs's play more like a series of tableaux than a fully developed tragedy.

Despite Marianne's early disappearance from the scene, her fate is conspicuously remembered in the third of the play's three epilogic "morals": the first warns that princes should expel all hypocrites and flatterers from the court and beware of hasty judgments; the second that whoever falsely accuses another will eventually fall into the trap he has contrived for another; but the third and most elaborately developed sternly inculcates the lesson that women who speak defiantly to their husbands will kindle jealousy and mistrust which the wives, however virtuous and honorable, cannot easily still. In the final lines of the play this moral receives the author's explicit imprimatur: "Aus dem volgt gar vil ungemachs / In ehling standt, so spricht Hans Sachs" ("from this [i.e., female insubordination] proceeds much trouble in the married state; so says Hans Sachs"; epilogue, lines 41–42). These sentiments sound like an anticipation of the Chorus in *The Tragedy of Mariam*, but on the whole, the blunt patriarchal moralism of the *Tragedia . . . der Wütrich König Herodes* serves as a foil to the more complex presentation of Mariam in Cary's tragedy.

Alexandre Hardy, a precursor of Corneille, was a significant figure in the emergence of French neoclassical drama, and his powerful and intriguing *Mariamne* particularly invites comparison with Cary's nearly contemporary tragedy. Whereas Cary dramatizes a crisis in the union of Herod and Mariam, Hardy presents the marriage as compelled and violently repugnant to Mariam from the outset. The psychological density of Hardy's tragedy is striking. Herod, who embraces (and frequently articulates) the principles of Machiavellian statecraft, has married Mariamne to secure his throne but finds himself tormented by his inability to win her genuine affection; he is self-divided before as well as after Mariamne's death ("Sa perte me conserve, & sa perte me pert," 4.2.23; "Her death preserves me, and her death destroys me"), and his obsessive attempts to prove she has cuckolded him seem rooted in a sense of inadequacy ("Il te falloit un Dieu, presomptueuse, afin / Que ton ambition excessive prist fin, / Afin de rencontrer un Espoux de ta sorte," 3.1.409–11; "It would have taken a god, presumptuous woman, / To satisfy your excessive ambition / And furnish you with the husband you desired" [or "a husband of your own sort"]). Mariamne longs for death as a release, but at the same time she is tormented by the uncertainty of when Herod's destructive rage will finally turn on her. In their final conversation, she virtually goads him into ordering her execution. *Mariamne* has other striking features (including a scene in which Salome seduces the cupbearer into perjury by appealing to his sense of loyalty to Herod and the good of the state) but never raises the issues of male and female power which are arguably at the center of *The Tragedy of Mariam*. Dolce's, Sachs's, and Hardy's tragedies provide evidence not only of how widely disseminated the story of Herod and Mariam was during the Renaissance but also of what different emphases the story could accommodate.

ENGLISH "CLOSET" DRAMAS

Soon after her marriage in 1549, Jane (also known as Joanna) Lumley, the young daughter of a politically active Catholic nobleman, penned an English translation of Euripides' *Iphigeneia at Aulis.* Her translation emphasizes female heroism and self-sacrifice in ways that make it a fascinating forerunner of Cary's *Mariam.* We have no evidence that Cary knew—or even knew of—the manuscript of the first extant translation of a classical drama by an Englishwoman (or, indeed, an Englishman); but Margaret Arnold has recently argued that Lumley's drama was intended for a "domestic" audience of readers and even spectators, and it is an open question whether a later woman writer such as Cary, who shared Lumley's class status as well as her religion, might have seen a copy of her play.[68] The text was first printed in 1909, from an autograph copy—the only one known to scholars—preserved in the British Library (MS Reg. 15. A.).[69]

Working, evidently, from both the original Greek and Erasmus's Latin translation of the play published in 1506 (and printed, as Margaret Arnold notes, on facing pages with the Greek text in the British Library copy of Euripides' *Iphigeneia at Aulis* which bears the Lumley autograph), Jane Lumley recreates a drama which stresses a daughter's willingness to value her country over her life. As Elaine Beilin remarks, Lumley thus offers a classical female parallel to the ideal of Christian male virtue set forth in a work by Erasmus, *The Institution of a Christian Prince,* which Jane's husband, John, translated at about the same time she was probably making her version of *Iphigeneia.*[70]

But Jane Lumley may well have chosen Iphigeneia's story not only to paint a portrait of female virtue but also to explore a situation of familial conflict that bore striking resemblances to dilemmas in her own aristocratic patriarchal family. Jane's father, Henry Fitzalen, twelfth earl of Arundel, was a leader of the Catholic nobility who plotted to place Mary, Queen of Scots, on the English throne and who also betrayed his wife's niece, the Lady Jane Grey, in a way that helped bring about her execution. Jane Lumley thus had ample reason, as Margaret Arnold notes, to reflect on plots in which young women were sacrificed to further goals that male leaders deemed desirable. Although Agamemnon agonizes—as Cary's Herod does—over his decision to kill a beloved woman, Lumley's play ultimately rationalizes, or at least distracts our attention from, the father's terrible judgment by imbuing the daughter's embrace of her fate with Christian significance. Erasmus had already given "implicitly Christian diction" to passages in his translation of the Greek, and Lumley, as Elaine Beilin shows, provides striking English parallels:[71] "I wolde counsell you therfore to suffer this troble paciently," Iphigeneia says to her mother, urging her not to be angry with her father, "for I muste nedes die, and will suffer it willingelye."[72] And she further counsels the Grecian women to sing songs of her death and lead her to the altar of Diana's temple, "that withe my blode I maye pacifie the wrathe of the goddes against you."[73] Like Cary's Mariam, Lumley's Iphigeneia partly succeeds in rhetorically transforming herself from a political victim to a Christlike martyr.

Although we can only speculate about Cary's knowledge of Lumley's play, we can be more certain that she knew most of the plays based on classical stories and written—for publication, but not for the stage—by members of the circle of Mary Sidney, countess of Pembroke. Influenced by the French dramatist Robert Garnier, writers such as Fulke Greville, Thomas Kyd, Samuel Daniel, and Lady Mary herself wrote dramas in an elite, quite untheatrical "Senecan" style which, according to most literary historians, exerted little influence on the later English theater.[74]

Typically "concerned with issues of public morality, treated philosophically, didactically, or politically,"[75] these plays address questions of government, "not only in the public world of the state," as Nancy Gutierrez has observed, "but also in the private world of the family."[76] Indeed, the closet dramas written before 1603 (the year of Queen Elizabeth's death) give more weight to women and the domestic sphere than to "the political dilemmas of men in public life," whereas the opposite is true—with the notable exception of *Mariam*—in closet dramas written after 1603.[77] All of these plays consist mainly of long speeches delivered antithetically in a mixture of heroic couplets and unrhymed iambic pentameter. Battles and deaths, albeit gruesomely described, tend to be reported by messengers rather than represented. Two of these plays, which use material from Plutarch's account of Antony and Cleopatra, are especially important for Cary's *Mariam*.

Perhaps in response to her famous brother Sir Philip Sidney's call for a more decorous, neoclassical style of English drama in his *Defence of Poetry* (written sometime between 1579 and 1583, posthumously published in 1595), the countess of Pembroke undertook in 1590 to translate Robert Garnier's *Marc Antoine* (1578) in a mixture of blank and rhymed verse. Her play, first published in 1592 by William Ponsonby under the title *Antonius* (in a volume which also included her translation of Philippe Mornay's *Discourse of Life and Death*), was reprinted by the same publisher in 1595 as *The Tragedie of Antonie*. Following Garnier's French closely, Mary Sidney brought to English readers a play dramatizing the noble pathos of Antony's and Cleopatra's death scenes. The play begins with Antony berating Cleopatra for fleeing with her boats from the battle of Actium, and hence contributing, along with Antony's passion-driven decision to follow her boats, to their fateful loss of political power. Garnier's and Mary Sidney's plays go on, however, to demand our admiration for the eloquent Cleopatra as she laments her mistake, remains steadfast in her love for Antony, and finally resolves to commit suicide rather than become Caesar's prisoner. With its complex characterization of the passionate Egyptian queen, *Antonie* is considerably more sympathetic to her than the source story in Plutarch's *Lives of the Noble Romans*.

In a drama "apparently suggested by the countess as a companion piece to her translation,"[78] Samuel Daniel goes even further in ennobling Cleopatra and, by implication, his patroness, who is, he writes in his preface, the "starre of wonder my desires first chose / To guide their travels in the course I use."[79] Daniel's play picks up where Mary Sidney's leaves off—with Cleopatra still alive in her tomb with the body of her beloved Antony—and traces her final moments with considerable psychological finesse. Torn between her desire for death and her sense of duty to her children, she finally chooses to follow Antony and, thereby, to defend her "glory" from the attacks it would have suffered in a Roman "triumph." Cleopatra's first words (in the long opening soliloquy of the play), like her last, at the end of act 4, dramatize her concern with "life beyond ... life";[80] and the play rings complex changes on this theme of immortality. A desire for worldly fame, which is appropriate for Cleopatra as a pagan heroine, is by no means condemned in the play though it is ironically counterpointed, in the Chorus's final speech, with the Christian notion of a heavenly afterlife. Having insisted, like Edgar at the conclusion of Shakespeare's *King Lear,* that future generations will never see human "worth" like that displayed by their forebears in this play, the Egyptian Chorus then turns, in its final stanza, to address an implicitly Christian divinity, "all-seeing light, / High President of Heaven" (lines 1758–59). This final stanza sounds a traditional Christian note of *contemptus mundi* and defines Cleopatra's greatness, retroactively, as self-destructive pride: "Are these the bounds y'have given ... / That limit Pride so short?" the Chorus rhetorically asks (lines 1763, 1765). Yet Daniel's characterization of the Chorus, like Mary Sidney's and Elizabeth Cary's, does not allow us to grant full authority to its perspective at any point in the drama (see the discussion below in "The Chorus and Conventional Wisdom"). And Daniel's play, like his noble patroness's *Antonie,* offers a compelling portrait of a flawed but ultimately noble heroine eager to shape her own "fame."

Cary's *Mariam* seems indebted in numerous ways to Sidney's and Daniel's dramas about Cleopatra and Antony. Herod's expressions of uxorious passion recall those of Antony in both earlier English closet dramas, and those dramas' versions of Cleopatra arguably influence Cary's portrait not only of Mariam but also of Salome, Mariam's enemy and chief dramatic foil, and of the vexed relation between them. The actual references to Cleopatra in Cary's play present her as a sensual "antitype" to Mariam,[81] and hence as a character apparently closer to Plutarch's (and Shakespeare's) dangerous Egyptian than to Daniel's and Sidney's noble queen. But the very fact that Cleopatra's reputation—like that of Elizabeth Tudor both during her lifetime and after her death—was still being actively debated in Renaissance England might have contributed to Cary's decision to write a play thematically concerned with a woman's right to fame and a "public voice."

THE "SOCIAL TEXT" OF HENRY VIII'S DIVORCE

As a play explicitly concerned with the legitimacy of divorce and allegorically concerned with religious faith and martyrdom, Cary's *Mariam* alludes in multiple ways to a major and controversial event of the English Reformation period, the divorce of Henry VIII from Catherine of Aragon and the consequent splitting of the Church of England from the Church of Rome. The printed texts that testify to widespread cultural preoccupation with this double "divorce" include polemical religious works as well as some humanist dramas concerned with Herod and John the Baptist. The execution of John the Baptist, which, as we have seen, involved the historical Herod Antipas and which is mentioned, albeit with different details, in Josephus as well as in the Gospels, would have been of particular interest to writers struggling with conflicts between their sense of political duty and their own religious beliefs, especially if those beliefs inclined to Catholicism.

To appreciate the allegorical significance of the Herod–John the Baptist story during the Tudor-Stuart era, we need to elaborate on the history, particularly the complex marital history, of Herod Antipas; he becomes, for both Catholics and Protestants, a central figure in the disputes about the legitimacy of Henry VIII's divorce from Catherine of Aragon. That divorce paved the way for the long reign of a Protestant queen whom Catholics continued to regard, long after her accession, as the "bastard" offspring of an incestuous union between Henry VIII and Anne Boleyn.

Herod Antipas, son of Herod the Great and his fourth wife, Malthace, fell in love with Herodias after he was married to someone else. Herodias happened to be the granddaughter of Herod the Great and his second wife, Mariam; hence she was a half-niece of Antipas. As if this impediment were not enough, she was also married to Herod Antipas's half-brother,

Herod II. Her daughter Salome was married to Philip, another of Antipas's half-brothers. To marry Herodias, Antipas divorced his wife and
took Herodias from Herod II. According to the Gospels, John the Baptist denounced this act saying, "It is not lawful for thee to have thy
brother's wife" (Mark 6:18). It was, however, Herodias, not Herod, who
then sought vengeance on John, for Herod, Mark reports, respected the
prophet, knowing "that he was a just man and a holy" (6:20). Herod
ordered John's death only because of a rash oath sworn to Herodias's
daughter on the occasion of the king's birthday feast. Although her name
isn't mentioned in the Gospels, this was the Salome who became famous
in art, literature, and music as the dancer of the "seven veils." According
to Mark, her dancing so pleased Herod that he promised her whatever she
desired. She consulted with her mother and requested the Baptist's head.
Herod ordered John beheaded in prison, and when the head was brought
to Salome, she gave it to her mother in a relay that artists as well as psy-
choanalytic critics have found compelling. For our purposes, the major allegorical riches of the gospel versions of this story (which contrast
with Josephus's spare account of how Herod executed John to prevent "rebellion") are the parallels they suggest, on the one hand, between a composite figure of Herod (both Antipas and the ten-times-married Herod
the Great) and Henry VIII and, on the other, between a composite figure
of a dangerous woman (Herodias, Salome, and also, potentially, Mariam)
and Anne Boleyn.

The story of John the Baptist's death was a locus of interpretive dispute because it was deployed both against and for Henry's divorce in texts
written not only during his reign but also during that of his daughter
Elizabeth and her heir, James, son of a beheaded Catholic queen and a
man feared, by some of his Protestant subjects, as a closet Papist. One
of Henry's own chief arguments in support of his divorce was the
illegitimacy of his marriage to Catherine on the grounds that she was the
widow of his elder brother, Arthur. Catholic writers like Nicolas Sanders,
whose major polemical work, *De origine et progressu schismatis Anglicani*, was
probably written in the 1530s but was first published in 1585, refuted this
argument by insisting that the law invoked by John the Baptist forbidding
marriage with a brother's widow (or wife) was in Henry's case "inappli-
cable," "partly because the marriage of Arthur and Catherine was never

perfected [i.e., consummated], partly because, even if that were not certain, Arthur was now dead."[82] Sanders pointedly remarks that Henry and Catherine were crowned together "on the feast of St. John the Baptist" (5), and he goes on to project the problem of incest onto Henry's alliance with Anne Boleyn. Anne, according to Sanders and many Catholic polemicists, was really Henry's daughter, her mother having been his mistress before he took up with Anne's elder sister Mary.[83] Further bolstering his analogy and his case against Henry's divorce and remarriage (and consequent break with the Catholic Church), Sanders remarks that Anne was "amusing in her ways" and compares her, as a "good dancer," to Salome (25).

Nicholas Harpsfield, in *A Treatise on the Pretended Divorce between Henry VIII and Catharine of Aragon* (probably written during Mary's reign) inveighs against "abusing" John the Baptist's "name and authority for the furtherance of the divorce" but, at the same time, links Herod and Henry as lascivious adulterers.[84] Harpsfield also develops the connection between Anne and Salome. The latter "dancing, devilish damsel" was aptly punished, he writes, by a miraculous beheading as she walked one day on the ice. When it broke under her feet, "by and by was she drowned, all saving the very neck, which did hang between the great pieces of ice. The head thus being above, the body beneath in the water, wagging and removing to and fro, did represent and exhibit a marvellous spectacle and a strange kind of dancing" (251). This striking image alludes to Anne Boleyn's own beheading; in addition, that emphasis on the "wagging" motion of Salome's head points to a cultural association central to *Mariam*, the association between female wantonness and female speech. As an anonymous play of 1607 showed, the female tongue (personified by a character named Lingua) needed to be locked up and guarded so that it would not "wagge abroad."[85] Anne Boleyn, like Cary's characters Mariam and Salome, broke the cardinal rule for women to be chaste, silent, and obedient; and Anne, like Mariam a second wife abhorred and openly denounced by the cast-off first wife, was executed for adultery by her "tyrannical" husband. A recent biography of Anne Boleyn by Retha Warnicke argues persuasively that Anne was truly innocent of adultery but—like Mariam—guilty of displeasing her lord and husband. The drama surrounding Anne Boleyn, as heroine or villainess of the "Reformation" or

"Schism," depending on one's views, arguably informs Cary's play much more deeply than critics have allowed. If aspects of the figure of Anne Boleyn are seen in the characterizations of *both* Mariam and Salome, then readers may better understand why those female speakers sometimes seem to be two versions of the same character even as they occupy apparently antithetical moral positions.

As mentioned above, the topical drama of Henry's divorce appears not only in polemical religious tracts Cary might well have known but also in a set of plays by humanist authors about the murder of John the Baptist. Like the Corpus Christi plays, the humanist plays focus on Herod's career as an allegorically rich story of pagan tyranny attacking Christian innocence; and they also share with the cycles and the Bible a tendency to conflate the three main historical Herods into a single wicked figure. Unlike the vernacular cycles, however, these humanist plays were written in Latin for elite audiences and performed in schools and the Inns of Court. This set of plays includes Jacob Schoepper's *Ectrachelisitis, sive Johannes decollatus* (published in Cologne in 1546); Nicholas Grimald's *Archipropheta* (published in Cologne in 1548 but, according to Rebecca Bushnell, probably written in 1546 at Oxford);[86] and George Buchanan's *Baptistes, sive calumnia* ("The Baptist, or Calumny," probably written in Bordeaux between 1541 and 1544, and first published in England in 1577). Even more closely related to the medieval morality play and the "Mirror for Magistrates" tradition than to the cycles, these humanist dramas offered didactic warnings against tyranny to both rulers and subjects. However, as Bushnell observes in *Tragedies of Tyrants*, this type of drama exhibits a rhetorical instability characteristic of "statecraft" or *speculum* (mirror) literature. Though the plays appear to confirm a "conservative ideology of proper sovereignty and non-resistance [on the subject's part]," the tyrant's typically hyperbolic theatricality "contaminates the 'proper' acting that exemplifies the moral, thus splintering the image in the mirror" (80).

Buchanan's play is of particular interest for the reader of Cary's *Mariam* because both plays relate Herod's tyranny to his succumbing to the influence of a wicked female—Herodias in Buchanan's text, Salome in Cary's; moreover, both plays show a subject heroically resisting the tyrant and paying the ultimate penalty for that resistance. As John the Baptist boldly counters Herod and Herodias in Buchanan's play, so Mariam counters her husband, Herod, and his sister Salome in Cary's play. The parallels between the two dramas become even more interesting when we note that Buchanan invited his readers to find topical meanings in his biblical drama. In his preface Buchanan writes: "For if an event enacted many centuries ago is old, this will be reckoned among the old, but if we consider as new what is fresh from recent recollection, this will certainly be new."[87] To his pupil James VI of Scotland (later to be James I of England) Buchanan wrote more explicitly that his *Baptistes* was intended to call "young persons away from the popular taste for theatrical allegories towards the imitation of antiquity as well as endeavouring vigorously to incite in them a zeal for true religion, which at that time was everywhere persecuted."[88] The play most strikingly promoted the "true religion," Roman Catholicism, by implying strong analogies between the biblical characters and the major actors in the inaugurating drama of the English Reformation. Herod resembles King Henry VIII; Herod's second wife, Herodias, and her daughter, Salome, resemble Henry's second wife, Anne Boleyn; and John the Baptist, who criticized Herod's marriage to Herodias, resembles a famous counselor beheaded by Henry for refusing to approve of the king's divorce from Catherine of Aragon: to members of the Portuguese Inquisition Buchanan declared, "I represented the accusation and death of Thomas More . . . and I provided a portrait of tyranny at that time."[89]

For readers of Cary's *Mariam*, as for readers of the Shakespearean plays discussed by Leah Marcus in *Puzzling Shakespeare: Local Reading and Its Discontents*, there are significant rewards in the labor of excavating a distant historical subtext, especially when it raises issues still culturally contested today. As Marcus suggests, literary works may create a force field of topicality that exceeds any single political or religious allegory. The evidence suggesting that the figure of Anne Boleyn lurks behind both the heroine and the female villain of Cary's play certainly inhibits any simple historical decoding of *Mariam* or any easy assumptions about the beliefs of its author. Although she was probably leaning toward Catholicism when she wrote the play, we cannot infer from that supposition any stable attitude toward Anne Boleyn, the woman whom some Catholics excoriated as the catalyst of England's break with the Church of Rome. For a *female* reader of English history who was concerned with the "justice" of divorce law,

Anne Boleyn might have held unexpected points of fascination. At any rate, Cary places an overt demand for women's right to divorce in the mouth of the lustful and villainous Salome, while making a more oblique, and equally interesting, argument that, if the occasion demands principled disobedience, a "virtuous" woman like Mariam should be able to follow her conscience—as Thomas More did his own—rather than the orders of a king.

CARY'S *MARIAM*

The Chorus and conventional wisdom

The dramatis personae, absent from most extant copies of *Mariam*, minimally and unhelpfully identifies the Chorus as a "company of Jews," that is, as a more or less anonymous group of elders putatively representing the collective wisdom of the community. Their aloofness from the action redoubles their relative anonymity and gives to the stanzas that terminate each act the appearance of an impersonal authority which articulates the standards and perspective by which the conduct of the characters is to be judged. Yet, as in many classical tragedies—and as in another seventeenth-century instance of neoclassical tragedy, Milton's *Samson Agonistes*—their gnomic, conventional utterances seem somewhat off the mark, not only capricious and volatile in the application of general precepts but also inadequate to the psychological, spiritual, or even practical situation of the protagonist. The uneasy match between dramatic presentation and choric commentary thus suggests some characterization, if not of the Chorus, at least of its perspective.

The Chorus of act 1 runs against the grain of a reader's expectations in a particularly striking way. The first four stanzas, emphasizing the restlessness of those "minds that wholly dote upon delight," crave variety, and insatiably seek an ever higher degree of wealth and influence, suggest Salome, as the preceding act has represented her, and it is almost shocking to discover, in the fifth stanza, that all along the Chorus has been talking about Mariam. When Mariam explores, in the opening speech and the succeeding scene with her mother, Alexandra, the conflicting feelings evoked by Herod's death, the notion that she is simply a woman who doesn't know her own mind and despises what she already possesses (according to the Chorus she is one of those for whom "in a property contempt doth breed" and who "care for nothing being in their power") seems obtuse and reductive. Nevertheless, the misdirection of the reader may catalyze or reinforce a recognition that there is more affinity between Mariam and Salome, or their situations, than either woman would care to acknowledge. Each is trapped in a marriage that she urgently wishes to escape; while Mariam submits to the will of heaven or history and merely examines her response to the external event, Salome does not hesitate to seize, by any means at her disposal, the release she desires. In another respect, however, Salome is more conventional. As the Chorus might predict, she wishes to exchange one husband for another; Mariam's object of desire, if she has one, is autonomy, an ability to act upon her sense of what she knows, believes, and wishes that is unconstrained by her obligations to Herod, whether as wife or subject. Herod's slip of the tongue at 4.4.84, where he initially utters Mariam's name for Salome's, may underscore the connection between the two women that the Chorus has already implicitly established.

The choric stanzas terminating act 2 are preoccupied with counsels of prudence, cautioning against the ready and wishful reliance on reports of Herod's death in which nearly all the characters are implicated. At the end of act 3, however, the question of how much weight should be given to the Chorus's judgments becomes crucial, since these verses articulate the doctrine of wifely self-containment (" 'Tis not so glorious for her to be free, / As by her proper self restrain'd to be") and suggest that publishing her interiority in the form of extradomestic speech impairs her chastity as much as adulterous action would: "Her mind if not peculiar is not chaste." The quest for false glory, reputation, or the grace of "public language" adulterates the marital compact; true glory consists in marital self-renunciation, a total gift of body and mind. The Chorus complacently asserts the most all-encompassing aspirations of patriarchal control. Needless to say, the terms of the Chorus's program would proscribe not only Mariam's "frowardness" toward Herod—what we might call her passive aggressiveness—but even more strongly the enterprise of Elizabeth Cary or any other woman who might venture to assume the prerogatives of authorship.

Again it is Mariam who is explicitly condemned, as if the Chorus saw less threat to the patriarchal order in the flagrant transgressions of

Salome than in the specious virtue of Mariam. On the other hand, Salome has virtually a chorus of her own in the form of Constabarus and the sons of Babas. Constabarus's misogynistic tirade (4.6.309–50) has the same sententiousness as the Chorus's commentary, but its coarser rhetoric, reflecting the sting of personal betrayal, contrasts with the more dispassionate and ethically difficult reflections of the Chorus.

Both Constabarus and the Chorus are interested parties, but the ideologically mediated interests of the Chorus are less nakedly apparent. The stanzas at the end of act 4 uneasily negotiate the conflicting imperatives of aristocracy, patriarchy, Christianity, and classical (especially Stoic) philosophy as embodied in tragic decorum. The ethos of wifely submissiveness is partially assimilated to the Christianity adumbrated by the typological presentation of Mariam as female Christ or martyr, in acts 4 and 5: "The fairest action of our human life / Is scorning to revenge an injury" (4.8.629–30). At the same time, the emphasis is not quite Christian, since the suggested motives for scorning revenge are variously pride, nobility, and honor, rather than humility. Among the forms of baseness which the high-minded disdain is that of failing to discharge a "duty" (like that which a wife owes to a husband), so apparently even aristocratic hauteur leads, by the Chorus's interpretations, back to self-surrender. At the same time, the fifth stanza does not quite banish the possibility of active, and not simply moral, revenge: "But if for wrongs we needs revenge must have, / Then be our vengeance of the noblest kind." Can overcoming hatred, an act of Stoic self-conquest, create a kind of purified agency? It is hard to imagine what sort of enacted vengeance the Chorus would regard as acceptable on Mariam's part, but it may be noteworthy that throughout these stanzas separate agency, or at least "mind," the capacity for individual moral choice, seems to have been restored to women.

While the choric stanzas of act 5, which end the tragedy, speak with detached sympathy of the "guiltless Mariam," their generalizing emphasis on the unforeseen reversals of human fortune, on the extraordinary mutations that even a single day can effect, deflects attention from either the execution of Mariam or the crazed grief of Herod, which dominates the final act. Renaissance plays frequently set up a tension between flat, Polonius-like sententiousness and dramatizations of character and action (compare the treatment of Edgar's moralizing in *King Lear* or the couplet which ends Webster's *The Duchess of Malfi*), but in the case of *Mariam* the disparity between the moral adages of the Chorus and the experience of the heroine (and perhaps, by extension, the bad fit between conventional wisdom and the experience of all women) seems the very heart of Cary's dramatic vision.

STRUCTURE AND CHARACTERIZATION

In one respect, the Chorus's final emphasis on the exchange of positions provides an appropriate culmination to the dramatic and moral structure of *Mariam*. As insistently as Shakespeare's history plays, *Mariam* reminds its readers (or potential auditors) that the places which characters occupy have been occupied before them and that their relationships repeat earlier configurations. Even before the arrival of Doris in Jerusalem, the play draws attention to the fact that Mariam has displaced her in Herod's affections and that Mariam's son, Alexander, has displaced Antipater as heir to Herod's throne (1.2.131–39). Constabarus is the most explicit about the relay of roles: "I was Silleus, and not long ago / Josephus then was Constabarus now" (1.6.462–63). Although these lines are intended as a reproach to Salome, they also undercut our sympathy for Constabarus, and even Mariam is implicated in Herod's tyranny by her indifference to the misfortunes of Doris and her children. The victims of power in *Mariam* have recently been its none-too-scrupulous beneficiaries. (The thematics of substitution are reinforced by emphasis on Herod's descent from Esau, and the allusion is more double-edged than those who invoke it apparently recognize. Although the house of Herod has usurped the Maccabean throne, the "legitimate" heirs of Israel can only claim their right through Jacob—the "Supplanter," as the Geneva Bible glosses his name.) If *The History of the Life, Reign, and Death of Edward II* is rightly attributed to Elizabeth Cary, it provides additional evidence of her unsparing view of history: in the early part of the historical narrative Queen Isabel is sympathetically treated as a victim of Edward and his favorites, but when she ascends to power she is represented as a monster of cruelty, and the treatment of King Edward undergoes a symmetrical transformation so that he becomes an object of pathos.

Cary may suspect the worst of power as a determinant of behavior, but position does not adequately define nor circumscribe character in *Mariam*.

Mariam herself is, not surprisingly, the most complex figure in the drama. At times her downfall is seen as the direct result of her integrity: believing Herod dead, she achieves an unconditional sense of what she thinks and feels and a "public voice" in which to utter her newfound authority, and when he reappears she is unable to retreat within the boundaries of her previous subordination and dependence. After she has fully acknowledged her hatred of Herod (3.3.137–38 and 157–60), she cannot force herself to wear a mask of agreeable compliance.[90] At other times, however, Mariam's tragedy seems the result of arrogance and miscalculation: her self-righteousness and assertions of genealogical, even racial, superiority gratuitously aggravate Salome's animosity, and while in act 3 she renounces the use of smiles and gentle words to "enchain" and "lead [Herod] captive" (3.3.163–66) and declares reliance upon her "innocence" (171), at the end of act 4 she expresses dismayed surprise that her beauty has failed to save her life (4.8.525–28). Even her trust in the single virtue of chastity (561) is framed as a kind of narcissistic complacency. By the end of this soliloquy in act 4, she has apparently achieved the stance and aura of martyrdom which never desert her until the end of the play: "And therefore can they but my life destroy, / My soul is free from adversary's power" (569–70), and yet the following scene with Doris renews questions about the terms on which Mariam has shared in Herod's power. Although the final acts of *Mariam* increasingly fix its protagonist in a figural role as Christlike victim or martyr of integrity, at no point does the tragedy make her a merely symbolic figure as most earlier dramatic representations of the story of Herod and Mariam had done. Mariam's irreducibility contrasts with the simplified characterization of the female figures disposed around her, especially with the naked will to dynastic ascendancy of Alexandra, the wounded pride and maternal grievances of Doris as the rejected wife, and the submissively virtuous femininity of Graphina (who also seems to enact the "silence" of writing in relation to the more vocal public speech of Mariam; see endnote to 2.1.18 for further discussion of the play's presentation of Graphina).

Among these foils, Salome stands out with startling vividness. Her energetic contrivances mark her as a (perhaps unique) female descendant of the Vice tradition of medieval drama, a cousin to Richard III, Edmund, or Iago, whose plots create the plot, whose malevolently inventive activity is the very mainspring of the play's theatrical life. Like her male counterparts, Salome is subversively witty—a quality most evident in act 4, scene 7, where she both deflates Herod's hyperbolic blazons of Mariam and indefatigably prompts him to kill Mariam by various means. But her subversions, obviously, are more than verbal. Frankly claiming for women the male prerogative of divorce (1.5.334–39) and asserting the preeminence of will over law and tradition (1.6.454–55), she crosses millennia of boundaries and, like Alexander cutting the Gordian knot, suggests a strikingly direct alternative to Mariam's careful (and finally unsuccessful) negotiation of conflicting moral imperatives.

The associations of "Salome," as name and figure, are, as explained above, compound and confusing, but her cumulative aura of wickedness presumably contains the representation of her transgressive behavior, marking it as beyond the pale of respectable moral possibility. Yet her actions succeed where Mariam's fail. Salome ranges freely and victoriously in the central arena of the drama, enacting options that a Mariam (or an Elizabeth Cary) might imagine but never actually perform. Her theatrical energy reinforces the impression that Cary is, unofficially, intrigued rather than repelled by Mariam's evil twin. Unlike Cleopatra, Salome is not simply Mariam's antitype, a figure of manipulative sensuality, but the active double of Mariam's passive resistance to patriarchal power and to definition by the male. The huffy moralism of Constabarus does not offer a persuasive rebuff to Salome's license. His own moral position is not beyond reproach: he makes it clear that Salome once plotted on his behalf as she now plots on Silleus's, and while his deception of Herod in sheltering the sons of Babas can be understood as an expression of loyalty and friendship (to the sons of Babas, if not to his patron, Herod), it can also be seen as a prudent hedge against further political upheavals. (The point emerges more forcefully in Josephus's narrative.) The extravagant misogyny of 4.6.309–50 further undercuts his moral authority. Silleus seems even more of a cipher in relation to Salome: another blank, and more or less arbitrarily chosen, surface on which she can inscribe the shape of her desires.

As already suggested, Salome's dialogue with Herod in act 4, scene 7, has comic elements,[91] but it may be questionable whether the figure of Herod ever moves entirely beyond the sphere of comedy. Despite his ominous power to destroy, he spends much of the final two acts in the posture of a lovelorn swain, wavering in each successive resolution and mooning over the beauties and virtues he has condemned to extinction. The Herod of medieval English drama was a ranter—dismaying, to be sure, but too bombastic to inspire awe. Cary's Herod is a Petrarchan ranter as well. If Salome is right that Herod's "thoughts do rave with doting on the queen" (4.7.453), he is lunatic as soon as he enters the scene; his monomania certainly accelerates during the scene with Salome and begins a final precipitous downward spiral midway through the scene with the Messenger that constitutes the whole dramatic action of act 5 (see, in particular, lines 141 and 153–54). Herod's self-division and unstable rages suggest a comic version—perhaps a comic anticipation—of Othello, but Herod's madness has more of degradation than of pathos.

MARIAM AND SHAKESPEARE

Since the date of *Mariam*'s composition (as opposed to its publication) is open to debate and the extent of its circulation in manuscript is also a matter of speculation, it is difficult to make firm assertions about its relation to contemporary dramas including those by Shakespeare. Nevertheless, its themes and language suggest intertextual connections with *Antony and Cleopatra* and *Othello* in particular—whether these plays were among the sources and influences of Cary's tragedy or it was among theirs. Throughout *Mariam* Cleopatra clearly figures as antitype for the protagonist. Mariam (or her brother, Aristobulus), Alexandra suggests, might have occupied Cleopatra's place in Antony's affections, and Mariam later says that Cleopatra unsuccessfully tried to woo Herod away from her (4.8.537–44). Despite this explicit rivalry, Mariam specifically disavows Cleopatra's licentious means of achieving and maintaining power:

> Not to be empress of aspiring Rome,
> Would Mariam like to Cleopatra live:
> With purest body will I press my tomb,
> And wish no favours Anthony could give.   (1.2.199–202)

Of course, the contrast between Mariam and Cleopatra could easily derive from the tradition of non-Shakespearean plays that represented

Cleopatra and that were certainly among Cary's literary influences (see discussion above), but there are also some verbal affinities between *Mariam* and *Antony and Cleopatra*; see, for example, 1.1.57–58, 1.2.190–92, 3.3.175 of *Mariam* and further discussion of such parallels in the endnote to act 1, line 192. The disparagements of the "brown Egyptian" (1.2.190) or "Egyptian blowse" (5.1.195) either echo or anticipate the abuse that Cleopatra's Shakespearean enemies—including Antony, in his more hostile moments—heap upon her. The equivocal grief and conflicting impulses of Mariam's opening soliloquy also suggest the uneasy accommodation of politics and private feeling in Shakespeare's Roman plays: "What willingly he did confound he wail'd" (*Antony and Cleopatra*, 3.2.58).

Even more strongly, the drama of jealousy in *Mariam* invites comparison with *Othello*. Herod's maddened solipsism evokes the erosion, and intermittent recovery, of Othello's self-control. (In contrast, however, Herod physically enters the tragedy only in act 4, and the condensed representation of his jealousy and repentance may suggest the foreshortening through which Leontes' passions are staged in *The Winter's Tale*.) The question of the appropriate female response to male tyranny also links the plays: Salome seems to imagine for herself another life as a kind of Desdemona (see 1.4.292), but her frank assertion of women's prerogatives ("Are men than we in greater grace with Heaven? / Or cannot women hate as well as men?" [1.4.308–9]) is closer to the language of Emilia (*Othello*, 4.3.92–103). It is tempting to consider Salome as a female Iago but probably more accurate to say that the two figures have a common origin in the Vice tradition of the popular stage.

However, the most teasing possibility of connection between *Mariam* and *Othello* depends on the Folio text of *Othello*, 5.2.345–47, where Othello describes himself as "one whose hand / (Like the base Iudean) threw a pearl away / Richer than all his tribe." While editors have usually preferred the First Quarto reading ("base Indian") or explained the "base Iudean" as a reference to Judas Iscariot, the eighteenth-century critic Lewis Theobald saw in these lines an allusion to Herod and specifically cited *The Tragedy of Mariam* to support his reading.[92] If Shakespeare did indeed know Cary's tragedy, the plausibility of the Folio reading is strengthened, and in view of Herod's supposedly inferior Edomite origins, both "base" and "all his tribe" seem more pointedly relevant to Herod than to Judas.

The dramatic energy of *Mariam* makes the play seem more consonant with the popular stage than most "closet dramas" are; by the testimony of her biographer, Cary was an enthusiastic playgoer until her financial means were reduced. It may be reasonable, therefore, to suspect the influence of Shakespearean dramaturgy on her complex and flexible treatment of soliloquies, particularly those of the title character. Mariam's soliloquies (and, to some extent, even those of Salome and Herod) go beyond the expository function they seem to serve in most earlier neoclassical drama; they represent the speaker's process of thought, her reflective and by no means static exploration of her own situation. In the opening soliloquy, her apostrophes virtually populate the stage with the absent figures of domestic and political history. Moreover, just as Hamlet is surrounded by male characters who express some aspect or possibility of his own position and identity (Laertes, Fortinbras, Horatio, the First Player), Mariam is surrounded by women who express alternative relations to power, marriage, agency, and speech: Salome, Doris, Alexandra, Graphina, and, at least allusively, Cleopatra. Like Hamlet, Mariam is defined as much by her refusals as by her actions; despite Hamlet's verbal virtuosity and despite the "unbridl'd tongue" which even Mariam's admirers attribute to her, both characters tease their observers with the impression of a reserve of subjectivity imperfectly expressed by either their words or actions.

In its engagement with the popular theatrical imagination, as most fully embodied by the Corpus Christi plays and Shakespeare's tragedies, *Mariam* seems, like its heroine, to be rehearsing the issue of whether it should "with public voice run on"; the play remains poised on the threshold between the private antitheatrical formalism of closet drama and the public forms of dissemination, whether through print or performance. Despite its absence from the canon of theatrical history, *Mariam* may well represent a unique fusion of Shakespearean and neoclassical dramaturgy.

THE TEXTS OF *MARIAM* AND THE *LIFE*

THE 1613 QUARTO OF *MARIAM*

The quarto text of "The Tragedie of Mariam, the faire Queene of Jewry," dated 1613, was printed by Thomas Creede and published by Richard Hawkins, who had entered the play in the Register of the Stationers' Company on 17 December 1612. On the title page the author is identified only as "that learned, vertuous, and truly noble Ladie, E.C." Most copies of the quarto, printed in what W. W. Greg and A. C. Dunstan describe as "ordinary roman type . . . approximating to modern pica (20 ll. = 83 mm.)," appear to consist of eight four-leaf signatures, A–H, and signature I, containing two leaves. (In fact, what looks like signature A comprises leaves from two different quires, as explained below.) In addition, two extant copies, at the Huntington and Houghton libraries, contain a leaf of forematter marked A. The recto of this leaf, which occurs between the title page and the argument, bears the dedicatory sonnet addressed "To Dianaes Earthlie Deputesse, and my worthy Sister, Mistris Elizabeth Carye." Whether this name refers to one of Henry Cary's sisters or his sister-in-law (see first endnote to the Dedicatory Sonnet), this identification of the dedicatee goes far to erase the playwright's anonymity and presumably provides the reason for the suppression of this leaf of the quarto. The verso of this leaf contains "The names of the Speakers." In their edition of *Mariam,* Dunstan and Greg suggested this leaf was "to be regarded as an insertion made in a few presentation copies only, or else as an afterthought added after the bulk of the edition had already been sold," and other bibliographers and librarians have followed their lead. However, the more likely hypothesis is that the list of speakers was sacrificed when the dedicatory page was cancelled. Stubs are visibly present in the Eton Library copy and the Malone collection copy in the Bodleian Library. To judge from the report of variants, Greg and Dunstan consulted only the Bodleian copy designated G below for their 1914 edition. By the time W. W. Greg compiled his *Bibliography of the English Printed Drama* (1939), he had observed that one of the copies in the Bodleian preserved both the blank leaf and the stub of the cancelled leaf of preliminary matter and would presumably have revised his earlier description. Only the Huntington and Houghton copies have the original four-leaf gathering A. The double leaf including the title page was separately printed and should be designated π^2; it is not conjugate with the rest of gathering A. (The first leaf of π and the verso of π^2 are blank.) A few copies with the dedicatory leaf were presumably preserved for presentation or circulation within the Cary family; in theory, these copies represent the first issue of *Mariam*, and those which were offered for sale the second.

Both the printer and publisher of *The Tragedie of Mariam* were associated with other theatrical texts. Thomas Creede worked as a printer in London from 1593 to 1617: until 1600 at the sign of the Catherine Wheel in Thames Street, and from 1600 to 1617 at the Eagle and Child in the Old Exchange. He was employed by William Ponsonby, and among the notable early publications on which he worked are *The First part of the Contention betwixt the two famous houses of Yorke and Lancaster* (1594, a bad quarto of Shakespeare's *Henry VI*, Part II), the non-Shakespearean *The true Tragedie of Richard III* (also 1594), *The Lamentable Tragedy of Locrine* (1595), and *The Famous Victories of Henry V* (1598; a probable source for Shakespeare's *Henry IV* plays and *Henry V*). Creede printed the first and third quartos of *Richard III* for Andrew Wise in 1597 and 1602 and printed the second ("good") quarto of *Romeo and Juliet* for Cuthbert Burby in 1599. In 1600 he printed *The Chronicle History of Henry V* for Thomas Millington and John Busby, and a second version of this quarto in 1602. In 1602 he also printed the first ("bad") quarto of *The Merry Wives of Windsor*.[93]

The striking printer's emblem on the title pages of *Mariam* and several other books produced by Creede shows the naked, crowned figure of Truth being scourged by a hand which emerges from the clouds; the surrounding motto reads "Virescit Vulnere Veritas" ("Truth flourishes through injury"). This emblem is among those which Mary, Queen of Scots, and Bess of Hardwick embroidered while the latter was acting as the former's jailer, and it is tempting to infer something about Creede's religious or political alignments, but neither he nor Richard Hawkins has any identification with recusant or other theological literature.

Richard Hawkins, after serving an apprenticeship to Edmond Mattes, stationer of London, from 1604 to 1611, operated as a bookseller in London from 1613 to 1636. His place of business was in Chancery Lane near Sergeant's Inn. "The Tragedie of Mariam" was his first entry in the Stationers' Register. Subsequently, he published plays (including Beaumont and Fletcher's *The Maid's Tragedy*, 1630, and *A King and No King*, 1631) and miscellaneous literature. His last entry in the Stationers' Register is dated 6 December 1633.

Since the printer of *Mariam*, like his contemporaries, proofread and corrected books while they were already in press, each copy is potentially unique, and we have therefore inspected as many extant copies of the quarto as possible. The Dunstan and Greg edition was based only upon the three copies in the British Library, the Dyce copy in the Victoria and Albert Museum, the Eton College Library copy, and one of the copies in the Bodleian Library. For an account of the preliminary leaf with the dedicatory sonnet and the dramatis personae, Dunstan and Greg relied on photographs of the extra leaf in the White copy (now in the Huntington Library) and a catalogue description of the Huth copy, now in the Houghton Library. Since they neglected the Malone copy in the Bodleian, and the stub of the cancelled leaf is much less visible in the Eton copy, they mistakenly inferred that the preliminary matter in the Huth copy was an insertion, although, as noted above, Greg's later researches corrected that conclusion.

In the preparation of this edition we have consulted the three copies of the quarto at the British Museum (which, following Greg and Dunstan, we have designated A, B, and C; C lacks printer's signature I, although some hand has produced a facsimile of the missing pages in ink); three copies at the National Library of Scotland (D, E, and F); two at the Bodleian Library (G and M, the copy from the Malone Collection); and the single copies at each of the following locations: the National Library of Art, Victoria and Albert Museum (Dyce); Worcester College Library, Oxford (Wo); Eton College Library; the New York Public Library (NY); the Beinecke Library, Yale University (Y); the Elizabethan Club, Yale University (EC); the Houghton Library, Harvard University (Ho); the Boston Public Library (BP); the Folger Shakespeare Library (Fo); the Huntington Library (Hu); and the Newberry Library (N). (The Huntington copy is used for the Short-Title Catalogue microfilm.) Two of the later gatherings of the play, G and H, contain press corrections, and those in gathering H are of particular substantive interest. A census of all four corrections is hereby offered:

    1.   In some copies the catchword for the verso of G1 reads "Youlle" and in others, "Youl'e." It seems likely that the latter is the correction, though

neither form quite corresponds to "Youle," the initial word of G2 (that is, of 4.7.387).

Youlle   A, D, BP

Youl'e   B, C, E, F, G, M, Dyce, Wo, Eton, NY, Y, EC, Ho, N, Hu, Fo

2.   On the verso of G3 the final word of 4.7.509 appears as both "a new" and "anew." Presumably the latter is the correction.

a new   A, D, Y, BP

anew   B, C, E, F, G, M, Dyce, Wo, Eton, NY, EC, Ho, N, Hu, Fo

3 and 4.   On the verso of H4 a double variation occurs in 5.1.211 and 213. Copies read either "faine" or "fame" in both lines. (Even if it were possible to establish that one of these readings was certainly a correction, it might well be a printing-house emendation without authorial weight.)

faine   A, D, F, G, Dyce, Wo, Y, Ho, N

fame   B, C, E, M, Eton, NY, EC, BP, Hu, Fo

One of the Edinburgh copies (D, originally from the library of John Patrick Crichton Stuart, earl of Bute) contains a unique variant, the initial "I" of F3r (4.4.187), which apparently fell out of the form (that is, the page of type secured together in a chase, or wooden frame) before the other extant copies were printed.

The copy in the National Library of Art at the Victoria and Albert Museum has the additional interest of suggested emendations dating from 1826. Whatever their source, these notations, on the final page of the quarto, are editorially shrewd and occasionally recognize doubtful readings that escaped the eyes of Greg and Dunstan. Since this copy comes from the library of Alexander Dyce, we believe the emendations are in his hand, and have cited them, where relevant, in discussing textual cruxes.

THE MANUSCRIPT OF THE LADY FALKLAND: HER LIFE

The manuscript occupies twelve gatherings of four leaves (that is, two folded sheets per gathering) as well as a single leaf inserted in the third gathering. It is legibly written in a cursive Italian hand; many of the marginal glosses, which supply the names of the figures referred to in the narrative, are written in the same hand. Another series of marginal annotations, in a more angular hand, apparently belong to the biographer's brother Patrick. At some point in the history of this manuscript, it was severely cropped, but the cropping affected primarily this second layer of marginal commentary. Lines have been drawn through or across some sections of the text, although the material marked for deletion almost always remains readable. The deletions frequently represent false starts in the original biographer's narrative—the material is repeated a few lines later with minor alterations—but other deletions may signal later editorial decisions by the biographer, her brother, or even another reader of the manuscript; some do indeed suggest the intention to suppress potentially embarrassing details of family history. In addition to the biography, the Archives of the Département du Nord preserve other documents of the Cambray convent, dissolved at the time of the French Revolution, most notably a register with the entries extending from 1623 to 1725: "A Catalogue of ye names & ages of all those that have at any time entred into this monastery of our B^d Lady of Consolation in Canbray, as well as such as have beene & are religious profess'd, as of such as have lived for any time in ye Monastry & gon away from it." The catalogue records the entry, during 1638 and 1639, of four of Elizabeth Cary's daughters into the nunnery. One of these, as we have said—most probably Anne or Lucy—wrote the *Life*. We hope our readers will use their own interpretive skills to trace, and appreciate the talents of, the elusive daughter of Elizabeth Cary.

EDITORIAL PROCEDURES

This edition of *Mariam* and *The Lady Falkland: Her Life* is intended to serve several purposes: the treatment of the text and the annotations reflect those different aims. In the first place, we have wanted to make the play accessible to students, not only those with an interest in Renaissance drama but also those who may encounter the tragedy and/or biography in a course in history or women's studies. Therefore, we have chosen a modern-spelling format. No manuscript of *Mariam* exists, and the spellings of the 1613 text are as likely to reflect the preferences of the printing house as authorial choices. The seventeenth-century text uses predominantly spellings which would now be identified as "British," but its orthography is inconsistent; we have followed British forms throughout, but we have noted changes of spelling for the sake of normalization in the textual apparatus.

The punctuation is also modernized, although more conservatively; that is, we have altered the punctuation where we thought it might present obstacles or prove misleading to a twentieth-century reader, but we have retained the pointing of the seventeenth-century text, even where it differs from modern usage, if it did not seem to offer significant difficulty. We hope we have thus retained at least some of the advantages of seventeenth-century punctuation, which often signals a more fluid sense of syntax and a greater responsiveness to breath and phrasing than later usage. Where our punctuation depends on some decision between different possibilities of meaning in the 1613 text, we have explicitly discussed that decision in the notes.

Indeed, in the presentation of *Mariam* (though not of the *Life*) we have for pedagogical reasons foregrounded the whole process of (re)constructing a seventeenth-century text for modern readers, and our annotations therefore give more prominence to textual choices and emendations than most editions designed for the classroom. It seems to us useful to emphasize to students both in literature and in other disciplines the process of historical recovery and inference through which the texts of the past reach a modern reader. This open consideration of editorial decisions will also allow the more advanced student and the Renaissance or textual scholar to second-guess or to dispute the conclusions and choices at which we have arrived.

We have retained the classicizing scene divisions ("Actus Primus. Scena Prima," etc.), which sometimes indicate a break in the action, sometimes merely the entry of new characters, but we have numbered the lines of each act continuously. (The 1613 text has no line numbers; the Malone Society reprint of the play numbers the entire play, including scene headings and stage directions, continuously.) Where additional stage directions seemed potentially helpful, we have added them in square brackets.

Cary's major historical source was Josephus's *Antiquities*; occasionally she also seems to have referred to the same historian's *The Jewish War*. It seems probable that Cary used or consulted Thomas Lodge's 1602 translation of *The Famous and Memorable Workes of Josephus*, and the text of Lodge has therefore been used for direct quotations from Josephus. However, since Lodge's chapter divisions do not always correspond to those of standard Greek texts of Josephus (or of later translations), his translations have been cited by signature and page numbers; citations of Josephus also refer to the book, chapter, and paragraph divisions of standard editions.

Although our primary goal has been to produce a teaching text, we believe that this edition should also have value for the scholar. We have examined all the copies of the 1613 *Mariam* recorded in the second edition of the *Short-Title Catalogue* and have carefully considered the readings which Greg and Dunstan's 1914 edition flagged as "doubtful" (as well as the handwritten suggestions for emendation in Dyce's copy of *Mariam* in the Victoria and Albert Museum). All substantive alterations in the text are indicated by square brackets, and a complete list of variants is provided in the textual apparatus.

The notes at the foot of the page gloss unfamiliar words or difficult sense so that students who are first encountering *Mariam* can read the play without frequent recourse to the endnotes. These latter, more elaborate, annotations, included for the sake of the more advanced student (or the more sedulous novice), can be found following the text of the play. The notes frequently cite Shakespeare, but neither as a touchstone of literary value nor (except where explicitly indicated) as an instance of influence; we wished to supply examples of contemporary usage or allusion with which the widest range of readers would be familiar. In devoting such extensive commentary to *Mariam*, we are implicitly staking a claim for its inclusion in the mainstream canon of Renaissance drama. Since it has not yet achieved this status, we have also allowed ourselves the latitude to draw attention to local felicities or intricacies of Cary's dramatic construction; broader points about the achievement of *Mariam* are argued in the Introduction.

Although we believe that *The Lady Falkland: Her Life* has independent value as a historical document, we suspect that for most readers it will be an ancillary text to *Mariam*. *The Lady Falkland: Her Life* does exist as a manuscript, of which our text is essentially a transcription. However, stylistic nuance seems less crucial to its value, and although we have modernized the *Life* in accordance with the principles applied to *Mariam*, in this case we have not provided a full commentary on editorial procedure. On the other hand, we have recorded, in angle brackets, substantive manuscript erasures. It is not clear on what basis Richard Simpson, the biography's nineteenth-century editor, decided that Patrick Cary had deleted passages he found "too feminine"; little of the deleted material seems even stereotypically "feminine," nor is Patrick Cary's responsibility for the erasures self-evident. Some of the marginal annotations, which we have reproduced, appear to be in Patrick Cary's hand, but most are not; unless otherwise noted, the annotations are written in the same hand as the biographical narrative.

We have divided the text of the *Life* into paragraphs for greater ease of reading. The syntactical boundaries between sentences are looser than they would be in a historically later, or perhaps more public and formal, text, but we have not followed the example of the nineteenth-century version of the biography, which broke the flow of sentences into smaller units. The editorial annotations provide primarily simple glosses, biographical capsules, or historical reference points. Since some of the names that appear in the text have been variously modernized, we have retained the manuscript spellings; the footnotes, or occasionally square brackets, supply the most common or most likely modern spellings of these names.

NOTES

1. In their Introduction to the 1914 facsimile reprint of *Mariam*, A. C. Dunstan and W. W. Greg persuasively demonstrate that the "learned, vertuous, and truly noble Ladie, E.C." mentioned on the play's title page is indeed that Elizabeth Cary who was Lawrence Tanfield's daughter and Henry Falkland's wife (there were several other women with this name, variously spelled, alive in early seventeenth-century England).

2. Donald Foster, "Resurrecting the Author: Elizabeth Tanfield Cary," forthcoming in Jean Brink, ed., *Privileging Gender in Early Modern England*, n. 8. He has also found a copy, "partly in Anne's hand, of what appears to be the English translation of Blosius that Elizabeth Cary was working on during her last months (Colwich Abbey MS 36)."

3. Donald Foster has kindly shared with us, through personal communication and the manuscript of a forthcoming article, his evidence for believing Anne to be the author of the biography. Among his most compelling pieces of evidence is the remark, in the *Life*, that Anne "retain[ed] always more memory of what she owed her [mother]" than any of the other children (see below, 218). Barbara Lewalski also mentions Anne as the probable author, though without any discussion of the evidence; see Foster's "Resurrecting the Author: Elizabeth Tanfield Cary," n. 8, and Lewalski's "Writing Women and Reading the Renaissance," *Renaissance Quarterly* 44 (Winter 1991): 792–821, esp. 807, n. 34. While we find Foster's case for Anne very intriguing, the evidence seems to us

more complex than he allows; almost entirely "internal," so far as we now know, the evidence poses rhetorical and epistemological questions that elude certain answers. In our view, Lucy remains a likely candidate for authorship despite Foster's argument that the wording of her obituary clearly rules her out as the author of the *Life*. Referring to Lucy's conversion as a response to her mother's prayers and tears, the obituary states that the mother was "a woman of extraordinary piety, as will appear in the relation of her life, written by a person who knew her very well" (cited in the Appendix to *The Lady Falkland: Her Life, From a MS. in the Imperial Archives at Lille*, ed. R[ichard] S[impson] [London: Catholic Publishing and Bookselling Co., Ltd., 1861], 185; this Appendix will subsequently be cited as Appendix to the 1861 *Life*). Foster thinks the phrase "one who knew her very well" excludes Lucy from authorship of the *Life*, presumably because the rest of the obituary refers to Lucy in direct language. On the other hand, the inclusion of a reference to the biography in an extremely brief obituary is in itself suggestive, and the phrase could well be read as a coy reference *to* Lucy, in an era when women authors publicly concealed their identity but often revealed it, through coded allusions, to coterie audiences. The anonymous biography of Aphra Behn published in 1696 by "one of the fair sex" who claims to have known Behn "intimately" may well be partly by Behn herself, for instance, as R. A. Day has argued in "Aphra Behn's First Biographer," *Studies in Bibliography* 22 (1969): 227–40.

We are also less sure than Foster is that internal evidence from the manuscript points clearly to Anne's authorship; he infers, for instance, that since Anne was the only child present throughout the harrowing scenes when Henry Cary's gangrenous leg was amputated, the account of his ensuing death "cannot have come from the younger daughters"; but surely the four sisters exchanged information and narratives about their family during their years together at the convent. Arguments for Anne's authorship on the basis that only she could have been present at a given event seem to oversimplify the biography's complexly layered temporality and its mode of (at least arguably "collective") production. While Foster points to moments in the narrative that highlight Anne's "thoughts and innermost feelings," it is possible to see comparable inwardness (and perhaps a touch of retrospective self-accusation) in the anecdote concerning Lucy's malicious pleasure in reminding her mother of fast days when she was "set down hungry, and ready to put her meat in her mouth" (223–24). For a different argument that assigns authorship of the biography to Lucy, see Dorothy Latz, "*Glow-Worm Light*," 118–19.

Although we are not fully persuaded by Foster's arguments for Anne's indisputable authorship, we assent to his conclusion that the *Life* was probably written between 1643 (after Lucius Cary's death in 1642) and before 1650 (the year of Lucy's death). Both Foster and Elaine Beilin date the manuscript in its current form "c. 1655," and we accept that judgment (see Foster, "Resurrecting the Author," n. 7, and Beilin, *Redeeming Eve: Women Writers of the English Renaissance*, 158).

The dates for Lucy and Anne derive from information in the convent's record book, preserved at Lille. It gives the following information about their sisters: Elizabeth (1617–1683) was received into the convent as Augustina on 29 Oct. 1638. Mary (1621/22–1693) evidently retained her own name; although the convent register records her age as fourteen when she was received on 31 Aug. 1638, she was baptized on 9 Jan. 1621 (i.e., 1622 according to the revised calendar) and must have been sixteen at the time. Elizabeth and Mary remain possible, if less likely, candidates for the authorship of the biography.

4. Kurt Weber says that a "proper discount" should be made because the biography was written under "pious influences" (*Lucius Cary*, 11–12), but Weber, like most biographers of the Cary-Falkland family, makes extensive use of the *Life*, as Elaine Beilin remarks in one of the few sympathetic discussions of this text (see *Redeeming Eve*, 158 and 314, n. 15). In an earlier article, Beilin notes that the author of the *Life* shows considerable "sympathy for her mother and hostility to her father . . . but by no means does she cast one as a saint and the other as a sinner" ("Elizabeth Cary and *The Tragedie of Mariam*," 47, n. 5); Beilin further remarks that the biographer's credibility is "increased when we find that other sources [for example, the *DNB* entry on Henry Cary] corroborate the main drift of her characterizations, particularly that of her father." If anything, Beilin understates the complicated allegiances of the *Life*; when the biographer reports that "to her husband [Lady Falkland] bore so much respect that she taught her children, as a duty, to love him better than herself," she continues, perhaps surprisingly, "though she saw it was a lesson they could learn without teaching, and that all but her eldest son did it in a very high degree" (193). See also Donald Stauffer, who calls the biography a "notable piece of individualization" and remarks that its "subtle appraisals and almost brazen analyses of motives are written with a certain dry intelligence that puts to shame the effusive contemporary masculine biographers" (*English Biography before 1700*, 148–50).

5. Of the eleven children "born alive" to Elizabeth Cary, nine survived to adulthood. For names and dates, see the Chronology.

6. Donald Stauffer, *English Biography before 1700*, 148–50. For the best discussion of the biography to date, see Donald Foster, "Resurrecting the Author."

7. These letters are reproduced in the Appendix to Richard Simpson's 1861 edition of the biography and, even more fully, in Georgiana Fullerton's 1883 life of Elizabeth Cary (the chief contribution of the latter to the biographical record).

8. Kenneth Murdock, *Sun at Noon*, 10.

9. The *Life* states that she was married "at fifteen," and gives her birthdate as 1585 or 1586, which would mean she should have been married in 1600 or 1601. The *Complete Peerage* (5:240), however, gives the date of the marriage contract as June 1602, with the marriage occurring in the fall of that year; and this date corresponds with the *Life's* statement that Elizabeth was married "seven years without any child," since her first child was born in 1609. Both Beilin and Murdock

accept 1602 as the date of the Cary marriage; see *Sun at Noon*, 7, n. 1, and "Elizabeth Cary and the *Tragedie of Mariam*," 50.

10. Nancy Cotton Pearse, "Elizabeth Cary," 602.

11. Murdock, 16.

12. Ibid.

13. Carol Thomas Neely suggests (in a personal communication) that the seven-year delay before the birth of the Carys' first child—followed by ten other children "born alive"—may indicate that the marriage was not consummated during the period of Henry's frequent absences. In any event, it seems likely that *Mariam* was written before Elizabeth had children but not necessarily as early as 1605, the latest date Dunstan and Greg allow. They assert that the dedicatee of *Mariam* "must have been" the Elizabeth Bland Cary who married Henry Cary's brother Philip, and from this inference they conclude that the play *had* to have been written between 1602 (when Lodge's translation appeared) and 1605, when Philip was knighted, since after that date the title of "Mistris" assigned to the dedicatee in Cary's text would have been inappropriate for Philip's wife. Some recent critics have accepted this reasoning, but we agree with Elaine Beilin that the date of the play's writing remains problematic and that the dedicatee could well have been not Elizabeth the wife of Philip but rather Henry's own sister Elizabeth Cary. See Beilin's finely detailed discussion of the evidence for this identification in "Elizabeth Cary and *The Tragedie of Mariam*," esp. n. 6.

14. *The Second Maiden's Tragedy*, ed. W. W. Greg, 59.

15. Carol Neely suggests (in a personal communication) that Davies's life and career bear comparison with those of Henry Cary, Viscount Falkland. Like Falkland, he pursued much of his political career in Ireland (where James I sent him as solicitor-general in 1603) and was active in enforcing Irish conformity to Protestantism. The writings of Davies's eccentric wife, Eleanor Touchet, daughter of George, Baron Audley, were even more immediately religiously and politically troublesome than those of Elizabeth Cary; she wrote prophecies, which, however, were published only after the death of Davies (who, by her report, burned the first book of her revelations).

16. *The Complete Works of John Davies of Hereford*, ed. Grosart, 2:5.

17. Murdock, 20.

18. Ibid., 21.

19. Letter to Lord Conway, 5 April 1626, State Paper Office, Dublin, quoted in the Appendix to the 1861 *Life*, 132.

20. Falkland to Charles I, 8 Dec. 1626, State Paper Office, Dublin, quoted in the Appendix to the 1861 *Life*, 137.

21. When Elizabeth's father disinherited her, he settled the estate on her eldest son, Lucius, or, in the event of his death, on the next eldest son, thus ensuring the continuity of the patriarchal line. Tanfield had taken Lucius "to live with him from his birth" (192), thus asserting the grandfather's (and chief money provider's) rights over those of the son-in-law as well as the daughter. See

the brief account of the disinheritance in the *Life*, 195, as well as the supplemental information (mostly conjectural) in the Appendix to the 1861 *Life*, 127. It is worth noting that Sir Henry maintains, against the written accounts of both his wife and daughter, that Elizabeth's conversion, not her mortgaging of her jointure, was the prime cause of her disinheritance; he does so in a self-serving letter written in May 1627, when he was himself refusing to pay an allowance to his estranged wife. He argues that she "misreports" the facts in saying that "her father disinherited her for her obedience to me." He further claims that he never had a penny from her after her initial dowry payment (Appendix, 153; for Elizabeth's counterstatement, also in a letter, that the mortgaged jointure caused the disinheritance, see Appendix, 149).

22. Edward Hyde, earl of Clarendon, *Selections from Clarendon*, 52.

23. Ibid.

24. Kurt Weber, *Lucius Cary*, 224–25.

25. For accounts of Lucius Cary's life see Weber, *Lucius Cary*; Murdock, *Sun at Noon*, 39–268; and the two brief biographies by Edward Hyde, earl of Clarendon, from his *True Historical Narrative of the Rebellion. . . .* (1702–04) and *The Life of Edward Earl of Clarendon, By Himself* (1759), rpt. in *Selections from Clarendon*, ed. G. Huehns, 49–67.

26. Weber, 5.

27. See Foster, "Resurrecting the Author," esp. n. 27, for a discussion of this elegy, a complete text of which, not previously identified, Foster has located in Beinecke Library MS Poetry Box VI/28. Foster is publishing this funeral elegy with annotations in his forthcoming anthology *Women's Works: 1400–1800*. Kurt Weber also (and unequivocally) takes the elegy as Elizabeth's work. He refers to the copy in MS 2725 of the British Museum (*Lucius Cary*, 28).

28. Letter to "Right Honourable Sir" (probably Sir John Coke, Charles I's secretary), 20 Dec. 1626, State Paper Office, Dublin, quoted in Appendix to the 1861 *Life*, 139; see also Falkland's letter to the king of 8 Dec. 1626, in which he begs for the "confinement" of his "apostate" wife (a rather tactless description, since Charles's own queen was a Catholic), State Paper Office, Dublin, quoted in Appendix to the 1861 *Life*, 138.

29. See Elizabeth Cary's petition to Charles I of 18 May 1627, State Paper Office, Domestic, quoted in the Appendix to the 1861 *Life*, 148–51.

30. Elizabeth Cary Falkland, *The Reply of the Most Illustrious Cardinall of Perron*, sig. C2.

31. In 1689 this version of the text was reprinted, without the preface and dedication some critics have used to ascribe it to Elizabeth Cary, as *The Parallel: Or the History of the Life, Reign, Deposition, and Death, of King Edward the Second* (London: R. Baldwin, 1689). Donald Foster classifies the folio *History of the Life* as a "verse biography" and remarks that it is the only extant instance of a form Elizabeth Cary clearly favored (e.g., in the lost verse biographies of Tamburlaine and the female saints); but Foster also remarks that "irregularities in the verse

suggest that the printer found the lines thus arranged in his copy-text . . . since the text is considerably less readable when rearranged as verse, future editors will do well . . . to follow the folio text in printing the entire work as prose" ("Resurrecting the Author," n. 36). For a different account of the style of *The History of the Life*, see Donald A. Stauffer, "A Deep and Sad Passion," 300. The text alternates between prose and blank verse, with almost all of the latter presented as direct discourse. The shifts between prose and verse, Stauffer opines, are not so definite as those in Shakespeare's plays, "for the author had an iambic beat so strongly in his pulses that all his sentences tend to fall into the [iambic] pattern" (at this point in his argument, Stauffer agnostically withholds the feminine pronoun from the author).

32. This text was originally printed in London by Playford; it was reprinted in *Harleian Miscellany*, 10 vols., ed. Thomas Park (London: White and Murray, 1808–11), 1 (1808): 92–127.

33. Stauffer, "A Deep and Sad Passion," 295.

34. Ibid., 295, n. 7.

35. Tina Krontiris, "Style and Gender in Elizabeth Cary's *Edward II*," in *The Renaissance Englishwoman in Print*, 137–53.

36. See Krontiris, 140, on the contrast between the treatment of Queen Isabel in this text and those of previous authors.

37. Ibid., 149, n. 2.

38. Lewalski, *Writing Women in Jacobean England*, Appendix A, 317. Lewalski further suggests a post-Restoration date for the octavo when she notes that it "elaborates much more than the folio on the fate of the regicides and their punishment."

39. Ibid., 317.

40. Travitsky, "The *Feme Covert* in Cary's *Mariam*," in *Ambiguous Realities*, ed. Carole Levin and Jean Watson, 193, n. 3.

41. Foster, "Resurrecting the Author."

42. D. R. Woolf, "The True Date and Authorship of Henry, Viscount Falkland's *History of the Life, Reign, and Death of King Edward II*," 442.

43. Isobel Grundy suggests that this phrase may refer to Ireland in the 1620s, rather than to the English Civil War. She criticizes Woolf for ignoring Stauffer's stylistic analysis of *Edward II* and challenges his arguments for a date of composition that would definitively exclude the possibility of Elizabeth Cary's authorship (Grundy, "Falkland's *History of . . . King Edward II*," 82–83).

44. Woolf, 442.

45. Anthony Wood, *Athenae Oxonienses*, quoted in Woolf, 445.

46. Woolf, 441.

47. *The History of the Life*, "The Author's Preface to the Reader," 20 Feb. 1627, n.p.

48. *Reply to the . . . Cardinall of Perron*, sig. a2 verso and a2 recto; another commendatory poem expresses men's amazement "that a Womans hand alone

should raise / So vast a monument in thirty days" (sig. a3r). Lewalski discusses all these passages in *Writing Women*, 202 and 392, n. 82.

49. See Lewalski, *Writing Women*, 202 and 320; see also Beilin, *Redeeming Eve*, 316, n. 20.

50. Clarendon, 51.

51. Maurice Jacques Valency, *The Tragedies of Herod and Mariamne*, 6.

52. Dympna Callaghan, "Re-reading *The Tragedie of Mariam, the Faire Queene of Jewry*," in *Women, 'Race,' and Writing in the Early Modern Period*, ed. Margo Hendricks and Patricia Parker. Forthcoming (London: Routledge, 1993).

53. See David S. Katz, *Philo-semitism and the Readmission of the Jews to England, 1603–1655*, and J. Fines, "'Judaising' in the Period of the English Reformation— the Case of Robt. Bruern," *Transactions of the Jewish Historical Society of England*.

54. See C. J. Sisson, "A Colony of Jews in Shakespeare's London."

55. Valency, 20.

56. Josephus, *Antiquities of the Jews*, 16.5.4.

57. *Interpreter's Bible*, 2:593.

58. Valency, 26.

59. *Interpreter's Bible*, 2:592.

60. Ibid., 2:593.

61. Ibid., 2:592.

62. Valency, 33.

63. See V. A. Kolve, *The Play Called Corpus Christi*, 156–58, on the representation of Herod in the mystery cycles.

64. Valency, 32.

65. Cynthia Bourgeault, ed., *Herod the Great*, 9; see also Valency, 32–33.

66. Quoted from *The Tragedy of Hamlet*, 3.2.8–14, in *The Riverside Shakespeare*, ed. G. Blakemore Evans et al. (Boston: Houghton Mifflin, 1974), 1161. All citations of Shakespeare's plays are from this edition.

67. *The Chester Plays*, ed. H. Deimling, 201.

68. Margaret Arnold, "Jane Lumley's *Iphigeneia*: Self-Revelation of a Renaissance Gentlewoman to Her Audience," a paper presented at the 1990 meeting of the Shakespeare Association of America. In *Redeeming Eve*, Elaine Beilin considers Lumley's and Cary's plays together in her chapter on "The Making of a Female Hero," but Beilin does not here address the question of the circulation of Lumley's MS or whether Cary, as a fellow Catholic, might actually have seen Lumley's text.

69. See *Iphigenia at Aulis, Translated by Lady Lumley*, ed. Harold H. Child and W. W. Greg for the Malone Society Reprint Series (London: Charles Whittingham & Co., 1909).

70. John Lumley, who matriculated at Cambridge in May 1549 and married Jane soon thereafter, evidently pursued his classical studies with his wife; see Child and Greg's introduction to *Iphigenia at Aulis*, vii.

71. Beilin, *Redeeming Eve*, 156–57.

72. *Iphigenia at Aulis, Translated by Lady Lumley*, Malone Society edition, fol. 91v-92r, quoted in Beilin, 156.

73. Ibid., fol. 94v.

74. Gordon Braden, *Senecan Tragedy*, 171.

75. Beilin, *Redeeming Eve*, 313, n. 6.

76. Nancy Gutierrez, "Valuing *Mariam*," 237.

77. Ibid., 237 and n. 18.

78. Beilin, *Redeeming Eve*, 125.

79. Samuel Daniel, *The Tragedie of Cleopatra* (1594); in Grosart, 3:23.

80. Ibid., 1.1.2, in Grosart, 3:31.

81. Cary's allusive rendition of Cleopatra builds on the complex role which the (quasi-)historical Cleopatra plays in Josephus's narrative: at different moments Josephus reports that Cleopatra showed an amorous interest in Mariam's brother Aristobulus; that Herod was a potential erotic partner for Cleopatra; and that Mariam's mother had schemed to make a match between Mariam and Antony. All these triangulations involving Mariam and Cleopatra may link Cary's emphasis on Mariam's chastity to Plutarch's and also Samuel Daniel's portraits of Antony's Roman wife, Octavia, the historical rival of Cleopatra. (Daniel's fascinating short work *Octavia* rather surprisingly presents that heroine as an eloquent defender of women's rights [*Complete Works*, ed. Grosart, vol. 4].) Mariam's erotic and political rivalry with Cleopatra doubles her more explicitly dramatized rivalry for power with Salome.

82. Nicolas Sander[s], *Anglican Schism*, ed. and trans. David Lewis, bk. 1, ch. 1, p. 4.

83. Ibid., ch. 5, and Retha Warnicke, *Anne Boleyn*.

84. Nicholas Harpsfield, *A Treatise on the Pretended Divorce*, ed. Nicholas Pocock, 250.

85. *Lingua: or the Combat of the Tongue, and the five Senses for Superiority. A pleasant Comoedie* (London: G. Eld for Simon Waterston, 1607), act 5, scene 19, sig. N1 verso. This passage is mentioned by Catherine Belsey, *The Subject of Tragedy*, 181. For a useful discussion of the play, see Patricia Parker, "On the Tongue: Cross-gendering, Effeminacy, and the Art of Words," *Style* 23, no. 3 (Fall 1989): 445–65.

86. Rebecca Bushnell, *Tragedies of Tyrants*, 106.

87. George Buchanan, *Tragedies*, 134–35.

88. *Baptistes, sive calumnia*, sig. A2 recto–A3 verso; quoted in Bushnell, 103. Bushnell cites I. D. McFarland's translation from his *Buchanan* (London: Duckworth, 1981), 386.

89. Bushnell, 109.

90. One of the probable contexts for Mariam's reflections on plain speech, silence, and dissimulation is the Jesuit doctrine of "mental reservation," which justified Catholics' not telling the whole truth in times of danger.

91. For further discussion of the comic elements in the text, see Boyd M. Berry, "'Move thy tongue / For silence is a signe of discontent'; or, What's Comic in *The Tragedy of Mariam*?" (unpublished).

92. *Othello: A New Variorum Edition of Shakespeare*, ed. Horace Howard Furness (1886; reprint, New York: Dover, 1963), 327.

93. See the introduction to *Shakespeare's Plays in Quarto*, ed. Michael J. B. Allen and Kenneth Muir (Berkeley: Univ. of California Press, 1981) for more detailed comments on how these quartos relate to the Shakespearean textual tradition.

94. The emblem is very distinctively connected with, perhaps unique to, Creede. (However, see discussion of other possible occurrences and precedents in R. B. McKerrow, *Printers' and Publishers' Devices in England and Scotland 1485–1640* [London: printed for the Bibliographical Society at the Chiswick Press, 1913] and Bella C. Landauer, ed., *Printers' Mottoes . . . from the 15th Century to the Present* [New York: privately printed, 1926].)

The more common form of the motto Creede's emblem incorporates is "Virescit vulnere virtus" ("Virtue flourishes through injury"), and these are the words that accompany the emblem as embroidered by Mary, Queen of Scots, and Bess of Hardwick; see illustration 31 to Antonia Fraser, *Mary Queen of Scots* (London: Weidenfeld and Nicolson, 1969).

PART ONE

———

THE TRAGEDY OF MARIAM

T&HE TRAGEDIE OF·MARIAM,
THE FAIRE
Queene of Iewry.

Written by that learned,
vertuous, and truly noble Ladie,
E. C.

LONDON.
Printed by Thomas Creede, for Richard
Hawkins, and are to be folde at his shoppe
in Chancery Lane, neere vnto
Sargeants Inne.
1613.

The title page of the 1613 edition of *The Tragedy of Mariam.*
Courtesy The Newberry Library.

HISTORICAL BACKGROUND
TO THE EVENTS IN THE PLAY

The Argument of *Mariam* outlines the situation at the opening of the tragedy, but the drama often refers more allusively to the complex of political and familial relationships that precede its action. Historians give alternative accounts of the events (and causal sequences) that the play assumes; the following summary and subsequent annotations reflect the emphases of Josephus's *Antiquities*, which was Cary's primary historical source.

In 39 B.C. Herod was appointed King of the Jews by the Romans, and, after a military campaign, took possession of Jerusalem and his throne in 37 B.C. He thus displaced Antigonus, the last ruler of the Maccabean, or Hasmonean, dynasty, to which Mariam, his second wife, and her family belonged. Since Antigonus had seized power from his uncle Hyrcanus II, the grandfather of Mariam, also named Hyrcanus, welcomed his defeat and Herod's entry into Jerusalem.

During the siege of Jerusalem, the sons of Babas had been particularly active in their support of Antigonus and had spread calumnies against Herod. When the city was taken, Constabarus, or Costobarus (an Idumean who later became Herod's brother-in-law), was placed in charge of the gates and was supposed to prevent Herod's enemies from escaping. However, thinking that the standing and authority of Babas's sons might be helpful to him in subsequent changes of government, he concealed them for twelve years on his farms outside the city. (Since Constabarus swore to Herod ignorance of their fate, discovery of their whereabouts would provide evidence of double disloyalty [Josephus, *Antiquities*, 15.7.10].)

Despite Hyrcanus's support, Herod remained wary of his in-laws and their dynastic claims. To avoid giving the high priesthood to Hyrcanus, his chief potential rival for the throne, Herod had conferred it on an obscure Babylonian priest named Ananelus (or Hananel). To soothe the subsequent commotion in his own family (and particularly to appease the wrath of his mother-in-law, Alexandra) Herod subsequently, in a not unprecedented abuse of civil power, deprived Ananelus of the priesthood and gave it to his brother-in-law Aristobulus, then aged seventeen. However, according to Josephus, the populace so much admired Aristobulus's striking figure and noble aspect in performing his priestly offices; and so displayed their warm predispositions toward his family, that Herod became jealous. When Aristobulus had held the priesthood for only a year, at Herod's instigation he joined a nighttime swimming party in a fishpond, where Herod's accomplices held him under the water, as though playfully, until he drowned (35 B.C.) (*Antiquities*, 15.3.3). After Aristobulus's death, Ananelus regained the position of high priest.

The mild-tempered and apparently unambitious Hyrcanus had little interest in seeking to regain the throne, but after the defeat of Antony and Cleopatra at Actium, when the power of Herod, a friend of Antony, seemed unstable, Hyrcanus was incited by his daughter, Alexandra, to write to Malchus, the governor of Arabia, requesting asylum until Herod could be deposed and the family of the Maccabees advance its claim to the monarchy. The messenger, Dositheus, betrayed this correspondence to Herod, who denounced Hyrcanus to the Sanhedrin and eagerly seized the excuse to have Hyrcanus executed (30 B.C.) (*Antiquities*, 15.6.1–4).

Herod's distrust and tyranny extended to his own family as well as Mariam's. Josephus, the uncle of Herod and Salome, had been Salome's first husband. Out of ill will toward her sister-in-law, Salome told Herod that Josephus had committed adultery with Mariam. When Herod discovered that Josephus had revealed to Mariam the royal order to kill her if her husband died, he took this indiscretion as confirmation of Josephus's guilt and ordered him to be slain. After Josephus's death, Herod gave Constabarus both his sister in marriage and the governorship of Idumea and Gaza.

THE TRAGEDY OF MARIAM

THE FAIR QUEEN OF JEWRY

———

WRITTEN BY THAT LEARNED, VIRTUOUS, AND
TRULY NOBLE LADY, E.C.

THE NAMES OF THE SPEAKERS.

Herod, King of Judea
Doris, his first wife
Mariam, his second wife
Salome, Herod's sister
Antipater, his son by [Doris]
Alexandra, Mariam's mother
[Silleus], prince of Arabia
Constabarus, husband to Salome
[Pheroras], Herod's brother
Graphina, his love
[Babas'] first son
[Babas'] second son
[Ananell], the high priest
Sohemus, a counsellor to Herod
Nuntio[1]
Bu[tler], another messenger
Chorus, a company of Jews

[1] Messenger.

To Diana's Earthly Deputess, and My Worthy Sister,
Mistress Elizabeth Cary[†]

When cheerful Phoebus his full course hath run,
His sister's fainter beams our hearts doth cheer:
So your fair brother is to me the sun,
And you his sister as my moon appear.

You are my next belov'd, my second friend,   5
For when my Phoebus' absence makes it night,
Whilst to th'antipodes[2] his beams do bend,
From you, my Phoebe,[3] shines my second light.

He like to Sol, clear-sighted, constant, free,
You Luna-like, unspotted, chaste, divine: 10
He shone on Sicily, you destin'd be[†]
T'illumine the now obscurèd Palestine.
My first was consecrated to Apollo,
My second to Diana now shall follow.

E.C.

[†] For lines marked with a dagger, see Notes to the Play, pages 151–76.
[2] The other side of the earth.
[3] Phoebe and Luna (Latin for "moon," l. 10) are alternative names for Diana (as Sol, Latin for "sun," l. 9, and Phoebus are for Apollo).

THE ARGUMENT

Herod, the son of Antipater (an Idumean),[†] having crept by the favour of the Romans, into the Jewish monarchy, married Mariam, the [granddaughter][†] of Hircanus, the rightful king and priest, and for her (besides her high blood, being of singular beauty) he repudiated Doris, his former wife, by whom he had children.

This Mariam had a brother called Aristobulus, and next him and Hircanus, his grandfather, Herod in his wife's right had the best title. Therefore to remove them, he charged the [second][†] with treason: and put him to death; and drowned the [first][†] under colour of sport. Alexandra, daughter to the one, and mother to the other, accused him for their deaths before Anthony.

So when he was forced to go answer this accusation at Rome, he left the custody of his wife to Josephus, his uncle, that had married his sister Salome, and out of a violent affection (unwilling that any should enjoy her after him) he gave strict and private commandment, that if he were slain, she should be put to death. But he returned with much honour, yet found his wife extremely discontented, to whom Josephus had (meaning it for the best, to prove Herod loved her) revealed his charge.

So by Salome's accusation he put Josephus to death, but was reconciled to Mariam, who still bare[4] the death of her friends[5] exceeding hardly.

In this meantime Herod was again necessarily to revisit Rome, for Caesar having overthrown Anthony, his great friend, was likely to make an alteration of his[6] fortune.

In his absence, news came to Jerusalem that Caesar had put him to death; their willingness it should be so, together with the likelihood, gave this rumour so good credit, as Sohemus, that had succeeded Josephus' charge,[7] succeeded him likewise in revealing it. So at Herod's return, which was speedy and unexpected, he found Mariam so far from joy, that she showed apparent signs of sorrow. He still desiring to win her to a better

---

[4] Bore.
[5] Relatives.
[6] Herod's.
[7] Had in turn assumed Josephus's responsibilities.

humour, she, being very unable to conceal her passion, fell to upbraiding him with her brother's death. As they were thus debating, came in a fellow with a cup of wine, who, hired by Salome, said first, it was a love potion, which Mariam desired to deliver to the king: but afterwards he affirmed that it was a poison, and that Sohemus had told her somewhat,[8] which procured the vehement hate in her.

The king hearing this, more moved with jealousy of Sohemus, than with this intent of poison, sent her away, and presently after[9] by the instigation of Salome, she was beheaded.† Which rashness was afterward punished in him, with an intolerable and almost frantic passion for her death.

[8] Something.
[9] Soon afterward.

ACTUS PRIMUS. SCENA PRIMA.

MARIAM *SOLA*[10]

Mariam. How oft have I with public voice run on[†]
To censure Rome's last hero for deceit:
Because he wept when Pompey's life was gone,
Yet[11] when he liv'd, he thought his name too great.
But now I do recant, and, Roman lord,[†]   5
Excuse too rash a judgement in a woman:
My sex pleads pardon, pardon then afford,
Mistaking is with us but too too common.
Now do I find, by self-experience taught,
One object yields both grief and joy:[†]   10
You wept indeed, when on his worth you thought,
But joy'd that slaughter did your foe destroy.
So at his death your eyes true drops did rain,
Whom dead, you did not wish alive again.
When Herod liv'd, that now is done to death,   15
Oft have I wish'd that I from him were free:
Oft have I wish'd that he might lose his breath,
Oft have I wish'd his carcass dead to see.
Then rage and scorn had put my love to flight,
That love which once on him was firmly set: 20
Hate hid his true affection from my sight,
And kept my heart from paying him his debt.
And blame me not, for Herod's jealousy
Had power even constancy itself to change:
For he, by barring me from liberty,   25
To shun[12] my ranging, taught me first to range.
But yet too chaste a scholar was my heart,[†]

[10] Alone.
[11] Although.
[12] Prevent.

To learn to love another than my lord:
To leave his love, my lesson's former part,
I quickly learn'd, the other I abhorr'd.   30
But now his death to memory doth call
The tender love that he to Mariam bare:[13]
And mine to him; this makes those rivers fall,
Which by another thought unmoisten'd[14] are.
For Aristobulus, the [loveliest] youth†   35
That ever did in angel's shape appear,
The cruel Herod was not mov'd to ruth;
Then why grieves Mariam Herod's death to hear?
Why joy I not the tongue no more shall speak,
That yielded forth my brother's latest[15] doom: 40
Both youth and beauty might thy[16] fury break,†
And both in him did ill befit a tomb.
And, worthy grandsire, ill did he requite†
His high ascent, alone by thee procur'd,
Except[17] he murder'd thee to free the sprite   45
Which still he thought on earth too long immur'd.†
How happy was it that Sohemus' [mind]†
Was mov'd to pity my distress'd estate!
Might Herod's life a trusty servant find,[18]
My death to his had been unseparate.   50
These thoughts have power, his death to make me bear,
Nay more, to wish the news may firmly hold:
Yet cannot this repulse some falling tear,
That will against my will some grief unfold.

---

[13] Bore.
[14] That is, dried up.
[15] Final.
[16] That is, Herod's.
[17] Unless.
[18] That is, if Herod, while living, had inspired fidelity. . . .

And more I owe him for his love to me,   55
The deepest love that ever yet was seen:
Yet had I rather much a milkmaid be,
Than be the monarch of Judea's queen.†
It was for nought but love he wish'd his end
Might to my death but the vaunt-courier[19] prove: 60
But I had rather still be foe than friend,
To him that saves for hate, and kills for love.†
Hard-hearted Mariam, at thy discontent
What floods of tears have drench'd his manly face!
How canst thou then so faintly now lament   65
Thy truest lover's death, a death's disgrace:[20]
Ay, now, mine eyes, you do begin to right
The wrongs of your admirer and my lord.[21]
Long since you should have put your smiles to flight,
Ill doth a widowed eye with joy accord.   70
Why, now methinks the love I bare him then,
When virgin freedom left me unrestrain'd,
Doth to my heart begin to creep again,
My passion[22] now is far from being feign'd.
But, tears, fly back, and hide you in your banks,[23]   75
You must not be to Alexandra seen:
For if my moan be spied, but little thanks
Shall Mariam have, from that incensèd queen.

[19] Forerunner. Cf. *King Lear*, 3.2.5.
[20] That is, faint lamentation disgraces (fails in the emotional and formal decorum proper to) his death.
[21] "Your admirer" (that is, the admirer of Mariam's eyes, to which lines 67–68 are addressed) is Herod; his "wrongs" are presumably Mariam's failure to weep before this moment.
[22] Emotion.
[23] In lines 75–76 Mariam addresses her tears, imagined as a stream which has flooded or overflown its banks—that is, her eyes.

ACTUS PRIMUS. SCENA SECUNDA.

Mariam. Alexandra.

Alexandra. What means these tears? My Mariam doth mistake,

The news we heard did tell the tyrant's end: 80

What[24] weep'st thou for thy brother's [murd'rer's] sake?†

Will ever wight a tear for Herod spend?

My curse pursue his breathless trunk and spirit,

Base Edomite, the damnèd Esau's heir:

Must he ere Jacob's child the crown inherit?† 85

Must he, vile wretch, be set in David's chair?[25]

No, David's soul, within the bosom plac'd

Of our forefather Abram, was asham'd:†

To see his seat with such a toad disgrac'd,

That seat that hath by Judah's race been [fam'd].† 90

Thou fatal enemy to royal blood,[26]

Did not the murder of my boy suffice,

To stop thy cruel mouth that gaping stood,

But must thou dim the mild Hircanus' eyes?

My gracious father, whose too ready hand 95

Did lift this Idumean from the dust:†

And he, ungrateful caitiff,[27] did withstand[28]

The man that did in him most friendly trust.

What kingdom's right could cruel Herod claim,

Was he not Esau's issue, heir of hell? 100

Then what succession can he have but shame?

Did not his ancestor his birth-right sell?

Oh yes, he doth from Edom's name derive†

His cruel nature which with blood is fed:

---

[24] Why.

[25] Throne, metonymy for royal authority over the Jews.

[26] Lines 91–94 apostrophize Herod.

[27] Wretch.

[28] Oppose, stand as an enemy against.

That made him me of sire and son deprive,   105
He ever thirsts for blood, and blood is red.
Weep'st thou because his love to thee was bent,
And read'st thou love in crimson characters?
Slew he thy friends to work thy heart's content?
No: hate may justly call that action hers.   110
He gave the sacred priesthood for thy sake
To Aristobulus, yet doom'd him dead:
Before his back the ephod warm could make,
And ere the miter settled on his head:†
Oh, had he given my boy no less than right,   115
The double oil should to his forehead bring
A double honour, shining doubly bright;
His birth anointed him both priest and king.
And say my father and my son he slew
To royalize by right your prince-born breath:²⁹   120
Was love the cause, can Mariam deem it true,
That Mariam gave commandment for her death?†
I know by fits he show'd some signs of love,
And yet not love, but raging lunacy:
And this his hate to thee may justly prove,   125
That sure he hates Hircanus' family.
Who knows if he, unconstant wavering lord,
His love to Doris³⁰ had renew'd again?
And that he might his bed to her afford,
Perchance he wish'd that Mariam might be slain.   130
[*Mariam.*] Doris! Alas, her time of love was past,
Those coals were rak'd in embers long ago
[Of] Mariam's love, and she was now disgrac'd,†
Nor did I glory in her overthrow.

²⁹ Either make Mariam heir apparent or ensure succession to her (their) son.
³⁰ The name of Herod's first wife (see Argument); according to Josephus (*Antiquities*, XIV, xii, 1; Lodge, Ll iv verso), she was "of his owne nation" but of a lower rank.

He not a whit his first-born son esteem'd,   135
Because as well as his he was not mine:[31]
My children only for his own he deem'd,[32]
These boys that did descend from royal line.
These did he style his heirs to David's throne;
My Alexander, if he live, shall sit   140
In the majestic seat of Solomon;[†]
To will it so, did Herod think it fit.
Alexandra. Why, who can claim from Alexander's brood[†]
That gold-adornèd lion-guarded chair?
Was Alexander not of David's blood?[†]   145
And was not Mariam Alexander's heir?
What more than right could Herod then bestow,[†]
And who will think except for more than right[33]
He did not raise them, for they were not low,
But born to wear the crown in his despite: 150
Then send those tears away that are not sent
To thee by reason, but by passion's power:
Thine eyes to cheer, thy cheeks to smiles be bent,
And entertain with joy this happy hour.
Felicity, if when she comes, she finds   155
A mourning habit, and a cheerless look,
Will think she is not welcome to thy mind,
And so perchance her lodging will not brook.[34]
Oh, keep her whilst thou hast her; if she go,
She will not easily return again: 160
Full many a year have I endur'd in woe,

---

[31] That is, because Antipater was not my son as well as his own.

[32] He considered as his own (or as legitimate heirs) only those children that I bore to him.

[33] In this context "more than right" seems to mean "less than right," or at least "less than righteous reasons"; cf. "more than reason," line 215. See endnote to this line for further discussion.

[34] Accept, put up with.

Yet still have su'd her presence to obtain:
And did not I to her as presents send
A table,[35] that best art did beautify,
Of two, to whom Heaven did best feature lend,   165
To woo her love by winning Anthony?
For when a prince's favour we do crave,
We first their minions' loves do seek to win:
So I, that sought Felicity to have,
Did with her minion Anthony begin.[†]   170
With double sleight I sought to captivate
The warlike lover, but I did not right:
For if my gift had borne but half the rate,[36]
The Roman had been overtaken quite.
But now he farèd like a hungry guest,   175
That to some plenteous festival is gone;
Now this, now that, he deems to eat were best,
Such choice doth make him let them all alone.
The boy's large forehead first did fairest seem,
Then glanc'd his eye upon my Mariam's cheek: 180
And that without comparison did deem,
What was in either but he most did like.[†]
And, thus distracted,[37] either's beauty's might
Within the other's excellence was drown'd:
Too much delight did bare[38] him from delight,[†]   185
For either's love the other's did confound.

---

[35] Picture, portrait.

[36] Value.

[37] The implied subject of this phrase is probably Antony, literally (as the Latin ety-mology of the word suggests) drawn in different directions, but also confused, agitated, even crazed. Conceivably, however, it is the power of beauty that is drawn apart or dispersed and thus diminished.

[38] The semantic range of this word probably includes "bear" (carry away), "bare" (strip), and "bar" (deprive of or debar from); "bare" is a possible seventeenth-century spelling for all three meanings.

Where if thy portraiture had only gone,[39]
His life from Herod, Anthony had taken:
He would have lovèd thee, and thee alone,
And left the brown Egyptian clean forsaken,   190
And Cleopatra then to seek had been[40]
So firm a lover of her wanèd face:†
Then great Anthonius' fall we had not seen,
By her that fled to have him hold the chase.†
Then Mariam in a Roman's chariot set,   195
In place of Cleopatra might have shown:
A mart of beauties[41] in her visage met,
And part in this, that they were all her own.†
Mariam. Not to be empress of aspiring Rome,
Would Mariam like to Cleopatra live: 200
With purest body will I press my tomb,
And wish no favours Anthony could give.†
Alexandra. Let us retire us, that we may resolve
How now to deal in this reversèd state:
Great are th'affairs that we must now revolve,   205
And great affairs must not be taken late.[42]

ACTUS PRIMUS. SCENA TERTIA.

MARIAM. ALEXANDRA. SALOME.

Salome. More plotting yet? Why, now you have the thing
For which so oft you spent your suppliant breath:
And Mariam hopes to have another king.
Her eyes do sparkle joy for Herod's death.   210
Alexandra. If she desir'd another king to have,

---

[39] If thy portrait alone had gone.
[40] That is, would have lacked, would have had to seek.
[41] Market or assortment of beauties, displayed as if for sale.
[42] With a possible aural pun on "light" (that is, lightly).

She might before she came in Herod's bed
Have had her wish. More kings than one did crave
For leave to set a crown upon her head.
I think with more than reason[43] she laments,   215
That she is freed from such a sad annoy:
Who is't will weep to part from discontent?
And if she joy, she did not causeless joy.[44]
Salome. You durst not thus have given your tongue the rein,
If noble Herod still remain'd in life: 220
Your daughter's betters far, I dare maintain,
Might have rejoic'd to be my brother's wife.
Mariam. My betters far! Base woman, 'tis untrue,
You scarce have ever my superiors seen:
For Mariam's servants were as good as you,   225
Before she came to be Judea's queen.
Salome. Now stirs the tongue that is so quickly mov'd,
But more than once your choler[45] have I borne:
Your fumish[46] words are sooner said than prov'd,
And Salome's reply is only scorn.   230
Mariam. Scorn those that are for thy companions held.
Though I thy brother's face had never seen,
My birth thy baser birth so far excell'd,
I had to both of you the princess been.
Thou parti-Jew, and parti-Edomite,   235
Thou mongrel: issu'd from rejected race,
Thy ancestors against the Heavens did fight,†
And thou like them wilt heavenly birth disgrace.
Salome. Still twit you me with nothing but my birth,†
What odds betwixt your ancestors and mine?   240

[43] Unreasonably.
[44] And if she did rejoice, she would not be without a cause for rejoicing.
[45] Anger.
[46] Irascible.

Both born of Adam, both were made of earth,†
And both did come from holy Abraham's line.
Mariam. I favour thee when nothing else I say,
 With thy black acts I'll not pollute my breath:
 Else to thy charge I might full justly lay   245
 A shameful life, besides a husband's death.
Salome. 'Tis true indeed, I did the plots reveal,
 That pass'd betwixt your favourites and you:†
 I meant not, I, a traitor to conceal.
 Thus Salome your minion Joseph slew.   250
Mariam. Heaven, dost thou mean this infamy to smother?
 Let slander'd Mariam ope thy closèd ear:
 Self-guilt hath ever been [suspicion's] mother,†
 And therefore I this speech with patience bear.
 No, had not Salome's unsteadfast heart   255
 In Josephus' stead her Constabarus plac'd,†
 To free herself she had not us'd the art
 To slander hapless Mariam for unchaste.
Alexandra. Come, Mariam, let us go: it is no boot[47]
 To let the head contend against the foot.†   260

ACTUS PRIMUS. SCENA QUARTA.

SALOME *SOLA*

Salome. Lives Salome to get so base a style[48]
 As "foot" to the proud Mariam? Herod's spirit
 In happy time for her endured exile,[49]
 For did he live, she should not miss her merit:[50]
 But he is dead: and though he were my brother,   265

---

[47] Use.
[48] Epithet or name.
[49] That is, spirit's exile from its body; contrast lines 45–46 earlier in this act.
[50] She would get what she deserves.

His death such store of cinders cannot cast
My coals of love to quench: for though they smother
The flames a while, yet will they out at last.
Oh blest Arabia, in best climate plac'd,†
I by the fruit will censure of the tree:†   270
'Tis not in vain thy happy name thou hast,
If all Arabians like Silleus⁵¹ be.†
Had not my fate been too too contrary,
When I on Constabarus first did gaze,
Silleus had been object to mine eye: 275
Whose looks and personage must [all eyes] amaze.
But now, ill-fated Salome, thy tongue
To Constabarus by itself is tied:
And now, except I do the Hebrew wrong,
I cannot be the fair Arabian bride: 280
What childish lets⁵² are these? Why stand I now
On honourable points? 'Tis long ago
Since shame was written on my tainted brow:⁵³
And certain 'tis, that shame is honour's foe.
Had I upon my reputation stood,   285
Had I affected an unspotted life,
Josephus' veins had still been stuff'd with blood,
And I to him had liv'd a sober wife.
Then had I never⁵⁴ cast an eye of love
On Constabarus' now detested face,   290
Then had I kept my thoughts without remove:
And blush'd at motion of the least disgrace:†

---

⁵¹ Chief minister of Obodas, king of Arabia.

⁵² Obstacles.

⁵³ That is, since she blushed, but the suggestion of a brand of shame is also present (cf. l. 294). The ambiguity extends to the following line, which can mean either that shamefastness, or modesty, is an enemy to worldly advancement, or—a sense that Salome would probably reject—that shame, in the sense of disgrace, is incompatible with honor.

⁵⁴ Then I never would have. . . .

But shame is gone, and honour wip'd away,
And Impudency on my forehead sits:
She bids me work my will without delay,   295
And for my will I will employ my wits.
He loves, I love; what then can be the cause
Keeps me [from] being the Arabian's wife?
It is the principles of Moses' laws,
For Constabarus still remains in life.   300
If he to me did bear as earnest hate,
As I to him, for him there were an ease;
A separating bill[55] might free his fate
From such a yoke that did so much displease.
Why should such privilege to man be given?†   305
Or given to them, why barr'd from women then?
Are men than we in greater grace with Heaven?
Or cannot women hate as well as men?
I'll be the custom-breaker: and begin
To show my sex the way to freedom's door,   310
And with an off'ring will I purge my sin;
The law was made for none but who are poor.†
If Herod had liv'd, I might to him accuse
My present lord. But for the future's sake[56]
Then would I tell the king he did refuse   315
The sons of Babas in his power to take.†[57]
But now I must divorce him from my bed,
That my Silleus may possess his room:[58]
Had I not begg'd his life, he had been dead,†
I curse my tongue, the hind'rer of his doom,   320
But then my wand'ring heart to him was fast,

---

[55] That is, a bill of divorcement; see Deuteronomy 24:1, which presents sending such a bill as an exclusively masculine privilege.

[56] Simply for the sake of my future husband (possibly *any* future husband, not just Silleus). . . .

[57] Capture. See Historical Background, paragraph 3.

[58] Place.

Nor did I dream of change: Silleus said,
He would be here, and see, he comes at last.
Had I not nam'd him, longer had he stay'd.

ACTUS PRIMUS. SCENA QUINTA.

SALOME. SILLEUS.

Silleus. Well found, fair Salome, Judea's pride!   325
  Hath thy innated[59] wisdom found the way
  To make Silleus deem him deified,
  By gaining thee, a more than precious prey?
Salome. I have devis'd the best I can devise;
  A more imperfect means was never found: 330
  But what cares Salome? It doth suffice
  If our endeavours with their end be crown'd.
  In this our land we have an ancient use,
  Permitted first by our law-giver's[60] head:
  Who hates his wife, though for no just abuse,   335
  May with a bill divorce her from his bed.
  But in this custom women are not free,
  Yet I for once will wrest it; blame not thou
  The ill I do, since what I do's for thee,
  Though others blame, Silleus should allow.   340
Silleus. Thinks Salome, Silleus hath a tongue
  To censure her fair actions? Let my blood
  Bedash my proper[61] brow, for such a wrong,
  The being yours, can make even vices good:
  Arabia, joy, prepare thy earth with green,   345
  Thou never happy wert indeed till now:
  Now shall thy ground be trod by beauty's queen,

---

[59] Native, inborn.
[60] Moses'.
[61] Own.

Her foot is destin'd to depress thy brow.
Thou shalt, fair Salome, command as much
As if the royal ornament were thine: 350
The weakness of Arabia's king is such,
The kingdom is not his so much as mine.[†]
My mouth is our Obodas' oracle,
Who thinks not aught but what Silleus will.[†]
And thou, rare creature, Asia's miracle,   355
Shalt be to me as it: Obodas' still.[62]
Salome. 'Tis not for glory I thy love accept,
Judea yields me honours worthy store:[63]
Had not affection in my bosom crept,
My native country should my life deplore.[64]   360
Were not Silleus he with whom I go,
I would not change my Palestine for Rome:
Much less would I a glorious state to show
Go far to purchase an Arabian tomb.
Silleus. Far be it from Silleus so to think,   365
I know it is thy gratitude requites
The love that is in me, and shall not shrink
Till death do sever me from earth's delights.[†]
Salome. But whist;[65] methinks the wolf is in our talk.[66]
Begone, Silleus. Who doth here arrive?   370
'Tis Constabarus that doth hither walk;
I'll find a quarrel, him from me to drive.
Silleus. Farewell, but were it not for thy command,
In his despite Silleus here would stand.

---

[62] The sense of lines 354–56 is difficult and may indicate textual corruption. As they stand, they might be paraphrased, "Thou shalt be to *me* as an oracle, and that oracle, expressing our combined wills, shall still have power to govern Obodas."

[63] A worthy supply of honors.

[64] I would deplore [the loss of] my native country as long as I lived.

[65] Hush.

[66] This phrase probably means "Sharp ears are listening," but the wolflike disposition of the lovers also makes it a comment on the predatory character of their conversation.

ACTUS PRIMUS. SCENA SEXTA.

SALOME. CONSTABARUS.

Constabarus. Oh Salome, how much you wrong your name,   375
  Your race, your country, and your husband most!
  A stranger's private conference[67] is shame,
  I blush for you, that have your blushing lost.†
  Oft have I found, and found you to my grief,
  Consorted with this base Arabian here: 380
  Heaven knows that you have been my comfort chief,
  Then do not now my greater plague appear.
  Now by the stately carvèd edifice
  That on Mount Sion makes so fair a show,[68]
  And by the altar fit for sacrifice,   385
  I love thee more than thou thyself dost know.
  Oft with a silent sorrow have I heard
  How ill Judea's mouth doth censure thee:
  And did I not thine honour much regard,
  Thou shouldst not be exhorted thus for me.   390
  Didst thou but know the worth of honest fame,
  How much a virtuous woman is esteem'd,
  Thou wouldest like hell eschew deservèd shame,
  And seek to be both chaste and chastely deem'd.
  Our wisest prince did say, and true he said,   395
  A virtuous woman crowns her husband's head.†
Salome. Did I for this uprear thy low estate?
  Did I for this requital beg thy life,
  That thou hadst forfeited to hapless fate,
  To be to such a thankless wretch the wife?†   400
  This hand of mine hath lifted up thy head,
  Which many a day ago had fall'n full low,

[67] Private conversation with a stranger; cf. act 3, lines 227–29 and 242.
[68] The temple of Jerusalem.

Because the sons of Babas are not dead;
To me thou dost both life and fortune owe.
Constabarus. You have my patience often exercis'd,   405
Use make my choler[69] keep within the banks:
Yet boast no more, but be by me advis'd.
A benefit upbraided[70] forfeits thanks:
I prithee, Salome, dismiss this mood,
Thou dost not know how ill it fits thy place: 410
My words were all intended for thy good,
To raise thine honour and to stop disgrace.
Salome. To stop disgrace? Take thou no care for me,
Nay, do thy worst, thy worst I set not by:[71]
No shame of mine is like to light on thee,   415
Thy love and admonitions I defy.
Thou shalt no hour longer call me wife,
Thy jealousy procures my hate so deep:
That I from thee do mean to free my life,
By a divorcing bill before I sleep.   420
Constabarus. Are Hebrew women now transformed to men?
Why do you not as well our battles fight,
And wear our armour? Suffer this, and then
Let all the world be topsy-turvèd quite.†
Let fishes graze, beasts [swim], and birds descend,†   425
Let fire burn downwards whilst the earth aspires:
Let winter's heat and summer's cold offend,
Let thistles grow on vines, and grapes on briars,
Set us to spin or sew, or at the best
Make us wood-hewers, water-bearing wights:†   430

---

[69] That is, "May habit make my anger ... " or perhaps a direct apostrophe to "Use": "Habitual self-discipline, make my anger. ..." ("Use" could also mean "proper behavior" or "formality.") If "make" were emended to "makes," the line could also mean "Use (habit) make[s] my anger. ..."

[70] Made a grounds of reproach to its beneficiary.

[71] Care not for.

For sacred service let us take no rest,
   Use us as Joshua did the Gibonites.†
Salome. Hold on your talk, till it be time to end,
   For me I am resolv'd it shall be so:
   Though I be first that to this course do bend,   435
   I shall not be the last, full well I know.
Constabarus. Why then be witness Heav'n, the judge of sins,
   Be witness spirits that eschew the dark:
   Be witness angels, witness cherubins,
   Whose semblance sits upon the holy Ark:†   440
   Be witness earth, be witness Palestine,
   Be witness David's city, if my heart
   Did ever merit such an act of thine:
   Or if the fault be mine that makes us part.
   Since mildest Moses, friend unto the Lord,   445
   Did work his wonders in the land of Ham,[72]
   And slew the first-born babes without a sword,
   In sign whereof we eat the holy lamb:†
   Till now that fourteen hundred years are past,
   Since first the Law[73] with us hath been in force:†   450
   You are the first, and will, I hope, be last,
   That ever sought her husband to divorce.
Salome. I mean not to be led by precedent,
   My will shall be to me instead of Law.
Constabarus. I fear me much you will too late repent,   455
   That you have ever liv'd so void of awe:
   This is Silleus' love that makes you thus
   Reverse all order: you must next be his.
   But if my thoughts aright the cause discuss,
   In winning you, he gains no lasting bliss;   460
   I was Silleus, and not long ago†

---

[72] That is, Egypt; see Genesis 10:6.
[73] That is, the law of Moses.

Josephus then was Constabarus now:
When you became my friend[74] you prov'd his foe,
As now for him you break to me your vow.†
Salome. If once I lov'd you, greater is your debt: 465
  For certain 'tis that you deserved it not.
  And undeservèd love we soon forget,
  And therefore that to me can be no blot.
  But now fare ill,[75] my once belovèd lord,
  Yet never more belov'd than now abhorr'd.   *Exit Salome.*   470
Constabarus. Yet Constabarus biddeth thee farewell.
  Farewell, light creature. Heaven forgive thy sin:
  My prophesying spirit doth foretell
  Thy wavering thoughts do yet but new begin.
  Yet I have better scap'd than Joseph did,   475
  But if our Herod's death had been delay'd,
  The valiant youths that I so long have hid,
  Had been by her, and I for them, betray'd.†
  Therefore in happy hour did Caesar give
  The fatal blow to wanton Anthony: 480
  For had he lived, our Herod then should live,
  But great Anthonius' death made Herod die.
  Had he enjoyed his breath, not I alone
  Had been in danger of a deadly fall:
  But Mariam had the way of peril gone,   485
  Though by the tyrant most belov'd of all—
  The sweet-fac'd Mariam, as free from guilt
  As Heaven from spots, yet had her lord come back,
  Her purest blood had been unjustly spilt,
  And Salome it was would work her wrack.   490
  Though all Judea yield her innocent,
  She often hath been near to punishment. [*Exit.*]

---

[74] Lover.
[75] That is, rather than farewell; cf. line 472.

Chorus. Those minds that wholly dote upon delight,
  Except[76] they only joy in inward good,
  Still hope at last to hop upon the right,[77]   495
  And so from sand they leap in loathsome mud.
    Fond[78] wretches, seeking what they cannot find,
    For no content attends a wavering mind.

If wealth they do desire, and wealth attain,
  Then wondrous fain[79] would they to honour leap: 500
  [If] mean degree they do in honour gain,†
  They would but wish a little higher step.
    Thus step to step, and wealth to wealth they add,
    Yet cannot all their plenty make them glad.

Yet oft we see that some in humble state,   505
  Are cheerful, pleasant, happy, and content:
  When those indeed that are of higher state,
  With vain additions do their thoughts torment.†
    Th'one would to his mind his fortune bind,
    Th'other to his fortune frames his mind.   510

To wish variety is sign of grief,
  For if you like your state as now it is,
  Why should an alteration bring relief?
  Nay, change would then be fear'd as loss of bliss.
    That man is only happy in his fate   515
    That is delighted in a settled state.

Still Mariam wish'd she from her lord were free,
  For expectation of variety:†
  Yet now she sees her wishes prosperous be,

---

[76] Unless.
[77] That is, to land on the right foot or side, superstitiously associated with a prosperous outcome. "Hop" supplies a playful verbal link between "hope" and "leap."
[78] Foolish.
[79] Willingly.

She grieves, because her lord so soon did die.   520
   Who can those vast imaginations feed,
   Where in a property[80] contempt doth breed?

Were Herod now perchance to live again,
She would again as much be grieved at that:
All that she may,[81] she ever doth disdain,   525
Her wishes guide her to she knows not what.
   And sad must be their looks, their honour sour,
   That care for nothing being[82] in their power.

ACTUS SECUNDUS. SCENA PRIMA.

PHERORAS AND GRAPHINA.†

Pheroras. 'Tis true, Graphina, now the time draws nigh
Wherein the holy priest with hallowed right,[1]
The happy long-desired knot shall tie,
Pheroras and Graphina to unite:
How oft have I with lifted hands implor'd   5
This blessed hour, till now implor'd in vain,
Which hath my wished liberty restor'd,
And made my subject self my own again.
Thy love, fair maid, upon mine eye doth sit,
Whose nature hot doth dry the moisture all,   10
Which were in nature, and in reason fit
For my [monarchal] brother's death to fall:†
Had Herod liv'd, he would have pluck'd my hand
From fair Graphina's palm perforce: and tied
The same in hateful and despisèd band,   15

---

[80] In relation to what is actually possessed. Cf. the proverb "Familiarity breeds contempt."
[81] Whatever she can do or possess.
[82] That is.
[1] Also "rite."

For I had had² a baby to my bride:
Scarce can her infant tongue with easy voice
Her name distinguish³ to another's ear:†
Yet had he liv'd, his power, and not my choice,
Had made me solemnly the contract swear.   20
Have I not cause in such a change to joy?
What though she be my niece, a princess born?
Near blood's without respect: high birth a toy,
Since love can teach [us] blood and kindred's scorn.†
What booted it⁴ that he did raise my head,   25
To be his realm's copartner, kingdom's mate?
Withal, he kept Graphina from my bed,
More wish'd by me than thrice Judea's state.
Oh, could not he be skilful judge in love,
That doted so upon his Mariam's face?   30
He, for his passion, Doris did remove;
I needed not a lawful wife displace.
It could not be but he had power to judge,
But he that never grudg'd a kingdom's share,
This well-known happiness to me did grudge: 35
And meant to be therein without compare.
Else had I been his equal in love's host,⁵
For though the diadem on Mariam's head
Corrupt the vulgar judgments, I will boast
Graphina's brow's as white, her cheeks as red.   40
Why speaks thou not, fair creature? Move thy tongue,†
For silence is a sign of discontent:
It were to both our loves too great a wrong

---

² Would have had.
³ Make distinct.
⁴ What use or benefit was it.
⁵ Suggesting, perhaps, not just a multitude but an army, who march under love's banners.

If now this hour do find thee sadly bent.[6]

Graphina. Mistake me not, my lord, too oft have I   45
Desir'd this time to come with wingèd feet,
To be enrapt with grief when 'tis too nigh.
You know my wishes ever yours did meet:
If I be silent, 'tis no more but fear
That I should say too little when I speak: 50
But since you will my imperfections bear,
In spite of doubt I will my silence break:
Yet might amazement tie my moving tongue,
But[7] that I know before Pheroras' mind.
I have admired[8] your affection long: 55
And cannot yet therein a reason find.
Your hand hath lifted me from lowest state,
To highest eminency wondrous grace,[9]
And me your handmaid have you made your mate,
Though all but you alone do count me base.[†]   60
You have preserved me pure at my request,
Though you so weak a vassal might constrain[†]
To yield to your high will; then last not best,[†]
In my respect a princess you disdain;
Then need not all these favours study crave,   65
To be requited[10] by a simple maid?
And study still, you know, must silence have.
Then be my cause for silence justly weighed,
But study cannot boot nor I requite,
Except your lowly handmaid's steadfast love   70

---

[6] Inclined to sadness.
[7] Except.
[8] Wondered at.
[9] Which would be a wondrous grace even to one in the most eminent social station.
[10] Won't repaying all these favors require application (or earnest thought and effort) . . . ?

And fast[11] obedience may your mind delight,
  I will not promise more than I can prove.
Pheroras. That study needs not let Graphina smile,[12]
  And I desire no greater recompense:
  I cannot vaunt me in a glorious style,   75
  Nor show my love in far-fetch'd eloquence:
  But this believe me, never Herod's heart
  Hath held his prince-born beauty-famèd wife
  In nearer place than thou, fair virgin, art,
  To him that holds the glory of his life.[†]   80
  Should Herod's body leave the sepulchre,
  And entertain the sever'd ghost again,[†]
  He should not be my nuptial hinderer,
  Except he hinder'd it with dying pain.
  Come, fair Graphina, let us go in state,   85
  This wish-endearèd time to celebrate. [*Exeunt.*]

ACTUS SECUNDUS. SCENA SECUNDA.

CONSTABARUS AND BABAS' SONS.

Babas' First Son. Now, valiant friend, you have our lives redeem'd,
  Which lives, as sav'd by you, to you are due:
  Command and you shall see yourself esteem'd,
  Our lives and liberties belong to you.   90
  This twice six years, with hazard of your life,
  You have conceal'd us from the tyrant's sword:
  Though cruel Herod's sister were your wife,
  You durst in scorn of fear this grace afford.
  In recompense we know not what to say,   95
  A poor reward were thanks for such a merit,[13]

---

[11] Firm.
[12] Need not hinder Graphina from smiling.
[13] An inversion: "Thanks would be a poor reward. . . ."

Our truest friendship at your feet we lay,
The best requital to a noble spirit.
Constabarus. Oh, how you wrong our friendship, valiant youth!
  With friends there is not such a word as "debt": 100
  Where amity is tied with bond of truth,[14]
  All benefits are there in common set.[†]
  Then is the golden age with them renew'd,
  All names of properties[15] are banish'd quite:
  Division, and distinction, are eschew'd: 105
  Each hath to what belongs to others right.[16]
  And 'tis not sure so full a benefit,
  Freely to give, as freely[17] to require:
  A bounteous act hath glory following it,
  They cause the glory that the act desire. 110
  All friendship should the pattern imitate,
  Of Jesse's son and valiant Jonathan:[†]
  For neither sovereign's nor father's hate
  A friendship fix'd on virtue sever can.
  Too much of this, 'tis written in the heart, 115
  And [needs] no amplifying with the tongue:
  Now may you from your living tomb depart,
  Where Herod's life hath kept you overlong.
  Too great an injury to a noble mind,
  To be quick buried;[18] you had purchas'd[19] fame, 120
  Some years ago, but that you were confin'd,
  While thousand meaner did advance their name.
  Your best of life, the prime of all your years,

---

[14] In the sense of "troth" (trust, fidelity, loyalty).

[15] All designations or assertions of individual and exclusive ownership.

[16] Each has a right to what belongs to other friends.

[17] Nobly (in a manner appropriate to the freeborn) as well as without constraint. "To require" means primarily "to ask," though the overtone of need is also relevant.

[18] Buried alive.

[19] Would have acquired.

Your time of action is from you bereft.
Twelve winters have you overpass'd in fears: 125
Yet if you use it well, enough is left.
And who can doubt but you will use it well?
The sons of Babas have it by descent:[20]
In all their thoughts each action to excel,
Boldly to act, and wisely to invent.   130
Babas' Second Son. Had it not like the hateful cuckoo been,
Whose riper age his infant nurse doth kill:†
So long we had not kept ourselves unseen,
But Constabarus safely[21] cross'd our will:
For had the tyrant fix'd his cruel eye   135
On our conceal`ed faces, wrath had sway'd
His justice so, that he had forc'd us die.
And dearer price than life we should have paid,
For you, our truest friend, had fall'n with us:
And we, much like a house on pillars set,†   140
Had clean depress'd our prop, and therefore thus
Our ready will with our concealment met.
But now that you, fair lord, are dangerless,
The sons of Babas shall their rigour show:
And prove it was not baseness did oppress   145
Our hearts so long, but honour kept them low.
Babas' First Son. Yet do I fear this tale of Herod's death
At last will prove a very tale indeed:
It gives me strongly in my mind,[22] his breath
Will be preserv'd to make a number bleed: 150
I wish not therefore to be set at large,
Yet peril to myself I do not [fear]:†

---

[20] Heredity.

[21] Dunstan and Greg suggest emending to "Constabarus' safety," but the phrase can also be understood as "Constabarus, for the sake of safety (ours, as well as his own), thwarted our inclination."

[22] I have a strong presentiment.

Let us for some days longer be your charge,[23]
Till we of Herod's state the truth do hear.

Constabarus. What, art thou turn'd a coward, noble youth,   155
  That thou beginn'st to doubt undoubted truth?

Babas' First Son. Were it my brother's tongue that cast this doubt,
  I from his heart would have the question out
  With this keen falchion,[24] but 'tis you, my lord,
  Against whose head I must not lift a sword: 160
  I am so tied in gratitude.

Constabarus.   Believe
  You have no cause to take it ill;
  If any word of mine your heart did grieve,
  The word dissented from the speaker's will.
  I know it was not fear the doubt begun,   165
  But rather valour and your care of me;
  A coward could not be your father's son.
  Yet know I doubts unnecessary be:
  For who can think that in Anthonius' fall,
  Herod his bosom friend should scape unbruis'd?[†]   170
  Then, Caesar, we might thee an idiot call,
  If thou by him should'st be so far abus'd.

Babas' Second Son. Lord Constabarus, let me tell you this,
  Upon submission Caesar will forgive:
  And therefore though the tyrant did amiss,   175
  It may fall out that he will let him live.
  Not many years agone it is since I,
  Directed thither by my father's care,
  In famous Rome for twice twelve months did [lie],[†]
  My life from Hebrews' cruelty to spare.   180
  There though I were but yet of boyish age,
  I bent mine eye to mark, mine ears to hear,

[23] Responsibility.
[24] Curved broadsword.

Where I did see Octavius, then a page,
When first he did to Julius' sight appear:†
Methought I saw such mildness in his face,   185
And such a sweetness in his looks did grow,
Withal, commix'd with so majestic grace,
His [phys'nomy]²⁵ his fortune did foreshow:
For this I am indebted to mine eye,
But then mine ear receiv'd more evidence,   190
By that I knew his love to clemency,
How he with hottest choler²⁶ could dispense.
Constabarus. But we have more than barely heard the news,
It hath been twice confirm'd. And though some tongue
Might be so false with false report t'abuse,   195
A false report hath never lasted long.
But be it so that Herod have his life,
Concealment would not then a whit avail:
For certain 'tis, that she that was my wife,
Would not to set her accusation fail.   200
And therefore now as good the venture give,
And free ourselves from blot of cowardice
As show a pitiful desire to live,
For, who can pity but they must despise?
Babas' First Son. I yield, but to necessity I yield;   205
I dare upon this doubt engage mine arm:²⁷
That Herod shall again this kingdom wield,
And prove his death to be a false alarm.
Babas' Second Son. I doubt²⁸ it too: God grant it be an error,
'Tis best without a cause to be in terror: 210

---

²⁵ This emendation of the 1613 text ("Phismony") is a contraction of "physiognomy";
cf. act 2, line 352.

²⁶ Anger.

²⁷ I dare to promise my arm in defense against this outcome (which you doubt), or,
simply, I bet my arm that what I fear ("doubt") is true.

²⁸ Fear.

And rather had I, though my soul be mine,
My soul should lie,[29] than prove a true divine.[30]
Constabarus. Come, come, let fear go seek a dastard's nest,
Undaunted courage lies in a noble breast.† [*Exeunt.*]

ACTUS SECUNDUS. SCENA TERTIA.

DORIS AND ANTIPATER.

Doris. [You] royal buildings, bow your lofty side,†   215
And [stoop] to her that is by right your queen:†
Let your humility upbraid the pride
Of those in whom no due respect is seen:
Nine times have we with trumpets' haughty sound,†
And banishing sour leaven from our taste,   220
Observ'd the feast that takes the fruit from ground.†
Since I, fair city, did behold thee last,
So long[31] it is since Mariam's purer cheek
Did rob from mine the glory, and so long
Since I return'd my native town to seek: 225
And with me nothing but the sense of wrong,
And thee, my boy, whose birth, though great it were,
Yet have thy after fortunes prov'd but poor:
When thou wert born, how little did I fear
Thou should'st be thrust from forth thy father's door!   230
Art thou not Herod's right begotten son?
Was not the hapless Doris Herod's wife?
Yes: ere he had the Hebrew kingdom won,
I was companion to his private life.
Was I not fair enough to be a queen?   235

[29] I would rather have my fears prove groundless, even if they make me a liar. . . .
[30] Prophet.
[31] That is, nine years.

Why, ere thou wert to me, false monarch, tied,
My lack of beauty might as well be seen,
As after I had liv'd five years thy bride.
Yet then thine [oaths] came pouring like the rain,†
Which all affirm'd my face without compare: 240
And that if thou might'st Doris' love obtain,
For all the world besides thou didst not care.
Then was I young, and rich, and nobly born,
And therefore worthy to be Herod's mate:
Yet thou ungrateful cast me off with scorn,   245
When Heaven's purpose rais'd your meaner fate.
Oft have I begg'd for vengeance for this fact,³²
And with dejected³³ knees, aspiring hands
Have pray'd the highest power to enact
The fall of her that on my trophy³⁴ stands.   250
Revenge I have according to my will,
Yet where I wish'd this vengeance did not light:
I wish'd it should high-hearted Mariam kill,
But it against my whilom³⁵ lord did fight.
With thee, sweet boy, I came, and came to try   255
If thou before his bastards might be plac'd
In Herod's royal seat and dignity.
But Mariam's infants here are only grac'd,³⁶
And now for us there doth no hope remain:
Yet we will not return till Herod's end   260
Be more confirm'd. Perchance he is not slain;
So³⁷ glorious fortunes may my boy attend.

³² Deed.
³³ In the etymological sense "thrown down."
³⁴ The spoils of my ruin, with the suggestion of a Roman triumph.
³⁵ Former.
³⁶ Here only Mariam's children are graced.
³⁷ Under those circumstances.

For if he[38] live, he'll think it doth suffice,
That he to Doris shows such cruelty:
For as he did my wretched life despise,   265
So do I know I shall despisèd die.
Let him but prove as natural to thee,
As cruel to thy miserable mother:
His cruelty shall not upbraided be
But in thy fortunes.[39] I his faults will smother.†   270
Antipater. Each mouth within the city loudly cries
That Herod's death is certain: therefore we
Had best some subtle hidden plot devise,
That Mariam's children might subverted be,
By poison's drink, or else by murderous knife,   275
So we may be advanc'd, it skills[40] not how:
They are but bastards, you were Herod's wife,
And foul adultery blotteth Mariam's brow.†
Doris. They are too strong to be by us remov'd,
Or else revenge's foulest spotted face   280
By our detested[41] wrongs might be approv'd,[42]
But weakness must to greater power give place.
But let us now retire to grieve alone,
For solitariness best fitteth moan. [*Exeunt.*]

[38] That is, Herod.
[39] If the punctuation of the 1613 text is retained, as here, "But" means "Except," and the lines may be paraphrased as follows: "I won't seek any recompense or satisfaction for his cruel treatment of me except in your better fortunes," or "Only the contrasting luster of your better fortunes will be a reproach to his former cruelty (to both you and me)." If line 270 is repunctuated with a comma after "fortunes," as Dunstan and Greg suggest, the second line would mean, "In your prosperity I will suppress your father's faults," or "I will bury his faults in (rejoicing at) your good fortunes."
[40] Matters.
[41] Detestable.
[42] Otherwise (if we had the power to avenge ourselves), revenge, even its ugliest form, might be justified ("approv'd") by the hateful wrongs we have suffered.

ACTUS SECUNDUS. SCENA QUARTA.

SILLEUS AND CONSTABARUS.

Silleus. Well met, Judean lord, the only wight[43]   285
　Silleus wish'd to see. I am to call
　Thy tongue to strict account.
Constabarus.　　　　　　　　For what despite
　I ready am to hear, and answer all.
　But if directly[44] at the cause I guess
　That breeds this challenge, you must pardon me:[45]   290
　And now some other ground of fight profess,
　For I have vow'd, vows must unbroken be.
Silleus. What may be your [exception]? Let me know.†
Constabarus. Why, aught concerning [Salome]; my sword†
　Shall not be wielded for a cause so low,   295
　A blow for her my arm will scorn t'afford.†
Silleus. It is for[46] slandering her unspotted name,
　And I will make thee in thy vow's despite,
　Suck up the breath that did my mistress blame,
　And swallow it again to do her right.   300
Constabarus. I prithee give some other quarrel ground
　To find beginning; rail against my name,
　Or strike me first, or let some scarlet wound
　Inflame my courage, give me words of shame;
　Do thou our Moses' sacred laws disgrace,   305
　Deprave our nation, do me some despite:
　I'm apt enough to fight in any case,
　But yet for Salome I will not fight.
Silleus. Nor I for aught but Salome: my sword,

---

[43] Creature.
[44] Accurately.
[45] Excuse me from fighting you.
[46] The cause of my challenge is.

That owes his service to her sacred name,   310
Will not an edge for other cause afford,
In other fight I am not sure of fame.
Constabarus. For⁴⁷ her, I pity thee enough already,
For her, I therefore will not mangle thee:
A woman with a heart so most unsteady   315
Will of herself sufficient torture be.
I cannot envy⁴⁸ for so light a gain;
Her mind with such unconstancy doth run:
As with a word thou didst her love obtain,
So with a word she will from thee be won.   320
So light as her possessions for most day⁴⁹
Is her affections lost, to me 'tis known:†
As good go hold the wind as make her stay,†
She never loves but till she call her own.⁵⁰
She merely is a painted sepulchre,   325
That is both fair, and vilely foul at once:
Though on her outside graces garnish her,
Her mind is fill'd⁵¹ with worse than rotten bones.†
And ever ready lifted is her hand,
To aim destruction at a husband's throat: 330
For proofs, Josephus and myself do stand,
Though once on both of us she seem'd to dote.

---

⁴⁷ Because of.

⁴⁸ Probably: envy you (although the intransitive construction tends to make the statement more general and impersonal: I cannot feel envy).

⁴⁹ The phrasing of this line (and of the following one) is somewhat obscure, though the general sense is that the possession of Salome's affections for most time (presumably, for the longest time among her various lovers) has little value, and therefore the loss of her affections also weighs little (is light, also in the sense of easy to bear). "Most day" suggests the duration of her love is to be measured in hours, certainly not more than days. If the plural of "possessions" is not an error, it may anticipate the plural of "affections" in the next line or it may suggest "prepossessions."

⁵⁰ That is, she loves only until she possesses her desire; cf. act 1, lines 522 –23.

⁵¹ The 1613 reading "fild" may mean "filed," that is, "defiled" (cf. Macbeth, 3.1.64), instead of or as well as "filled."

Her mouth, though serpent-like it never hisses,
Yet like a serpent, poisons where it kisses.
Silleus. Well, Hebrew, well, thou bark'st, but wilt not bite.[†]   335
Constabarus. I tell thee still for her I will not fight.
Silleus. Why then, I call thee coward.
Constabarus.   From my heart
  I give thee thanks. A coward's hateful name
  Cannot to valiant minds a blot impart,
  And therefore I with joy receive the same.   340
  Thou know'st I am no coward: thou wert by[52]
  At the Arabian battle th'other day,
  And saw'st my sword with daring valiancy,
  Amongst the faint Arabians cut my way.
  The blood of foes no more could let it shine,   345
  And 'twas enamelèd with some of thine.
  But now have at thee; not for Salome
  I fight, but to discharge a coward's style:[53]
  Here 'gins the fight that shall not parted be,
  Before a soul or two endure exile.[†] [*They fight.*]   350
Silleus. Thy sword hath made some windows for my blood,
  To show a horrid crimson phys'nomy:[54]
  To breathe[55] for both of us methinks 'twere good,
  The day will give us time enough to die.
Constabarus. With all my heart take breath, thou shalt have time,   355
  And if thou list, a twelvemonth; let us end:
  Into thy cheeks there doth a paleness climb,
  Thou canst not from my sword thyself defend.
  What needest thou for Salome to fight?
  Thou hast her, and may'st keep her, none strives for her:[†]   360
  I willingly to thee resign my right,

---

[52] At hand.
[53] Name.
[54] Physiognomy, face.
[55] Take a rest.

For in my very soul I do abhor her.
Thou seest that I am fresh, unwounded yet,
Then not for fear I do this offer make:
Thou art with loss of blood to fight unfit,   365
For here is one, and there another take.[56]
Silleus. I will not leave, as long as breath remains
  Within my wounded body: spare your words,
  My heart in blood's stead courage entertains,
  Salome's love no place for fear affords.   370
Constabarus. Oh, could thy soul but prophesy like mine,
  I would not wonder thou should'st long to die:
  For Salome, if I aright divine,
  Will be than death a greater misery.
Silleus. Then list,[57] I'll breathe[58] no longer.
Constabarus.   Do thy will;   375
  I hateless fight, and charitably kill. Ay, ay,† *They fight.*
  Pity thyself, Silleus, let not death
  Intrude before his time into thy heart:
  Alas, it is too late to fear, his breath†
  Is from his body now about to part.   380
  How far'st thou, brave Arabian?
Silleus.   Very well,
  My leg is hurt, I can no longer fight:
  It only grieves me, that so soon I fell,
  Before fair Salom's wrongs I came to right.[59]
Constabarus. Thy wounds are less than mortal. Never fear,   385
  Thou shalt a safe and quick recovery find:
  Come, I will thee unto my lodging bear,

---

[56] Here (in this fight) each combatant (gives and) takes in turn. (Constabarus courteously suggests that he and Silleus are equally matched, although the preceding lines indicate that Silleus has had the worse of the combat. Presumably, since Silleus is now wounded, even such give-and-take would harm him more than Constabarus.)

[57] Hear me.

[58] Pause; with a possible secondary sense of "live," anticipating lines 379–80.

[59] Before I succeeded in righting fair Salome's wrongs.

I hate thy body, but I love thy mind.

Silleus. Thanks, noble Jew, I see a courteous foe,

Stern enmity to friendship can no art:[60]   390

Had not my heart and tongue engag'd me so,

I would from thee no foe, but friend depart.

My heart to Salome is tied [too] fast[†]

To leave her love for friendship, yet my skill

Shall be employ'd to make your favour last,   395

And I will honour Constabarus still.

Constabarus. I ope my bosom to thee, and will take

Thee in as friend, and grieve for thy complaint:

But if we do not expedition[61] make,

Thy loss of blood I fear will make thee faint. [*Exeunt.*]   400

Chorus. To hear a tale with ears prejudicate,[62]

It spoils the judgment, and corrupts the sense:[†]

That human error, given to every state,[63]

Is greater enemy to innocence.[64]

It makes us foolish, heady, rash, unjust,   405

It makes us never try before we trust.[†65]

It will confound the meaning, change the words,

For it our sense of hearing much deceives:

Besides, no time to judgment it affords,

To weigh the circumstance our ear receives.   410

The ground of accidents[66] it never tries,

But makes us take for truth ten thousand lies.

---

[60] Enmity knows ("can," in its Old English etymological sense) no way or method to arrive at friendship.

[61] Haste.

[62] Prejudiced.

[63] Which affects every disposition (and possibly every social level).

[64] Is more dangerous to those who are naive or unworldly (as well as guiltless; the emphasis on judgment in this context makes guiltlessness a secondary consideration).

[65] Test our conclusions before we rely on them.

[66] The basis of appearances (as "accidental" or nonessential phenomena).

[handwritten: warning to Sillers]

Our ears and hearts are apt to hold for good
That[67] we ourselves do most desire to be:
And then we drown objections in the flood   415
Of partiality, 'tis that[68] we see
    That makes false rumours long with credit pass'd,[69]
    Though they like rumours must conclude at last.

The greatest part of us, prejudicate,
With wishing Herod's death do hold it true: 420
The being once deluded doth not bate[70]
The credit to a better likelihood due.[71]
    Those few that wish it not, the multitude
    Do carry headlong, so they doubts conclude.[72]

They[73] not object[74] the weak uncertain ground,   425
Whereon they[75] built this tale of Herod's end:
Whereof the author scarcely can be found,
And all because their wishes that way bend.
    They think not of the peril that ensu'th,
    If this should prove the contrary to truth.   430

On this same doubt, on this so light a breath,
They pawn their lives and fortunes. For they all
Behave them as the news of Herod's death

---

  [67] That which.

  [68] That is, that partiality.

  [69] The line puns on both senses of "credit": *belief* gives false rumors extended *currency* or (economic) value.

  [70] Abate, lessen.

  [71] In the context of this stanza, lines 421–22 seem to mean that once burnt is *not* twice shy, and "better" means "more desired or desirable" (like the news of Herod's death). In a wider context, they also suggest that the possibility of deception does not undercut the authority of more probable or rational ("better") inferences about the truth.

  [72] They (the minority who don't wish for a particular event and therefore might be more skeptical of its report) surrender or give up their doubting.

  [73] Those few.

  [74] Don't offer as an objection.

  [75] The greatest part.

They did of most undoubted credit call:
　　But if their actions now do rightly hit,[76]　　　　　　　　　435
　　Let them commend their fortune, not their wit.

ACTUS TERTIUS. SCENA PRIMA.

PHERORAS. SALOME.

Pheroras. Urge me no more Graphina to forsake,
　　Not twelve hours since I married her for love:
　　And do you think a sister's power can make
　　A resolute decree so soon remove?[1]
Salome. Poor minds they are that honour not affects.[2]　　　　　5
Pheroras. Who hunts for honour happiness neglects.
Salome. You might have been both of felicity
　　And honour too in equal measure seiz'd.[3]
Pheroras. It is not you can tell so well as I,
　　What 'tis can make me happy or displeas'd.　　　　　　　10
Salome. To match for neither beauty nor respects[4]
　　One mean of birth, but yet of meaner mind,
　　A woman full of natural defects—
　　I wonder what your eye in her could find.
Pheroras. Mine eye found loveliness, mine ear found wit,　　　15
　　To please the one, and to enchant the other:
　　Grace on her eye, mirth on her tongue doth sit,
　　In looks a child, in wisdom's house a mother.

[76] Hit the mark, succeed.

[1] The verb is intransitive, meaning "cancel itself."

[2] "That honour not affects" could mean "who do not aspire to honor" as well as "who are not affected by honor." Salome, who means "honour" in the worldly sense of exalted position, no doubt intends the first of these meanings (as Pheroras's response appears to assume). The second meaning could be construed as a reproach to Salome, who is unaffected by considerations of honor in its less material sense; cf. act 1, lines 281–84.

[3] Possessed.

[4] Considerations of fortune; cf. *King Lear*, 1.1.248.

Salome. But say you thought her fair, as none thinks else,
  Knows not Pheroras, beauty is a blast:[5]   20
  Much like this flower which today excels,
  But longer than a day it will not last.
Pheroras. Her wit exceeds her beauty.
Salome.   Wit may show
  The way to ill as well as good, you know.
Pheroras. But wisdom is the porter of her head,   25
  And bars all wicked words from issuing thence.
Salome. But of a porter, better were you sped,[6]
  If she against their entrance made defence.†
Pheroras. But wherefore comes the sacred Ananell,†
  That hitherward his hasty steps doth bend?   30
  Great sacrificer, y'are arrivèd well,
  Ill news from holy mouth I not attend.[7]

ACTUS TERTIUS. SCENA SECUNDA.

PHERORAS. SALOME. ANANELL.

Ananell. My lips, my son, with peaceful tidings bless'd,
  Shall utter honey to your list'ning ear:
  A word of death comes not from priestly breast,   35
  I speak of life: in life there is no fear.
  And for the news I did the Heavens salute,
  And fill'd the Temple with my thankful voice:
  For though that mourning may not me pollute,†
  At pleasing accidents I may rejoice.   40
Pheroras. Is Herod then reviv'd from certain death?

---

  [5] Brief gust, but the word also anticipates the following lines, telescoping the metaphorical blossoming and destruction of a flower into a single moment. (*OED* gives "A blasted bud or blossom" as an additional meaning [7] of "blast.")
  [6] Provided.
  [7] Don't expect.

Salome. What? Can your news restore my brother's breath?

Ananell. Both so, and so, the King is safe and sound,

  And did such grace in royal Caesar meet:

  That he, with larger style⁸ than ever crown'd,   45

  Within this hour Jerusalem will greet.

  I did but come to tell you, and must back

  To make preparatives for sacrifice:

  I knew his death your hearts like mine did rack,

  Though to conceal it prov'd you wise. *Exit.*   50

Salome. How can my joy sufficiently appear?

Pheroras. A heavier tale did never pierce mine ear.

Salome. Now Salome of happiness may boast.

Pheroras. But now Pheroras is in danger most.

Salome. I shall enjoy the comfort of my life.   55

Pheroras. And I shall lose it, losing of my wife.

Salome. Joy, heart, for Constabarus shall be slain.

Pheroras. Grieve, soul, Graphina shall from me be ta'en.

Salome. Smile, cheeks, the fair Silleus shall be mine.

Pheroras. Weep, eyes, for I must with a child combine.⁹   60

Salome. Well, brother, cease your moans. On one condition

  I'll undertake to win the King's consent:

  Graphina still shall be in your tuition,¹⁰

  And her with you be ne'er the less content.

Pheroras. What's the condition? Let me quickly know,   65

  That I as quickly your command may act:

  Were it to see what herbs in Ophir grow,

  Or that the lofty Tyrus might be sack'd.†

Salome. 'Tis [not] so hard a task: It is no more

  But tell the King that Constabarus hid   70

  The sons of Babas, done to death¹¹ before:

---

⁸ Grander title.

⁹ Marry.

¹⁰ Protection, safekeeping.

¹¹ That is, supposedly executed.

And 'tis no more than Constabarus did.
And tell him more that [we] for Herod's sake,
Not able to endure [our] brother's foe,†
Did with a bill our separation make,   75
Though loath from Constabarus else to go.
Pheroras. Believe this tale for told, I'll go from hence
In Herod's ear the Hebrew to deface:
And I that never studied eloquence,
Do mean with eloquence this tale to grace. *Exit.*   80
Salome. This will be Constabarus' quick dispatch,
Which from my mouth would lesser credit find:
Yet shall he not decease without a match,
For Mariam shall not linger long behind.
First, jealousy—if that avail not, fear—   85
Shall be my minister to work her end:
A common error moves not[12] Herod's ear,
Which doth so firmly to his Mariam bend.
She shall be chargèd with so horrid crime,
As Herod's fear shall turn his love to hate: 90
I'll make some swear that she desires to climb,
And seeks to poison him for his estate.[13]
I scorn that she should live my birth t'upbraid,
To call me base and hungry Edomite:
With patient show her choler I betray'd,†   95
And watch'd the time to be reveng'd by sleight.[14]
Now tongue of mine[15] with scandal load her name,
Turn hers to fountains, Herod's eyes to flame:
Yet first I will begin Pheroras' suit,
That he my earnest business may effect: 100

---

[12] The report of an ordinary fault would not anger.
[13] That is, his royal position, which Mariam will be represented as coveting.
[14] Trick, stratagem.
[15] Now let my tongue (or possibly Salome directly addresses and admonishes her tongue, "Now, tongue of mine, with scandal load . . . ").

And I of Mariam will keep me mute,
Till first some other doth her name detect.[16]
Who's there, Silleus' man? How fares your lord,
That your aspects[17] do bear the badge of sorrow?
Silleus' Man. He hath the marks of Constabarus' sword,   105
And for a while desires your sight to borrow.
Salome. My heavy curse the hateful sword pursue,
My heavier curse on the more hateful arm
That wounded my Silleus. But renew
Your tale again. Hath he no mortal harm?   110
Silleus' Man. No sign of danger doth in him appear,
Nor are his wounds in place of peril seen:
He bids you be assured you need not fear,
He hopes to make you yet Arabia's queen.
Salome. Commend my heart to be Silleus' charge,   115
Tell him my brother's sudden coming now
Will give my foot no room to walk at large,
But I will see him yet ere night, I vow. [*Exit.*]

ACTUS TERTIUS. SCENA TERTIA.

MARIAM AND SOHEMUS.

Mariam. Sohemus, tell me what the news may be
That makes your eyes so full, your cheeks so blue?   120
Sohemus. I know not now how to call them. Ill for me
'Tis sure they are: not so, I hope, for you.
Herod—
Mariam.   Oh, what of Herod?
Sohemus.   Herod lives.
[*Mariam.*] How! Lives? What, in some cave or forest hid?†

---

[16] Expose (to scandal).
[17] Countenance.

Sohemus. Nay, back return'd with honour. Caesar gives   125
  Him greater grace than e'er Anthonius did.
Mariam. Foretell the ruin of my family,
  Tell me that I shall see our city burn'd:
  Tell me I shall a death disgraceful die,
  But tell me not that Herod is return'd.   130
Sohemus. Be not impatient, madam, be but mild,
  His love to you again will soon be bred.
Mariam. I will not to his love be reconcil'd,
  With solemn vows I have forsworn his bed.
Sohemus. But you must break those vows.
Mariam.   I'll rather break   135
  The heart of Mariam. Cursed is my fate:
  But speak no more to me, in vain ye speak†
  To live with him I so profoundly hate.
Sohemus. Great queen, you must to me your pardon give,
  Sohemus cannot now your will obey: 140
  If your command should me to silence drive,
  It were not to obey, but to betray.
  Reject and slight my speeches, mock my faith,
  Scorn my observance, call my counsel nought:[18]
  Though you regard not what Sohemus saith,   145
  Yet will I ever freely speak my thought.
  I fear ere long I shall fair Mariam see
  In woeful state, and by herself undone:
  Yet for your issue's sake more temp'rate be,
  The heart by affability is won.   150
Mariam. And must I to my prison turn again?
  Oh, now I see I was an hypocrite:
  I did this morning for his death complain,
  And yet do mourn, because he lives, ere night.
  When I his death believ'd, compassion wrought,   155

---

[18] This word, spelled here as in the 1613 text, probably represents both *nought* (nothing) and the closely related *naught* (worthless, poor).

And was the stickler[19] 'twixt my heart and him:
But now that curtain's drawn from off my thought,
Hate doth appear again with visage grim:
And paints the face of Herod in my heart,
In horrid colours with detested look:†   160
Then fear would come, but scorn doth play her part,
And saith that scorn with fear can never brook.[20]
I know I could enchain him with a smile:
And lead him captive with a gentle word,
I scorn my look should ever man beguile,   165
Or other speech than meaning[21] to afford.
Else Salome in vain might spend her wind,
In vain might Herod's mother whet her tongue:
In vain had they complotted and combin'd,
For I could overthrow them all ere long.   170
Oh, what a shelter is mine innocence,
To shield me from the pangs of inward grief:
'Gainst all mishaps it is my fair defence,
And to my sorrows yields a large relief.
To be commandress of the triple earth,†   175
And sit in safety from a fall secure:
To have all nations celebrate my birth,
I would not that my spirit were impure.
Let my distressèd state unpitied be,
Mine innocence is hope enough for me. *Exit.*   180
Sohemus. Poor guiltless queen! Oh, that my wish might place
A little temper[22] now about thy heart:
Unbridled speech is Mariam's worst disgrace,†

---

[19] A stickler was a "moderator or umpire at a tournament, wrestling or fencing match. . . . Hence, one who intervenes as a mediator between combatants or disputants" (*OED*).
[20] Put up with (with a suggestion of "endure as company" or "consort with").
[21] That is, what I mean.
[22] Moderation.

And will endanger her without desert.†23
I am in greater hazard. O'er my head,   185
The fatal axe doth hang unsteadily:†
My disobedience once discoverèd
Will shake it down: Sohemus so shall die.
For when the King shall find, we thought his death
Had been as certain as we see his life: 190
And marks withal I slighted so his breath,24
As to preserve alive his matchless wife—
Nay more, to give to Alexander's hand†
The regal dignity; the sovereign power,
How I had yielded up at her command,   195
The strength of all the city, David's Tower—†
What more than common death may I expect,
Since I too well do know his cruelty?
'Twere death a word of Herod's to neglect;
What then to do directly contrary?   200
Yet, life, I quit thee with a willing spirit,
And think thou could'st not better be employ'd:
I forfeit thee for her that more doth merit,
Ten such25 were better dead than she destroy'd.
But fare thee well, chaste queen, well may I see   205
The darkness palpable, and rivers part:†
The sun stand still, nay more, retorted26 be,†
But never woman with so pure a heart.
Thine eyes' grave majesty keeps all in awe,
And cuts the wings of every loose desire:†   210
Thy brow is table27 to the modest law;

---

23 Her deserving it.
24 That is, his command.
25 That is, such as me.
26 Turned backward in its course.
27 That is, a table (or tablet) on which laws are engraved (possibly evoking the tables
on which Moses brought the Ten Commandments from Mount Sinai, Exodus 31:18).

Yet though we dare not love, we may admire.[†]
And if I die, it shall my soul content,
My breath in Mariam's service shall be spent.

Chorus. 'Tis not enough for one that is a wife   215
To keep her spotless from an act of ill:
But from suspicion she should free her life,[†]
And bare[28] herself of power as well as will.
    'Tis not so glorious for her to be free,
    As by her proper[29] self restrain'd to be.[†]   220

When she hath spacious ground to walk upon,
Why on the ridge should she desire to go?
It is no glory to forbear alone[30]
Those things that may her honour overthrow.
    But 'tis thankworthy if she will not take   225
    All lawful liberties for honour's sake.

That wife her hand against her fame doth rear,
That more than to her lord alone will give
A private word to any second ear,
And though she may with reputation live,   230
    Yet though most chaste, she doth her glory blot,
    And wounds her honour, though she kills it not.

When to their husbands they themselves do bind,
Do they not wholly give themselves away?
Or give they but their body, not their mind,   235
Reserving that, though best, for others' prey?
    No sure, their thoughts no more can be their own,
    And therefore should to none but one be known.

---

[28] The spelling used in the 1613 text allows the possibility that, for a seventeenth-century reader, it meant "bar" as well as (or even instead of) "bare."
[29] That is, own.
[30] Only.

Then she usurps upon another's right,
That seeks to be by public language grac'd: 240
And though her thoughts reflect with purest light,
Her mind if not peculiar[31] is not chaste.
   For in a wife it is no worse to find,
   A common[32] body than a common mind.

And every mind, though free from thought of ill, 245
That out of glory[33] seeks a worth to show,
When any's ears but one therewith[34] they fill,
Doth in a sort her pureness overthrow.
   Now Mariam had (but that to this she bent)[35]
   Been free from fear, as well as innocent. 250

ACTUS QUARTUS. SCENA PRIMA.

ENTER HEROD AND HIS ATTENDANTS.

Herod. Hail, happy city, happy in thy store,[1]
  And happy that thy buildings such we see:
  More happy in the Temple where w'adore,
  But most of all that Mariam lives in thee. [*Enter Nuntio.*]†
  Art thou return'd? How fares my Mariam? [How?]† 5
Nuntio. She's well, my lord, and will anon[2] be here
  As you commanded.
Herod.   Muffle up thy brow,

---

[31] Privately owned or exclusive property.
[32] Shared, public; associations of the word with class or social status (low-born, coarse, etc.) are also relevant.
[33] From a desire for glory or fame (cf. "by public language grac'd," l. 240), possibly with a suggestion of vainglory, like the Latin *gloria*.
[34] That is, with their worth or value, as manifest in speech.
[35] If not for her inclination to reveal herself in speech.
[1] Plenty.
[2] Soon.

Thou day's dark taper.[3] Mariam will appear,
And where she shines, we need not thy dim light,
Oh, haste thy steps, rare creature, speed thy pace: 10
And let thy presence make the day more bright,
And cheer the heart of Herod with thy face.
It is an age since I from Mariam went,
Methinks our parting was in David's days:[†]
The hours are so increas'd by discontent,   15
Deep sorrow, Joshua-like, the season stays:[†]
But when I am with Mariam, time runs on,
Her sight can make months minutes, days of weeks:
An hour is then no sooner come than gone
When in her face mine eye for wonders seeks.   20
You world-commanding city,[4] Europe's grace,
Twice hath my curious eye your streets survey'd,
I have seen the statue-fillèd place,
That once if not for grief had been betray'd.[†]
I all your Roman beauties have beheld,   25
And seen the shows your ediles[5] did prepare;
I saw the sum of what in you excell'd,
Yet saw no miracle like Mariam rare.
The fair and famous Livia, Caesar's love,[†]
The world's commanding mistress did I see: 30
Whose beauties both the world and Rome approve,
Yet, Mariam, Livia is not like to thee.
Be patient but a little while, mine eyes,[†]
Within your compass'd[6] limits be contain'd:

[3] Candle; that is, the sun, imagined, proleptically, as darkened by the appearance of Mariam.

[4] Rome.

[5] Roman officials in charge of, among other things, public works and games.

[6] Circumscribed, duly measured; but "compass'd" can also mean circular or arched and may further suggest the shape of the sockets.

That object straight shall your desires suffice,   35
From which you were so long a while restrain'd.
How wisely Mariam doth the time delay,
Lest sudden joy my sense should suffocate:
I am prepar'd, thou need'st no longer stay:
Who's there? My Mariam, more than happy fate?[†]   40
Oh no, it is Pheroras. Welcome, brother.
Now for a while I must my passion smother.

ACTUS QUARTUS. SCENA SECUNDA.

HEROD. PHERORAS.

Pheroras. All health and safety wait upon my lord,
   And may you long in prosperous fortunes live
   With Rome-commanding Caesar at accord,   45
   And have all honours that the world can give.
Herod. Oh brother, now thou speak'st not from thy heart,
   No, thou hast struck a blow at Herod's love:
   That cannot quickly from my memory part,
   Though Salome did me to pardon move.[7]   50
   Valiant Phasaelus, now to thee farewell,[†]
   Thou wert my kind and honourable brother:
   Oh hapless hour, when you self-stricken fell,
   Thou father's image, glory of thy mother.
   Had I desir'd a greater suit of thee   55
   Than to withhold thee from a harlot's bed,
   Thou would'st have granted it: but now I see
   All are not like that[8] in a womb are bred.
   Thou would'st not, hadst thou heard of Herod's death,
   Have made his burial time thy bridal hour: 60
   Thou would'st with clamours, not with joyful breath,

[7] Urge.
[8] Alike who.

116

Have show'd the news to be not sweet but sour.

Pheroras. Phasaelus' great worth I know did stain

  Pheroras' petty valour: but they lie

  (Excepting you yourself) that dare maintain   65

  That he did honour Herod more than I,

  For what I show'd, love's power constrain'd me show,

  And pardon loving faults⁹ for Mariam's sake.

Herod. Mariam, where is she?

Pheroras.   Nay, I do not know,

  But absent use of her fair name I make: 70

  You have forgiven greater faults than this,

  For Constabarus, that against your will

  Preserv'd the sons of Babas, lives in bliss

  Though you commanded him the youths to kill.†

Herod. Go, take a present order for his death,   75

  And let those traitors feel the worst of fears:

  Now Salome will whine to beg his breath,

  But I'll be deaf to prayers: and blind to tears.

Pheroras. He is, my lord, from Salome divorc'd,†

  Though her affection did to leave him grieve: 80

  Yet was she by her love to you enforc'd

  To leave the man that would your foes relieve.

Herod. Then haste them to their death. [*Exit Pheroras.*] I will requite

  Thee, gentle Mariam—Salom, I mean.

  The thought of Mariam doth so steal my spirit,   85

  My mouth from speech of her I cannot wean.

ACTUS QUARTUS. SCENA TERTIA.

HEROD. MARIAM.

Herod. · And here she comes indeed: happily met,

  My best and dearest half: what ails my dear?†

---

⁹ Faults committed for the sake of love.

Thou dost the difference[10] certainly forget
'Twixt dusky habits[11] and a time so clear.[12]   90
Mariam. My lord, I suit my garment to my mind,
    And there no cheerful colours can I find.
Herod. Is this my welcome? Have I long'd so much
    To see my dearest Mariam discontent?[†]
    What is't that is the cause thy heart to touch?   95
    Oh speak, that I thy sorrow may prevent.
    Art thou not Jewry's queen, and Herod's too?
    Be my commandress, be my sovereign guide:
    To be by thee directed I will woo,
    For in thy pleasure lies my highest pride.   100
    Or if thou think Judea's narrow bound
    Too strict a limit for thy great command:
    Thou shalt be empress of Arabia crown'd,
    For thou shalt rule, and I will win the land.
    I'll rob the holy David's sepulchre[†]   105
    To give thee wealth, if thou for wealth do care:
    Thou shalt have all they did with him inter,
    And I for thee will make the Temple bare.
Mariam. I neither have of power nor riches want,
    I have enough, nor do I wish for more: 110
    Your offers to my heart no ease can grant,
    Except they could my brother's life restore.
    No, had you wish'd the wretched Mariam glad,
    Or had your love to her been truly tied:
    Nay, had you not desir'd to make her sad,   115
    My brother nor my grandsire had not died.
Herod. Wilt thou believe no oaths to clear thy lord?
    How oft have I with execration sworn:[†]
    Thou art by me belov'd, by me ador'd,

---

[10] Incongruity.
[11] Clothes.
[12] Fair or unclouded (giving "time" the secondary sense of "weather"), cheerful, serene.

Yet are my protestations heard with scorn.   120
Hircanus plotted to deprive my head
Of this long-settled honour that I wear:
And therefore I did justly doom him dead,
To rid the realm from peril, me from fear.
Yet I for Mariam's sake do so repent   125
The death of one whose blood she did inherit:
I wish I had a kingdom's treasure spent,
So I had ne'er expell'd Hircanus' spirit.
. . . .†

As I affected[13] that same noble youth,[14]   130
In lasting infamy my name enroll
If I not mourn'd his death with hearty truth.
Did I not show to him my earnest love,
When I to him the priesthood did restore,
And did for him a living priest remove,   135
Which never had been done but once before?†
Mariam. I know that, mov'd by importunity,
   You made him priest, and shortly after die.
Herod. I will not speak, unless to be believ'd,
   This froward[15] humour will not do you good:†   140
   It hath too much already Herod griev'd,
   To think that you on terms of hate have stood.
   Yet smile, my dearest Mariam, do but smile,
   And I will all unkind conceits exile.
Mariam. I cannot frame disguise, nor never taught   145
   My face a look dissenting from my thought.
Herod. By Heav'n, you vex me, build[16] not on my love.
Mariam. I will not build on so unstable ground.†
Herod. Nought is so fix'd, but peevishness may move.[17]

---

[13] Liked, felt affection for.
[14] Aristobulus.
[15] Sullen, peevish.
[16] That is, rely.
[17] Dislodge (also, possibly, persuade to anger).

Mariam. 'Tis better slightest cause than none were found.   150
Herod. Be judge yourself, if ever Herod sought
  Or would be mov'd a cause of change to find:
  Yet let your look declare a milder thought,
  My heart again you shall to Mariam bind.
  How oft did I for you my mother chide,   155
  Revile my sister, and my brother rate:[18]
  And tell them all my Mariam they belied;
  Distrust me still, if these be signs of hate.

ACTUS QUARTUS. SCENA QUARTA.

[ENTER BUTLER.]

Herod. What hast thou here?
Butler.   A drink procuring love,
  The queen desir'd me to deliver it.   160
Mariam. Did I? Some hateful practice[19] this will prove,
  Yet can it be no worse than Heavens permit.
Herod. [To the Butler.] Confess the truth, thou wicked instrument
  To her outrageous will, 'tis [poison] sure:[†]
  Tell true, and thou shalt scape the punishment,   165
  Which, if thou do conceal, thou shalt endure.
Butler. I know not, but I doubt it be no less,
  Long since the hate of you her heart did seize.
Herod. Know'st thou the cause thereof?
Butler.   My lord, I guess
  Sohemus told the tale that did displease.   170
Herod. Oh Heaven! Sohemus false! Go, let him die,
  Stay not to suffer him to speak a word: [Exit Butler.]
  Oh damnèd villain, did he falsify
  The oath he swore ev'n of his own accord?

[18] Berate, scold vehemently.
[19] Plot.

Now do I know thy falsehood, painted devil, 175
Thou white[20] enchantress. Oh, thou art so foul,†
That hyssop cannot cleanse thee, worst of evil.†
A beauteous body hides a loathsome soul.
Your love Sohemus, mov'd by his affection,
Though he have ever heretofore been true, 180
Did blab forsooth, that I did give direction,†
If we were put to death to slaughter you.†
And you in black revenge attended[21] now
To add a murder to your breach of vow.

Mariam. Is this a dream?

Herod.   Oh Heaven, that 'twere no more, 185
I'll give my realm to who can prove it so:
I would I were like any beggar poor,
So I for false my Mariam did not know—
Foul pith contain'd in the fairest rind
That ever grac'd a cedar. Oh, thine eye 190
Is pure as Heaven, but impure thy mind,
And for impurity shall Mariam die.
Why didst thou love Sohemus?

Mariam.   They can tell
That say I lov'd him, Mariam says not so.

Herod. Oh, cannot impudence the coals expel, 195
That for thy love in Herod's bosom glow?
It is as plain as water, and denial
Makes of thy falsehood but a greater trial.
Hast thou beheld thyself, and could'st thou stain
So rare perfection? Even for love of thee 200
I do profoundly hate thee. Wert thou plain,
Thou should'st the wonder of Judea be.

---

[20] Fair-seeming. The phrasing continues the meditation on hypocrisy contained in the preceding line's play on the common Renaissance notion of a "white devil" (see endnote to l. 176).

[21] Waited.

But oh, thou art not. Hell itself lies hid
Beneath thy heavenly show. Yet never wert thou chaste:†
Thou might'st[22] exalt, pull down, command, forbid,   205
And be above the wheel of fortune plac'd.[23]
Hadst thou complotted Herod's massacre,
That so thy son a monarch might be styl'd,
Not half so grievous such an action were,
As once to think, that Mariam is defiled.   210
Bright workmanship of nature sulli'd o'er,
With pitchèd[24] darkness now thine end shall be:
Thou shalt not live, fair fiend, to cozen more,
With [heav'nly] semblance, as thou cozen'dst me.†
Yet must I love thee in despite of death,   215
And thou shalt die in the despite of love:
For neither shall my love prolong thy breath,
Nor shall thy loss of breath my love remove.
I might have seen thy falsehood in thy face;
Where could'st thou get thy stars that serv'd for eyes   220
Except by theft, and theft is foul disgrace?
This had appear'd before, were Herod wise,
But I'm a sot, a very sot, no better:
My wisdom long ago a-wand'ring fell,
Thy face, encount'ring it, my wit did fetter,   225
And made me for delight my freedom sell.
Give me my heart, false creature, 'tis a wrong,
My guiltless heart should now with thine be slain:
Thou hadst no right to [lock] it up so long,
And with usurper's name I Mariam stain.   230

[22] Had the power or might have had the power.
[23] Be exempt from changes of fortune (cf. 3.3.176). Traditional representations of the wheel of fortune showed a monarch at the top and a beggar at the bottom, indicating the reversals its revolution might bring.
[24] Pitchy, pitch-black.

Enter Butler.

Herod. Have you design'd[25] Sohemus to his end?

Butler. I have, my lord.

Herod.   Then call our royal guard
  To do as much for Mariam. [*Exit Butler.*] They offend
  Leave[26] ill unblam'd, or good without reward. [*Enter Soldiers.*]
  Here, take her to her death. Come back, come back,   235
  What meant I to deprive the world of light:
  To muffle Jewry in the foulest black,
  That ever was an opposite to white?
  Why, whither would you carry her?

Soldier.   You bade
  We should conduct her to her death, my lord.   240

Herod. Why, sure I did not, Herod was not mad.
  Why should she feel the fury of the sword?
  Oh, now the grief returns into my heart,
  And pulls me piecemeal: love and hate do fight:
  And now hath love acquir'd the greater part,   245
  Yet now hath hate affection conquer'd quite.
  And therefore bear her hence: and, Hebrew, why
  Seize you with lion's paws the fairest lamb
  Of all the flock? She must not, shall not, die.†
  Without her I most miserable am,   250
  And with her more than most. Away, away,
  But bear her but to prison, not to death:
  And is she gone indeed? Stay, villains, stay,
  Her looks alone preserv'd your sovereign's breath.
  Well, let her go, but yet she shall not die;   255
  I cannot think she meant to poison me:
  But certain 'tis she liv'd too wantonly,
  And therefore shall she never more be free. [*Exeunt.*]

[25] Assigned or dispatched.
[26] That is, who leave.

ACTUS QUARTUS. SCENA QUINTA.

Butler. Foul villain, can thy pitchy-coloured soul
   Permit thine ear to hear her causeless doom,   260
   And not enforce thy tongue that tale control,[27]
   That must unjustly bring her to her tomb?
   Oh, Salome, thou hast thyself repaid
   For all the benefits that thou hast done:
   Thou art the cause I have the queen betray'd,   265
   Thou hast my heart to darkest falsehood won.
   I am condemned, Heav'n gave me not my tongue
   To slander innocents, to lie, deceive:
   To be the hateful instrument to wrong,
   The earth of greatest glory to bereave.   270
   My sin ascends and doth to Heav'n cry,[†]
   It is the blackest deed that ever was:
   And there doth sit an angel notary,
   That doth record it down in leaves of brass.[†]
   Oh, how my heart doth quake: Achitophel,   275
   Thou founds[28] a means thyself from shame to free:[†]
   And sure my soul approves[29] thou didst not well;[†]
   All follow some, and I will follow thee. [*Exit.*]

ACTUS QUARTUS. SCENA SEXTA.

CONSTABARUS, BABAS' SONS, AND THEIR GUARD.

Constabarus. Now here we step our last, the way to death;
   We must not tread this way a second time: 280
   Yet let us resolutely yield our breath,
   Death is the only ladder, Heav'n to climb.

[27] Hold in check or overmaster.
[28] In ordinary seventeenth-century usage, "found'st."
[29] Finds by experience or, having sifted the evidence, confirms. The sense of *commends* might also be relevant, if the line were emended as discussed in the endnote to line 277.

Babas' First Son. With willing mind I could myself resign,
   But yet it grieves me with a grief untold:
   Our death should be accompani'd with thine,   285
   Our friendship we to thee have dearly sold.[30]
Constabarus. Still wilt thou wrong the sacred name of friend?
   Then should'st thou never style[31] it friendship more:
   But base mechanic[32] traffic[33] that doth lend,
   Yet will be sure they[34] shall the debt restore.   290
   I could with needless compliment return,
   [This] for thy ceremony I could say:†
   'Tis I that made the fire your house to burn,
   For but[35] for me she would not you betray.
   Had not the damnèd woman sought mine end,   295
   You had not been the subject of her hate:
   You never did her hateful mind offend,
   Nor could your deaths have freed [her] nuptial fate.†
   Therefore, fair friends, though you were still unborn,
   Some other subtlety devis'd should be: 300
   Whereby my life, though guiltless, should be torn.
   Thus have I prov'd, 'tis you that die for me,
   And therefore should I weakly now lament,
   You have but done your duties;[36] friends should die
   Alone their friends' disaster to prevent,†   305
   Though not compell'd by strong necessity.
   But now farewell, fair city, never more
   Shall I behold your beauty shining bright:

---

[30] *We . . . sold:* has cost you dear.

[31] Call.

[32] Vulgar, low; a term typically applied to those involved in manual labor or trade.

[33] Commerce.

[34] Those to whom money or a commodity is lent.

[35] Except.

[36] It would be weak of me to lament when you have only done your duties (or lament *that* you have done your duties), and it would be weak of me to do no more than lament your deaths (rather than joining you in death). A full stop or semicolon after "lament" would make the clauses more autonomous and produce a slightly different emphasis.

Farewell, of Jewish men the worthy store,[37]
But no farewell to any female wight.[38]   310
You wavering crew: my curse to you I leave,
You had but one to give you any grace:
And you yourselves will Mariam's life bereave;
Your commonwealth doth innocency chase.[39]
You creatures made to be the human curse,   315
You tigers, lionesses, hungry bears,
Tear-massacring[40] hyenas: nay, far worse,[†]
For they for prey do shed their feignèd tears.
But you will weep (you creatures cross[41] to good),
For your unquenchèd thirst of human blood: 320
You were the angels cast from Heav'n for pride,[†]
And still do keep your angels' outward show,
But none of you are inly beautified,
For still your Heav'n-depriving pride doth grow.
Did not the sins of [man] require a scourge,[†]   325
Your place on earth had been by this[42] withstood:[43]
But since a flood no more the world must purge,[†]
You stay'd in office of a second flood.
You giddy creatures, sowers of debate,
You'll love today, and for no other cause   330
But for[44] you yesterday did deeply hate;
You are the wreck of order, breach of laws.
[Your] best are foolish, froward,[45] wanton, vain,[†]
Your worst adulterous, murderous, cunning, proud:[†]

---

[37] Stock, number.
[38] Creature.
[39] Drive out.
[40] Who weep while they slaughter.
[41] At odds with, opposed to.
[42] By this time.
[43] Refused or denied.
[44] Except that.
[45] Sullen, peevish.

And Salome attends the latter train,[46]   335
Or rather [she] their leader is allow'd.
I do the sottishness of men bewail,
That do with following you enhance your pride:
'Twere better that the human race should fail,
Than be by such a mischief multiplied.†   340
Cham's servile curse to all your sex was given,
Because in Paradise you did offend:†
Then do we not resist the will of Heaven,
When on your wills like servants we attend?
You are to nothing constant but to ill,   345
You are with nought but wickedness indued:
Your loves are set on nothing but your will,
And thus my censure I of you conclude.
You are the least of goods, the worst of evils,
Your best are worse than men: your worst than devils.   350
Babas' Second Son. Come, let us to our death: are we not bless'd?
Our death will freedom from these creatures give:
Those trouble-quiet[47] sowers of unrest,
And this I vow, that had I leave to live,
I would forever lead a single life,   355
And never venture on a devilish wife. [*Exeunt.*]

ACTUS QUARTUS. SCENA SEPTIMA.

HEROD AND SALOME.

Herod. Nay, she shall die. Die, quoth you? That she shall:
But for the means. The means! Methinks 'tis hard
To find a means to murder her withal,
Therefore I am resolv'd she shall be spar'd.   360

---

[46] Set or class of persons (*OED, sb¹*, 11); the verb "attends" also activates the sense of "train" as "retinue."
[47] Peace-disturbing.

Salome. Why, let her be beheaded.

Herod.   That were well,

  Think you that swords are miracles like you?[†]

  Her skin will ev'ry curtl'ax[48] edge refell,[49]

  And then your enterprise you well may rue.

  What if the fierce Arabian notice take   365

  Of this your wretched weaponless estate:

  They[50] answer, when we bid resistance make,

  That Mariam's skin their falchions did rebate.[51]

  Beware of this, you make a goodly hand,

  If you of weapons do deprive our land.   370

Salome. Why, drown her then.

Herod.   Indeed, a sweet device.

  Why, would not ev'ry river turn her course

  Rather than do her beauty prejudice,[52]

  And be reverted[53] to the proper source?

  So not a drop of water should be found   375

  In all Judea's quondam[54] fertile ground.

Salome. Then let the fire devour her.

Herod.   'Twill not be:

  Flame is from her deriv'd[55] into my heart:

  Thou nursest flame, flame will not murder thee,

  My fairest Mariam, fullest of desert.   380

Salome. Then let her live for me.[56]

---

  [48] "Any heavy slashing sword . . . sometimes taken by persons unfamiliar with the weapon for some kind of battle-ax" (*OED*). A falchion (l. 368) was a curved broadsword with a convex cutting edge, although the term was loosely applied, especially in poetic diction, to any sword.
  [49] Repel, force back.
  [50] That is, the citizens of Jerusalem.
  [51] Make dull, blunt.
  [52] Injury.
  [53] Withdrawn or driven back.
  [54] Once.
  [55] Conveyed; drawn off or diverted (like water into a channel).
  [56] As far as I'm concerned.

Herod.   Nay, she shall die:
  But can you live without her?
Salome.   Doubt you that?
Herod. I'm sure I cannot; I beseech you try:
  I have experience but I know not what.
Salome. How should I try?
Herod.   Why, let my love be slain,   385
  But if we cannot live without her sight
  You'll find the means to make her breathe again,
  Or else you will bereave my comfort quite.
Salome. Oh ay: I warrant you. [*Exit.*]
Herod.   What, is she gone,
  And gone to bid the world be overthrown?   390
  What, is her heart's composure hardest stone?
  To what a pass are cruel women grown! [*Re-enter Salome.*]
  She is return'd already: have you done?
  Is't possible you can command so soon
  A creature's heart to quench the flaming sun,†   395
  Or from the sky to wipe away the moon?
Salome. If Mariam be the sun and moon, it is:
  For I already have commanded this.
Herod. But have you seen her cheek?
Salome.   A thousand times.
Herod. But did you mark it too?
Salome.   Ay, very well.   400
Herod. What is't?
Salome.   A crimson bush, that ever limes⁵⁷
  The soul whose foresight doth not much excel.
Herod. Send word she shall not die. Her cheek a bush—
  Nay, then I see indeed you mark'd it not.
Salome. 'Tis very fair, but yet will never blush,   405
  Though foul dishonours do her forehead blot.†

---

⁵⁷ Entraps (as with birdlime smeared on twigs). "Crimson bush" appears to be suggested by a subliminal association with "blush," a word that surfaces in line 405.

Herod. Then let her die, 'tis very true indeed,
  And for this fault alone shall Mariam bleed.
Salome. What fault, my lord?
Herod.   What fault is't? You that ask,
  If you be ignorant I know of none.   410
  To call her back from death shall be your task,
  I'm glad that she for innocent is known.
  For on the brow of Mariam hangs a fleece,†
  Whose slenderest twine is strong enough to bind
  The hearts of kings; the pride and shame of Greece,   415
  Troy-flaming Helen's not so fairly shin'd.†
Salome. 'Tis true indeed, she lays them[58] out for nets,
  To catch the hearts that do not shun a bait:
  'Tis time to speak: for Herod sure forgets
  That Mariam's very tresses hide deceit.†   420
Herod. Oh, do they so? Nay, then you do but well,
  In sooth I thought it had been hair:†
  Nets call you them? Lord, how they do excel,
  I never saw a net that show'd so fair.
  But have you heard her speak?
Salome.   You know I have.   425
Herod. And were you not amaz'd?
Salome.   No, not a whit.
Herod. Then 'twas not her you heard; her life I'll save,
  For Mariam hath a world-amazing wit.
Salome. She speaks a beauteous language, but within
  Her heart is false as powder:[59] and her tongue   430
  Doth but allure the auditors to sin,
  And is the instrument to do you wrong.

---

[58] The strands of her hair.

[59] Probably gunpowder (cf. *Romeo and Juliet*, 3.3.132, and 5.1.64); Salome suggests that Mariam is treacherously mined within. (The sense of "powder" as a cosmetic fits "within" less comfortably and is at most secondary but may contribute another version of falsehood.)

Herod. It may be so: nay, 'tis so: she's unchaste,
  Her mouth will ope to ev'ry stranger's ear:[†]
  Then let the executioner make haste,   435
  Lest she enchant him, if her words he hear.
  Let him be deaf, lest she do him surprise
  That shall to free her spirit be assign'd:
  Yet what boots[60] deafness if he have his eyes?
  Her murderer must be both deaf and blind.   440
  For if he see, he needs must see the stars
  That shine on either side of Mariam's face:
  Whose sweet aspect will terminate the wars,
  Wherewith he should a soul so precious chase.[61]
  Her eyes can speak, and in their speaking move;   445
  Oft did my heart with reverence receive
  The world's mandates. Pretty tales of love
  They utter, which can human bondage weave.
  But shall I let this heaven's model[62] die,
  Which for a small self-portraiture she[63] drew?   450
  Her eyes like stars, her forehead like the sky,
  She is like Heaven, and must be heavenly true.
Salome. Your thoughts do rave with doting on the queen.
  Her eyes are ebon-hued, and you'll confess:
  A sable star hath been but seldom seen.   455
  Then speak of reason more, of Mariam less.
Herod. Yourself are held a goodly creature here,
  Yet so unlike my Mariam in your shape
  That when to her you have approachèd near,
  Myself hath often ta'en you for an ape.   460
  And yet you prate of beauty: go your ways,
  You are to her a sun-burnt blackamoor:[†]

[60] Help is.
[61] That is, from its body.
[62] Accurate image.
[63] Heaven.

Your paintings[64] cannot equal Mariam's praise,
Her nature is so rich, you are so poor.
Let her be stay'd from death, for if she die,   465
We do we know not what to stop her breath:[65]
A world cannot another Mariam buy;†
Why stay you ling'ring? Countermand her death.†
Salome. Then you'll no more remember what hath pass'd,
Sohemus' love and hers shall be forgot?   470
'Tis well in truth: that fault may be her last,
And she may mend, though yet she love you not.
Herod. Oh God: 'tis true. Sohemus—earth and Heav'n,
Why did you both conspire to make me curs'd:
In coz'ning[66] me with shows and proofs unev'n?[67]   475
She show'd the best, and yet did prove the worst.
Her show was such, as had our singing king,
The holy David, Mariam's beauty seen,
The Hittite had then felt no deadly sting,
Nor Bethsabe had never been a queen.[68]   480
Or had his son, the wisest man of men,
Whose fond delight did most consist in change,†
Beheld her face, he had been stay'd[69] again;
No creature having her, can wish to range.
Had Asuerus seen my Mariam's brow,   485
The humble Jew, she might have walk'd alone:
Her beauteous virtue should have stay'd below,

[64] The effect you achieve by cosmetics.
[65] We don't know what it means to kill her (with an echo of Luke 23:34, "they know not what they do").
[66] Deceiving, cheating.
[67] Unjust.
[68] As poet of the Psalms, David is the "singing king." In 2 Samuel 11 after Bathsheba ("Bethsabe"), the wife of Uriah the Hittite, has conceived a child by the king, David orders Uriah placed in the front lines of battle "that he may be smitten, and die." After the death of Uriah, Bathsheba married David and became the mother of Solomon.
[69] Restrained, checked in his course of change.

Whiles Mariam mounted to the Persian throne.†
But what avails it all? For in the weight[70]
She is deceitful, light as vanity: 490
Oh, she was made for nothing but a bait,
To train[71] some hapless man to misery.
I am the hapless man that have been train'd
To endless bondage. I will see her yet:
Methinks I should discern her if she feign'd;   495
Can human eyes be daz'd by woman's wit?
Once more these eyes of mine with hers shall meet,
Before the headsman do her life bereave:
Shall I forever part from thee, my sweet,
Without the taking of my latest leave?   500
Salome. You had as good resolve to save her now,
I'll stay her death; 'tis well determinèd:[72]
For sure she never more will break her vow,
Sohemus and Josephus both are dead.
Herod. She shall not live, nor will I see her face;   505
A long-heal'd wound a second time doth bleed:
With Joseph I remember her disgrace,
A shameful end ensues[73] a shameful deed.
Oh, that I had not call'd to mind anew
The discontent of Mariam's wavering heart: 510
'Twas you: you foul-mouth'd Ate,[74] none but you,
That did the thought hereof to me impart.
Hence from my sight, my black tormentor, hence,
For hadst not thou made Herod unsecure,

[70] Scales.
[71] Entice, lead astray.
[72] Resolved.
[73] Follows, succeeds.
[74] The Homeric personification not merely of discord but also of delusion and blind, reckless impulse (*Iliad* 19.91–94, 126–31). In the Elizabethan period she appears as the prologue to George Peele's *The Arraignment of Paris* (1584) and figures largely in book 4 of Spenser's *The Faerie Queene* (1596).

I had not doubted Mariam's innocence,   515
  But still had held her in my heart for pure.
Salome. I'll leave you to your passion: 'tis no time
  To purge me now, though of a guiltless crime. *Exit.*
Herod. Destruction take thee: thou hast made my heart
  As heavy as revenge; I am so dull,   520
  Methinks I am not sensible of smart,
  Though hideous horrors at my bosom pull.
  My head weighs downwards: therefore will I go
  To try if I can sleep away my woe.[†] [*Exit.*]

ACTUS QUARTUS. SCENA OCTAVA.

Mariam. Am I the Mariam that presum'd so much,   525
  And deem'd my face must needs preserve my breath?
  Ay, I it was that thought my beauty such,
  As it alone could countermand my death.
  Now death will teach me: he can pale as well
  A cheek of roses as a cheek less bright,   530
  And dim an eye whose shine doth most excel,
  As soon as one that casts a meaner light.
  Had not myself against myself conspir'd,
  No plot, no adversary from without
  Could Herod's love from Mariam have retir'd,   535
  Or from his heart have thrust my semblance out.
  The wanton queen that never lov'd for love,
  False Cleopatra, wholly set on gain,
  With all her sleights did prove, yet vainly prove,[75]
  For her the love of Herod to obtain.   540
  Yet her allurements, all her courtly guile,
  Her smiles, her favours, and her smooth deceit
  Could not my face from Herod's mind exile,

[75] Try.

But were with him of less than little weight.
That face and person that in Asia late   545
For beauty's goddess, Paphos' queen,[76] was ta'en:
That face that did captive[77] great Julius' fate,
That very face that was Anthonius'[78] bane,[79]
That face that to be Egypt's pride was born,
That face that all the world esteem'd so rare:[†]   550
Did Herod hate, despise, neglect, and scorn,
When with the same, he Mariam's did compare.
This made that I improvidently wrought,
And on the wager even my life did pawn:
Because I thought, and yet but truly thought,   555
That Herod's love could not from me be drawn.
But now, though out of time,[80] I plainly see
It could be drawn, though never drawn from me,[†]
Had I but with humility been grac'd,
As well as fair I might have prov'd me wise: 560
But I did think because I knew me chaste,
One virtue for a woman might suffice.
That mind for glory of our sex might stand,
Wherein humility and chastity
Doth march with equal paces hand in hand.   565
But one, if single seen, who setteth by?[81]
And I had singly one, but 'tis my joy,
That I was ever innocent, though sour:
And therefore can they but my life destroy,
My soul is free from adversary's power.[†] *Enter Doris.*   570
You princes great in power, and high in birth,

---

[76] Paphos, on Cyprus, was the site of a famous temple devoted to the worship of Aphrodite (or Venus).
[77] Take captive.
[78] "Great Julius" and "Anthonius" are Julius Caesar and Mark Antony respectively.
[79] Destruction.
[80] Not in season, too late.
[81] Takes account of.

Be great and high, I envy not your hap:[82]
Your birth must be from dust, your power on earth;
In Heav'n shall Mariam sit in Sara's lap.[83]
Doris. Ay, Heav'n—your beauty cannot bring you thither,[†]   575
Your soul is black and spotted, full of sin:[†]
You in adult'ry liv'd nine year together,
And Heav'n will never let adult'ry in.
Mariam. What art thou that dost poor Mariam pursue,
Some spirit sent to drive me to despair?   580
Who sees for truth that Mariam is untrue?[†]
If fair she be, she is as chaste as fair.
Doris. I am that Doris that was once belov'd,
Belov'd by Herod, Herod's lawful wife:
'Twas you that Doris from his side remov'd,   585
And robb'd from me the glory of my life.
Mariam. Was that adult'ry? Did not Moses say,
That he that being match'd did deadly hate:
Might by permission put his wife away,
And take a more belov'd to be his mate?   590
Doris. What did he hate me for: for simple truth?
For bringing[84] beauteous babes, for love to him?[†]
For riches, noble birth, or tender youth?
Or for no stain did Doris' honour dim?
Oh, tell me, Mariam, tell me if you know,   595
Which fault of these made Herod Doris' foe?
These thrice three years have I with hands held up,
And bowèd knees fast nailèd to the ground,
Besought for thee the dregs of that same cup,
That cup of wrath that is for sinners found.[†]   600

[82] Lot, fortune.
[83] A feminine counterpart to the "bosom of Abraham"; cf. act 1, lines 87–88, and the endnote to act 1, line 97.
[84] That is, bringing forth; giving birth to.

And now thou art to drink it: Doris' curse
Upon thyself did all this while attend,
But now it shall pursue thy children worse.
Mariam. Oh, Doris, now to thee my knees I bend,
That heart that never bow'd to thee doth bow: 605
Curse not mine infants, let it thee suffice,
That Heav'n doth punishment to me allow.
Thy curse is cause that guiltless Mariam dies.
Doris. Had I ten thousand tongues, and ev'ry tongue
Inflam'd with poison's power, and steep'd in gall: 610
My curses would not answer for my wrong,
Though I in cursing thee employ'd them all.†
Hear thou that didst Mount [Gerizim] command,†
To be a place whereon with cause to curse:
Stretch thy revenging arm, thrust forth thy hand, 615
And plague the mother much: the children worse.
Throw flaming fire upon the baseborn heads
That were begotten in unlawful[85] beds.
But let them live till they have sense to know
What 'tis to be in miserable state: 620
Then be their nearest friends their overthrow,
Attended be they by suspicious hate.
And, Mariam, I do hope this boy of mine
Shall one day come to be the death of thine.† *Exit.*
Mariam. Oh! Heaven forbid. I hope the world shall see, 625
This curse of thine shall be return'd on thee:
Now, earth, farewell, though I be yet but young,
Yet I, methinks, have known thee too too long. [*Exit.*]

Chorus. The fairest action of our human life
Is scorning to revenge an injury: 630
For who forgives without a further strife,

[85] That is, unsanctified by marriage.

His adversary's heart to him doth tie.
 And 'tis a firmer conquest truly said,[86]
 To win the heart than overthrow the head.

If we a worthy enemy do find,   635
To yield to worth, it must be nobly done:[87]
But if of baser metal[88] be his mind,
In base revenge there is no honour won.
 Who would a worthy courage overthrow,
 And who would wrestle with a worthless foe?   640

We say our hearts are great and cannot yield;
Because they cannot yield it proves them poor:
Great hearts are task'd[89] beyond their power but seld,†[90]
The weakest lion will the loudest roar.
 Truth's school for certain doth this same allow,   645
 High-heartedness doth sometimes teach to bow.

A noble heart doth teach a virtuous scorn:
To scorn to owe a duty[91] overlong,
To scorn to be for benefits forborne,[92]
To scorn to lie, to scorn to do a wrong,   650
 To scorn to bear an injury in mind,
 To scorn a freeborn heart slavelike to bind.

But if for wrongs we needs revenge must have,
Then be our vengeance of the noblest kind:†
Do we his body from our fury save,   655
And let our hate prevail against our mind?

---

[86] It is truly said to be a firmer conquest.

[87] It is a noble act to yield to a worthy enemy (and thereby surrender the prospect of revenge).

[88] Also meaning *mettle* (although *mettle* and *metal*, of which the former is an alternate spelling and figurative application, are difficult to distinguish in a play of this period).

[89] Burdened, taxed.

[90] Seldom.

[91] That is, not repay an obligation.

[92] Treated leniently from gratitude for former kindnesses.

What can 'gainst him a greater vengeance be,
Than make his foe more worthy far than he?

Had Mariam scorn'd to leave a due unpaid,†
She would to Herod then have paid her love: 660
And not have been by sullen passion sway'd.†
To fix her thoughts all injury above
  Is virtuous pride. Had Mariam thus been prov'd,[93]
  Long famous life to her had been allow'd.

ACTUS QUINTUS. SCENA PRIMA.

Nuntio. When, sweetest friend,[1] did I so far offend
  Your heavenly self, that you my fault to quit
  Have made me now relator of [your] end,
  The end of beauty, chastity and wit?
  Was none so hapless in the fatal place   5
  But I, most wretched, for the queen t'choose?
  'Tis certain I have some ill-boding face
  That made me cull'd to tell this luckless news.
  And yet no news to Herod: were it new
  To him, unhappy 't had not been at all:[2]   10
  Yet do I long to come within his view,
  That he may know his wife did guiltless fall:
  And here he comes. Your Mariam greets you well.
Enter Herod.
Herod. What? lives my Mariam? Joy, exceeding joy!
  She shall not die.
Nuntio.   Heav'n doth your will repel.[3]   15
Herod. Oh, do not with thy words my life destroy,

---

[93] Turned out to be virtuously proud.
  [1] The messenger is apostrophizing Mariam.
  [2] If Herod were ignorant of the event I report (the execution of Mariam), there would be no bad news to report.
  [3] Reject or resist.

I prithee tell no dying-tale: thine eye
Without thy tongue doth tell but too too much:
Yet let thy tongue's addition make me die,
Death welcome comes to him whose grief is such.   20

Nuntio. I went amongst the curious gazing troop,
   To see the last of her that was the best:
   To see if death had heart to make her stoop,
   To see the sun-admiring phoenix' nest.†
When there I came, upon the way I saw   25
   The stately Mariam not debas'd by fear:
   Her look did seem to keep the world in awe,
   Yet mildly did her face this fortune bear.

Herod. Thou dost usurp my right, my tongue was fram'd
   To be the instrument of Mariam's praise: 30
   Yet speak: she cannot be too often fam'd:
   All tongues suffice not her sweet name to raise.

Nuntio. But as she came she Alexandra met,
   Who did her death (sweet queen) no whit bewail,
   But as if nature she did quite forget,   35
   She did upon her daughter loudly rail.† ⁴

Herod. Why stopp'd you not her mouth? Where had she words
   To [darken] that, that Heaven made so bright?†
   Our sacred tongue no epithet affords
   To call her other than the world's delight.   40

Nuntio. She told her that her death was too too good,
   And that already she had liv'd too long:
   She said, she sham'd to have a part in blood
   Of her that did the princely Herod wrong.

Herod. Base pickthank⁵ devil! Shame, 'twas all her glory,   45
   That she to noble Mariam was the mother:
   But never shall it live in any story—
   Her name, except to infamy, I'll smother.

---

⁴ Utter abuse.
⁵ Flattering, sycophantic.

What answer did her princely daughter make?

Nuntio. She made no answer, but she look'd the while,　　　　50
　As if thereof she scarce did notice take,
　Yet smil'd, a dutiful, though scornful, smile.†

Herod. Sweet creature, I that look to mind do call;[6]
　Full oft hath Herod been amaz'd withal.
　[Go on.]

[*Nuntio.*]† She came unmov'd, with pleasant grace,　　　　55
　As if to triumph her arrival were:
　In stately habit, and with cheerful face:†
　Yet ev'ry eye was moist but Mariam's there.
　When justly[7] opposite to me she came,
　She pick'd me out from all the crew:　　　　60
　She beckon'd to me, call'd me by my name,
　For she my name, my birth, and fortune knew.

Herod. What, did she name thee? Happy, happy man,
　Wilt thou not ever love that name the better?
　But what sweet tune did this fair dying swan†　　　　65
　Afford thine ear? Tell all, omit no letter.

Nuntio. "Tell thou my lord," said she—

Herod.　　　　　　　　　　　　Me, meant she me?
　Is't true,[8] the more my shame: I was her lord,†
　Were I not mad, her lord I still should be:†
　But now her name must be by me ador'd.　　　　70
　Oh say, what said she more? Each word she said
　Shall be the food whereon my heart is fed.†

Nuntio. "Tell thou my lord thou saw'st me loose my breath."†

Herod. Oh, that I could that sentence[9] now control.[10]

Nuntio. "If guiltily, eternal be my death"—　　　　75

---

[6] Remember.

[7] Precisely.

[8] Possibly, this phrase should be understood as a question and punctuated "Is't true?" Otherwise, it means, "If it is true."

[9] Both utterance and death sentence.

[10] Overrule (a legal sense; see *OED v.,* 5b).

Herod. I hold her chaste ev'n in my inmost soul.

Nuntio. "By three days hence, if wishes could revive,

  I know himself would make me oft alive."[†]

Herod. Three days: three hours, three minutes, not so much,

  A minute in a thousand parts divided;[†]   80

  My penitency for her death is such,

  As in the first[11] I wish'd she had not died.

  But forward in thy tale.

Nuntio.   Why, on she went,

  And after she some silent prayer had said,

  She did as if to die she were content,[†]   85

  And thus to Heav'n her heav'nly soul is fled.

Herod. But art thou sure there doth no life remain?

  Is't possible my Mariam should be dead?

  Is there no trick to make her breathe again?

Nuntio. Her body is divided from her head.   90

Herod. Why, yet methinks there might be found by art

  Strange ways of cure; 'tis sure rare things are done

  By an inventive head, and willing heart.

Nuntio. Let not, my lord, your fancies idly run.

  It is as possible it should be seen,   95

  That we should make the holy Abraham live,

  Though he entomb'd two thousand years had been,[†]

  As breath again to slaughter'd Mariam give.

  But now for more assaults prepare your ears—

Herod. There cannot be a further cause of moan,   100

  This accident shall shelter me from fears:

  What can I fear? Already Mariam's gone.

  Yet tell ev'n what you will.

Nuntio.   As I came by,

  From Mariam's death, I saw upon a tree

  A man that to his neck a cord did tie:[†]   105

  Which cord he had design'd his end to be.

---

[11] That is, the first minute or first thousandth of a minute.

When me he once discern'd, he downwards bow'd,
And thus with fearful voice [he] cried aloud,
"Go tell the King he trusted ere he tried,[†]
I am the cause that Mariam causeless died."   110
Herod. Damnation take him, for it was the slave
  That said she meant with poison's deadly force
  To end my life that she the crown might have:[†]
  Which tale did Mariam from herself divorce.[†]
  Oh, pardon me, thou pure unspotted ghost,   115
  My punishment must needs sufficient be,
  In missing that content I valued most:
  Which was thy admirable face to see.
  I had but one inestimable jewel,[†]
  Yet one I had no monarch[12] had the like,   120
  And therefore may I curse myself as cruel:
  'Twas broken by a blow myself did strike.
  I gaz'd thereon and never thought me bless'd,
  But when on it my dazzl'd eye might rest,
  A precious mirror made by wondrous art,   125
  I priz'd it ten times dearer than my crown,
  And laid it up fast folded in my heart:
  Yet I in sudden choler cast it down,
  And pash'd it all to pieces: 'twas no foe
  That robb'd me of it; no Arabian host,   130
  Nor no Armenian guide hath us'd me so:
  But Herod's wretched self hath Herod cross'd.
  She was my graceful moiety;[13] me accurs'd,
  To slay my better half and save my worst.
  But sure she is not dead, you did but jest,   135
  To put me in perplexity a while;
  'Twere well indeed if I could so be dress'd:[14]

---

[12] Yet one I *did* have of which no monarch. . . .
[13] Half; cf. following line and act 4, line 88, and the endnote to act 4, line 88.
[14] Rebuked, "straightened out."

I see she is alive, methinks you smile.

Nuntio. If sainted Abel yet deceasèd be,†

    'Tis certain Mariam is as dead as he.   140

Herod. Why, then go call her to me, bid her now†

    Put on fair habit, stately ornament:

    And let no frown o'ershade her smoothest brow,

    In her doth Herod place his whole content.

Nuntio. She'll come in stately weeds[15] to please your sense,   145

    If now she come attir'd in robe of Heaven:

    Remember, you yourself did send her hence,

    And now to you she can no more be given.

Herod. She's dead, hell take her murderers, she was fair,†

    Oh, what a hand she had, it was so white,   150

    It did the whiteness of the snow impair:[16]

    I never more shall see so sweet a sight.

Nuntio. 'Tis true, her hand was rare.

Herod.   Her hand? her hands;

    She had not singly one of beauty rare,†

    But such a pair as here where Herod stands,   155

    He dares the world to make to both compare.

    Accursèd Salome, hadst thou been still,[17]

    My Mariam had been breathing by my side:

    Oh, never had I, had I had my will,

    Sent forth command, that Mariam should have died.   160

    But, Salome, thou didst with envy vex,[18]

    To see thyself outmatchèd in thy sex:

    Upon your sex's forehead Mariam sat,

    To grace you all like an imperial crown,†

    But you, fond fool, have rudely push'd thereat,   165

    And proudly pull'd your proper glory down.

    One smile of hers—nay, not so much—a look

---

[15] Garments.

[16] That is, make it seem less pure or dazzling by its superior whiteness.

[17] Quiet.

[18] In this intransitive form, "vex" means fret, grieve.

Was worth a hundred thousand such as you.
Judea, how canst thou the wretches brook,[19]
That robb'd from thee the fairest of the crew? 170
You dwellers in the now deprivèd land,
Wherein the matchless Mariam was bred:
Why grasp not each of you a sword in hand,
To aim at me your cruel sovereign's head?
Oh, when you think of Herod as your king, 175
And owner of the pride of Palestine,
This act to your remembrance likewise bring:
'Tis I have overthrown your royal line.
Within her purer veins the blood did run,
That from her grandam Sara she deriv'd, 180
Whose beldame age the love of kings hath won;†
Oh, that her issue had as long been liv'd.
But can her eye be made by death obscure?[20]
I cannot think but it must sparkle still:
Foul sacrilege to rob those lights so pure, 185
From out a temple made by heav'nly skill.
I am the villain that have done the deed,
The cruel deed, though by another's hand;
My word, though not my sword, made Mariam bleed,
Hircanus' grandchild [died] at my command— 190
That Mariam that I once did love so dear,
The partner of my now detested bed.
Why shine you, sun, with an aspect so clear?†
I tell you once again my Mariam's dead.
You could but shine,[21] if some Egyptian blowse, 195
Or Aethiopian dowdy lose her life:†
This was—then wherefore bend you not your brows?—

[19] Endure.
[20] Dark.
[21] You would do nothing other than shine in this way . . . (he is implying that Mariam's death deserves to be signalled by a more spectacular event, such as an eclipse, for example).

The King of Jewry's fair and spotless wife.
Deny thy beams, and, moon, refuse thy light,
Let all the stars be dark, let Jewry's eye   200
No more distinguish which is day and night:
Since her best birth did in her bosom die.
Those fond idolaters, the men of Greece,
Maintain these orbs are safely governèd:†
That each within themselves have gods apiece,   205
By whom their steadfast course is justly led.
But were it so, as so it cannot be,
They all would put their mourning garments on:
Not one of them would yield a light to me,
To me that is the cause that Mariam's gone.   210
For though they feign their Saturn melancholy,† 22
Of sour behaviours, and of angry mood:
They feign him likewise to be just and holy,
And justice needs must seek revenge for blood.
Their Jove, if Jove he were,23 would sure desire,   215
To punish him that slew so fair a lass:†
For Leda's beauty set his heart on fire,
Yet she not half so fair as Mariam was.

---

22 The following lines play upon the mythological attributes of the Greek and Roman gods. The influence of the planet Saturn was said to produce cold and gloomy temperaments (possibly because of Saturn's association, as a Roman agricultural god, with the earth); hence the adjective *saturnine*. On the other hand, Saturn also presided over the Golden Age, a time of prosperity, piety, and justice. Jupiter (or Jove) (ll. 215–17), who dethroned his father Saturn as ruler of the gods, was equally well known for erotic appetites; to rape Leda (l. 217), he transformed himself to a swan. Mars, the god of war (l. 219), was the adulterous lover of Venus, the goddess of love and beauty (l. 223); Paphos on Cyprus was one of Venus's shrines (l. 231). Apollo, or Sol (l. 220), was god not only of the sun but also of medicine ("physic," l. 222). Hermes (l. 224, or "Mercurius," l. 233), messenger of the gods, was also the god of eloquence and commerce (thus of "wit" as both verbal inventiveness and shrewdness). "Cinthia" (l. 234), or Diana, was goddess of the moon (the "night's pale light," l. 225) and patroness of chastity; Herod may be implying that the light of the moon is "pale" in comparison not only to the sun but also to Mariam's "brighter brow" (l. 234; cf. Herod's similar claim about Mariam's outshining the sun in act 4, ll. 7–9).

23 If he truly had supreme authority (or if he truly existed).

And Mars would deem his Venus had been slain;
Sol to recover her would never stick:[24]   220
For if he want the power her life to gain:
Then physic's god is but an empiric;[25]
The queen of love would storm[26] for beauty's sake;[27]
And Hermes too, since he bestow'd her wit;
The night's pale light for angry grief would shake,   225
To see chaste Mariam die in age unfit.
But, oh, I am deceiv'd, she pass'd[28] them all
In every gift, in every property:[29]
Her excellencies wrought her timeless[30] fall,
And they rejoic'd, not griev'd, to see her die.   230
The Paphian goddess did repent her waste,[31]
When she to one such beauty did allow:
Mercurius thought her wit his wit surpass'd,
And Cinthia envi'd Mariam's brighter brow.
But these are fictions, they are void of sense;[32]   235
The Greeks but dream, and dreaming falsehoods tell:
They neither can offend nor give defence,[†33]
And not by them it was my Mariam fell.
If she had been like an Egyptian black,
And not so fair, she had been longer liv'd: 240
Her overflow of beauty turnèd back,[34]

,[24] Hesitate.
    [25] Quack.
    [26] Rage.
    [27] That is, for grief or anger at the destruction of such beauty.
    [28] Surpassed.
    [29] Quality.
    [30] Untimely (but also "eternal," suggesting that the memory of this event will be immortal).
    [31] That is, Venus's prodigality or wasteful generosity (but a suggestion of the wastefulness of Mariam's destruction also seems obliquely present in the phrase).
    [32] Meaning (and perhaps physical—that is, sensible—reality as well).
    [33] They can neither do harm nor afford anyone protection.
    [34] In the context of the two preceding lines (which seem a final allusion to Cleopatra), the "overflow" of line 241 may evoke the annual flooding of the Nile.

And drown'd the spring from whence it was deriv'd.
Her heav'nly beauty 'twas that made me think
That it with chastity could never dwell:†
But now I see that Heav'n in her did link   245
A spirit and a person[35] to excel.
I'll muffle up myself in endless night,
And never let mine eyes behold the light.
Retire thyself, vile monster, worse than he†
That stain'd the virgin earth with brother's blood.[36]   250
Still in some vault or den enclosèd be,
Where with thy tears thou may'st beget a flood,
Which flood in time may drown thee: happy day
When thou at once shalt die and find a grave;
A stone upon the vault someone shall lay,   255
Which monument shall an inscription have,
And these shall be the words it shall contain:
Here Herod lies, that hath his Mariam slain. [*Exit.*]

Chorus. Whoever hath beheld with steadfast eye,
The strange events of this one only day:†   260
How many were deceiv'd, how many die,
That once today did grounds of safety lay!
  It will from them all certainty bereave,
  Since twice six hours so many can deceive.[37]

This morning Herod held for surely dead,[38]   265
And all the Jews on Mariam did attend:
And Constabarus rise[39] from Salom's bed,
And neither dream'd of a divorce or end.

---

[35] Body, physical appearance.
[36] Cain; see Genesis 4:8–12.
[37] Mislead, ensnare, delude.
[38] Either, elliptically, "This morning Herod [was] considered surely dead," or "This morning [metonymically, all those who held an opinion this morning] considered Herod surely dead."
[39] That is, did rise.

Pheroras joy'd[40] that he might have his wife,
And Babas' sons for safety of their life.   270

Tonight our Herod doth alive remain,
The guiltless Mariam is depriv'd of breath:
Stout Constabarus both divorc'd and slain,
The valiant sons of Babas have their death,
    Pheroras sure his love to be bereft,   275
    If Salome her suit unmade had left.[41]

Herod this morning did expect with joy,
To see his Mariam's much belovèd face:
And yet ere night he did her life destroy,
And surely thought she did her name disgrace.   280
    Yet now again, so short do humours last,
    He both repents her death and knows her chaste.

Had he with wisdom now her death delay'd,
He at his pleasure might command her death:
But now he hath his power so much betray'd,[42]   285
As all his woes cannot restore her breath.
    Now doth he strangely, lunaticly rave,
    Because his Mariam's life he cannot save.

This day's events were certainly ordain'd,
To be the warning to posterity: 290
So many changes are therein contain'd,
So admirably strange variety.
    This day alone, our sagest Hebrews shall
    In after times the school of wisdom call.

FINIS

---

[40] Rejoiced.

[41] Pheroras would certainly have been deprived of his beloved if Salome had not petitioned Herod on his behalf. (Pheroras, who has escaped the consequences of Herod's unexpected return, is included among the—at least potential—victims of the day's events, but the syntax suggests this inclusion requires some strain.)

[42] Proved false to, exposed to punishment. The line suggests self-betrayal.

NOTES TO THE PLAY

DEDICATORY SONNET

Dedication. Sir Henry Cary's brother Philip (1579–1631) married Elizabeth Bland of Carleton, Yorkshire, in 1609, and Dunstan and Greg concluded that it is to this sister-in-law, who shared her name, that Elizabeth Cary addressed the dedication of *Mariam*. However, Elaine Beilin has argued that the metaphors of the sonnet, emphasizing the sibling relationship of Phoebus and Phoebe, suggest that one of Henry Cary's own sisters was the dedicatee (see "Elizabeth Cary and *The Tragedie of Mariam*," esp. note 6). His sister Elizabeth married Sir John Savile in 1586 but might still, in this context, have been addressed by her original name. If the comparison to Diana suggests an unmarried woman, his sister Jane, who did not marry until 1627, is also a possibility, though this identification requires the supplementary hypothesis that the printer misapplied the name "Elizabeth" to the heading of the sonnet.

11. Elizabeth Cary had written an earlier tragedy (her "first," line 13), set in Syracuse, Sicily; the play is no longer extant and its subject is unknown. Apparently, not only *Mariam* but also this earlier play had circulated among Cary's contemporaries, who were aware of their authorship. John Davies of Hereford, who seems to have been Cary's handwriting tutor when she was a girl, refers to both tragedies in his dedication to *The Muses Sacrifice* (London, 1612); Cary shares the joint dedication with Lucy, countess of Bedford, and Mary Herbert, countess of Pembroke and Sir Philip Sidney's sister. Davies praises Cary by saying: "Thou mak'st Melpomen proud, and my Heart great / of such a Pupill, who, in Buskin fine, / With Feete of State, dost make thy Muse to mete / the Scenes of Syracuse and Palestine." (Melpomene was the muse of tragedy and buskins the thick-soled boots that Greek and Roman actors wore when they presented tragic dramas; "mete" means *measure* or *traverse*.)

ARGUMENT

Par. 1. *Idumean*: When John Hyrcanus I (nephew of Judas Maccabeus and the great-great-grandfather of Mariam) conquered the kingdom of Idumea (or, in Hebrew, Edom) to the south of Judea, its inhabitants converted to Judaism to avoid exile, but the Jews regarded them as only "half-Jews," and Herod's Idumean origins made him an unpopular governor (and, accordingly, more dependent on the Romans, his patrons).

[*granddaughter*]: The first sentence of the following paragraph makes it clear that "daughter" (in the 1613 text) should be emended to "granddaughter."

Par. 2. [*second*]: The printed text reads "first," but it is evident from the sources in Josephus that Hyrcanus is intended. See Historical Background, especially paragraph 5.

[*first*]: In this instance, the printed text says "second," but the sources make clear that Cary (or whoever wrote the Argument) is referring to Aristobulus. (The events to which the Argument alludes occurred in the opposite sequence, and this chronology may, in part, account for the confusion in the sentence. See Historical Background, especially paragraph 4.)

Par. 7. *she was beheaded*: In emphasizing the form of Mariam's execution, the Argument reinforces the traditional association of Salome with the decapitation of John the Baptist (and tacitly links Mariam's fate with Christian martyrdom); see Matthew 14:1–11. However, this tradition is rich in confusions; see "Biblical and Historical Herods" in the Introduction.

ACT I

Scene One

1. Although the sense of the first line is clearly continued by the second, in the 1613 text this line is punctuated with a question mark. While in the seventeenth century the intermediate pointing, or punctuation, of questioning or reflective speeches is not unusual and question marks are placed where modern usage would prescribe exclamation points, here the pause and the note of interrogation may be significant. In the opening line of the play Mariam seems to question the propriety of her own frank speech, one of the tragedy's recurrent issues, and the terms in which she expresses her hesitation also raise questions about how "public" and its implicit antithesis, "private," are to be understood. Even Mariam's physical situation is equivocal: by convention, she is alone (*sola*), but if the play is even notionally dramatic, she is speaking *to* an audience as well as herself and *on* a public stage. See the Introduction for further discussion of this initial line. (On rhetorical questions, see also Harry Levin, *The Question of Hamlet* [New York: Oxford University Press, 1959], 19–20, and chapter 1, "Interrogation," passim.)

5. Lines 5–8, addressed to Julius Caesar, are the first of many apostrophes (addresses to absent, abstract, or personified entities) through which the speak-

ing characters of *Mariam* create much of the play's imagined, as well as historical, world. Plutarch records, in his *Lives* of both Pompey and Julius Caesar, that
when the head of Pompey, Caesar's chief rival for domination of the Roman re-
public and its emergent empire, was sent to him by the Egyptians, Caesar
turned away from the loathsome present and burst into tears over Pompey's
signet ring. At the time of the play's events, Julius Caesar himself has been as-
sassinated, and his political heirs, preeminently Mark Antony and Octavius
Caesar, have been squabbling over the territories dominated by Rome—that is,
the emerging Roman Empire. As the Argument indicates, the defeat of Herod's
patron, Mark Antony, casts doubt on Herod's continued authority and even
life. On the politics of Roman mourning, see *Antony and Cleopatra*, 3.2.54–59, as
well as 5.1 passim.

   In their supplementary introduction to Oxford's 1992 reprint of the Dunstan
and Greg text, Marta Straznicky and Richard Rowland suggest that the opening soliloquy is influenced by Cary's reading of Montaigne, which is mentioned
in the *Life* (268). One of Montaigne's Essais (1.38) is entitled "Comme nous
pleurons et rions d'une mesme chose" ("How we weep and laugh at the same
thing").

   10. Here, as elsewhere, Dunstan and Greg note that the line is metrically de-
fective; that is, it lacks two syllables for a regular iambic pentameter line. As
Shakespeare frequently illustrates, deviation from this metrical norm is not unusual in drama, and whether or not *Mariam* was intended for performance, it
seems to have been written with an ear for dramatic inflection, variety, and emphasis; the metrically truncated lines may well represent deliberate choices. The
shortened lines tend to receive more weight and emphasis, as in this instance,
where the summary of Mariam's state of mind produces a *sententia* (an aphorism
expressing a general truth, which may be detached from its immediate dramatic
context).

   27. The repetition of "range" (to roam about like game—or dogs—on a
stretch of hunting grounds) in line 26 probably activates the pun on "heart"
and "hart," which is frequent in Renaissance poetry. See, for example, Wyatt's
"They flee from me" or "The long love that in my thought doth harbor," line
9. The hart is a male deer, but in Wyatt's "Whoso list to hunt I know where
is an hind," a deer also represents a woman who has become royal property.
This poem was not published until the nineteenth century, but it circulated in
manuscript, and Cary might have seen it. Like *Mariam*, the poem alludes topi-
cally to Anne Boleyn—or possibly even to Mary Boleyn, Anne's older sister
and a previous mistress of Henry VIII; Mary eventually married Henry Cary's
great-uncle.

   35. The 1613 text reads "lowlyest," and although "lowliest" (that is, hum-
blest, most submissive) is plausible, Josephus's consistent emphasis on Aristobulus's beauty recommends the emendation "loveliest," proposed by Dunstan
and Greg.

41. *Brake* as a verb is not recorded before the nineteenth century, but an aural pun on the noun *brake* (as curb or bridle) still seems possible.

43. Lines 43–46 are another apostrophe, this time addressed to the dead Hyrcanus.

46. Cf. *Richard III*, 1.1.119.

47. Rhyme (line 49) as well as sense makes it clear that "maide," the reading of the printed text, should be emended.

58. Cf. *Antony and Cleopatra*, 4.15.73–75: "No more but [e'en] a woman, and commanded / By such poor passion as the maid that milks / And does the meanest chares." Cf. also Queen Elizabeth's 1576 speech to Parliament: "If I were a milkmaid with a pail on my arm, whereby my private person might be little set by, I would not forsake that poor state to match with the greatest monarch" (as quoted in J. E. Neale, *Elizabeth I and Her Parliaments, 1559–1581* [London: Jonathan Cape, 1953], 366).

62. Cf. *Othello*, 5.2.42.

Scene Two

81. Dunstan and Greg suggest that "What" should be "Why," but in seventeenth-century usage *what* can mean *why*, and the emendation lessens the exclamatory force of the line. (Inserting a comma after "What" would produce another plausible reading of the line.)

The reading of the printed text "murthers" (murders) has been emended to "murthrers" (or in modernized form "murd'rer's"). The modernization, however, disrupts the rather marked sequence of *th* sounds in line 81.

85. The Idumeans, or Edomites, were said to be the descendants of Esau, generally despised for selling his birthright to his younger brother, Jacob, for a mess of pottage (see Genesis 25:29–34). In relation to this play, with ixs presentation of women's varied relations to political and dynastic power, it may be significant that Jacob obtains his father's blessing and ultimate ascendancy over Esau through the contrivance of his mother, Rebecca (Genesis 27).

88. "In the bosom of Abraham," as a metaphor for "gathered to his forefathers," is derived from the story of the beggar Lazarus and the rich man (Luke 16:22). Cf. Shakespeare, *Richard III*, 4.3.38, or his play with the phrase in *Henry V*, 2.3.9–10 (both works were published in quarto versions by Thomas Creede, the printer of *Mariam*, though the phrase was common).

90. The printed text reads "fain'd," but in seventeenth-century handwriting *m* is easily mistaken for *n* and vice versa (the so-called minim error). Cf. the similar confusion in act 5, lines 211 and 213.

96. Alexandra may be referring to Hyrcanus's permitting Herod to ally with the royal blood of his family through Mariam. The lines may also allude to an incident in which Herod, early in his career, was brought before the Sanhedrin

(state council) for slaying Hezekiah, a robber captain. Hyrcanus, as high priest, deferred the trial and privately urged Herod to leave Jerusalem. Moreover, after Herod had driven Antigonus (Hyrcanus's nephew and the last Maccabean, or Hasmonean, king) out of Judea, Hyrcanus greeted his entry into Jerusalem with garlands.

103. The traditional etymology derived *Edom* from a root meaning "red"; see Genesis 25:30.

114. See Exodus 28 for the priestly vestments, especially the elaborately described ephod, 28:6–14, a kind of linen apron (possibly covering the entire torso, as Cary seems to understand it). In modern translations, "turban," rather than "miter," designates the headpiece. "Double oil" (line 116) refers to the anointing of the priest (as well as the king); Exodus 29:7.

122. Dunstan and Greg propose changing "Mariam" in this line to "Herod," which would certainly be an easier reading. It is, however, possible to understand "Mariam" as an indirect object ("Was it love that gave a death sentence to Mariam?"), rather than as subject of "gave commandment."

133. The 1613 text reads "If." Dunstan and Greg suggest either "Of" or "In" as possible emendations. Whatever the reading of the initial word in line 133, the image in lines 131–32 is paradoxical, if not ominous, since it represents Herod's love of Mariam (or Mariam's of Herod) as ashes that extinguish flame rather than, as proverbially, one fire driving out another (cf. *Coriolanus*, 4.7.54). "Now" in line 133 presumably means "when I came to favor" and seems to evoke a historical present tense, but "was" immediately jogs the temporal sequence again. Both the metaphor and the confused temporality suggest that, despite Mariam's attempt to distinguish her situation from Doris's, the two figures are, even in her own mind, already conflated. In act 4, scene 8, the dialogue between Mariam and Doris emphasizes their exchange of positions.

141. Years after the events represented in the tragedy, Herod, believing informers' tales of his son Alexander's treachery, had both him and his younger brother, Aristobulus, strangled, and thus left the succession to Antipater, his son by Doris.

143. This Alexander, Mariam's father, was killed at Pompey's orders in 49 B.C. He was the son of Aristobulus II (who ruled the Jews from 67 to 63 B.C.) and married his cousin Alexandra, uniting the two lines of descent in the House of the Maccabees.

145. The emphasis on the name of Mariam's father may be significant in relation to the play's presentation of Mariam as a kind of anti-Cleopatra. Cleopatra, like all the Ptolemies, claimed descent from one of Alexander the Great's Macedonian generals; thus, the Ptolemies were, by extension, heirs to Alexander's authority.

147. Alexandra seems to be arguing that, since the throne belongs to Mariam's children by right, no one should think that Herod's presumption in "exalting"

them reflects anything but a distortion that aggrandizes his own authority at the expense of true lineal claims to kingship. Or perhaps she is dismissing the possibility that anyone could impugn their claim as relying on something other than—"more than"—true lineal right, such as Herod's favor or partiality to his own offspring. The "not" in line 149 further complicates the syntax and meaning, although, like a double negative, it may simply give more emphasis to Alexandra's argument. It may also suggest that if Herod *refuses* to elevate his children by Mariam, he will certainly have transgressed against right. Cf. also Alexandra's appeal to "right" in line 115.

170. The Roman Dellius seems to have suggested to Alexandra this snare for the notoriously lascivious disposition of Mark Antony (83–30 B.C.), the favorite, or "minion," of Felicity (apparently a close relative of the more familiar Renaissance deity Fortune). According to Josephus (*Antiquities*, 15.2.6), although Antony avoided the provocation of asking for the wife of Herod, he did send for the sixteen-year-old Aristobulus. Herod, fearing either the increased influence of Aristobulus's family or the uproar that would ensue in Judea if Antony took sexual liberties with someone so well born, refused the request.

182. The final word in this line is, in the 1613 edition, "leeke"; Dunstan and Greg suggest emending it to "seeke," but it may merely reflect contemporary pronunciation of *like*. The lines may be paraphrased: he judged incomparable what he found most pleasing in each of them.

185. A version of the Ovidian topos, "Inopem me copia fecit" ("Plenty has made me poor"), *Metamorphoses* 3.466, widely imitated in the Renaissance.

192. This line may contain one of the passage's specific connections with *Antony and Cleopatra*; cf. 2.1.21. This entire passage seems to be either a sustained allusion to Shakespeare's *Antony and Cleopatra* (for example, in its metaphorical connection between appetite for food and sexual desire and its emphasis on Cleopatra's dusky complexion and the brows [or forehead] as the seat of beauty) or one of the sources for Shakespeare's tragedy.

194. See *Antony and Cleopatra*, 3.10.10–21.

198. Dunstan and Greg suggest emending "And part" to "Apart" (that is, singular or distinctive), although the line could be paraphrased as "And part [of the excellence of her beauties] lay in this: they were hers by nature—all her own, not borrowed or cosmetic like those of Cleopatra." If the line does require emendation, Dyce's suggestion (in his annotated copy in the National Art Library, Victoria and Albert Museum) seems more attractive and economical: "past" (that is, *surpassed*) for "part."

202. Lines 199–200 allude to Cleopatra's successive affairs with Julius Caesar and Mark Antony, each of whom aspired to (and might have shared with a consort) supreme power over the Roman Empire. Since Cleopatra's suicide is a recent event as Mariam speaks, it is presumably association of ideas that prompts line 201.

Scene Three

237. See the first endnote to the Argument and endnote to line 85, above. In the Hebrew prophets, especially, Edom's continued conflict with Israel (and occupation of southern Judea) is considered to be an offense against the divine will; see particularly Ezekiel 25:13, 35, as well as Jeremiah 49:7–22, Amos 1:11–12, and Obadiah 1. Josephus attributes the hostility of both Salome and Herod's mother to Mariam's taunts about the meanness of their birth (*Antiquities*, 15.3.9).

239. This line could be either an assertion or a question, and the comma from the 1613 text has been retained to preserve the ambiguity.

241. Hebrew wordplay may underlie Salome's argument. The name *Adam, adamah* (meaning "earth") and *Adom* (meaning "red," from which the nation of Edom gets its name; see endnotes to lines 85 and 237 above) all come from the same Hebrew root.

248. See Historical Background, paragraph 6, on Salome's complaints to Herod against Josephus. In referring to "favourites," Salome may be loosely generalizing her accusations, but she may also be including Sohemus among Mariam's favorites and suggesting, proleptically, that she will denounce him too.

253. "Suspicious," the reading of the 1613 text, appears to have resulted from an inversion or misreading of the *n* in *suspicions*.

Here Mariam strikes back by insinuating that Salome suspects that Josephus was Mariam's lover because of her own infidelities; however, the following lines, while continuing the topic of Salome's fickleness, suggest that her accusation is merely strategic.

256. Since Cary alters "Josephus" to "Joseph" (as well as "Salome" to "Salom") according to the metrical needs of the line, Dunstan and Greg suggest that "Josephus'" might be emended to "Joseph's."

For Constabarus, see the Argument, paragraph 3, and Historical Background, paragraph 6.

260. Quasi-proverbial; cf. *Tempest*, 1.2.469–70: "What, I say, / My foot my tutor?" The phrase also activates the common metaphor of the state as body politic, with the ruler as head. For the inscription of social hierarchy upon the body, cf. also *Coriolanus*, 1.1.96–160, as well as the Introduction to Peter Stallybrass and Allon White, *The Politics and Poetics of Transgression* (Ithaca: Cornell University Press, 1986).

Scene Four

269. Salome plays on the name Arabia Felix (or *eudaimon*), which Ptolemy and other ancient geographers gave to the fertile part of Arabia south of the Gulf of Aqaba. (Cf. *Paradise Lost*, 4. 159–65, and Milton's source in Diodorus Siculus, 3.44.4.)

270. See Matthew 7:17–20: "A good tree cannot bring forth evil fruit, neither can a corrupt tree bring forth good fruit. . . . Wherefore by their fruits ye shall know them."

272. According to Josephus (*Antiquities*, 16.7.6; Lodge, Qq ii recto), he "was a craftie fellow, & in the prime of his youth, and very beautifull." In Josephus's account Salome was already a widow when she and Silleus were mutually smitten. (Silleus eventually declined marriage when Herod made conversion to Judaism a condition for the match.)

292. Cf. *Othello*, 1.3.95–96.

305. Salome's argument parallels Emilia's speech in *Othello*, 4.3.92–103.

312. The first seven chapters of Leviticus make elaborate prescriptions for offerings (see especially chapters 5 and 6 on offerings for particular sins). The satirical butt of these lines is not so much Hebrew observances as conventional, externalized piety of any kind. The charge that law (or religious restrictions, as a form of law) could be waived or eased for the wealthy was pertinent to the social context and grievances of Cary's era. Cf. Dekker and Webster, *Sir Thomas Wyatt* (1607), 5.1.99f.: "Great men like great Flies, through Lawes Cobwebs breake, / But the thin'st frame, the prison of the weake"; see R. W. Dent, *Proverbial Language in English Drama Exclusive of Shakespeare, 1495–1616*, 463, for other uses of this proverb.

316. The name "Babas" occurs in a variety of forms ("Baba," "Babas," and "Babus") in the 1613 text. In the Greek text of Josephus the name is "Baba," but "Babas" is the form that Thomas Lodge uses in his translation of Josephus's *Workes*, which Cary evidently knew and consulted. For the sake of consistency we have used "Babas" throughout the text, though alterations are noted in the textual collation.

319. While governor of Idumea, Constabarus had sought to make himself independent of Herod's authority by asking Cleopatra to obtain the kingdom for him from Antony. Cleopatra's intercession was unsuccessful, and when Herod learned of it, only the entreaties of Salome and her mother managed to preserve Constabarus's life. See *Antiquities*, 15.7.9.

Scene Five

352. Josephus reports that Obodas was "a slouthfull man, and one given to idlenes," who entrusted most of his affairs to Silleus (*Antiquities*, 16.7.6; Lodge, Qq iii recto).

354. "Who" probably refers back to "Obodas." In the 1613 text line 355 ends with a question mark. If this line is understood as an independent question, then Dunstan and Greg's suggestion that "not" might be emended to "on" is plausible.

368. Silleus echoes the marriage ceremony in the Book of Common Prayer, "till death do us part," though his emphasis on pleasure may express something further of his character.

Scene Six

378. Cf. lines 282–83.

396. Constabarus quotes Proverbs 12:4, traditionally attributed to King Solomon. See also the chapter on the conjugal crown in Karen Newman, *Fashioning Femininity*.

400. See endnote to line 319, above.

424. *OED* records the verb *topsy-turvèd* as a back-formation from *topsy-turvy*. On the other hand, "topsie turued," the reading of the 1613 text, may simply indicate that the *n* in *turned* has been inverted.

425. The immediate context of the words "beastes, swine" ("fishes graze," "birds descend") invites this emendation of the 1613 text.

430. In the 1613 text the penultimate word is "waters-bearing," which makes tenable sense but also makes the line difficult to pronounce. It seems likely that the terminal *s* in "waters" results from contamination by the other plurals in the phrase.

432. That is, enslave us, make us hewers of wood and drawers of water; cf. line 430 and Joshua 9.

440. See Exodus 25:18–20, where God instructs Moses in the construction and adornment of the tabernacle.

448. See Exodus 12, especially 12:12 and 12:21–27.

450. Most Christian theologians assigned two thousand years to the era between the promulgation of the Law and the incarnation of Christ, and the events of the play occur in 29 B.C. Constabarus's figure corresponds most closely to the chronology of Philo Judaeus (which differs from that of Josephus). On Philo, Josephus, and disparate accounts of Biblical chronology, see Sir Thomas Browne, *Pseudodoxia Epidemica* (1646), bk. 6, ch. 1.

461. Scanning the first foot of this line as a trochee produces the appropriate inflection.

464. In line 464 "his" means Josephus's, and in line 465 "him" refers to Constabarus; but the syntactically vague alignment of pronouns with antecedents reinforces Constabarus's assertion that the men in Salome's life are interchangeable.

478. Constabarus continues, unawares, his prophecy through line 490 and thus describes the shape of the succeeding plot.

501. In the 1613 text this word is "Of," which makes possible, though elliptical, sense ("If they gain an intermediate degree of honor . . ."), but Dunstan and Greg's suggested emendation has been adopted here. The next line plays upon the buried etymology (and literal French meaning) of *degree* as "step."

508. Compare, among other Renaissance eulogies of moderate desire, Meliboeus's praise of the pastoral life in Spenser, *Faerie Queene*, bk. 6, canto 9, st. 20ff. (Spenser here follows Tasso's *Jerusalem Delivered* [7.8–13].) Horace is the most conspicuous classical source for such idealizations of the "humble state"; see, for example, *Odes* 2.18.

518. The chorus imputes to Mariam motives similar to Salome's as described by Constabarus in act 1, line 474.

ACT 2
Scene One

Sc. head. Pheroras was Herod's younger brother and partner in many of the dignities and revenues of the kingdom. The subplot of Pheroras and Graphina derives from a brief comment in Josephus's *Jewish War* (1.24.5) that, after the death of his first wife (a younger sister of Mariam's), Pheroras refused marriage with Herod's eldest daughter because he had fallen in love with a slave girl. The name and character of Graphina are Cary's inventions (see Introduction and endnote to line 18, below).

12. Although Greg and Dunstan don't note it as a doubtful reading, the 1613 text's "monachall" has been emended to "monarchal" (royal). (In the copy in the National Library of Art, Victoria and Albert Museum, Dyce also notes this correction.)

Pheroras offers a pseudophysiological explanation of why he can't cry for Herod's death: the heat of his passion—which enters through his eyes with the sight of Graphina—dries up the moisture of his tears. The failure of Pheroras's tears recalls Mariam's soliloquy that opens act 1; cf. especially lines 33–34.

18. Pheroras plays upon the Latin etymology of "infant" (*infans*, speechless), and allusive connections between speech, silence, and writing supply a thematic structure for the scene. Later in the speech, lines 41–42, Pheroras talks about Graphina as if she shares in the speechlessness of her royal rival; indeed, her name may be intended to evoke writing (*graphesis* in Greek) as a "silent" form of speech. The emphasis on her position of handmaiden (lines 59, 70) also suggests the traditional presentation of writing as ancillary (literally, in the position of a handmaiden) to spoken discourse.

24. "Us" is a conjectural addition to this line (suggested by Dunstan and Greg), since the meter is unusually rough without some such insertion.

41. "Speaks" may be a shortened form of *speak'st* or *speakest*.

60. Cf. "for he has regarded the low estate of his handmaiden" (Luke 1:48).

62. The word refers primarily to Graphina's feudal and sexual subordination to Pheroras as her lord and master, but it also puns biblically on *vessel*, thus alluding both to woman as the "weaker vessel" (1 Peter 3:7) and to human fragility (Psalms 31:12) or subjection to the divine will (Acts 9:15, Romans 9:22–23).

63. Dunstan and Greg suggest emending "best" to "lest" (that is, *least*), but the less familiar phrase also makes sense: Graphina says that rejecting a princess is *not* the best or greatest of the favors Pheroras has granted her.

80. Dyce (in his notes in the Victoria and Albert copy of *Mariam*) plausibly suggests emending "the" to "thee" (producing the meaning "him who considers you the glory of his life"), but "the" also makes sense: "him who embraces the glory of his life [namely, thee]."

82. That is, severed from the body, a notion that again allies death with divorce or exile.

Scene Two

102. Citing sources including Pythagoras, Euripides, and Terence, Erasmus set the ancient proverb "Amicorum communia omnia" ("Between friends all is common") at the head of his collection of *Adagia* (1508).

112. The friendship between David ("Jesse's son") and Jonathan, the son of Saul, is narrated in 1 Samuel 18:4, 20:1–42 and 2 Samuel 1:17–26; it defied the authority of Saul as both king and father.

132. The cuckoo hides its eggs in other birds' nests, and its offspring displace the other young birds in the nest. For the notion that the cuckoo also kills its foster parent, see Pliny, *Natural History*, bk. 10, 11, and cf. *King Lear*, 1.4.215–16. "Infant nurse" means "nurse of his infancy."

140. The phrasing may recall Judges 16:26–30.

152. Emended from "leare" in the 1613 text.

170. See Argument, paragraph 5, and Historical Background, paragraph 5.

179. The rhyme word "I" in line 177 indicates that the 1613 reading, "live," should be emended to "lie," with the same meaning.

184. Octavius (later Augustus Caesar, 63 B.C.–A.D. 14) was the great-nephew of Julius Caesar, who eventually adopted him as his heir. Octavius's first public appearance was at the age of twelve, when he delivered a funeral oration for his grandmother Julia, Julius Caesar's sister; perhaps this is the moment to which Babas's son refers. Suetonius reports that "Augustus' eyes were clear and bright, and he liked to believe that they shone with a sort of divine radiance; it gave him profound pleasure if anyone at whom he glanced keenly dropped his head as though dazzled by looking into the sun" (para. 79; *The Twelve Caesars*, trans. Robert Graves [Baltimore: Penguin Books, 1957], 94). Suetonius tells several anecdotes of Octavius's youthful promise (para. 94; esp. pp. 101–2) and devotes sections 51–56 of his biography to Octavius's clemency and courtesy (pp. 79–82).

214. The line is hypermetrical, and it seems possible that "a" (which also weakens the sententious ring of the couplet) is an unauthorized insertion.

Scene Three

215. The 1613 text reads "Your," which could refer to Jerusalem, but the second "your" in the line ("your lofty side") makes more sense if the apostrophe is addressed to the buildings themselves.

216. "Scope," in the 1613 text, could be a second object of "bow," meaning something like *extent* (and making "side / And scope" a hendiadys for "extensive walls"), but we have followed Dyce's suggested emendation. In contemporary handwriting, a *t* could easily have been mistaken for a *c*.

219. See Numbers 10:10 for the proclamation of sacred feasts by trumpets.

221. See Leviticus 23:5–14. On the day after the final sabbath of the feast of unleavened bread (associated with Passover, at Exodus 12:14–20), the offering of first fruits took place, that is, at the beginning of the barley harvest in April.

239. The 1613 text reads "oath," but a plural here, as suggested by Dunstan and Greg, seems more probable.

270. In Renaissance physiology the womb, or "mother," was thought capable of moving upward to cause a feeling of suffocation or hysteria (etymologically derived from the Greek word for *womb*); cf. *King Lear*, 2.4.56–58. Accordingly, the associative connection between "mother" and "smother," expressed by this rhyme, was strong.

278. Although the terms of Antipater's indignation at his dispossession are dramatically apt, these lines may also allude to charges that, because Catherine of Aragon was still living when Henry VIII remarried, Anne Boleyn was an adulteress and Elizabeth I a bastard.

Scene Four

293. In the 1613 text this word is "expectation," but the meter, as well as the sense, suggests that it should be emended to "exception," as Dunstan and Greg propose. The "exception" is the grounds on which Constabarus will refuse to fight (lines 289–90).

294. The 1613 text has the shortened form, "Salom," but the meter makes an emendation desirable here.

296. Cf. the attitude of Albany toward Goneril in act 4, scene 2, of *King Lear*.

322. This phrase might be emended to "affection's [or affections'] loss," as Dunstan and Greg suggest, but in seventeenth-century idiom "affections lost" conveys the same meaning.

323. Proverbial; cf. Wyatt, "Since in a net I seek to hold the wind" ("Whoso list to hunt I know where is an hind," line 8, *Collected Poems of Sir Thomas Wyatt*, ed. Muir and Thomson, p. 5).

328. See Matthew 23:27: "Woe unto you, scribes and Pharisees, hypocrites! for ye are like unto whited sepulchres, which indeed appear beautiful outward, but are within full of dead men's bones, and of all uncleanness."

335. Cf. the general address to Shylock as a dog, *Merchant of Venice*, 1.3.111, 117–22, 127–28; and 3.3.6–7.

350. Cf. act 1, lines 262–63.

360. This line appears hypermetrical, although the first two words might be condensed into "Thou'st." It is metrically irregular in any case, and its extra stresses invite a heavy, flat (possibly contemptuous) delivery.

376. After "kill," the 1613 text reads, "I, I, they fight," which has been emended to make the last two words a stage direction. However, "I, I," (or "Ay, ay") falls outside of the rhyme scheme. While these letters may indicate the exclamatory cries of Constabarus (or of both combatants) during the duel,

they may also represent a compositor's confused interpretation of some graphic device in the manuscript—for example, a parenthesis—used to indicate a stage direction.

379. Dunstan and Greg suggest this phrase might be emended to "it is too late, I fear," but the emendation seems unnecessary. The phrase implies "The fatal event has already occurred."

393. Emended, as Dunstan and Greg propose, from "so" in the 1613 text. (However, "so" suggests an alternative syntax, which looks back to the preceding lines, and therefore may not be a misprint.)

402. Cf. Deuteronomy 16:19.

406. The phrase is proverbial, but cf. also *Othello*, 1.3.1–43, a scene in which the Venetian senators "try" by reason initial reports about the Turkish fleet.

ACT 3

Scene One

28. Cf. *Othello*, 3.3.136–41.

29. See Historical Background, paragraph 4. Although Josephus reports that Ananelus "had familiar acquaintance" with Herod (*Antiquities*, 15.3.1) the history of their relationship makes it possible to suspect some undertones of irony in his report of the "good news" that Herod lives, especially at lines 49–50.

Scene Two

39. See Leviticus 21:1–2.

67–68. The Hebrew scriptures frequently refer to Ophir as a source of gold, and in 1 Kings 21 the fleet of Hiram also brings "almug wood" (probably sandalwood) and precious stones from Ophir. Its location has been variously identified as the west coast of Arabia and India (for the latter, see Josephus, *Antiquities*, 1.6.4; according to Thomas Browne [*Pseudodoxia Epidemica*, bk. 2, ch.2], it "is supposed to be Taprobana or Malaca in the Indies"). Pheroras's speech suggests Cary imagined it as one of the more remote locations. Tyre (or Tyrus), on the coast of Lebanon, was the chief city of Phoenicia. Its beauty and power are celebrated, and its destruction lamented, in Ezekiel 27.

74. In the 1613 text "we" in line 73 reads "he" and "our" in line 74 reads "his." These pronouns make little sense, especially since there is no reference in either the play or the sources to a brother of Constabarus. These emendations, proposed by Dunstan and Greg, are not wholly satisfactory—they represent a unique assumption on Salome's part of the royal "we"—but they provide the most economical means of making reasonably coherent sense of the lines.

95. Possibly Salome means that by pretending to be patient she has exposed Mariam's anger or bad temper (as displayed in upbraiding Salome) to

punishment. Conceivably, "her" might be emended to "no," indicating that Salome had concealed her own anger while waiting for an opportunity to be avenged.

Scene Three

124. The 1613 text presents this line as a continuation of Sohemus's speech, but the line clearly belongs to Mariam, and a new speech heading has been supplied.

137. There is no terminal punctuation for this line in the 1613 text, so the final phrase is enjambed with the following line to mean, "In vain you urge me to live with him. . . . " However, it is also possible to supply a period at the end of line 137 and read line 138 as an exclamation.

160. Lines 158–60 present the mind as a kind of stage populated by personified emotions. In line 161 scorn either enters and makes her contribution to the inner drama after fear or takes fear's place and speaks instead of her.

175. This phrase (with the following lines) is probably an allusive repetition of Mariam's comparison of herself to Cleopatra; see 1.2.199–202. Its diction parallels that of *Antony and Cleopatra*, 1.1.12.

183. Sohemus echoes Josephus; see Introduction and Appendix, 15.7.6.

184. Catherine Belsey comments that the contradictions in Sohemus's speech, " 'guiltles,' 'disgrace,' 'without desart'—are symptomatic of the play's consistent unease about its heroine's right to speak" (*The Subject of Tragedy*, 173).

186. Probably an allusion to the sword of Damocles. When Damocles, a courtier to Dionysius of Syracuse, praised the happiness of a king too lavishly, Dionysius illustrated the precariousness of a ruler's fortunes by inviting Damocles to a banquet and seating him beneath a sword suspended by a single hair.

193. Dunstan and Greg believe this name should be emended to "Alexandra's," but it seems as likely that Sohemus would surrender royal authority to Alexander, Mariam's son (and thus to Mariam, as his guardian), as to her mother. "Her" in line 195 would thus refer to Mariam, rather than to Alexandra.

196. Sohemus's use of this place-name is an anachronism. Herod built an extensive palace-fort by the western wall of Jerusalem (near the Jaffa Gate), but it was the Crusaders, conquering Islamic Jerusalem in 1099, who conferred the name of "David's Tower" on part of this structure.

206. This line alludes to one of the plagues of Egypt (Exodus 10:21) and to the parting of the Red Sea (Exodus 14:21–22).

207. In Joshua 10:12–14, Joshua commands the sun to stand still at Gibeon while the men of Israel avenge themselves on their enemies.

210. The clipped wings evoke the personification of desire as Cupid or Eros, god of love.

212. Cf. the eulogy which Antonio, steward and future husband of the Duchess of Malfi, delivers (*The Duchess of Malfi* [1613–14], 1.1.200–19).

217. Cf. Stefano Guazzo, *Civile Conversation*, trans. George Pettie and Bartholomew Yong (1581–86): "It is not sufficient to be honest and innocent in deed, if she doe not likewise avoyde all suspicion (in respect of the world) between being naught and being thoughte naught" (New York: Alfred Knopf, 1925, vol. 3–4, 31).

220. Both interrupting and intensifying "herself," the word "proper" draws additional attention to the exploration, in this Chorus, of the ways in which the self of the wife is both her own and not her own; her *proper*, or self-defined, identity is compromised by being the *property* of someone else. See also Catherine Belsey on the play's presentation of a "wife's right to speak, to subjectivity" (*The Subject of Tragedy*, 171–75).

ACT 4
Scene One

4. In the 1613 text this stage direction appears at the end of line 5. Although the former placement probably indicates that the entrance occurs as line 5 begins, we have relocated the stage direction in accordance with modern conventions.

5. In the 1613 text, line 5 ends with "Mariam?" but the rhyme scheme suggests that something is missing. We have added "How?" as proposed by Dunstan and Greg. One could, however, argue that the rhyme scheme was deliberately ruptured for dramatic effect.

14. Although schemes of biblical chronology differed (see endnote to act 1, line 450), the span Herod evokes is roughly a thousand years.

16. See endnote to act 3, line 207. The 1613 text uses an alternative form of Joshua's name in the compound "*Iosualike*."

24. Dunstan and Greg suggest that "greefe" in the 1613 text should be emended to "geese" (alluding to the tradition that when the Gauls attempted to scale the Capitol in 390 B.C., the sacred geese of Juno gave the alarm by cackling and clapping their wings; see Livy, 5.47). Since the original can plausibly be glossed (for example, Rome would have been betrayed to the Volscians except for the grief which Coriolanus felt at the sight of his mother's pleading for the city's salvation), we have chosen to retain the 1613 reading.

29. When Augustus fell in love with Livia Drusilla (c. 55 B.C.–A.D. 29), he forced her husband to divorce her and, after divorcing his own wife, Scribonia, married her himself. Suetonius reports she was the one woman Caesar, although notoriously unfaithful, loved throughout his life ("Life of Augustus," para. 62, *The Twelve Caesars*, p. 84).

The echo of line 21 in line 30 makes Livia virtually the embodiment of Rome itself. Personifications of Rome as a powerful woman, either an idealized mistress or a reviled "Whore of Babylon," appear frequently in Renaissance writing. See, for instance, Spenser's *Ruines of Rome* (1591), a translation of Du Bellay's *Les*

Antiquitez de Rome (1558), and Wayne Rebhorn's "Du Bellay's Imperial Mistress," *Ren Q*, Winter 1980, 33(4): 609–22.

33. In the 1613 text lines 33–34 are punctuated: "Be patient but a little, while mine eyes / Within your compass limits be contain'd:" but this pointing suggests that the compositor misunderstood their syntax. Herod addresses lines 33 through 36 to his eyes, and the text has been repunctuated accordingly.

40. These phrases might plausibly be repunctuated "my Mariam? More than happy fate!"

Scene Two

51. During Herod's war against Antigonus, the last of the Hasmonean kings (see Historical Background), Phasaelus, the brother whom Herod apostrophizes in lines 51–62, was captured and threatened with death. Rather than die at the hands of his enemies, Phasaelus dashed his head against a rock. By some accounts, before dying he heard the news that Herod had escaped, and he declared himself happy, knowing that someone was still living to avenge him. (See Josephus, *Antiquities*, 14.13.10; *Jewish War*, 1.13.10.) His father and mother were, respectively, Antipater and Cypros, also the parents of Herod and Pheroras.

74. Pheroras slyly pretends that Herod has known and forgiven what he is just now learning.

79. "Salome" is substituted for "Salom" (the 1613 reading) for metrical reasons. "Her affection," in the following line, means "she, with her affectionate nature."

Scene Three

88. In Philip Sidney's *Arcadia* (1590), bk. 3, the dying Argalus addresses his wife, Parthenia, as "My deare, my deare, my better halfe."

94. Cf. Josephus (*Antiquities*, 15.7.2; Lodge, sig. Oo i recto); see Appendix, 15.7.2.

105. Nehemiah (3:16) locates the "tombs of David" near the pool of Siloam and the King's Garden (that is, somewhere in the southern part of the Citadel, or City, of David, rather than at the traditional site of the Tomb of David in modern Jerusalem). For Cary, however, the relevant citations to the Tomb of David come from Josephus's *Antiquities*. John Hyrcanus I (see endnote to the first paragraph of the Argument) "opening Davids monument (who surpassed all other kings in riches during his time), drewe three thousand talents out of the same" (13.8.4; Lodge, sig. Hh vi recto). After the death of Mariam, when her sons were already young men, Herod, who had spent "lavishly much and many summes of money, both at home and abroad," secretly entered the sepulcher and, though he found no money, took away the furniture of gold and other precious goods stored in the tomb. When he ventured further, "where the bodies of Salomon and David were intombed . . . fire came out of those secret places, and consumed" two of his guards. Frightened by the consequences of his sacrilege,

Herod built an expensive propitiatory monument of white stone at the mouth of the sepulcher (16.7.1; Lodge, sig. Qq ii recto).

118. The context suggests that this word should mean "solemn oath," but all of the uses recorded by the *OED* reflect only its sense as "curse." Perhaps this language suggests that Herod cannot protest even love without imprecations, but in Latin *exsecratio* can mean either "curse" or, by extension, "oath with an imprecation."

129. The gap in the rhyme scheme, as well as the elliptical syntax of the sentence, indicates a missing line.

136. According to Josephus, it had been done twice before: "The first that transgressed this ordinance was Antiochus Epiphanes, who dispossessed Josuah, and preferred his brother Onias to his place. The second was Aristobulus, who tooke it away from his brother Hircanus, and usurped it himselfe" (*Antiquities,* 15.3.1; Lodge, Nn i recto). The Seleucid king Antiochus IV Epiphanes attempted to suppress the practice of Judaism and provoked the Maccabean rebellion; see also Daniel 10:21–39. Aristobulus II, who reigned from 67 to 63 B.C., was the great-uncle and not the brother of Mariam; the brother whom he deprived of office was Hyrcanus, Mariam's grandfather.

140. Cf. Josephus, *Antiquities,* 15.7.4 (Lodge, Oo i verso); see Appendix, 15.7.4. The pseudonymous Joseph ben Gorion (see Introduction, 18) asserts Herod was the first to depose a high priest.

148. Cf. Matthew 7:26–27.

Scene Four

164. The 1613 text reads "passion." Dramatic clarity and the Josephan source (*Antiquities,* 15.7.4) support Dunstan and Greg's proposed emendation, which has therefore been adopted. On the other hand, "passion" might represent a metonymic substitution of cause for effect; cf. line 168.

176. According to a Renaissance proverb, "The white devil is worse than the black." R. W. Dent records the earliest dramatic use of the phrase "white devil" as in Cyril Tourneur's *The Revenger's Tragedy* (3.5.145), published in 1607, after the conjectural date of *Mariam*'s composition. However, Dent notes that the phrase is common in religious literature before that date and that John Harington also uses "white divels" in the commentary to his 1591 translation of Ariosto's *Orlando Furioso.* Harington applies the term to women, and it is usually assumed that the title of Webster's *The White Devil* (1612) also refers to a woman, Vittoria Corombona. See Dent, *John Webster's Borrowing* (Berkeley: University of California Press, 1960), 69–70.

177. The Hebrew scriptures prescribe this aromatic herb for various ritual uses, including the purification of lepers (Leviticus 14:4).

181. The phrasing here seems influenced by Lodge's translation of Josephus (*Antiquities,* 15.7.1; Lodge, Oo i recto); see Appendix, 15.7.1.

182. "Slaughter" may allude to Herod's association with the slaughter of the innocents at Bethlehem (Matthew 2:16–18).

204. This line has two extra syllables, and Dunstan and Greg therefore propose that "never" should be omitted. As it stands, Herod's *cri de coeur* expresses retrospective disillusionment; the omission of "never" would make it a kind of protest, attempting to preserve the past or a hypothetical future. Although the metrical difficulty is not sufficient to justify altering the text, the emended version would effectively introduce the following lines, which recall the power Mariam once exercised over (and through) Herod.

214. The 1613 text reads "heavy" (possibly meaning "sad, sorrowful"), but the emendation proposed by Dunstan and Greg seems to fit the context better. Cf. *Othello*, 2.3.350–51 (as well as 3.3.278–79 and 4.2.35–37).

249. Once Mariam is condemned by Herod, the play increasingly, in acts 4 and 5, associates her death with that of Christ, in this instance, as the Lamb of God (see, e.g., John 1:29 and Revelation 5:12). See Beilin, *Redeeming Eve*, 171–72.

Scene Five

271. Cf. the blood of Abel crying out to heaven (Genesis 4:10) and Claudius at prayer (*Hamlet*, 3.3.36), where Claudius also invokes the murder of Abel, 37–38.

274. Possibly the book of which the prophet Daniel is told (Daniel 12:1–4; see also Revelation 10). Cf. Shakespeare and Fletcher, *Henry VIII*, 4.2.45–46: "Men's evil manners live in brass, their virtues / We write in water." For "leaf of brass" see also *Titus Andronicus*, 4.1.102–3. (Among the seventeenth-century associations of "leaves of brass" might have been the tablets used for funerary inscriptions in churches.)

276. Achitophel counseled Absalom in his rebellion against his father, King David, advising him, among other things, to publicly appropriate the royal concubines. When Absalom rejected his strategic advice (which might have made the rebellion successful), he went home and hanged himself (2 Samuel 17:23). *The Jerusalem Bible* notes that (apart from soldiers who killed themselves to thwart the enemy) his is the only suicide recorded in the Hebrew scriptures, exclusive of the Apocrypha. However, in *Biathanatos* Donne considers the death of Samson as a suicide. See the Introduction to John Donne, *Biathanatos*, ed. Michael Rudick and M. Pabst Battin (New York: Garland Publishing, 1982), esp. pp. lxv–lxvi, lxxvii–lxxxii, for further discussion of how Donne understands the "suicides" of Samson and other biblical figures.

277. As the text stands, it is somewhat perplexing, and Dunstan and Greg propose that "didst not" be emended to "didest" so that the Butler endorses the suicide of Achitophel. However, it is possible that the line means, "I truly believe you did evil (and therefore appropriately freed yourself from shame through death)" or that lines 277–78 together mean, "Even though my soul judges your suicide wrong, I will follow your example."

Scene Six

292. Dunstan and Greg suggest that "Tis" in the 1613 text should be emended to "Thus." We have preferred "This," which requires a smaller alteration to the text and can be understood as introducing the following two lines; "for thy ceremony" means "in response to your formal or courteous self-blame."

298. The 1613 text reads "your" and requires emendation. Dunstan and Greg propose "our," which requires the least graphic alteration. Nevertheless, the insistent focus on Salome in these lines makes "her" the slightly more likely pronoun.

305. Friends should be willing ("not compell'd by strong necessity") to die solely to avert the destruction of their friends. Constabarus may also be reasoning that "Since you will do your duties by dying on my account (as I have proved), I should be willing to die for you (not merely 'weakly now lament'), even were I not compelled—as, in fact, I am." However, since his death will not prevent his "friends' disaster," the two parts of the thought seem somewhat disjunct. Constabarus's argument conforms with the common opinion of sixteenth-century Roman Catholic moral theologians, who elaborate on the biblical text "Greater love hath no man than this, that a man lay down his life for his friends" (John 15:13).

317. According to Pliny (*Natural History*, 8.44), hyenas could imitate the human voice; they were also said to sob hypocritically over their victims as they consumed them.

321. In effect, Constabarus says that women are demons (cf. line 350). Accounts of the fall of the angels were elaborated from biblical passages including Isaiah 14:12–15 and Revelation 12:7–9. That pride or ambition led to their fall was commonplace; cf. Shakespeare and Fletcher, *Henry VIII*, 3.2.440–41.

325. In the 1613 text this word is "many," but the misogyny of this passage, as well as the meter, indicates that the correct reading is "man."

327. See Genesis 9:11: "And I will establish my covenant with you; neither shall all flesh be cut off any more by the waters of a flood; neither shall there any more be a flood to destroy the earth."

333. Emended from "You" in the 1613 text because parallelism with the following line's "Your" makes better sense than the repetition of "You" from the preceding line, which the printer may have assumed.

334. Constabarus speaks for a long tradition of misogyny. For general discussion of stock antifeminist themes, see Katharine Rogers, *The Troublesome Helpmate*, Linda Woodbridge, *Women and the English Renaissance*, and Katherine Henderson and Barbara McManus, eds., *Half Humankind*.

340. Cf. Posthumus's misogynist tirade, *Cymbeline*, 2.5.1ff.

342. "Cham's servile curse" is an extraordinary condensation of the curses pronounced against Eve after the fall (Genesis 3:16) and against Canaan (apparently conflated with his father Ham, or Cham) after Ham summons his brothers to observe the drunken nakedness of their father, Noah (Genesis 9:22, 25).

The curse of "Cham" is slavery (and later interpreters also saw in this curse the "cause" of black skin; see Sir Thomas Browne's refutation of this absurdity in *Pseudodoxia Epidemica*, bk. 6, ch. 11). Presumably, Constabarus associates this servitude with Eve's punishment after the fall ("thy desire shall be to thy husband, and he shall rule over thee," Genesis 3:16); lines 343–44 confirm that he is discussing the proper hierarchy of authority.

Scene Seven

362. The notes in Dyce's copy of *Mariam* suggest that "miracles" should be changed to "merciless." Since Herod implies that Salome is a miracle of cruelty, the emendation, though ingenious, is unnecessary. (Cf. the implied contrast between Iago's cruelty and the less "mortal natures" of inanimate threats, *Othello*, 2.1.68–73.)

395. Cf. *Othello*, 5.2.7–13: "But once put out thy light, / Thou cunning'st pattern of excelling nature. . . . "

406. Cf. Salome's self-description, 1.4.282–84.

413. Mariam's tresses are implicitly compared to the golden fleece that hung in a sacred grove of Colchis. This fleece of a winged ram, sent from Olympus to rescue Phrixus from sacrifice, prompted Jason's expedition in the Argo; many of the Argonauts were recruited from among the "kings" of Greece. Cf. the comparison of Portia's "sunny locks" and Belmont to the golden fleece and Colchis, *Merchant of Venice*, 1.1.169–72.

416. The object of the Trojan War was, at least ostensibly, to recover Helen, the queen of Sparta, who had been abducted by (or had eloped with) Paris, prince of Troy; the ten-year siege by the Greeks culminated in the conquest and burning of Troy. Lines 413–16 connect Mariam with the two most famous epic enterprises of ancient Greece.

420. The focus on women's hair, as both glory and seductive lure, is pervasive in Renaissance poetry; its genealogy includes St. Paul's injunctions that women keep their heads covered in the church (1 Corinthians 11:4–6, 13–15).

422. Dunstan and Greg note that this line is two syllables short, and Dyce's notes propose inserting "only" before "hair," but the line may be deliberately truncated. The brevity and metrical flatness of the line give it not only more emphasis but also a mildly comic spin.

434. Cf. act 1, line 378, and act 3, lines 227–29, 242.

462. The comparison of Salome to a "blackamoor" activates common Renaissance associations between blackness and female "vice." Dympna Callaghan discusses this passage and its "racialization" of female beauty in "Re-reading *The Tragedie of Mariam*." For the cultural association between blackness and failures of female virtues, see Karen Newman, "And Wash the Ethiop White: Femininity and the Monstrous in *Othello*," in *Fashioning Femininity*, 71–94.

Ptolemy's *Tetrabiblos* (2.2) and Ovid's myth of Phaethon (*Metamorphoses*, 2.235–36) are among the ancient sources of the theory that the pigmentation of black skin results from overexposure to the sun. This notion had wide currency during the sixteenth century (for example, in Thomas Newton's *The Touchstones of Complexion*, 1565); *The Merchant of Venice*, 2.1.1–3, also alludes to this belief. At the same time, however, the accounts of explorers reporting lighter-skinned people inhabiting the same climates as Negroes began to challenge such explanations; Sir Thomas Browne attempts to refute climatic theories in *Pseudodoxia Epidemica*, bk. 6, ch. 10. In England, at least, the conflation of blacks and moors (encapsulated in the word *blackamoor*) probably dated back to the fourteenth-century *Mandeville's Travels*, which described the inhabitants of Mauretania (Moors) as black; Gower's *Confessio Amantis* (1390) uses "Moor" as a synonym for "Negro." (For further discussion of these topics, see also Elliot H. Tokson, *The Popular Image of the Black Man in English Drama, 1550-1688* [Boston: G. K. Hall, 1982], and Anthony Gerard Barthelemy, *Black Face, Maligned Race: The Representation of Blacks in English Drama from Shakespeare to Southerne* [Baton Rouge: Louisiana State University Press, 1987].)

467. Cf. *Othello*, 5.2.144–46.

482. On the wisdom of Solomon, see 1 Kings 4:29–34; on the number of his wives and concubines (and his fickleness in religion as well as love), see 1 Kings 11:1–8.

488. Chapter 2 of the Book of Esther narrates how Esther (the "humble Jew") "found grace and favour" in the sight of Ahasuerus (Xerxes I, 485–464 B.C.), king of Persia.

524. According to the daughter who wrote her biography, this was Cary's own refuge from grief: "Her greatest sign of sadness . . . was sleeping, which she was used to say she could do when she would, and then had most will to when she had occasion to have sad thoughts waking; which she much sought to avoid, and it seemed could (for the most part) do it, when she gave herself to it" (*Life of Lady Falkland*, 196).

Scene Eight

550. Lines 547–50, which emphasize Cleopatra's face through anaphora, may recall the famous line of Faustus when he sees the image of Helen of Troy: "Was this the face that launched a thousand ships, / And burnt the topless towers of Ilium?" (Marlowe, *Doctor Faustus*, 5.1.109–10).

558. Line 559 completes the sense of the previous line and might be punctuated with a period or semicolon. However, it also functions as a transition to the thought that begins in 560, and we have retained the original comma, which seems more compatible with the syntactical fluidity of these lines.

570. "Adversary" (as the literal meaning of *Satan*) carries specifically theological overtones. Freedom of conscience (including, if sometimes only tacitly, the

right to religious dissent) was often expressed in similar terms during the seventeenth century. Cf. "Tho my body be confin'd his prisoner, / Yet my mind is free" (in the anonymous play *Swetnam the Woman Hater Arraigned by Women* [1620], 2.1.97–98) or the Lady's speech to Comus: "Thou canst not touch the freedom of my mind / With all thy charms, although this corporal rind / Thou hast immanacl'd, while Heav'n sees good" (in Milton's *A Maske* [1645], 663–64).

575. The 1613 text reads, "I heau'n, your beauty." Dunstan and Greg suggest emending "I" to "In," but "I" was a common spelling of "Ay," and "In heav'n" produces redundancy with "thither."

576. Cf. *Hamlet*, 3.4.89–91. Doris's accusation in the following lines suggests a parallel between Mariam and Anne Boleyn, viewed as adulterous by many opponents of Henry VIII's divorce.

581. Dunstan and Greg propose emending "sees" to "says." Although this change might produce slightly preferable sense ("Who asserts as true" rather than "Who perceives as true"), the difference does not seem strong enough to warrant emendation.

592. The 1613 text has no comma after "babes," and it is certainly possible to understand Doris as saying that she has borne children for love of Herod. However, the series of phrases beginning "for" in lines 591–94 encourages the division of line 592 into two such phrases.

600. Cf. Isaiah 51:17 ("Awake, awake, stand up, O Jerusalem, which hast drunk at the hand of the Lord the cup of his fury") or Revelation 16:19, where God gives to Babylon "the cup of the wine of the fierceness of his wrath."

612. Doris's role in this scene resembles that of Queen Margaret in *Richard III*, act 1, scene 3; her reproaches to Mariam are in the key of Margaret's address to Queen Elizabeth: "Poor painted queen, vain flourish of my fortune!" (240). Prolific in curses, refusing their respective exiles, Doris and Margaret represent both the claims of the past and the encroachment of a threatening, spectral future.

613. "Gerarim" in the 1613 text appears to be a mistake for "Gerizim." Mount Gerizim and Mount Ebal are twin mountains flanking the pass of Shechem in central Palestine; however, in Deuteronomy (11:29) it is Mount Gerizim which is named as the place on which to set the blessing for obeying God's commandments, and Mount Ebal as the place to set the curse for disobedience. (Later, the Samaritans built a temple on Mount Gerizim as a rival to that of Jerusalem. It was first desecrated by Antiochus Epiphanes [see endnote to act 4, line 136, and, in the Apocrypha, 2 Maccabees 6:2] and then destroyed by John Hyrcanus I [see endnotes to the first paragraph of the Argument]. Perhaps this ill-starred history contributes to the confusion of the two mountains.)

624. Doris becomes, like Queen Margaret, an accurate prophet of her enemies' misfortunes. A series of slanders, instigated by Antipater ("this boy of mine"), enraged Herod against Alexander and Aristobulus, his sons by Mariam.

Pheroras and Salome were willing instruments in this campaign; among other things, Salome made damaging use of domestic secrets extracted from her daughter, who was married to Aristobulus. The sense of "friends" (line 621) as "relatives" is probably pertinent here.

643. In the 1613 text this line and the next are punctuated "Great hearts are task'd beyond their power, but seld / The weakest lion . . . ," so that enjambment produces the sense that the weakest lion seldom roars loudest. Although Dunstan and Greg apparently do not perceive a difficulty here, such an assertion not only runs against the grain of the stanza's argument but also sounds counterproverbial. We have therefore repunctuated to make line 643 end-stopped.

654. Proverbially, the noblest vengeance is forgiveness. In the lines that follow, merely to forgo the enactment of vengeance (to save "his body from our fury") is not enough; unless genuine forgiveness accompanies this restraint, we are allowing hate to "prevail against our mind" and falling short of the moral superiority that constitutes the "noblest kind" of revenge. Cf. also biblical injunctions to leave vengeance to God: Deut. 32:35 and Rom. 12:19.

659. Cf. line 648 as well as St. Paul's discussion (I Cor. 7:3–5) of wives' and husbands' mutual obligations, often read as enjoining a specifically sexual "marriage debt."

661. There is no period after "sway'd" in the 1613 text. Dunstan and Greg do not propose adding one, but since the absence of terminal punctuation produces enjambment ("sway'd to fix . . . "), they do suggest that "Is" in line 663 should be emended to "In." However, in the context of the Chorus as a whole, it scarcely seems that fixing one's thoughts above all resentment of injuries would be the result of "sullen passion," and "To fix her thoughts all injury above / Is virtuous pride" is virtually a summary of the third stanza of the Chorus.

ACT 5
Scene One

24. The mythical Arabian bird, sacred to the sun, was said to live 540 years, after which it built a nest and set itself on fire. A new phoenix was regenerated from the ashes of the old. (Cf. Pliny, *Natural History*, 9.2, and *Paradise Lost*, 5.272–75.) In Christian iconography, the phoenix became an emblem of resurrection and a symbol of Christ.

36. Cf. Josephus, *Antiquities*, 15.7.5 (Lodge, Oo i verso–Oo ii recto); see Appendix, 15.7.5.

38. "Darken" is emended from "darke" (as suggested by Dunstan and Greg), for both metrical and idiomatic reasons.

52. Cf. Josephus, ibid.

55. The 1613 text reads: "*Nun.*: Go on, she came unmov'd," etc., but "Go on" obviously belongs to Herod.

57. Cf. Josephus (ibid.), who reports that she showed "a constant be-ha[v]iour; and [went] to her death without a chaunge of colour, so that those that beheld her, perceived in her a kind of manifest courage and nobilitie, even in her utmost extremitie."

65. The swan was believed to sing chiefly (or exclusively) before its own death (see, e.g., Aristotle, *History of Animals*, 11.9). Cf. *Merchant of Venice*, 3.2.44–45, and *Othello*, 5.2.247–48.

68. In a personal communication, Carol Neely suggests that the language here may have some connection, whether of echo or anticipation, with Othello's "I have no wife" (5.2.97) and perhaps, more subliminally, with the iteration of "Lord" in *Othello*, 5.2.84–90, and Desdemona's final "Commend me to my kind lord" (5.2.125).

69. In the 1613 text this line reads, "Were I not made her Lord, I still should be." A strained paraphrase of this line is possible: for example, "Had I not had authority over her, I would still be her husband." However, we have adopted the emendation suggested by Dunstan and Greg.

72. Emphasizing speech as the food of love, Herod gives a distinctive turn to a familiar Petrarchan trope (cf. Sidney, *Astrophil and Stella*, 87, line 2, or Shakespeare, *Sonnets*, 75, line 1).

73. "Loose" may be simply a variant spelling of *lose*. On the other hand, it may emphasize the persistence (or resumption) of Mariam's agency and volition in her final moments; that is, she does not simply lose the breath of life but releases it.

78. The span of time in which Mariam imagines herself revived in Herod's thoughts and desires probably alludes to the three days in which Jesus was cru-cified, entombed, and resurrected.

80. Cf. *As You Like It*, 4.1.44–45.

85. "Did" may mean "acted," or it may be a seventeenth-century spelling of "died." Cf. line 190 of this scene, in which "did" in the 1613 text more clearly re-quires modernization (or emendation) as "died."

97. According to the chronology of events in the Hebrew scriptures which the play elsewhere assumes (see endnote to act 1, line 450), "two thousand years" is roughly the time that has elapsed since Abraham's death.

105. Cf. the fate of Judas as narrated by Matthew (27:5).

109. Cf. act 2, line 416.

113. In Josephus's account (*Antiquities* 15.7.4), Mariam is never accused of as-piring to the throne; her hatred of Herod, and thus her supposed attempt to poison him, is imputed to her resentment of Herod's orders to Sohemus (to ex-ecute her after his own death). Her reproaches to Herod for his role in the deaths of her brother and grandfather are also mentioned in this section of Josephus, and perhaps Herod thought desire to avenge her relatives was another motive for plotting against him.

114. Cf. Shakespeare and Fletcher, *Henry VIII*, 2.1.76, where Buckingham calls his impending decapitation "the long divorce of steel." In *Mariam* the verb evokes both Mariam's struggles to preserve the wholeness of her body and spirit and Salome's (proscribed) remedy for the loss of self in marriage.

119. Proverbs 31:10 declares a good wife more precious than jewels. Cf. *Othello*, 5.2.346–47: "one whose hand / (Like the base Indian) threw a pearl away / Richer than all his tribe." The Folio text of Othello reads "Iudean" [Judean], and Theobald, one of Shakespeare's eighteenth-century editors, argued both that "Judean" was preferable to the First Quarto reading "Indian" and, citing the *Tragedy of Mariam*, that it referred to Herod's destruction of Mariam.

139. In typological readings of the Bible, the death of the innocent shepherd Abel (Genesis 4:2–8) was understood as a prefiguration of Jesus' sacrificial death, and Abel was sometimes known in Roman Catholic hagiology as St. Abel.

141. From this point to the conclusion of the act, Herod appears to wander in and out of madness. Cf. Josephus, *Antiquities*, 15.7.7 (Lodge, Oo ii recto); see Appendix, 15.7.7.

149. The staccato syntax and rhythm of this line anticipate Webster's *Duchess of Malfi* (probably written in 1613–14), 4.2.263: "Cover her face. Mine eyes dazzle. She died young."

154. Herod's language oddly echoes Mariam's argument about the impotence and vulnerability of one virtue only: "But one, if single seen, who setteth by?" (act 4, line 566). However, Herod's literal-minded insistence that, after all, Mariam had *two* hands seems a further symptom of his fragile purchase on reality.

164. That is, she is the summit, or perfection, of her sex. Cf. Proverbs 12:4: "A virtuous woman is a crown to her husband." Here, however, Mariam does honor to all women, rather than to her husband.

181. Cf. Genesis 12:10–20 and 20:1–18. To judge by the information Genesis supplies on the relative ages of Abraham and Sarah, Sarah is at least sixty-five when Pharaoh is stirred by her beauty and eighty-nine when she attracts the attention of Abimelech, king of Gerar. The most neutral meaning of "beldame" is "grandmotherly." While the term is often unflattering (see *OED* 3), this representation of Sarah may animate its etymological sense of *belle dame* (fair lady). Whether or not Cary knew of the importance of the mother's identity in Jewish genealogies, the emphasis on the matriarchal, rather than patriarchal, descent of Mariam's nobility is noteworthy. Cf. "Sara's lap," 4.8.574 and note.

193. "Aspect" is stressed on the second syllable.

196. Another pair of unflattering references to Cleopatra (who is not only Egyptian but "Aethiopian," because of her supposedly dark complexion; cf. act 1, line 190). "Blowse" originally referred to a beggar's whore and then, by association, to a coarse-complexioned, bloated woman; a "dowdy" is a shabby, dull-looking woman.

204. In the Ptolemaic conception of the universe, the "orbs" were the hollow spheres, nestled within one another, on which the planets were fixed. Intelligences, or spirits, were said to guide and impel the revolution of these spheres. However, the lines which follow associate the intelligence of each heavenly sphere (Saturn, Jupiter, Mars, the sun, Venus, Mercury, and the moon) with the classical deity of the corresponding celestial body. (Although Herod refers to the Greeks, the names he gives, with the exception of "Hermes," are those of Roman, rather than Greek, deities.)

211. The extant copies of Mariam are about equally divided between those which read "faine" (feign) in lines 211 and 213 and those which read "fame." (See the textual collation for a full census of the copies we have examined.) Both readings are plausible, and either could represent a correction of the error in reading minims that produced the other. (Cf. the similar problem at act 1, line 90, and corresponding note.) There are no other press corrections in this form that might help to determine which is the original reading. However, the emphasis of Herod's speech on the fictiveness of the Greek gods (see the emphatic language at lines 235–37) favors "faine" as the corrected and preferable reading.

216. Cf. the description of Cleopatra as a "lass," Antony and Cleopatra, 5.2.316.

237. The strong statement that the gods are fictions invites additional interpretations; poetry, rightly understood as fictive, gives no offense but cannot defend itself against critical or polemical misrepresentations. Cf. Sidney's Defence of Poetry, "for the poet, he nothing affirms, and therefore never lieth" (Miscellaneous Prose, ed. Katherine Duncan-Jones and Jan van Dorsten [Oxford: Oxford University Press, 1973], 102) as well as Puck's epilogue to Midsummer Night's Dream, 5.1.423–29: "If we shadows have offended. . . . "

244. The misogynistic lore that beauty and chastity are incompatible was commonplace. See, e.g., John Lyly, Euphues and His England, 2.209, "Who knoweth not how rare a thing it is (Ladies) to match virginitie with beautie?" and As You Like It, 1.2.37–39.

249. Herod is addressing himself. Cf. Josephus, Antiquities, 15.7.7 (Lodge, Oo ii recto): "the kings discontents being . . . increased, he at last hid himselfe in a solitarie wildernesse; where afflicting himselfe incessantly, at last he fell into a most grievous sicknes."

260. The Chorus emphasizes the tragedy's conformity to the unity of time, as neoclassical critics conceived it.

PART TWO

———

THE LADY FALKLAND

Elizabeth Taunfield wife of S.ʳ Henry Carey 1.ˢᵗ Lord Falkland. From an Original picture at Burford Priory.

Elizabeth, Lady Falkland, by T. Athow from a painting by
Paul Van Somer. Sutherland Collection, Ashmolean Museum,
Oxford. Reproduced by permission of the Ashmolean.

CHRONOLOGY OF
ELIZABETH CARY'S LIFE AND WORKS

ca. 1585   Elizabeth Tanfield born.

1602   Elizabeth marries Henry Cary.

Lodge's translation of Josephus's *Antiquities of the Jews*.

1602–8   Probable range of dates for the composition of *Mariam*.

1603   Death of Queen Elizabeth I; James VI of Scotland accedes to the English throne as James I.

1605   Henry Cary captured in battle in the Netherlands; remains a Spanish prisoner for three years (see notes 20 and 21 to the *Life*).

1609   Elizabeth and Henry's first child, Catherine, born; m. James, second earl of Home, in 1622 and died in childbirth after the accident recorded in the *Life* (p. 202).

1610   First son, Lucius Cary, born; m. Lettice Morison in 1630. He became the second Viscount Falkland and died at the Battle of Newbury, 1643, during the Civil War.

1612   Cary's play "set in Palestine" mentioned in dedication of Sir John Davies's *The Muses Sacrifice*.

Mariam licensed at the Stationers' Register on December 17.

1613   Quarto publication of *The Tragedie of Mariam, the Faire Queene of Jewry*, printed by Thomas Creede for the bookseller Richard Hawkins.

	Second son born and named Lorenzo (or Laurence) after his maternal grandfather; his father's recent captivity might have influenced the form of the name; d. 1642.
1614?	Birth of Victoria Cary; served as maid of honor to Queen Henrietta Maria, m. Sir William Uvedale of Wickham, in the county of Hampshire.
1615	Birth of Anne Cary; received into the convent at Cambray as Clementia on 8 March 1639; d. 1693.
1616	Birth of Edward Cary (died as an infant).
1617	Birth of Elizabeth Cary; received into the convent at Cambray as Augustina on 29 Oct. 1638; d. 1683.
1619	Birth of Lucy Cary; received into the convent at Cambray as Magdalena on 31 Aug. 1638; d. 1650.
1621/22	Birth of Mary Cary; evidently retained her own name when received into the convent at Cambray at the age of sixteen on 31 Aug. 1638; d. 1693 (see note 3 to the Introduction).
1622–29	Henry Cary serves as Lord Deputy of Ireland.
1624	Birth of Patrick Cary; after returning to England, he married Susan Uvedale, a niece of his brother-in-law, in 1652; d. 1656 (see note 180 to biography for further details).
1625	Death of James I and accession of Charles I.
	Birth of Henry Cary (took the name of Placid upon joining a religious order); followed his brother Patrick back to England, and his admission to Lincoln's Inn was recorded 28 Sept. 1654: "Henry Cary, 4th [surviving] son of Henry Lord Viscount Falkland, dec'd." The date of his death is uncertain but probably occurred in 1656.
	Elizabeth Cary leaves her husband in Ireland; shortly thereafter her conversion to Catholicism becomes public and she is disinherited by her father.
1627	Elizabeth Cary petitions King Charles I for release from his command that she live with her mother in Burford; also begs the king to command Lord Falkland's agent to pay her a weekly allowance.
1630	Elizabeth Cary publishes—with a preface in her own name dedicating the work to Queen Henrietta Maria—her

translation of *The Reply of the Most Illustrious Cardinall of Perron, to the Answeare of the Most Excellent King of Great Britaine,* printed by Martin Bogard of Douay. All but approximately twelve copies of the impression were burned when they arrived in England from France. The presentation copy is preserved in the Bodleian Library.

1633	Henry Cary, Viscount Falkland, dies.
1636	Elizabeth Cary arranges for the abduction of her two youngest sons from the house of Lucius Cary (now Viscount Falkland) and the influence of William Chillingworth.
Oct. 1639	Elizabeth Cary dies.
1642	Outbreak of the English Civil War.
1643–49	*Life* written.
Ca. 1655	MS of *Life* preserved in Lille copied.

THE LADY FALKLAND:
HER LIFE

___

BY ONE OF HER DAUGHTERS

She was born the year of our Lord 1585 or 6 in Oxfordshire at the Priory of Burford, her father's house, who was a lawyer, afterwards a judge, and Lord Chief Baron. His name was Laurence Tanfild;[1] his father was a younger brother, who dying left him a child, giving him all he had, which was not much; but what it was, his mother parted amongst his sisters and herself, breeding him well; and as soon as his age would permit sent him to Lincoln's Inn[2] to study law, where as soon as he was capable of practice, she left him to shift for himself, nor did he ever question what she had done, nor ever seek to recover anything, but contented himself with his own industry, and to provide for himself by following his profession; though when he was married he was earnestly solicited to the con-

---

[1] Lawrence Tanfield was admitted to the Inner Temple (one of the Inns of Court where candidates for the practice of law could qualify) in 1569 and became a serjeant-at-law in 1603. He represented the borough of New Woodstock in Oxfordshire from 1584 to the end of Elizabeth's reign and was returned to Parliament for the city of Oxford in 1603–04. He was knighted in 1604 and served as Chief Baron of the Exchequer from 1607 until his death in 1625.

[2] A marginal note in Patrick Cary's handwriting is lined through; it was also partially cropped by the binding of the MS. However, enough is legible to indicate that Patrick was pointing out that Lawrence Tanfield was a member of the Inner Temple (as indicated by the naming of Tanfield Court in the Temple) and that Lincoln's Inn was merely "where [he] lay" (i.e., lived) while he was a student.

trary by his wife, who had much power with him in other things, but could not prevail in this.

He was called to the bar at eighteen year old; the first cause he pleaded was against Queen Elizabeth, of whose counsel was M[r] Ploydon[3] the famous lawyer. It was the cause of a kinsman and friend of his, who would not have trusted it in the hands of so young a man, but that it was refused by all others for these two reasons; but he [Tanfield] had no credit to lose, nor could he lose any by being overthrown in his beginning by so learned a man, it being enough for him to have pleaded against him; and thinking the cause most just and the man whose it was his friend, he as little feared being against the Queen. He discharged himself so well of it, that he carried the cause; and showed so much freedom and courage in pleading, that the same M[r] Ploydon met him coming out of the hall and embracing him said, the law was like one day (if he lived) to have a great treasure of him and England an excellent judge.

When he could avoid it, he never sat upon life and death; but when he did, he made a most strict inquiry into the cause, hearing diligently all that could be said, nor did he ever pronounce sentence of death, without sweating exceedingly and trembling. That which might give him the more apprehension in this might be this accident, of which he was an eyewitness: When he was a young lawyer going the western circuit, at one of the towns where the [as]sizes[4] is kept, the judge, having condemned amongst the criminals a priest,[5] the day of general execution being to be the next day after his departure, he gave order to have the priest

---

[3] Edmund Plowden (1518–85) was widely considered by his contemporaries the greatest and most honest lawyer of his day, and he published influential commentaries on English common law (London, 1571). Queen Elizabeth shared the general respect for his abilities, but his adherence to Roman Catholicism inhibited his appointment to offices of public trust.

[4] Square brackets indicate punctuation or other alterations made by the editors in the interest of greater clarity for the modern reader. Angle brackets in the text or the notes indicate material that was crossed out in the original. This deleted material sometimes contributes revealingly to the narrative; more generally, the editors have wished to provide a record of all potentially significant features of the manuscript.

[5] That is, a Roman Catholic priest.

dispatched the day before the rest, before he should leave the town. Having eat his breakfast and being ready to take horse, he asked if it were done? & was answered no, and that if he pleased, it would be more convenient to let it be done at the ordinary time with the rest. He with an oath said he would not dine till the priest were executed, and commanding it to be done presently, stayed to hear it was done, which having heard and taken horse, he was no sooner up, but his horse, at all other times most gentle (as those of judges commonly are), began to curvet, threw him off of his back, casting his head against a stone, where his brains were dashed out. This same thing, it may be, might incline him to be less forward to persecute Catholics (which he never was),[6] though he did seem to tell it (which he did frequently) but only as an example on too bloody a mind.

In other matters of justice he would not hear his nearest friend speak, yet many about him were said to be great bribe takers; and some that might know did affirm it was their ordinary practice to take a bribe and, if the cause did chance to go on that side, keep it (though they neither had spoke nor durst speak one word);[7] if on the contrary, give it back; and that many times they took on both, being sure one would get the suit, and then send back the loser's. He did so entirely ⟨give⟩ apply himself to this profession, and it did so swallow him up, that being said to be excellent in it, he was nothing out of it. He left the care of all his own affairs ⟨so⟩ entirely to his wife and servants, not affording himself so much to them, as to look over his evidences when he bought land, a matter so within his own element.[8]

---

[6] *Deleted marginal annotation in the manuscript*: ⟨Unreasonably he hath been charged with it.⟩

[7] *Deleted marginal annotation*: ⟨Unjustly his having been charged with bribery makes the digression.⟩ (According to the *Dictionary of National Biography*, Lawrence Tanfield had the reputation of a "hard unjust man," but the activities of his wife, who allegedly took bribes to influence her husband's decisions, might have affected such perceptions. The biographer may be referring in veiled terms ["many about him"] to her practices; the details of the biography supply, at least obliquely, an unattractive general picture of Lady Tanfield.)

[8] *Deleted marginal annotation*: ⟨Unjustly his having been taxed with making unjust bargains makes this.⟩

Her mother's name was Elizabeth Symondes.[9] She was their only child. She was christened Elizabeth. She learnt to read very soon and loved it much. When she was but four or five year old they put her to learn French, which she did about five weeks and, not profiting at all, gave it over. After, of herself, without a teacher, whilst she was a child, she learnt French, Spanish, Italian, which she always understood very perfectly. She learnt Latin in the same manner (without being taught) and understood it perfectly when she was young, and translated the Epistles of Seneca out of it into English; after having long discontinued it, she was much more imperfect in it, so as a little afore her death, translating some (intending to have done it all had she lived) of Blosius[10] out of Latin, she was fain to help herself somewhat with the Spanish translation. Hebrew she likewise, about the same time, learnt with very little teaching; but for many year neglecting it, she lost it much; yet not long before her death, she again beginning to use it, could in the Bible understand well, in which she was most perfectly well read. She then learnt also, of a Transylvanian, his language, but never finding any use of it, forgot it entirely. She was skilful and curious in working,[11] ⟨but⟩ never having been helped by anybody; those that knew her would never have believed she knew how to hold a needle unless they had seen it.

Being once present when she was ⟨about⟩ ten year old, when a poor old woman was brought before her father for a witch, and, being accused for having bewitched two or 3 to death, the witness not being found convincing, her father asked the woman what she said for herself? She falling down

---

[9] She was the daughter of Giles and Catherine Symondes of Clay, in the county of Norfolk. Her maternal uncle, Sir Henry Lee, figured conspicuously in the ceremonies of the Elizabethan court, especially the Accession Day Tilts, which he organized in the queen's honor.

[10] The Flemish monk and mystic Louis de Blois (1506–66), known as Blosius, entered the Benedictine monastery of Liessies in Hainaut at the age of fourteen and became its abbot in 1530. He refused the archbishopric of Cambray and devoted himself to the reform of his monastery and the composition of devotional works, including *Institutio Spiritualis* (Spiritual Instruction), *Consolatio Pusillanimium* (Comfort for the Fainthearted), *Sacellum Animae Fidelis* (Sanctuary of the Faithful Soul), and *Speculum Monachorum* (A Mirror for Monks).

[11] That is, in needlework.

before him trembling and weeping confessed all to be true, desiring him to be good to her and she would mend. Then he asking her particularly, did you bewitch such a one to death? she answered yes. He asked her how she did it? One of her accusers, preventing her, said, "Did not you send your familiar in the shape of a black dog, a hare or a ⟨toad?⟩ cat, and he finding him asleep, licked his hand, or breathed on him, or stepped over him, and he presently came home sick and languished away?" She, quaking, begging pardon, acknowledged all, and the same of each particular accusation, with a several manner of doing it. Then the standers-by said, what would they have more than her own confession? But the child, seeing the poor woman in so terrible a fear, and in so simple a manner confess all, thought fear had made her idle,[12] so she whispered her father and desired him to ask her whether she had bewitched to death Mᵣ John Symondes of such a place (her uncle that was one of the standers-by). He did so, to which she said yes, just as she had done to the rest, promising to do so no more if they would have pity on her. He asked how she did it? She told one of her former stories; then (all the company laughing) he asked her what she ailed to say so? told her the man was alive, and stood there. She cried, "Alas, sir, I knew him not, I said so because you asked me." Then he, "Are you no witch then?" ⟨(says he)⟩ "No, God knows," says she, "I know no more what belongs to it than the child newborn." "Nor did you never see the devil?" She answered, "No, God bless me, never in all my life." Then he examined her what she meant to confess all this, if it were false? She answered they had threatened her if she would not confess, and said, if she would, she should have mercy showed her—which she said with such simplicity that (the witness brought against her being of little force, and her own confession appearing now to be of less) she was easily believed innocent, and [ac]quitted.

She having neither brother nor sister, nor other companion of her age, spent her whole time in reading; to which she gave herself so much that she frequently read all night; so as her mother was fain to forbid her servants to let her have candles, which command they turned to their own profit, and let themselves be hired by her to let her have them, selling them

---

[12] Delirious or incoherent.

to her at half a crown apiece, so was she bent to reading; and she not having money so free, was to owe it them, and in this fashion was she in debt a hundred pound afore she was twelve year old, which with two hundred more ⟨afore⟩ for the like bargains and promises she paid on her wedding day; this will not seem strange to those that knew her well. When she was twelve year old, her father (who loved much to have her read, and she as much to please him) gave her Calvin's *Institutions*[13] and bid her read it, against which she made so many objections, and found in him so many contradictions, and with all of them she still went to her father, that he · said, "This girl hath a spirit averse from Calvin."

At fifteen year old,[14] her father married her to one Sir Harry Cary (son to sir Edward Cary of Barkhamsteed in Harfordshire),[15] then Master of the Jewel House to Queen Elizabeth. He married her only for being an heir, for he had no acquaintance with her (she scarce ever having spoke to him) and she was nothing handsome, though then very fair. The first year or more she lived at her own father's; her husband about that time went into Holland, leaving her ⟨there⟩ still with her own friends.[16] He, in the time they had been married, had been for the most part at the court or his father's house, from her, and ⟨so⟩ had heard her speak little, and those letters he had received from her had been indited by others, by her mother's appointment, so he knew her then very little.

Soon after his being gone, his mo[ther must][17] needs have her to her, and, her friends not being able to satisfy the mother-in-law[18] with any excuse, were fain to send her; though her husband had left her with them till his return, knowing his own mother well, and desiring (though he did not care for his wife) to have her be where she should be best content. Her mother-in-law having her, and being one that loved much

---

[13] *Institutes of the Christian Religion*, first published in 1536 but later revised and enlarged, outlines the essential tenets of Calvinist theology.

[14] On the date of the marriage, see p. 4 and note 9 of the Introduction.

[15] Berkhampstead, Hertfordshire. Because of inconsistencies in seventeenth-century (and subsequent) orthography, we have retained proper names as they appear in the MS but have supplied, in the footnotes or brackets, more familiar forms as necessary.

[16] Relatives (a common Renaissance usage).

[17] The bracketed words are cropped in the MS.

[18] Katherine, Lady Cary, *née* Paget.

to be humored, and finding her not to apply herself to it, used her very hardly, so far, as at last, to confine her to her chamber; which seeing she little cared for, but entertained herself with reading, the mother-in-law took away all her books, with command to have no more brought her; then she set herself to make verses. There was only two in the whole house (besides her own servants) that ever came to see her, which they did by stealth: one of her husband's sisters[19] and a gentlewoman that waited on her mother-in-law. (To the first of them, she always, all her life after, showed herself a very true friend in all occasions wheresoever she was able ⟨to⟩; of the other (being gone from her mother-in-law's service) she never gave over to take care till she died, she [the gentlewoman] having continual recourse to her when she had need, who ever provided her places with her children or friends, and helped her in the meantime.) But her husband returning (who had been taken prisoner in the Low Countries by the Spaniards,[20] and carried prisoner into Spain, where he was kept *a year*[21] whilst his father was raising his ransom), all this was soon at an end, he being much displeased to see her so used.

In his absence he had received some letters from her, since she came from her mother, which seemed to him to be in a very different style from the former, which he had thought to have been her own. These he liked much, but believed some other did them, till, having examined her about it and found the contrary, he grew better acquainted with her and esteemed her more. From this time she writ many things for her private recreation, on several subjects, and occasions, all in verse (out of which

[19] Jane Cary, subsequently Jane Barrett, Lady Newburgh.

[20] In October 1605 Henry Cary was captured near the junction of the Ruhr and Rhine when a small force of Italians defeated three times as many English and Dutch troops, led by Maurice of Nassau. His actual captors were Spanish allies of the Italians. Ben Jonson's Epigram No. 66, "To Sir Henry Cary," celebrates his valor in holding his ground (and thus being captured) when most of his comrades fled.

[21] *Marginal annotation in Patrick Cary's hand:* Almost 3 years he was abroad and in prison. This S[r]. William Uvedale told me who went over with him: and both with my Lord of Hartford, then Ambassador for Q. Eliz[abeth], to seal the treaty of Peace at Cambresis [Cambray] (I take it) with Flanders & after went to Holland and was taken by D. Luis de Velasco. [In 1605 Sir Edward Seymour, earl of Hertford, was ambassador extraordinary at Brussels. Sir William Uvedale married Patrick's older sister Victoria.]

she scarce ever writ anything that was not translations). One of them was after stolen out of that sister-in-law's (her friend's) chamber and printed, but by her own procurement was called in. Of all she then writ, that which was said to be the best was the life of Tamberlaine[22] in verse.

She continued to read much, and when she was about twenty year old, through reading, she grew into much doubt of her religion. The first occasion of it was reading a Protestant book much esteemed, called Hooker's *Ecclesiastical Polity*.[23] It seemed to her, he left her hanging in the air, for having brought her so far (which she thought he did very reasonably), she saw not how, nor at what, she could stop, till she returned to the church from whence they were come. This was more confirmed in her by a brother of her husband's[24] returning out of Italy, with a good opinion of Catholic religion. His wit, judgment and ⟨company⟩ conversation she was much pleased withal. He was a great reader of the Fathers, especially S[t] Augustine, whom he affirmed to be of the religion of the Church of Rome. He persuaded her to read the Fathers also (what she had read till then having been for the most part poetry and history, except Seneca, and some other such, whose Epistles it is probable she translated afore she left her father's house, because the only copy of it was found by her son in her father's study)—which she did upon his persuasion, all that she could meet with in French, Spanish or Italian. It may be she might then read some in Latin, but for many year only in the others.

Her distrust of her religion increased by reading them, so far as that at two several times she refused to go to church for a long while together. The first time she satisfied herself she might continue as she was, having a great

---

[22] Timur i Leng (Timur the Lame), or Tamerlane (1336–1405), the Mongol conqueror whose exploits had been dramatized by Christopher Marlowe in *Tamburlaine the Great*, Parts I (1587?) and II (1588?).

[23] *Of the Laws of Ecclesiastical Polity*, by Richard Hooker (1553–1600), vindicates the role of the episcopacy in the Church of England against the attacks of Presbyterians. Its first four books appeared in 1593 and its fifth in 1597; the final three books appeared posthumously, in 1648 and 1662.

[24] *Marginal annotation*: His Bro[ther]: Adulphus [or Adolphus, 1577–1609. He represented the borough of St. Albans, Hertfordshire, in Parliament from 1601 until his death, and was knighted in 1604.]

mind to do so. The second time, going much to the house of a Protestant bishop,[25] which was frequented by many of the learnedest of their divines (out of the number of whose chaplains, those of the King's were frequently chosen, and some of their greatest bishops), she there grew acquaint[ed][26] with many of them, making great account of them, and using them with much respect (being ever more inclined to do so to any for their learning and worth, than for their greatness of quality, and she had learnt in the Fathers, and histories of former Christian times to bear a high reverence to the dignity they pretended to). By them she was persuaded she might lawfully remain as she was, she never making question for all that but that to be in the Roman Church were infinitely better and securer. Thus (from the first) she remained about two and twenty year, flattering herself with good intentions. She was in the house of the same bishop divers times present at the examination of such beginners, or receivers, of new opinions, as were by them esteemed heretics, where some (strangers to her), wondering to see her, asked the bishop how he durst trust that young lady to be there? who answered, he would warrant she would never be in danger to be an heretic, so much honor and adherence did she ever render to authority, where she ⟨conceived⟩ imagined it to be, much more where she knew it to be.

She was married seven year without any child; after, had eleven born alive.[27] When she had some children, she and her husband went to keep house by themselves, where she, taking the care of her family, which at first was but little, did seem to show herself capable of what she would apply herself to. She was very careful and diligent in the disposition of the affairs of her house of all sorts; and she herself would work hard, together with her women and her maids, curious pieces of work, teaching them and directing all herself; nor was her care of her children

---

[25] *Marginal annotation*: The Bishop of Durham afterwards York, Docter Neale. [Richard Neile, 1562–1640, was a prominent member of Laud's party (see note 129). He was successively dean of Westminster (1605), bishop of Rochester (1608), bishop of Winchester (1628), and archbishop of York (1631).]

[26] Cropped in the MS.

[27] See the Chronology for details of Elizabeth and Henry Cary's six daughters and five sons.

less, to whom she was so much a mother that she nursed them all herself, but only her eldest son[28] (whom her father took from her to live with him from his birth), and she taught 3 or 4 of the eldest. After, having other occasions to divert her, she left that to others, of whose care long experience might make her confident, for she never changed her servants about them, and whilst she was with them she was careful nothing in that kind might be wanting.

Her first care was (whether by herself or others) to have them soon inclined to the knowledge, love, and esteem of all moral virtue; and to have them according to their capacities instructed in the principles of Christianity, not in manner of a catechism (which would have instructed them in the particular Protestant doctrines, of the truth of which she was little satisfied), but in a manner more apt to make an impression in them (than things learnt by rote and not understood), as letting them know, when they loved anything, that they were to love God more than it; that he made it, and them, and all things; they must love him, and honour him, more than their father; he gave them their father, he sent them every good thing, and made it for them; the King was his servant, he made all kings, and gave them their kingdom[s?].[29] If they would be good, he would give them better things, than any they had, or saw here, and so for the rest—which kind of familiar teaching made those of them that were apt to it have soon so great a sense of good and ill, that once one of her elder sons, whom she taught herself, being yet extremely young, she having with an oath threatened to whip him (of which he was very dreadfully apprehensive) and after pardoning him, the child begged of her to save her oath. She much pleased with him for his innocent care of her was more resolved not to do it; but he so feared her being forsworn that, with tears in his eyes and on his knees, he continued to beg that ⟨same⟩ which he trembled at; nor was there other way to ⟨soothe?⟩ satisfy the child but by doing as she had sworn.

Being once like to die, whilst she had but two or 3 children, and those very little, that her care of them might not die with her, she writ (directed

---

[28] Lucius Cary (1610–43), who became the second Viscount Falkland (1633) and secretary of state (1641); he died at the Battle of Newbury, 20 September 1643. See the Introduction for further details of his life and career.

[29] The MS is cropped at this point.

to her two eldest, a daughter and a son) a letter of some sheets of paper (to be given them when they were come to a more capable age), full of such moral precepts as she judged most proper for them,[30] and such effect had this care of hers in the mind of her eldest daughter[31] (for the forming of whose spirit and her instruction (though she were of a good nature) she had taken extraordinary pains, and ever found her again the most dutiful and best loving of all her children), that being married afore she was thirteen year old, and going then to live in the house of her mother-in-law (in which she yielded a great obedience to her father's will) where she lived till her death (which was between sixteen and seventeen year old, in childbed of her first child), she being exceedingly beloved by her mother-in-law and all her family, her own mother asked her what she had done to gain all their affections in so great a degree? She said, indeed, she knew not anything that she did, unless that she had been careful to observe, as exactly as she could, the rule she had given her, when she took her leave of her at her first going from her: that wheresoever conscience and reason would permit her, she should prefer the will of another before her own.

Neither did she neglect to have those that were of a bigness capable of it (whilst she was with them) learn all those things that might be fit for them. She always thought it a most misbecoming thing in a mother to make herself more her business than her children and, whilst she had care of herself, to neglect them. Her doing was most contrary to this, being excessive in all that concerned their clothes or recreation, and she that never (not in her youth) could take care or delight in her own fineness, could apply herself to have too much care and take pleasure in theirs.

To her husband she bore so much respect that she taught her children, as a duty, to love him better than herself; and, though she saw it was a lesson they could learn without teaching, and that all but her eldest son did it in a very high degree, it never lessened her love or kindness to any

---

[30] The dangers of childbirth in the seventeenth century fostered the genre of the "mother's legacy" or "instructions." For other instances, see Antonia Fraser, *The Weaker Vessel*, 69–70; all of "The Pain and the Peril" (Part 1, ch. 4) is relevant to the terrors of pregnancy and childbearing during the period.

[31] *Marginal annotation*: Her Daughter Humes. [Catherine Cary, the eldest child of Elizabeth and Henry Cary, married James, second earl of Home.]

of them. He was very absolute, and though she had a strong will, she had learnt to make it obey his. The desire to please him ⟨would⟩ had power to make her do that, that others would have scarce believed possible for her: as taking care of her house in all things (to which she could have no inclination but what his will gave her); the applying herself to use and love work;[32] and, being most fearful of a horse, both before and after, she did (he loving hunting and desiring to have her a good horsewoman) for many year ride so much, and so desperately, as if she had had no fear but much delight in it; and so she had, to see him pleased, and did really make herself love it as long as that lasted. But after (as before) she neither had the courage, nor the skill, to sit upon a horse; ⟨and he left to desire it, after her having had a fall from her horse (leaping a hedge and ditch being with child of her fourth child, when she was taken up for dead though both she and her child did well), she being continually after as long as she lived with him either with child or giving suck⟩.

Dressing was all her life a torture to her, yet because he would have it so, she willingly supported it, all the while she lived with him, in her younger days, even to tediousness; but all that ever she could do towards it, was to have those about her that could do it well, and to take order that it should be done, and then endure the trouble; for though she was very careful it should be so, she was not able to attend to it at all, nor ever was her mind the least engaged in it, but her women were fain to walk round the room after her (which was her custom) while she was seriously thinking on some other business, and pin on her things and braid her hair; and while she writ or read, curl her hair and dress her head; and it did sufficiently appear how alone for his will she did undergo the trouble by the extraordinary great carelessness she had of herself after he was angry with her, from which time she never went out of plain black, frieze or coarse stuff, or cloth.

Where his interest was concerned, she seemed not able to have any consideration of her own; which amongst other things, she showed in this: a considerable part of her jointure (which upon her marriage had been made sufficiently good) having been reassumed to the crown, to which it had formerly belonged, a greater part of it (being all that

[32] That is, needlework.

remained, but[33] some very small thing) she did on his occasions consent to have mortgaged; which act of hers did so displease her own father that he disinherited her upon it, putting before her, her two eldest (and then only) sons, tying his estate on the eldest and, in case he failed,[34] on the second. She showed herself always no less ready to avoid whatsoever might displease him. Of this all her life she gave many proofs; and after she was a Catholic, when he would neither speak to her nor see her, she forbore things most ordinarily done by all, and which she did much delight in, for hearing from some other that he seemed to dislike it; and where she did but apprehend it would not please him, she would not do the least thing, though on good occasion; so as she seemed to prefer nothing but religion and her duty to God before his will. The rules which she did, in some things she writ (and in her opinions), seem to think fit to be held in this, did displease many as overstrict. She did always much disapprove ⟨a⟩ the practice ⟨with⟩ of satisfying oneself with their conscience being free from fault, not forbearing all that might have the least show, ⟨of unfit⟩ or suspicion, of uncomeliness, or unfitness; what she thought to be required in this she expressed in this motto (which she caused [to be inscribed][35] in her daughter's wedding ring): be and seem.

In this time she had some occasions of trouble, which afflicted her so much as twice to put her into so deep melancholy ⟨⟨while she was with child of her 2^d and 4th child) that she lost the perfect use of her reason, and was in much danger of her life. She had ground for the beginning of her apprehensions, but she giving full way to them (which were always apt to go as far as she would let them), they arrived so far as to be plain distractedness. It is like she at first gave the more way to it at those times, thinking her husband would then be most sensible of her trouble, knowing he was extraordinary careful of her when she was with child or gave suck, as being a most tenderly loving father.⟩ One of these times for fourteen days together she eat nor drunk nothing in the world, but only a little beer with a toast, yet without touching the toast, so as

---

[33] Except.
[34] That is, died without issue.
[35] Cropped in the MS.

being great with child and quick, the child left to stir, and she became as flat as if she had not been with child at all. Yet after, coming out of her melancholy, the child and she did well.

From this time she seemed so far to have overcome all sadness that she was scarce ever subject to it on any occasion (but only once), but always looked on the best side of everything, and what good every accident brought with it. Her greatest sign of sadness (after) was sleeping, which she was used to say she could do when she would, and then had most will to when she had occasion to have sad thoughts waking; which she much sought to avoid, and it seemed could (for the most part) do it, when she gave herself to it; and she could well divert others in occasions of trouble, having sometimes with her conversation much lightened the grief of some, suddenly, in that which touched them nearliest. This occasion of her own trouble being past, she did so far pardon the causers of it as to some of them she showed herself a most faithful and constant friend, to others so careful a provider and reliever in their necessities that she was by some (that knew her but afar off, and were not witness of what she had suffered) thought almost guilty of their faults.

She continued the care of her house till, her husband being made Controller of the King's Household, she came to live frequently at his lodgings at court; and her father-in-law dying, their family being increased, she put it into the hands of others. She continued her opinion of religion, and bore a great and high reverence to our Blessed Lady, to whom, being with child of her last daughter[36] (and still a Protestant) she offered up that child, promising if it were a girl it should (in devotion to her) bear her name, and that as much as was in her power, she would endeavour to have it be a nun. Whilst she yet gave suck to the same child, she went into Ireland, with her lord[37] and all her children, except her eldest daughter (who, just before her going, was married into Scotland). Being there, she had much affection to that nation, and was very desirous

---

[36] Mary Cary. Baptismal records indicate she was born in 1621, although the register of the Benedictine convent at Cambray says that she was fourteen when she entered the nunnery in 1638.

[37] Henry Cary, First Viscount Falkland and a protégé of the duke of Buckingham, served as lord deputy, or viceroy, of Ireland from 1622 to 1629. Much of his tenure was

to have made use of ⟨her⟩ what power she had on any occasion in their behalf, as also in that of any Catholics. She there learnt to read Irish in an Irish Bible; but it being very hard (so as she could scarce find one that could teach it) and few books in it, she quickly lost what she had learnt.

Here chiefly the desire of the benefit and commodity of that nation set her upon a great design. It was to bring up the use of all trades in that country, which is fain to be beholding to others for the smallest commodities. To this end she procured some of each kind to come from those other places where those trades are exercised (as several sorts of linen and woollen weavers, dyers, all sorts of spinners, and knitters, hatters, lace makers, and many other trades) at the very beginning; and for this purpose she took of beggar children (with which that country swarms) more than 8 score prentices, refusing none above seven year old, and taking some less. These were disposed to their several masters and mistresses to learn those trades they were thought most fit for, the least amongst them being set to something, as making points, tags, buttons, or lace, or some other thing. They were parted in their several rooms and houses, where they exercised their trades, many rooms being filled with little boys or girls, sitting all round at work; besides those that were bigger, for trades needing more understanding and strength. She brought it to that pass that they there

---

occupied with the enforcement, largely unsuccessful, of edicts against the Roman Catholic clergy. In the early years of Charles I's reign, when he needed money for the army in Ireland, he was willing, despite the opposition of his bishops, to accord a certain measure of toleration (or "graces") in exchange for financial support from the Irish gentry. However, Falkland's last proclamation as viceroy (1 April 1629) forbade the operation of religious orders in Ireland; secular clergy and laypeople were not affected by this order.

Falkland encountered equal frustration in other areas of his policy. He favored continued plantation, or colonization, as the best bulwark of English power in Ireland, but in Leinster this design brought him into collision with the clan of the O'Byrnes, and a royal commission dismissed the charges of conspiracy and rebellion he had leveled against Phelim McFeagh O'Byrne and his sons.

Bagwell reports (*Ireland under the Stuarts* [London: Holland Press, 1963], vol. 1, 184) that during his entire term of office Falkland received no remittance from England yet managed to increase governmental revenues by 14,000 pounds. He acquired no land of his own in Ireland and, unlike many similarly unpopular English officials, he derived no personal profit from his tenure as lord deputy. (For further details, see Bagwell, 169–89.)

made broadcloth so fine and good (of Irish wool, and spun and weaved and dyed and dressed there) that her Lord, being Deputy, wore it.

Yet it came to nothing; which she imputed to a judgment of God on her, because the overseers made all those poor children go to church; and she had great losses by fire and water (which she judged extraordinary, others but casual).[38] Her workhouse, with all that was in it, much cloth and much materials, was burnt; her fulling mills carried away; and much of her things spoiled with water—all which when she was a Catholic she took to be the punishment of God for the children's going to church, and that therefore her business did not succeed. But others thought it rather that she was better at contriving than executing, and that too many things were undertaken at the very first, and that she was fain (having little choice) to employ either those that had little skill in the matters they dealt in, or less honesty, and so she was extremely cozened,[39] which she was most easily, though she were not a little suspicious in her nature; but chiefly the ill order she took for paying money in this (as in all other occasions). Having the worst memory, in such things, in the world, and wholly trusting to it (or them she dealt with), and never keeping any account of what she did, she was most subject to pay the same thing often (as she hath had it confessed to her, by some, that they have (in a small matter) made her pay them the same thing five times in five days). Neither would she suffer herself to be undeceived by them that stood by and saw her do it frequently; rather suspecting they said it out of dislike of her designs, and to divert her from them; and the same unwillingness she had to see she was cozened, in all things on which she was set with such violence (as she was on all the things she undertook, which were many), which violence in all occasions made her ever subject to necessities (even when she had most), and made her continually pawn and sell anything she had (though it were a thing she should need (almost) within an hour after) to procure what she had a mind to at the present: the same violence made her subject to make great promises to those that assisted her in those things

---

[38] That is, she attributed to God's intervention events that others regarded as merely accidental and random.

[39] Deceived or cheated.

which, being many, could not always be performed. It made her, too, to acknowledge small things, done at the instants she desired them, so great (and without regarding to whom it was) that, if it chanced to be to such as would claim a requital according to the acknowledgement (and not the worth of the thing), at a greater distance, looking on it with truer eyes, what she had said could not always be stood to.

About these works, after the beginning of them, her lord seemed often displeased with her; yet rather with the manner of ordering it than the thing itself, which she knew not how to mend. It would have been in his power easily to have made her give over; but she conceived what he showed in it was rather not to engage his own credit in the success of it, than that he desired to have her leave it; and in this she after saw herself not deceived; for, some letters of his, to others, came after to her hands, where she saw he highly praised that for which he had often chidden her, and that he affirmed it would have been to the exceeding great benefit of that kingdom, could it have been well prosecuted.

To all her lord's ⟨kindred⟩ sisters (especially that sister, her friend), kindred, friends, or any that had relation to him, she always showed herself most kind and respective; and most careful and ready to use her power, when and wheresoever she had any, to do them any courtesy; and this much more than to those that had relation to herself; but her own fath[er][40] and mother she always used with very much respect; so far, as for the most part (all her life), to speak to her mother (when she was sitting) on her knees, which she did frequently fo[r][40] more than an hour together; though she was but an ill kneel[er][40] and a worse riser: she loved them both much, though her mother was never kind to her, especially after her being a Catholic. All her friends were able to employ her to the uttermost of her power; and to her friends she continued so to their very deaths, at which she was always present when she could—afore she was a Catholic, for their comfort, (apprehending much the desolateness of seeing oneself then left); after, the rather that she might be ready to assist them, if God should give them light and grace to desire to be so; (and for the same cause she visited some others even in infectious and noisome diseases (as she would fain have done that sister-in-law she loved so much, who died of the small

---

[40] Cropped in the MS.

pox in extremity), she being nothing pleased with their affection that leave their friends to die alone; nor theirs that must not hear a dead friend named, she loving much to speak of hers.[ )]

Nor was she any way sparing to her servants, when any occasion ⟨of⟩ for their advantage was offered. When they were very young (of which kind she often took even children), she was very careful they should be well brought up, and to have them learn rather those things that might after be profitable or graceful to themselves than what was useful for her. Of any of whom she had once taken care, she never left to do so ´(when they had need of her care) till she saw them, or they her, in their graves. She was more inclined to have much affection (as she would confess) to those for whom she had done than for those that had done for her; as finding much more delight in obliging than in being obliged; yet she was never ungrateful, neither in not acknowledging, nor in not requiting where she had means and occasion.

In Ireland she grew acquainted with my Lord Inchequin[41] ⟨a Ca⟩ an exceeding good Catholic and the first (at least knowing one) she had yet met. She highly esteemed him for his wit, learning, and judgment, though he were but about nine-and-twenty year old when he died. Her lord did the same, admiring him much as a man of so sincere and upright a conscience that he seemed to look on whatsoever was not lawful as not possible: he did somewhat shake her supposed security in esteeming it lawful to continue as she was.

She was ⟨alw⟩ ever very diligent, when she heard of any that had been turned Protestants, to search out their motives, if they were not apparent, as for the most part they are. Amongst her lord's chaplains, there was one[42] who had been of the Society of Jesus (then a Protestant dean), whose life seeming very moral, and he accounted learned and ⟨as⟩ an excellent preacher, there not appearing any evident cause for his turning (for though he were now married and had a benefice, he had been a Protestant long enough before either not to have ⟨them⟩ his marriage or promotion

---

[41] Probably Dermod O'Brien, fifth Baron Inchiquin, who died in 1624.

[42] *Marginal annotation*: Dean Hacket. [John Hacket, 1592–1670, became chaplain to King James in 1623. After the Restoration he was made bishop of Coventry and Lichfield.]

suspected to be the occasion of it), she could not be quiet till she had inquired of himself (having observed in him that he never in his sermons
spoke against Catholic relig[ion],[43] as most that are fallen do, but only
exhorted to a good life), earnestly urging him to tell her the truth in this;
and he told her that indeed being a Jesuit and desiring to be sent to Rome
(which place, he said, had to them every way much advantage of all
others) and his desire being refused, his superiors contrarily sent him into
Scotland (being his own country, but of all others to them the most
dangerous and incommodious) and that he being most unwilling to go
thither, out of the desire he had to find some way how he might avoid so
hard (as it seemed to him) an obedience, began to look into Protestant
religion, and then satisfied himself as she saw, but this was truly ⟨his⟩ the
first motive of his search into religion. With this answer she remained well
satisfied, leaving to wonder as she had done before.

The eldest of two sons[44] she had there (being her last children), in
devotion to the great patron of the country, she called by his name,
who she did believe did take them both into his protection, assisting them
with his prayers, she living to see them both Catholics. Soon after she
was churched[45] of the younger of them, she came out of Ireland, having
been there three year, and about two year after the beginning of her works
(which were not then dissolved, but were quickly after). She brought
with her out of Ireland her eldest unmarried daughter and her 3
youngest children, leaving the rest with her lord there, who was so
tenderly careful that he could well supply the part both of father and
mother. By a violent tempest at sea they were once driven back, being
in great danger to be cast away, the child at her breast (she sitting upon the
hatches) had his breath struck out of his body by a wave, and remained
as dead a quarter of an hour. After arriving safe, and having first kissed

---

[43] Cropped in the MS.

[44] Patrick and Henry.

[45] "Churching" was a ceremony of thanksgiving for the safe delivery of a child, but in
its origins it was also a ritual to "cleanse" the woman after childbirth (cf. Leviticus
12:4–8). Milton's Sonnet XIX ("Methought I saw my late espousèd saint"), lines 5–6,
indicates that the latter associations were still active in the seventeenth century; see also
Fraser, *Weaker Vessel*, 72.

her Majesty's hands (who was not long before come into England),[46] she retired to her mother's for fear of the plague (then very hot), carrying with her (besides the rest) her married daughter, great with child; who in the journey, being carried over a narrow bridge by a gentleman of her mother's (who out of particular care desired to carry her), his foot slipping, fell into the water; but he in the fall (taking only care of her) cast himself so along in the water that she fell upright with her feet on his breast; and she seeing them all troubled for fear of her, and he especially (who had long served her father and mother) much afflicted at it, she would not acknowledge feeling any hurt nor being frightened, but at the end of her journey the same night fell sick, and within a week died, being first delivered, almost three months afore her time, of a daughter, which lived three hours and was christened. Had it lived, the mother [Elizabeth Cary] was resolved to have nursed her daughter's child together with her own, not yet weaned. Her daughter died in her arms.

She[47] never gave much way to grief in any such occasion, and did here comfort herself the more through her daughter's affirming (being perfectly awake, as they thought, and as perfectly in her senses, for all they could perceive) that there stood by her bed a bright woman clothed in white having a crown on he[r] head; which she then assuredly believed to be our Blessed Lady, and persuaded her daughter the same; but yet a little after, dying, she often repeated with a sad lamentable mournful voice, "Woe is me, is there no remedy?"; which her mother (not judging to be only the apprehension of death, she having showed herself all the time (and when she was most in danger) much more desirous of, and careful for, the preservation of her child's life than her own) did persuade herself was some sight she had of what she was to suffer (as she hoped) in purgatory (which, with all other points of Catholic religion, she then believed), both which opinions she did continue to hope to be true after she was a Catholic; out of the consideration of the good inclination her daughter had for Catholic religion for as much as she knew of it; which she had received from her, whom only she had heard speak for it; but many against it, living amongst

[46] Henrietta Maria, the French Catholic bride of the future Charles I, arrived in England in 1625.

[47] The text from "She never gave much way" to "where it was due" appears on a leaf inserted into the third gathering of the MS of the biography.

most earnest Scotch Puritans; and how little account she made of what they said in this she (a few days afore she died) showed, reprehending one that spoke much against them, since she could know nothing of them but what the Scotch ministers said, which nobody with sense could believe; and, besides, the little means she had had possibly to know her obligation to be one, never having been acquainted with any; and her short, innocent life not being without some matter for the exercise of her patience, and much for a high obedience, which she continually rendered where it was due.

She coming again to London, where she frequented the house of the bishop (spoken of before), and having her house frequented by the same divines, began to settle herself to continue as she was, though with less satisfaction daily; and esteeming them to be, as they pretended,[48] truly priests (never yet having heard the contrary, that being a truth they most unwillingly hear of any), she was desirous (at least) to do as like Catholics in all and to draw as near them as she could. To this end she resolved to go to confession to one of them, making choice for the purpose of one of the King's chaplains (who had been one of this bishop's)[49] whom she every way much esteemed. He (as it pleased God) excused himself at the present, as not being used to take confessions, but that he would take time to prepare himself for it by studying casuists,[50] being to go into the country (or going a purpose) for half a year; but before his return she had (God be thanked) made a confession somewhat more to the purpose, for going much to my last Lord of Ormond's[51] she there met and grew acquainted

---

[48] Claimed (not necessarily suggesting insincerity).

[49] *Marginal annotation:* Doctor Cousens. [John Cosin, 1594–1672, a protégé of Bishop Neile. He eventually became bishop of Durham in 1660.]

[50] That is, theologians who applied the general principles of Christian doctrine to specific cases (as a confessor would need to do). From a Protestant perspective, the emphasis of such theology on the force of particular circumstances showed excessive ingenuity and produced moral laxity; its practice of "special pleading" was especially associated with the Jesuits.

[51] Walter Butler, eleventh earl of Ormonde (1569–1633), of Kilcash in Ireland, was confined to the Fleet Prison from 1617 to 1625 for refusing to surrender family estates that James I had awarded to a cousin of the earl's. After his release, he and his grandson (who succeeded him in the title) resided in Drury Lane, but soon after the eleventh earl retired to Ireland. According to Bagwell (*Ireland under the Stuarts*, vol. 1, 140), his piety earned him the nickname "Walter of the beads and rosaries."

with some Catholics and priests. The first she knew was Mr Coshet, a Scotch Minum,[52] then Fathers Dunstans, the white, and black[53]⟨, and others⟩, by whom (especially, as it is thought, by black Father Dunstan) she was soon convinced (yet after some disputes at which had been present some friends of hers) of the danger and unsecurity of her present state, on what pretense soever; and had been as soon reconciled,[54] but that she was desired by a lady, her friend (my Lady Denby),[55] (who had heard some of the disputations) to expect her a little, promising her that after hearing one more dispute, she would be reconciled together with her; which having heard, she desired another, ⟨and then she would⟩ with the same promise; and after that another, and then she would; delaying her thus for little less than half a year, yet never being able to resolve to do ⟨it⟩ as she promised; which she seeing, determined to stay no longer for her, but making herself ready for reconciliation (which she intended to dispatch without farther delay), meaning to be reconciled by white father Dunstan,[56] he being the first Benedictine (to which order she ever bore most peculiar devotion) she had known. She therefore in the morning went to court (where this lady lived) to advertise her that if she would now dispose herself to do the same, she might. Otherwise she would expect her no farther; she was resolved. The other continued to make her old request with much earnestness, but, seeing herself now not to prevail as before but that she [Elizabeth Cary] told her she neither could, nor would, by no means put it off longer, the lady said, "Well, I have you now in the court,

---

[52] That is, a Minum friar, belonging to the mendicant order founded by St. Francis of Paula (ca. 1416–1507).

[53] "White Father Dunstan" was Dunstan Everard, who later attended Charles II in Jersey and is said to have enjoyed the favor of that king. He died in 1650. "Black Father Dunstan" was Dunstan Pettinger, who died at London in Drury Lane in 1665, at the age of seventy-nine, possibly of the plague. He was "surnamed afterwards Capt. Bold and White" (see *A Chronicle of the English Benedictine Monks . . . , Being the Chronological Notes of Dom. Bennet Weldon, O.S.B.* [London, 1881]).

[54] Throughout the biography, this word frequently means reunited with, or restored to the communion of, the Roman Catholic Church.

[55] Susan Villiers Feilding, Lady Denbigh, was the sister of James Villiers, first duke of Buckingham and powerful favorite of James I. Later, as first lady of the bedchamber, she followed Henrietta Maria to Oxford and then to Paris and eventually, in France, became a Roman Catholic. She is also known as the patron of Richard Crashaw.

[56] Father Dunstan Everard. See note 53.

and here I will keep you. You shall lie in my chamber and shall not go forth," giving order to have a bed set up there for her. She was amazed to see herself thus surprised, little expecting it, but thought it best then to seem content to stay there. The lady, either believing her to be so indeed, or (by making some show as if she herself would perhaps go with her (as she had formerly promised), when she had been within to speak with someone) making herself sure she would, at least, stay for her return, left her alone; who, suspecting (as it was truly) that the lady was gone to fetch one that should confirm her stay, let not this opportunity slip, but got her ways in the lady's absence, going with all speed to my Lord of Ormond's, and, as before she meant to be reconciled within some few days, she now durst expect no other time (not knowing what hindrance might happen) but, finding black Father Dunstan[57] there, she was, the soonest she could, reconciled by him in my Lord of Ormond's stable (who continued her ghostly father till he was taken)[58] and, as soon as she had done, in the afternoon returns to court to this lady, telling her, she was now content to stay with her as long as she pleased, for all was done. ⟨She⟩ the Lady, much troubled at it, goeth presently to a near and powerful friend of her own,[59] and tells him; he as instantly to the King,[60] who showed himself highly displeased. They straight seek most earnestly to persuade her that whilst it was yet unknown she should return, but seeing her not moved neither by persuasions nor displeasures, they let her go home; whither she was soon followed by Secretary Cooke[61] with a command from the King to her to remain confined to her house during his Majesty's pleasure. So as had she not done as she did, she had been prevented, for she saw herself confined (which continued six weeks), no Catholic daring to come near her, her household being wholly Protestant. Thus God delivering her (after having long mercifully expected her) from that most dangerous deceit, in which it may be feared too many have lost themselves dying so, and others living lost the light they had.

---

[57] *Marginal annotation*: Pettenger [See note 53]
[58] That is, arrested.
[59] *Marginal annotation*: The Duke of Buckingham.
[60] Charles I.
[61] Sir John Coke, 1563–1644, who served as one of the principal secretaries of state from 1625 to 1639.

The day after her reconciliation, the same divine that was to have been her confessor came to town, and to visit her, and having heard from her all that had been done, fell into so great and violent a trouble that casting himself on the ground, he would not rise nor eat from morning till night, weeping even to roaring; using for arguments (to make her return) the disgrace of their company, and that she would hurt others, making them afraid of them, and that everyone would say this was the end of those that received their opinions, but seeing he no way prevailed with her (but ⟨to⟩ only to sit fasting with him all day), he went his way, coming no more to her. ⟨Nor⟩ No more did none of her former acquaintance of that kind; yet she used alway those that were deserving of them more respectfully than ordinary, and had her house after frequented by some others who, being moral and of good parts, were very welcome thither; and indeed out of her love and esteem of learning, she had a most particular devotion and desire to their conversions, having principally (as she professeth in the Epistle to the reader) for the sakes of the scholars of Oxford and Cambridge (who do not generally understand French) translated Cardinal Perone's[62] works.

Her lord's agent in England, without staying to expect order from his lord (who yet, as soon as he knew what had passed, was exceedingly angry with her), immediately stops her allowance,[63] so as she (who never was much aforehand) was in a little while brought to some extremity, being constrained to send her children ⟨and those that⟩ (for her eldest daughter[64] was gone from her before, to court, being one of the first English maids that had the honor to serve her Majesty)[65] and those that

---

[62] Jacques Davy du Perron (1556–1618), although the child of Calvinist parents who had sought refuge in Switzerland, renounced Protestantism in 1576 and began a brilliant career at the French court. A man of wide literary, philosophical, and scientific attainments, he took holy orders during the 1580s and was appointed bishop of Evreux in 1591. From the 1590s onward he devoted his energies to combating the progress of Protestantism and became a famous preacher and prolific controversialist. In 1606 he received the archbishopric of Sens. For Elizabeth Cary's translation of Perron, see Introduction and Bibliography.

[63] On 18 May 1627 Elizabeth Cary petitioned the king to compel this agent to pay her a weekly allowance (see Introduction, p. 11 and note 29).

[64] Anne Cary.

[65] Henrietta Maria.

waited on them, ⟨to d⟩ abroad to their friends to dinners and suppers, not being willing to part with them altogether, till they should be taken from her, which they were very soon by her lord's command to her chief servant,[66] who together with them took away all her old servants (but only one young maid,[67] whom she had brought up from a child (and who now is so happy as to be a choir nun amongst the English Teresians at Antwerp), ⟨which⟩ who would not leave her lady, though she herself were then a Protestant), and also all even the least things that were in the house, as beer, coal, wood, or whatsoever ⟨were movable⟩ else was movable, leaving her confined, alone, and in this necessity. Yet not withstanding this cruelty showed to her, when after she knew that in his letters to her lord he [her lord's agent] had always spoke of her with much respect and honour, and had never made those complaints which others falsely had (increasing by it her lord's anger) but had ever seemed to think her only blamable in the wrong he conceived she did her lord and herself in changing her religion, she was in her nature much more inclined to be pleased with him for this than displeased for the other, so much greater did she esteem the benefits of (but) forbearing to seek (unjustly) to increase her lord's displeasure than the injury of reducing her to such want; which was in such extremity, as she had not meat of any sort to put in her mouth, which being a thing then wholly strange to her, she having hitherto been very far from all personal want, she was willing to conceal it, being ashamed to do otherwise. Yet not to let her faithful servant suffer in it, she sent her to my Lord of Ormond's to meals, but with a charge to conceal her case; and she, to give her lady what help she could and yet obey her, did from the table privately take and put into a handkercher some pieces of piecrust or bread or other such thing, which bringing home to her were all she had to live on some days (so much did she seem to be forgotten by all the world, and all the friends she ever had had), but her maid, no longer able to endure to see her in such extremity, made it known at my Lord of Ormond's, from whose table after, during her confinement, they daily sent her dishes of meat.

[66] *Marginal annotation*: (Mʳ Hitchcock.)
[67] *Marginal annotation*: (Besse Poulter.)

In this time she was so desolate (who had been long used to much company) that one Mr Chaperlin, a very honest Catholic gentleman, coming to see her (being the first that had ventured upon it), bringing her a Catholic book of devotion (the first she had ever had), she was so much joyed and comforted by his visit that till her death she ever acknowledged it, as a great benefit, saying an Ave Mary for him for the most part whensoever she went to her prayers. After this she was visited by some others, and my Lady Manners,[68] a Catholic cousin of hers, seeing the state she was in, told it to my Lady ⟨Carlisl⟩ of Carlile[69] (for the occasion of this confinement, having come from that part where, in any other matter, she would most readily and assuredly have sought help (towards the King), made her she could not look towards the succour of any friend of her own),[70] who advertised the King in what necessity she was, and that, being deprived of her liberty, she could not seek remedy. And that there had not been any that had done thus much before to his Majesty in her behalf, had been the only cause her confinement had continued so long; for the King wondered she was still confined, it having been far from his intention, but that he had not been put in mind of her before, and he presently gave her leave to go abroad at her pleasure. In this time of her being first a Catholic, my Lady of Banbury[71] (being herself one) showed herself her great friend (who had been long well acquainted with her), relieving very much her necessities, as she

---

[68] Cecily Tufton Manners, second wife of Francis, sixth earl of Rutland, and step-mother of the duchess of Buckingham.

[69] Lucy Percy Hay, countess of Carlisle (1599–1660), whose beauty and wit were celebrated by various poets of the Caroline court. Later, as a member of the aristocratic Presbyterian party, she played a major role in the intrigues of the Civil War.

[70] The narrative here is somewhat tangled and perhaps perplexing. Under other circumstances, the biographer suggests, Lady Falkland would have sought help from the king, but he is the "occasion" of (that is, has ordered) her confinement. (The phrasing may also suggest that the Buckinghams and/or Lady Denbigh, ordinarily her allies, had engineered the order.) Correspondence from the State Papers indicates that the king had ordered her confined to her mother's house; the biography implies he might have regarded this (or any other) order for confinement as a temporary measure.

[71] Elizabeth Knollys Howard, Lady Banbury (1586–1658), daughter of the earl of Suffolk. In 1632 she married Lord Vaux and adopted Roman Catholicism, the religion of her second husband.

hath acknowledged in verses made on the Annunciation of our Blessed
Lady, and directed to my Lady of Banbury.

The terror of a confinement having wrought nothing on her, her friends
(who she again frequented as before) began to renew their persuasions; and
first by a high authority[72] there was sent her from court a paper writ by ⟨a
Protestant⟩ one of their bishops of arguments, pretended examples, and
authorities, to prove that, were Catholic religion true, yet it were lawful to
communicate with them, which paper was by Father Benet Price[73] (with
whom she then grew acquainted, and who lent her much in her great need,
and who was a very good friend to her in all) sent over to Father Leander,[74]
who answered it, and that so satisfactorily that she, having returned the answer to the hand from whence she had received the paper, was sent to by
the bishop (the author of it) to desire her not to publish it; which she (not
to displease beyond necessity) did not. From many others she was
earnestly pressed with these considerations (which some had begun to lay
before her by letters before the end of her confinement): the disgracing her
lord; undoing him and her children; separating herself from them (for it
was certain, that as he would not permit them to live with her, no more
would he ever suffer her to live with him); that she never had so much grace
and favour where it was most for her advantage (⟨being⟩ even from the
King himself) as before her changing her religion, and by which she might
have had power most to benefit her lord, all which she might regain with
increase by coming back. These were their chief arguments on all parts, yet
some of them did withal desire there might be an appointed disputation
at which she should be present, which was done for their satisfaction, at
the house of my Lord Newburgh (that sister-in-law her friend's husband),

---

[72] *Marginal annotation*: (From the King).

[73] Father Benedict of St. Facundus, also known as Bennet Jones or William Price, who
served as Procurator at Rome as well as in various offices for the English mission. When
he died in London, in 1639, he held the title of Cathedral Prior of Winchester and had
been designated as the vice president of the English mission.

[74] Leander à Sancto Martino (1575–1635), whose secular name was John Jones, came
from a Welsh family and, as an undergraduate at St. John's College, Oxford, had shared
rooms with William Laud. A Benedictine monk, he became the first president general
of the English Benedictine congregation and also served as prior of Douay.

they providing for the purpose Doctor Wheatly,[75] she bringing Black Father Dunstan. There was present, besides themselves, Doctor Lany, my Lord Newburgh's Chaplain, since the King's;[76] which dispute (horribly falsified) was set out by Doctor Wheatly (who had indeed scarce done anything in it but rail) which he carrying to Doctor Lany to set his name to as a witness, he (⟨Doctor Lany⟩) showed himself so honest a man as not only to refuse it him; but also to persuade him not to set forth so false a thing; assuring him, that if the other gentleman (Father Dunstan) did set out a true relation contrary to his, and should demand his hand as a witness, he must and would give it him; all which did not detain him from printing it;[77] and the setting forth a true one was neglected.

About this time she procured the conversion of that young maid that served her [Bessie Poulter]. She had at first much ado to get her to see or speak with a priest, whom she seriously believed to be all witches (as she had heard from the Scotch ministers in their pulpits, she having lived in Scotland with her lady's eldest daughter), but at last by ⟨the⟩ means of Father Dunstan was converted and reconciled. He not long after was taken in her house by the procurement of the same servant that had left her in so much necessity (which same man on his deathbed sent to her for a priest, who not coming time enough (he being dead before one could possibly be gotten), he yet expressed much desire to have had him, and ⟨there⟩ earnestly commended to his wife to become a Catholic), but his lord, whose favour he thought to have gained by causing his [Father Dunstan's] taking, was displeased with him for it, his displeasure against his wife being much greater out of his taking himself to be much prejudiced by her turning and that she had by it disabled herself to advance his affairs (which otherwise (he esteemed) she might now have had more power to have done than ever) than for her only being a Catholic. He was also angry with her for making such haste to publish ⟨it⟩ her being so, which it was not her intention to have done (though she always joyed much

[75] Possibly William Whately (1583–1639), vicar of Banbury, whose deployment of his "able body and sound lungs" in preaching earned him the nickname of "the Roaring Boy of Banbury."

[76] Benjamin Laney (1591–1675), a devoted royalist and high churchman, eventually became bishop of, successively, Peterborough, Lincoln, and Ely.

[77] We have not been able to identify any surviving copies of this account.

to make profession of it), had not that accident spoken of before done it for her.[78] [What may have been mistaken in the order of anything, about her being first a Catholic, M^rs. . . . of her.][79]

Some of his servants too did make many false complaints to him against her, but by those who she most frequented she was always defended, and many of them (as my Lady the Duchess of Buckingham,[80] and my Lord Duke's mother[81] (who was herself then a Catholic), his sister, my Lady of Denby,[82] and her sister Newburgh and my Lord) did often write to him earnestly in her defence, but that which made those letters not work the effect they desired was his being informed by one of his servants (who had much more power with him than he deserved to have) that she did put impediments to his affairs at court, and did him ill offices to his friends there (all the letters of the same man to her lord full of railing at her came after to be seen by her), but she was so far from doing anything that might displease him, much ⟨less⟩ more that might disadvantage him (farther than religion constrained her), that some of her friends, having alleged to the [Privy] Council how very fit it was that her lord should allow her, at least, what might keep her from want of necessaries, and having to that end procured from their lordships, in her favour, an order by which he was commanded to allow her five hundred pound a year, she would never make use of it, nor so much as advertise him of it, knowing well how much it would displease him to see himself ordained to do that which he would not do voluntarily; and she desired in all things to do her uttermost to avoid the increase of his displeasure where with conscience she could,

[78] Presumably, this phrase refers to Lady Denbigh's spreading the news of Elizabeth Cary's conversion (see p. 205, above).

[79] Written in the margin, evidently for insertion in the body of the text, but severely cropped so that most of the second line is illegible. The insertion apparently lays the blame for Henry Cary's misapprehensions about his wife's conduct on false accounts supplied by an informant.

[80] Katherine Manners Villiers, daughter of the Roman Catholic earl of Rutland. James I forbade her marriage to the duke of Buckingham until after her at least nominal conversion.

[81] Mary Beaumont Villiers. As a widow, she was in 1618 created countess of Buckingham for life and and later married two more times. She was converted by the Jesuit John Fisher (alias Thomas Piercy), who was also responsible for William Chillingworth's conversion at Oxford.

[82] Susan Villiers Feilding; see note 55.

though here she suffered the more by it, for being blamed by her friends for not helping herself with the Council's order, they were the less forward to help her, and she only excused (to them) her not doing it, by assuring them she certainly believed, if he could well do it, he would of himself without that, but that she knew well in what case his estate was, and therefore was loath to press him, forbearing to say anything of her fearing to increase his anger by it, or any other thing that might have given them cause of dislike to him.

But to charge[83] others the less, and that her debts might not increase, she retired to a little old house that she took in a little town ten mile from London, the rather because her mother (her father being dead before her coming back into England), in whose house she had hitherto lived at London, desired she would leave it, being so displeased with her for being a Catholic that in all this time she was neither willing to help her nor hear of her. In this little house she lived for some time all alone with that young Catholic maid, the house being ready to fall on their heads, and had no other household stuff in it, ⟨but⟩ than a flock bed on the bare ground (which was also borrowed of a poor body in the town) and an old hamper which served her for a table, and a wooden stool. Here one Lent she lived for the most part (if not only) on the water in which fish had been boiled ⟨they living on the Thames side⟩ with bread ⟨sopped⟩ in it, and her woman eat the fish, who never before nor after could eat of any kind (but they living on the Thames side it was the cheapest thing, and easiliest had), and God rewarded her fidelity both to himself and to her lady (for remaining a Catholic and his servant, she might have easily procured a service (now at least) more to her commodity, would she have left her lady, being so handsome at everything she did that she could not have failed to find enow that would gladly have entertained such a servant) by making her able and contented to endure all so cheerfully, that both of them did affirm they were never more merry nor better content in their lives than they were then. ⟨She sometimes, transported with her own thoughts (as she was often wont to be), would forget herself where she was and how attended, and having designed many messages in her head, would call out for somebody to come to her, and receiving no answer, would cry out earnestly, "Who is there?

---

[83] Burden.

Will none of my people come near me?"—when, either remembering herself, or being put in mind by her sole servant how the case stood, they would both laugh most heartily.⟩

In this time she grew acquai[n]ted with Mr Clayton[84] who lent her the greatest part of what he had upon his first acquaintance with her, some before he had ever seen her; whom she always (and ⟨very?⟩ most justly) esteemed a very excellent friend, he being one of those very few who, contenting himself with what he had, kept himself wholly free from desires and pretenses by which (though he had but little) he seemed to have all his acquaintance obliged to him, and he to be so to none, for he made use of one friend only to do another a pleasure, retaining nothing to himself. My Lady of Banbury did also at this time furnish her with many things. In the time she lived at that little house she began her translation of Cardinal Peron's works, of which she translated the *Reply to the King's Answer*, in thirty days (as Mr Clayton who saw it affirms in his verses printed (without an name) before ⟨it⟩ her book). Sometime after she procured it to be printed, ⟨and⟩ dedicating it to her Majesty, but Doctor Abbotts,[85] then Lord of Canterbury, seized on it coming into England[86] and burnt it, but some few copies came to her hands. She likewise here begun the rest of his works which she finished long after but was never able to print it.

At length her mother dying,[87] that estate to which she was naturally heir being given in present to her eldest son (and some very small thing, only, to her), he did take some order to keep her out of so very great extremity. About this time she writ the lives of St Mary Magdalene, St Agnes Martyr, and St Elizabeth of Portingall[88] in verse, and both before and after many verses of our Blessed Lady (whose name she took in con-

---

[84] *Marginal annotation in a different hand from that in which the biography is written*: She was acquainted with Mr Clayton sooner. [The Bodleian copy of *The Reply of the Cardinall of Perron*, donated by James Clayton in 1635, records that he was formerly a fellow of St. John's College, Oxford.]

[85] George Abbot (1562–1633) was appointed to the see of Canterbury in March 1611.

[86] The translation was printed in Douay, 1630, by Martin Bogard.

[87] Lady Tanfield died in July 1629.

[88] Mary of Magdala, from whom Jesus had cast out "seven devils" (Luke 8:2), was the first to whom Jesus appeared after his resurrection (Mark 16:9; John 20:11–18); tradition

firmation which she received from the hand of my Lord of Calcedon)[89] and of many other saints.

She now seeing herself very much in debt, which she had been almost continually from her infancy (yet rather through a freeness of heart, which always went beyond what she had, and those other things spoken of before, than any voluntary neglect in it, for she was most sensible of it, especially after her being a Catholic; and she was never used to refuse to pay when she had it, but rather to thank those that then came for it, and never question what they then asked; but if they came when she had it not, she would be less pleased and more apt to question, but everyone knew her ill memory ⟨so⟩ in such things so well that, where conscience did not hinder it, they could not fear to claim what they pleased, and if they seemed willing to accept a promise to pay them at some other set time, ⟨they⟩ she would not stick to acknowledge whatsoever they claimed, and whilst she could not pay, she held herself highly obliged to pray for her creditors; and she was rather too forward ⟨to borrow⟩ in borrowing than anything backward in paying, never being accustomed to refuse, not even to give what was asked of her, whensoever she could; and when she had not anything to give, overfree to promise to those that would be satisfied with that; which promises, being most commonly to those nearest hand, were generally first served) and there not being ordinary means by which she might discharge

---

also, dubiously, identifies her with the woman "who was a sinner" and who anoints Jesus' feet (Luke 7:36–50) and sometimes with Mary of Bethany, the sister of Martha (Luke 10:39–42). The youthful Roman martyr St. Agnes refused marriage, consecrating her virginity to God; she was executed, ca. 304, by being stabbed in the throat. Elizabeth (or Isabel) of Portugal (1271–1336), the daughter of King Pedro III of Aragon, devoted much of her life to the service of God and the poor and founded such charitable institutions as a hospital, an orphanage, and a shelter for women. Although mistreated by her husband, King Diniz of Portugal, she was also conspicuous for her efforts as a peacemaker, attempting to reconcile her son Alfonso, who led a rebellion against his father, with King Diniz, and later acting as a mediator in the war between Alfonso (then King Alfonso IV) and Alfonso XI of Castile.

[89] Richard Smith (1566–1655) became a Roman Catholic while he was at Trinity College, Oxford, and went to Rome. In 1625 he was appointed vicar-apostolic for England and Scotland as bishop of Chalcedon. In 1630 information was supplied to the Privy Council that "Bishop of Smith of Chalcedon lived in the French Ambassador's house, in the chamber Lady Falkland's, besides divers Jesuits more"; it was presumably at this time that Elizabeth Cary was confirmed.

herself of these debts having but what would at most keep her for the present from necessity, ⟨out of the desire to be free ⟨herself⟩ from them, she again set herself on new designs, and suits at court and other things, having always a great inclination to have a working head, and⟩ she was by others drawn into some projects; and in these kind of businesses she consumed some years, with hope to get herself out of debt, but at the end of all she ever found herself a loser, though whilst she was bent upon them she would not see it.

In some part of these times her life and house were less well ordered or more confused, whilst she was so carried away with her businesses, ⟨and so swallowed up in them as to forget herself (which she was ever much inclined to, and she was seldom able for the earnestness of her thoughts to distinguish her own necessities, not discerning whether she were cold or hungry; calling for beer when she burnt herself at the fire; knowing she wanted something, and that somewhat troubled her, but not knowing what) and not having anybody about her that took care to call upon her and put her in mind, which she would have given them thanks for that would have done it and would have esteemed them her friends⟩ and the same she would generally do to them that would tell her of her faults; and for this consideration chiefly (that he was free in reprehending her) she did continue to have Father Benet Price for her ghostly father, when in many other respects it was very inconvenient to her, having Father Cuthbert the whilst in her own house,[90] and being fain to go abroad to seek the other, and for her failings towards God she could bow herself to receive reproof from any hand as most just, for through a great faith, and experience of what came from her of herself, and what from God, she seemed well to esteem her faults her own, and what good she might have done as his benefits, accounting thereby her obligation to him increased and not discharged. And that this confusedness was forgetfulness and not want of good intentions, a paper or two ⟨several papers⟩ which were found of hers in ⟨these times⟩ this time did show, wherein she did make a disposition of the day for herself, designing to all her duties a due

---

[90] For "Father Benet Price," see note 73. Father Cuthbert is introduced later in the narrative; see pp. 228–30 and note 110.

part, and expressly appointing to herself what prayers to say for the conversions of her lord and children, and for her creditors, and she always much esteemed and loved order ⟨when she remembered there was such a thing⟩.

She always seemed scarce able to do small things, but great ones by the grace of God she sometimes did. If in little matters she seemed somewhat subject to herself, in those of more importance she could and did command herself. She could be passionate in extremity for the least (even childish) things, but in more great hath many times showed much constancy and patience. She could give herself leave to apprehend a trifle as dreadful, whilst in great occasions she showed no sense of fear, especially where the service of God or conversion of souls was concerned. She seemed ⟨to⟩ not to have full power over herself in matter of diet (yet she could through the employment of her mind forget her necessities in it) but when strengthened by the precept of the Church, or that she had occasion to want (in that) immediately for God's cause, she seemed able to do anything; observing most exactly the fasts of the Church, never eating butter nor milk in Lent, as long as she was a Catholic (only the two Lents afore she died, when she was in a consumption), and some Lents she did confirm her observance of the obliged fast by resolving and observing some farther abstinence, as particularly one Lent when her table was filled with flesh for her Protestant children, she forbid herself anything with sugar in it, save on Sundays, which in the manner of her diet (especially Lenten) had a great part, and it is like her strict observance of Lent might be the less easy to her, she by *custom* and *nature* never drinking wine; of which she never drunk more than a spoonful at ⟨once, at⟩ any time.

Her lord coming into England, she was the more careful in some things to live rather in a little better fashion than she had, as avoiding in some measure the having occasion to have her wants relieved by others so much as they had been, knowing he would be less pleased at it, as disgraceful to him, though he would not then see her, and she did then set herself most seriously (notwithstanding his displeasure against her) to use all the means she could, by some friends of hers, to advantage his affairs. At length by the interposition of the power of her most Excellent Majesty (who was pleased to make herself ⟨the⟩ a mediatrix ⟨for⟩ of their reconciliation, and who both before and after by her royal charity relieved her and many other ways afforded her gracious assistance to her and hers), they were reconciled; yet continued to live as before, both for the better commodity of her exercising her religion, as also that his estate was now so broken and wasted (especially since the marriage of his eldest son against his will; by whose marriage he hoped and expected the repair of his fortune, and for that purpose was in a treaty, when he [Lucius Cary], by marrying himself to another, disappointed his hope)[91] that he could not conveniently have it otherwise. Besides, she being ⟨besides/ so⟩ entangled in those businesses and pretenses (before spoke of) could more freely prosecute them, remaining as she did, and yet though she had not anything from him, she did so much regard his will as not to seek remedy for her own need but by his leave; for being not able always to make what she had serve her, and in her occasions desiring to have recourse to the King for succour, she would not do it (though the fear of his discredit could not be there) till she knew he did not apprehend it would be any hindrance to his pretenses ⟨to the⟩ towards the King, and that he let her know he was very well content and desirous she should do it.

Being herself ⟨once? anew?⟩ friends with her lord, she seriously laboured to dispose him to be reconciled to his son, with whom he was very angry for his marriage, for this regard only, that he was by it frustrated of that supply which his estate (otherwise desperate) did necessarily require for the disengagement of it, he having always much outgone what he had.

Towards her other children (whom she now sometimes saw) she showed herself most kind, seeking by all means to gain some interest in them, being like not to have much more from them than she got by pleasing them; they esteeming what respect they did show her as a voluntary act, or at most a necessary civility, but not much of duty (though to have showed notably the contrary would have displeased their father, who, in his greatest anger towards her, loved to see his children respect her), and they would have taken it as a great injury if she had seemed to claim any authority over them; for having been left young by her, and not been a good while in her

---

[91] Viscount Falkland had hoped to marry his eldest son to the daughter of Sir Richard Weston, lord treasurer, but Lucius Cary frustrated this plan by marrying, in 1630, Lettice Morison, the daughter of Sir Richard Morison of Tooley Park, Leicestershire.

hands (especially three daughters) and now seeing her but when they would, as they had the whilest had from their father the care of both father and mother, so they paid to him the love and respect due to both, leaving her but a small part. (Only her eldest living daughter,[92] who came from her later, was elder, and a less while from her, seemed to retain always more memory of what she owed her, which daughter was ever loved best by her of all her children (till the others were Catholics) and loved her better again than any of them, having showed herself very zealous in her mother's defence at her return into Ireland, which she made with her little brothers and sister, a year after her mother was a Catholic, though she were now returned to court again.) She therefore did apply herself much to procure them that that might please them, and might make them willing to be with her, yet never durst speak to them of religion (farther than desiring some of them to add to their prayers the ⟨desire of knowing the truth⟩ asking of God the knowledge of the truth) and, had she done otherwise, she would but have made them weary of her. Yet she many times spoke of it afore them, as not of set purpose.

Her husband, having broken up his house and dispersed his children, did two year after, by the providence of God, call home his four younger daughters (who else had never been like to have come into the hands of their mother), and soon after, at the end of summer, waiting on the King[93] (then newly come out of Scotland) a-shooting in Tiballs Park,[94] fell from a stand and broke his leg, and instantly broke it in a second and a third place, with standing up upon it at the King's coming to him, who commanded his doctor and surgeon then waiting, not to leave him on any occasion till he was well. He was carried into a lodge in the park, whither he sent for his wife to him (who had, that summer, been some little time at his own house with him, which she had never been before, since their falling out; and he had then spoken of both their coming to live at home

---

[92] Anne Cary.

[93] Charles I.

[94] Theobalds Park in Hertfordshire was acquired by Sir William Cecil, Lord Burghley, in 1561; James I took this property in 1607 and forced Burghley's son, Robert Cecil, first earl of Salisbury, to accept Hatfield House in exchange. James I had died there in 1625.

together (for he himself lived for the most part at my Lord Newburgh's), designing a place for her chapel, and for her priest to live in). She came instantly from London, which was about twenty mile, making such haste that she slept not nor went to bed that night afore she came, and being come to him, she stayed with him day and night, watching with him and never putting off her clothes in all the time, but what sleep she got was for the most part in the daytime and sitting in his chamber in a chair, or lying on the ground on a pallet, which he made be brought in for her.

He was there visited by some few of his friends, ⟨but⟩ his daughter at court, one of his sisters, and my Lord Newburgh, but nobody stayed with him (besides 3 of his own servants) ⟨and⟩ but she, who left him not till his death; which was but a week after, for the surgeon, having undertaken the part of a bonesetter, pretended to set his leg, but failing in it, instead of being set, it gangrened. Then sending for Doctor Myarne[95] and Mr Aubert, the Queen's doctor and surgeon, and an hospital surgeon (as being most used to such occasions), they consulting resolved the leg was to be cut off just above his knee: which she would fain have had done by Mr Aubert, but he was persuaded to choose another. ⟨He looked on?⟩ Whilst they cut it off, he never changed his countenance, nor made any show of pain; no more he had not at the breaking of it (at which time he omitted not the least civility to anyone that spoke to [him])[96] nor all the time of the dressing of it, only when they went to search how far it was gangrened, he once frowned and cried, "Oh, softly!" She was also present; and in the very time it was a-cutting, his daughters from home and his two younger sons from school coming to see him, and not having heard in how much danger he was, hearing as they lighted that his leg was cutting off, one of them[97] shrieked out. He heard her, knew her voice, and took care to have her comforted, sending one forth to her from him; and as soon as ever it was done and he laid in his bed, he sent for them in; smiling on them, spoke cheerfully seeking to comfort them; then giving them his last blessing, sent them home.

---

[95] Sir Theodore Mayerne (1573–1655), a celebrated physician who frequently attended the families of both James I and Charles I.

[96] Possibly cropped in MS.

[97] *Marginal annotation*: M[other]. Clem[entia]: [Anne Cary].

When his leg was cut off he had no apprehension of death, on which morning he received the Protestant communion, but in the cutting they scaled the bone, and judging therefore it was more like to gangrene again than cure, they did not sear it, but stanched the blood for the present with a powder, not esteeming it likely he could support a new cutting without dying in it. Yet they let him not know his danger; the next morning, it bleeding again, they stanched it in the same manner. It doing the same about seven a clock that night, they could not get the doctor and two surgeons (for Sir Theodore Myarne, and M[r] Aubert were gone) to him from tables. At last coming, they told him there was no hope, and so offered no more to stop it, but let him bleed to death. He did not seem daunted at hearing this, though it was very unexpected to him (the more that they would not be drawn to try to do anything more to him), but speaking in French to his wife (because the surgeons, his servants, and chaplain were by), he first told her what he desired of the King, what of his own friends, and concerning his children and servants; and inquired concerning some business of hers, and a little after asked her (still in French, which he spoke ill enough) if her man were there, calling it "homme"; which she took only for an ill phrase, but having told him, he that used to wait on her abroad was there; and that he said he meant not him, she saw he meant her priest, and called him so to distinguish him ⟨for⟩ from a servant, she (not having provided one (as not fearing his death, at least not so suddenly), nor it not being possible to have one from London soon enough, nearer than which she knew not of any) told him there was no other there. He then asked if there were no way but legal.[98] She, kneeling by his bed, told him the best she could how to dispose himself interiorly, not having exterior means; but she durst not propose to him the professing himself to have a desire to be a Catholic, before the standers-by, not thinking it to be necessary, and fearing he might be too loving a careful father, and not have the courage to do that, for fear of prejudicing his children towards[99] their friends. He seemed to

---

[98] That is, he asked if there were no way for him to convert to Roman Catholicism except in the presence of a priest and with the ceremonies of the church.

[99] In relation to (that is, he was afraid of prejudicing relatives or friends against his children).

hearken to all she said, but spoke no more. He was bleeding to death more than three hours. He passed the most part of it in silence, especially towards the last; she the whilest praying by him, or speaking to him; and, he being very near death, one of the surgeons desired him to profess he died a Protestant, or else (he said), his lady being there and speaking much to him, it would be reported he died a papist. To this (which the man repeated three or four times) he only still turned away his head without answering him; but seeing he did not cease to bawl the same in his ears, he said to him at last, "Pray, do not interrupt my silent meditation"; which showed he could have said the other if he would, and this, of his refusing in this manner to say he died a Protestant, two of his Protestant servants ⟨ac⟩ that were present did acknowledge. He died presently after without sign of agony or strife, and seeming perfectly sensible to the last, being about 57 year old, and she about 47.[100] That that it is like might have chiefly inclined him to have a desire of being a Catholic, was reading her translation of Perone (which she had given him, and was found in his closet after his death, all noted by him) and the having talked with Mʳ Clayton of religion (which he had done often), whom he knew to be learned, judicious, and most sincere.

Seeing him dead, though she wept (for she truly loved him) ⟨much⟩, she was very present with herself (never being much transported with any grief in this kind, besides comforted with what signs he had given beyond her expectation, on which she could hope much [yet much lamenting the neglect of not having a priest ready][101]), and her first thoughts were to get her children ⟨into her hands⟩ to live with her (which she desired in order to their being Catholics) and that she might prevent any hindrance, and get their consent speedily, she ⟨so⟩ that night (as late as it was) ⟨borrowed my Lord of Tichbarn's[102] coach (her lord nor she having none there) and in it⟩ went ⟨to her/her lord's house, being nine mile off⟩, together with his dead body, in the dark, to his house where his daughters were,

---

[100] Sir Henry Cary died in 1633.

[101] Added in the margin.

[102] Possibly Sir Henry Tichborne, of Tichborne, Hampshire, best known for his military service at Drogheda in Ireland during the Civil War. The fourth son of Sir Benjamin Tichborne, Gentleman of the Privy Chamber to James I, he was knighted in 1623.

being nine mile; whither she came at three a clock in the morning. She sought at first to conceal it from her children, then to let them know he was past hope—at which seeing them so extremely troubled, to think she had left him alone a-dying, she confessed he was dead, seeking with all her power to comfort them.

She made haste to propose to them living with her, telling them their father desired it, and saying all she could imagine to incline them to it; and begging of them to promise her not to go from ⟨them⟩ her to any of their friends, if it should be desired; which they did, being (then) more strongly moved to it by the fidelity they thought their mother had showed to their father at his death beyond all his other friends, ⟨than⟩ and the thinking it his will, than by any other promise she could make them; and she esteemed herself to have obtained a great victory in their consents, though she had not any other means to defray this undertaken charge (which was not like to be small) but only hope in the providence of God. For, that she might not be wanting to her power in discharging her debts, there being some very little remainder of her jointure fallen to her by her lord's death, she instantly assigned it, to pay her debts ⟨to Father Benet⟩; and of two hundred pound a year more (which was all she had from her father and mother), she assigned one towards paying Mr Clayton, and of part of the sale of the goods of her lord's house she was to pay some debt of his (which she had a violent desire to have seen all wholly discharged (though, had she been able, she had no way any obligation to it), and she ⟨⟨that could hope strange things⟩⟩ did hope to do it; but this difference she always found in her hopes, that when they were built on human policies and industries, they did infallibly deceive her, though sometimes she brought them to probability; but when, in that that had more immediate relation to the service of God, she placed her confidence only in him, she did without fail experience his mercy to go beyond her hopes, though they seemed to be little less than impossibilities). And for help from others towards maintaining them, as little could she look for it, their own friends blaming her much for keeping them, as a wrong to her children to live at such uncertainties. And for such as had assisted her in her own necessities, when she was first a Catholic, as she had forborne such succour in her lord's time the more in consideration of him, she was now to do no less for them, who, had they known she had had anything from any stranger below the King and Queen, would never have endured it; besides that everyone was more ready to blame her than help her for drawing on herself so great and, as it seemed to all, so unnecessary a charge.

She then only sought to have her children with her, where they might have more occasion to come to the knowledge of the truth, and better means to follow it, trusting wholly in God for the rest, as well for their conversion as means to maintain them, having promised them (to make them willing to come to her) not to speak of religion to them till they should desire it; which they thought themselves sure they would never do; but she knew to speak, when they had no mind to hear, would but avert them from her and religion. So, doing thus much, together with her prayers (which were most earnest in this behalf), she thought she did all that lay in her, not doubting God would effect the rest; nor was she deceived in her great confidence, neither in her obtaining their conversion, nor in the discharge of the debts she incurred on this occasion.

She having asked Father Benet (then her ghostly father)[103] whether a Catholic might not have flesh dressed on fasting days for a Protestant to keep him in a place where he were likely to be converted, where he would not stay without it, and where some flesh was to be for ⟨sick⟩ infirm Catholics? he told her, such likelihood there might be of a conversion, as he judged it might be done, but if she asked for her own children, of whose there was not any, he would not say so. She made use of the first part of this answer, not thinking herself bound to take his word for the latter, and without it she knew they would never stay. Yet she did this only upon the strength of her confidence, not with any contempt of the ordinance of the Church, whose precepts had so full a power over her, as to give a check at an instant to her strongest appetites; and she did so heartily love them, and so truly joy in obeying them, that sometimes, having risen early and been all morning abroad ⟨at⟩ about her businesses, and finding herself at dinner time (it happening often to be on fasting days) at some of her Protestant friends' houses, where being made stay by importunity, and forgetting the fast (there being no sign of one to put her in mind), being set down hungry, and ready to put

---

[103] *Marginal annotation*: Bennet Price.

her meat in her mouth, one of her children[104] then Protestant would stop her, telling her of the fast. She would so sincerely rejoice to have scaped the unwilling breach of ⟨them⟩ it that it seemed not to leave place for the first motion of any reluctation, but with most hearty thanks, she would desire her to continue to do so, really loving her the better for having concurred to her observance of the Church's precept, though she saw well enough, she [her daughter] had no other end in it than to laugh when she had done, to see how suddenly she had stopped her in her haste, and had there either been more fish, or she [Elizabeth Cary] less hungry, she [her daughter] would have been like to have let her alone; but this happening many times, she being much subject to this forgetfulness, made her most unwilling to eat abroad, which she would do rarely after her lord's death, for when he lived (though she never loved it) she did it more frequently for his sake, where he was, and that she might do it the more freely, he himself would take care to remember her of her fast.

That Lent that she had flesh for them she fasted the more herself, living almost wholly (except on Sundays) on nettle porridge without butter, and cakes made only of flour, water, and salt, baked on the hearth. There was not one at her table that kept Lent but herself, the Catholics that were constantly at it eating all of them flesh for infirmity. Yet she was careful to have fish (not for herself, for ⟨though⟩ she could seldom take care for what was for herself only) but as well for stranger Catholics that might come, as for her children, if any of them would leave flesh and eat it, which when she perceived any of them do, she would be most glad, and would endeavour to have them have what they loved most of that kind, to invite them to it, using all the means she durst venture on to draw them to forbear flesh.

After her lord's death she never went to masques nor plays, not so much as at the court, though she loved them very much, especially the last extremely; nor to any other such public thing. Yet she continued to go very much abroad to court and other places about her businesses. As she herself avoided to dine and sup abroad, so she endeavoured much to have her children at home at those times, ⟨it⟩ chiefly because at

---

[104] *Marginal annotation:* D[ame]. Magd[alena]. [Lucy Cary].

her table she only hoped to have them hear of religion; for her two elder sons, being with her also that first winter, many of their friends (Oxford scholars and others) came much to her house, and were exceeding welcome to her (who always loved good company so much that the contrary was almost insupportable to her, especially at her table, where she loved to have her friends, and that they might esteem themselves as much at home as herself, and find nothing, as near as she could, troublesome or tedious to them, or that might hinder any from conversing freely; yet she could much better endure those whose company she liked not, when she thought they might really want a dinner, and that she had known them in a better case, than she could have done for their being anything at the present, there being no commodity to herself that she would have bought at such a rate). Their discourse ⟨at the table⟩ was frequently religion, there being those that were very capable on both sides, and she believed this discourse being mingled with others, and from those that were able to make any pleasant, would draw her daughters' attentions, whose conversion she sought in all; and indeed it did in some of them (by the grace of God) work imperceivably some disposition more than they made show of, and all of them found matter to reflect on after; though then they marked it not much; for they could not but see in general (besides many particulars) that either the Protestants said the same as the Catholics, taking their part entirely against their own side (as their eldest brother then did (who was so wholly Catholic in opinion then that he would affirm he knew nothing but what the Church told him; pretending for his being none, that though this seemed to him to be thus (and that he always disputed in the defence of it), yet he would not take upon him to resolve anything so determinately as to change his profession upon it till he was forty year old, but he did not live to see four-and-thirty; yet this good inclination ⟨had re⟩ towards religion he had had for some years, and had received it from the conversation of his mother and ⟨those⟩ the company he met at her house, having before believed but little, and he continued in the same mind till a little after, when, meeting a book of Socinus[105] his [i.e., Socinus's], it opened to him a new way), as

---

[105] Fausto Paolo Sozzini (1539–1604), known as Socinus, emphasized each believer's freedom to reach his or her own religious conclusions, and his intellectual, rationalist

also Mr Chillingworth[106] (who, having been a fellow of Trinity College in Oxford, and there by reading become a Catholic, went over to Doway to the Benedictine College,[107] where not shining so much as he expected (for he there found young students able to do that which gave him matter to admire ever after), he returned to Oxford a Protestant (at least no Catholic), where having, as it was said, preached at St Mary's,[108] and, there again becoming a Catholic or towards it, coming to London, he much frequented this house, and calling Protestants "we," and in his clothes being

---

approach encouraged the repudiation of much ecclesiastical tradition, including the doctrine of the Trinity. Socinianism as a movement borrowed Sozzini's name, rather than his specific teachings, and "in common parlance Socinianism was little else than the application of reason to Scripture" (Hugh Trevor-Roper, *Catholics, Anglicans and Puritans*, 95).

[106] Toward the end of 1628, William Chillingworth (1602–44), son of the mayor of Oxford and fellow of Trinity College, Oxford, was converted to Roman Catholicism by the Jesuit missionary Father Fisher. His godfather was William Laud, and according to John Aubrey, before his conversion, he acted as an Oxford informer for Archbishop Laud (*Aubrey's Brief Lives*, ed. Oliver Lawson Dick, 63). In 1630 he went to Douay but returned to England full of doubts about the dogmatic authority of the Roman church. It was not until 1634 that he again declared himself a Protestant, and it is during the period in the early 1630s when he remained at least outwardly a Catholic that the biography represents him. Although his apostasy made him especially obnoxious to Roman Catholics, his scrupulously self-questioning theological inquiries and his quest for a nonsectarian Christianity won him few friends among Protestants, either. He defended the necessity of personal religious conviction and the right of free inquiry, and was one of the central figures in the "Great Tew Circle" that gathered at Lucius Cary's Oxfordshire house. His major work, *The Religion of Protestants a Safe Way of Salvation* (1637), emerged from the discussions of this circle and argued that the Roman Catholic Church had distorted the original teachings of Christianity by unnecessary additions, underwritten by its claims to infallibility, and that, insofar as it had suffered fewer incrustations, the Church of England was the more authentic Christian church. However, his praise of Anglicanism was premised on its simplicity and freedom from theological prescription; he kept Calvinist doctrine at arm's length. Aubrey comments, "He never swore to all the points of the Church of England" and reports that Thomas Hobbes said Chillingworth "was like a lusty fighting fellow that did drive his enemies before him, but would often give his owne party smart back-blowes" (*Brief Lives*, 63–64). Aubrey describes him as "a little man, blackish haire, of a Saturnine complexion" (63). (For further discussion of Chillingworth and his theology, see Robert R. Orr, *Reason and Authority: The Thought of William Chillingworth* [London: Oxford Univ. Press, 1967] and, especially in relation to the milieu of Lucius Cary, Hugh Trevor-Roper, "The Great Tew Circle," in *Catholics, Anglicans and Puritans*.)

[107] In order to provide a supply of priests for England while it remained alienated from the Church of Rome, a missionary college or seminary was established at Douay in 1568.

[108] The University Church in High Street.

like an Oxford scholar⟨s⟩, he was secretly a Catholic, if not more secretly neither, but what he was known to be after, for in him there seemed to be a kind of impossibility of agreement between his heart and his tongue), and some others did the same, who were much Catholic in opinion) or else that those others, that were in very good earnest Protestants, as much as men with sense (though helped with a desire to be so) could be, did disagree amongst themselves laughing at one another's arguments, at least fain ever to break off in jest what was begun seriously, for though they were really Protestants, and such as could certainly say what was to be said, yet they ⟨would r⟩ were so judicious and honest, as rather to divert the discourse with a jest, when they had no more to say, than defend themselves with saying seriously any false or ridiculous thing. And here they had also occasion to mark, which they did reflect more on when their time was come, that those who, seriously touched in conscience with the desire of the truth, did begin to search after, did always end in Catholic religion, unless detained by some other respect, of which they were witness of too many.

What she did undergo to keep them with her, both from and for them, may well give them cause to acknowledge she was their mother in faith as well as in nature; for though they were by other reasons now than either their promise or her desire tied to stay with her, according to their several inclinations (as either of desiring to have their wills absolutely, or esteeming her house their proper natural place, where being they had not the least obligation to anybody), yet presuming on the vehement desire she had to keep them, they would (especially the two eldest), when with the greatest care and solicitude she did procure them all they desired, or that that she thought would please them, depriving herself secretly of things most necessary to furnish them with trifles at instants, if the least thing were not had for them on a sudden just when they desired it [(] not taking any heed to what she had done, but only to what they now desired and had not presently), threaten her they would be gone, and wonder she would offer to keep them when she was not able to do it. And ⟨though⟩ they could well think her extraordinary care but the part of a mother, whilst they scarce thought the duty of children theirs. And though she spared not any care nor pains to keep them as they desired in all things, and so as they knew well they should not have been in any other place, yet they seemed to think her ⟨only⟩ beholding to them for staying; and would on occasions, sometimes small enough, in which it seemed to them she did amiss and withal vexed them (for else they would not have been so zealous), reproach her with her religion as giving her leave to do anything; which would touch her very nearly, for as she most highly esteemed the high benefit of being a child of the Catholic Church, so she was most sensible of the great ingratitude of giving disedification in it, thereby seeming to cast a reproach upon the same church; and, confessing she had done ill, would (with tears in her eyes) ask pardon for the scandal she had given them.

In the enduring this she found not anyone to encourage her. Many or all seemed to tax her much even in conscience for burdening herself to no purpose and dressing flesh for them, but God seemed, by the success, to give an approbation to her act and a reward to her confidence in him; in virtue of which she had supported all with an incredible patience and constancy for near three quarters of a year, without the least sign of hope, but rather increase of the contrary in all but one[109] (who was the occasion of the conversion of all the rest), when yet within that time, without knowing how, she saw them all resolved to be Catholics, they being converted by Father Cuthbert,[110] without her knowledge, who was, by all the Catholics and Protestants that knew him and were capable of judging, esteemed to have an excellent wit and judgement, and to be an exceeding good scholar, her eldest son using to affirm of him, that if he had not had an admirable memory, and an extraordinary gift of making use of what he had read, he could not possibly have benefited himself so much in the time he could have studied, being no elder, for when he died four or five year after he was but about 33.

He had been a monk from sixteen or seventeen, and a very exemplary one, ⟨at⟩ about five-and-twenty was sent into England for his health, and had been twice or thrice recalled from thence before this (which he ever much desired, using to affirm himself (with St Anselm)[111] to be an

---

[109] *Marginal annotation*: D[ame]. Magd[alena]. [Lucy Cary].

[110] *Marginal annotation*: Breton [also known as John Fursden; he died on February 2, 1638].

[111] St. Anselm (1033–1109), the son of a Lombard noble, entered the monastery at Bec in Normandy in 1059. His appointment as archbishop of Canterbury (1093) brought him

owl out of his monastery), but by God's merciful providence was stayed. He there led a life of so much edification that it drew esteem and praise from the earnestest Protestants, and some such friends of theirs, who knew him, would often say, it was the sanctity of his life that had deceived them (but not that they esteemed it not real, for they believed him to be most sincere) and that had they met with any other than him, they had ne'er been papists; that they were sure there was no more such priests amongst them. And no question it did give an authority to his words, where there was occasion to rely on the truth of his saying in anything; and was the cause of their choosing him to speak to (to whom 3 of them had never spoke before at all), when they had by accident or rather God's especial providence, occasion to make question of religion; ⟨and⟩ when his humble sanctity did allay the apprehension they had to manifest their simplicities, which they could not have had the power to have done to any whom they had thought never so holy, had he not appeared to them, like him, not to be of the world; besides the assistance his prayer gave to his work. Yet he did no extraordinary outward thing (being ever sickly and careful to recover his health out of his desire to return to his monastery; yet so as, when the remedies he sought had a contrary effect, he seemed as fully content, as if it had been that that he had pretended[112]). Only he did observe much abstraction and recollection; and those ordinary things he did, seemed to receive a grace from within, appearing to proceed from, and be directed and ordered by, no ordinary interior.

His passing from a holy fear to that height of charity which expels fear, seemed to show itself apparently in that, about three year before he died, having a great and dangerous sickness, he showed in it (though with resignation and hope) much sense of fear, often encouraging himself by the memory and example of S[t] Hilarion in the same occasion;[113] and

---

into repeated conflict with William II and Henry I about the autonomy of the church. His best-known theological work, on the doctrine of atonement, is *Cur Deus Homo?* The life of St. Anselm by Eadmer reports the comparison (ch. 2, para. 8) quoted by Father Cuthbert. See *The Life of St. Anselm, Archbishop of Canterbury, by Eadmer,* ed. and trans. by R. W. Southern (Oxford: Clarendon Press, 1972), 70–71.

[112] Intended or aspired to.

[113] For more than fifty years, St. Hilarion (ca. 291–371) lived as a solitary, severely mortifying his flesh, in the desert of Palestine. Nevertheless, he suffered bitter spiritual

frequently with fear repeating that saying of St Paul, "Nihil conscius sum, sed in hoc non iustificatus sum";[114] and ever desiring those that came to see him to pray he might die in the state of grace. But after, coming to die of a consumption, at the beginning of which having given over hope of recovery and not judging his life to be long, or farther serviceable to his congregation, he desired at least to die in the service of God and it, and to that end besought his superior to impose on him the charge of assisting those sick of the plague (which was then in London); which being denied him, he from that time gave over all other study but of the Bible, the works of Blosius,[115] and his rule[116] (the spirit of which he daily more and more highly admired) spending from thence the rest of his life ⟨wholly⟩ entirely in order to his spirit, which he had ever much regarded, but ⟨to⟩ did now wholly and only attend ⟨it⟩ to it; and coming to die, he did earnestly desire death but most resignedly; and ⟨having⟩ whereas before he had much feared sudden death, he did now covet that by which he might most speedily pass to God, which with a great but humble confidence he hoped to do, cheerfully promising his prayers and help in the next world, to those that asked them, and in the continual exercise of love and resignation, having most devoutly received all the sacraments, and with great love to holy poverty desired that not the least of those little things he had, might be disposed of but by the will of his superior, after a strong agony of 3 hours, his senses and devotion continuing to the last, he died happily by the grace of God.

She was most exceedingly joyed at the resolution of her daughters, when she was made acquainted with it, which yet they kept from her, till by their

---

agonies, and after the death of St. Antony in 356, his contemplative peace was disturbed by many who sought his aid in effecting miracles. After moving repeatedly to escape both followers and persecutors, he found an inland refuge in Cyprus. There he achieved the serenity he had sought and died at the age of eighty. St. Jerome, who is the chief source of biographical details, reports his dying words as, "Depart, my soul; why do you hesitate? You have served Christ for seventy years, and do you now fear death?" (*Life of St. Hilarion, Hermit*, para. 45).

[114] 1 Corinthians 4:4 ("My conscience does not reproach me at all, but that does not prove that I am acquitted").

[115] See note 10.

[116] That is, the monastic rule of the order of St. Benedict, to which Louis de Blois belonged.

forbearing to go to church, it was suspected by their Protestant friends, and that they had as good as acknowledged it to them. They then professed it to her too, who either knew nothing afore, or durst not take any notice of it for fear of hindering it (⟨but though she might have some glimpse of hope it is like she did not know anything, for she could very hardly conceal what she knew⟩). Presently my Lord Newburgh (who was always very kind to them and careful of them, as being a true friend to their father's memory, and by a mistaken zeal most solicitous in such occasions) went to the King; from whom he procured a command to be sent by secretary Cooke[117] to her, to send her daughters to their brother. She told him she would herself carry her answer to the King, judging it her best and most secure way to seek either mercy or justice immediately from his Majesty; which she did by humbly representing how hard a dealing it would be to take her children from her, she desiring to have them with her, and they to stay, being able to choose (the youngest being twelve year old) and not having done anything to forfeit their natural liberty; and no less hard (without his committing any fault) to lay such a punishment upon her son as to charge him with four sisters and nothing to keep them, without asking his consent, and against their own wills ⟨which would make his house their prison, and himself their gaoler⟩; upon which the King was pleased to give her leave to keep them till she heard his farther pleasure. ⟨who a⟩ The King after sent to her son about it, who was not willing to have them against their own wills, which would but make his house their prison and himself their gaoler, and none of them were found willing; so as this only served to hasten their reconciliation, which else the apprehension of confession might have delayed, but now fearing to be taken from having means to execute it, and that they might, by the grace of the sacraments and being in the Church, have strength to stand more firm in what opposition might happen, they were speedily reconciled. Yet divers Catholics abroad did dissuade her and Father Cuthbert from venturing on it so suddenly, believing assuredly their friends would never rest till they got them from her, and then that as assuredly they would fall again; but she, that had had so much confidence when there was not the least sign of

[117] Sir John Coke; see note 61.

hope, could not want it now, and Father Cuthbert, that knew how little
the awe of a mother had swayed here, ⟨and⟩ or of how small force the desire to please had been, and that had seen all that had passed could not
doubt but the hand of God was in this change. Yet it was not long before
she saw herself in very much danger of losing what she had gained by God's
mercy with so much pain.

⟨Lord⟩ Mʳ Chillingworth ⟨who⟩ continually frequented her house,
⟨and⟩ of whom she made great account, for (besides his being one
of those to the thirst of whose conversion she was so strongly carried) he
had gained from her the great esteem of a saint, for his so free reproving
her (though he were the whilst himself most apprehensive of anything
that seemed to derogate from his esteem in all things, being ever com-
plaining of some conceived neglect, or that he was not respected equally
with them that were the most so). She heard him with much respect
seeking to raise the same belief in her daughters, before they were
Catholics, out of hope he might assist to make them so (and he had
been very busy, even to troublesomeness, about them; but God did effect
what he went about by a more faithful servant of his, and one that intended his glory only and the good of souls); after they were Catholics,
for their better establishment. But this man, of whom it is hard to know
(if ever he were a sound Catholic) when he began to change, yet it may
easily be thought that he was none from hence: both because after, brag-
ging of his own great charity, he did affirm, he had dissembled himself a
Catholic one half year for their sakes (and it was not so much after they
were reconciled before he fell openly) and that he (who could hardly
think anything well done that was not done by himself, and now saw this
that he had offered at effected by another (who meddled not in it but by
his prayers, till he was sought to), without his having any hand in it or
being made acquai[n]ted with it) did soon show signs of dislike of what
had passed, and from that time did seem to go seeking the drawing them
back, and that with so much closeness, subtlety, and so many forgeries,
that, as it may be well thought none but the devil could have invented, so
it may be certainly said ⟨nobo⟩ none but God could have delivered them
from. It was said he had undertaken this to their Protestant friends,
having missed of laying that obligation on their mother he seemed to
aim at in making them Catholics; which might well be it that had power

to make him descend so low as to make them so much his business, who
of themselves were most uncapable subjects for his glory; ⟨nor⟩ yet he
could not well pretend it to be charity that made him so humble, since
that would have made him take some pains with his own mother, whom
he had made a Catholic (a sign he was once truly so himself, though
God knows when), yet was so far from going about to make her other
that he seemed always (as she said) to give her hope of his own returning, in time.

She [Elizabeth Cary] then had raised in her children a⟨n⟩ high
opinion of him. He was much with them, and they heard him with an open
ear, as a confirmer and informer in Catholic religion. He the whilest ⟨was⟩
did with much diligence seek to gain knowledge and power on their spirits; and having at first cast forth some words, by which he seemed indi-
rectly to give them occasion to look a little back, soon (yet rather as not
being come by a right way than not arrived to a right place), and to propose himself for their most proper assistant, he having been a long
waverer, and they too speedy resolvers, he after was very inquisitive to learn
by what motives they were induced to become Catholics, or else to make
them receive some from him to rely on, that he might the easilier destroy
what he had built. He also showed himself a most officious assister of their
devotions. He sought to make them change their ghostly father for his
(who indeed had a greater opinion of him) and to persuade them to learn
some things for which he ⟨proposed⟩ offered himself for their master; and
to draw them to open their hearts to him in ⟨al⟩ any doubt or difficulty
they might have—all this that he might the better find (as it appeared by
what followed) somewhat to lay hold on, knowing by experience those that
are proud are easilier caught by what is first conceived in their own heads;
but they being more ready to hear him than to communicate themselves
to him (he never seeming so dead to the world, in their eyes, as to give them
that confidence), he could find nothing to fix on for some time. But at
length, having by a small occasion discovered that they had some little difficulty in something, not knowing well what to think of it, he here begins,
⟨not⟩ seeming to take the same difficulty from them, that he might engage
them to go on with him, and to have the more confidence of the simplicity and sincerity of his proceeding, of which ⟨(as⟩ (he made them believe)
they were witnesses of the beginning; but he ⟨made divers several persons

think,⟩ affirmed to divers others, severally, that some word ⟨they⟩ every one of them had said was that that gave him first occasion to doubt.

At first, then, he showed only some little dislike of that which he had perceived they were not forward to use; yet very reservedly; the whilest (as condemning the senselessness of Protestants) he began to propose to them what would be most reasonable to be thought, were it not for the authority of the Church, laying before them what he after followed; then spoke of the former thing with more dislike (but as not supposing the Church anyway concerned in it) and seemed to discover some other things somewhat blamable, but not charging the Church but private men's irregular devotions, till by degrees he made these things appear to them to be of more consequence, and many in number; and what he durst not say by himself as sounding yet too harsh, he did by counterfeited letters; as one, ⟨from⟩ pretended to be from a friend of his, who was inclined to be a Catholic; wherein he seemed to be diverted from religion by some things he found practised in matter of devotion; and advised him [Chillingworth] not to strain at a gnat in Protestant religion, and swallow a camel[118] in the Catholic. This he showed them, and after bragged of the deceit; another from my Lord of Canterbury to them, with a paper of motives for farther consideration of religion, which was not (as he said) to be so soon resolved on; ⟨who⟩ the foul copy[119] of which he after by mistake gave one of them.

After having made the things he spoke against seem strange enough to them, he began to say he saw not how so fully to excuse the Church, yet at the end of his discourse still professing himself a Catholic; and to prevent their speaking of what he said in this kind, he seemed to the rest to blame her that was the cause of their being ⟨a⟩ Catholics for doing so to those that would think the worse of him; that what they saw found fault with (especially as a breach of trust, or too much suspiciousness) in another they might avoid in themselves; and they being most confident of his sincerity, feared others would, if they knew it, judge worse of him than ⟨he deser⟩ they thought he deserved. He continued thus daily to go further (but by such (to them) imperceptible degrees) [that][120] at length he affirmed those things to be impious, nor could he see

[118] Matthew 23:24.
[119] Rough draft.

but that the Church was guilty of allowing and approving their practice; yet still affirming the doctrine the Church pretended to teach was good, but that it did use and approve the practice of things which were repugnant to that doctrine: ⟨yet⟩ but always showing to them a great desire to receive satisfaction in these things, and hope to do so when he should speak of them; which he would sometimes tell them he did of some (though he was not willing they should speak of what he said, because he should be blamed and suspected for dealing so freely with them that were new Catholics) and would show much joy to have received some plausible answer, but then would be sure to return soon, with some new discovery of the unsoundness of it; and they urging him to speak fully to others as he did to them and to let them hear him, that they might hear the answers too, he long delayed it, pretending not to be ready and that, to receive the more full satisfaction, he desired to furnish himself with all the objections he could; and of receiving satisfaction he ⟨made⟩ seemed to make no doubt; yet if he should not, and that, coming to the matter, he should prove these things to be as condemnable as he had said, and the Church as much engaged in them, and its authority remain overthrown, and that so the greatest part of its doctrine (whose chief foundation was, he said, its infallibility) should fall to the ground too; would they then be content, to retire from their mother's, to their brother's, and there by the help of their brother (as a Protestant) and himself (as a Catholic) begin a new inquiry into religion, they two debating between them, and then informing them, of all they should meet in their inquisition? He prevailed so far with one of them,[121] as to give her consent to this, she not perceiving what it was to admit such an "if"; and the rather for his conclusion, which was that, though he should not receive sufficient satisfaction from Catholics, notwithstanding he should[122] not doubt of the truth of the Church's doctrine, nor its authority, and so made no question but this search would end there again; yet having come too hastily to it, they were to go back that by

---

[120] Cropped in the MS.

[121] *Marginal annotation:* D[ame]. Aug[ustina]: [Elizabeth Cary].

[122] The phrase "notwithstanding he should" serves as the catchword bridging the seventh and eighth gatherings of the manuscript biography; at the end of the seventh gathering, however, the phrase is "he should notwithstanding."

a more thorough inquiry they might make a more immovable resolution;
he deceiving them with S^t ⟨Paul's⟩ Peter's saying, everyone ought to be able
to give a reason of his faith;[123] pretending upon it that it was not enough
to believe the right, unless they could defend the reasonableness of it; and
they, not discerning how easily they might (and how many things they did)
know for certain, which they ⟨could not prove⟩ were not capable of proving, ⟨did⟩ were the sooner deceived by him. Yet being from him, and in a
more quiet sight of what he had said, they did discern in⟨finit⟩numerable
contradictions in his words, and that all was only founded on supposi-
tions; and some unsincere dealings they did perceive in him; as affirming
to one of them[124] that all reasonable Protestants believed a point (of which
she showed herself very confident) and seemed to do the like himself, and
the same day gave another of them two sheets of paper of citations out of
St Augustine (as he pretended) against the same thing; and in some other
things they plainly saw he had juggled and had told them a formal set lie,
at least a most large equivocation, which they might well think much in
him that did pretend to so high truth as to reprehend the least of either of
those most sharply, alleging incessantly St Augustine's saying, one was not
to tell the least officious lie to save the whole world;[125] but after, when his
whole life was proved one great one, besides many others on occasions, he
could justify it with the words of St Paul, and say, he was all to all, to gain
all; a Catholic to a Catholic, and a Puritan to a Puritan, etc.[126] They could
therefore, being from him, easily resolve to hear him no more, but not so
easily execute it; the fear of judging or defaming him, with the confidence
that it was impossible one should willingly (for any motive in the world)
deal insincerely in such a matter, taking from them the means to cut off
the occasion.

---

[123] 1 Peter 3:15.

[124] *Marginal annotation*: D[ame]. Augustina.

[125] Since St. Augustine (bishop of Hippo, 354–430) believed that a lie could endanger
one's immortal soul, his teachings on lying are particularly stringent and absolute; see,
especially, *De mendacio* (395) and *Contra mendacium ad Consentium* (420). An "officious lie"
was the term, used by casuists among others, for a lie told out of kindness or to benefit
another.

[126] See 1 Corinthians 9:20–22.

She herself [Elizabeth Cary], who all this while had no suspicion of him, was warned by ⟨my Lord Craven⟩ a Protestant lord[127] that he was no Catholic, and that he would not let his brother (who Mr Chillingworth pretended to be making one) be anything in quiet; but having drawn him to resolve to be a Catholic, he would there stop him and draw him back again, till being ready to fix where he was before, he would again draw him on. This she, judging his Lordship had been misinformed, ⟨and therefore giving⟩ did not ⟨believing it⟩ believe it, yet told to Mr Chillingworth (as that lord desired her she would, and withal to forbid him his house from him), which he with much patience seemed to receive as a calumny cast on him for God's cause; but she soon found it truer (as it was all most true) than she thought.

For Mr Chillingworth, having (before his promised proofs) underhand procured that the motion of the removal of her daughters should again be proposed to them by my Lord Newburgh, the second (who before had given him a kind of conditional consent) was now (not suspecting him to have had any hand in this offer) drawn to acknowledge to my Lord ⟨of⟩ Newburgh (with whom Mr Chillingworth had dealt secretly, though he pretended not to be known to him) some fear of religion, and to yield to go to her brother's on the condition she might have a Catholic with her, naming Mr Chillingworth for the purpose, according to his instigation; but soon seeing she had gone farther than she meant (being the more inclined to do so, by Mr Chillingworth's seeking to make them fear it was shame, or want of courage, that did withhold them from drawing back, but having now done all she could apprehend hard in it, and that the execution of what was resolved on, was most easy every way, that fear being past); she perceived how she had been surprised (all their fears being built on his unproved supposals) and especially by seeing the foul copy of ⟨that that had been⟩ my Lord Canterbury's[128] paper (as it had been pretended to be ⟨in⟩ when it was given them at the same time with the motion of their removal) in his own hand, he himself giving it them by

---

[127] *Marginal annotation:* My Lord Craven [William Craven, 1606–97, earl of Craven, probably best known for his championship of Elizabeth of Bohemia].

[128] That is, the archbishop of Canterbury (probably George Abbot is meant; see note 85).

mistake, intending to have given them another paper; by which it was plain he had had a hand in this offer (having ⟨not⟩ not proved anything of what he had said) and that there must needs have been some deceit on his part, she recalled herself, refusing absolutely to go till his proofs were made. From which time, with somewhat more suspicion of him, they pressed him to delay no longer; and though he was most crafty in excusing himself and regaining a good opinion, he saw he could now defer ⟨no longer?⟩ it no farther: and he after said, he would have continued much longer a seeming Catholic, had not they by their urging him to declare himself, thrust him out.

And to find means to do this in a manner most for his purpose, he pretends to have been sent for by the Bishop of London,[129] feigning much apprehension of what should be the matter; commending himself to everyone's prayers, encourages himself as if in some conflict with fear (whilst my Lord of London never sent for him, nor thought of him, nor was he ever with him, as one of his chaplains affirmed of his own knowledge). He returns (as he pretended) from my Lord of London's, sad and full of thoughts, but would not tell why, but next morning, as being better resolved, seems more cheerful, and then professes openly that my Lord of London ⟨had examined⟩, examining him of what he had done hitherto (in matter of religion[ ]) and ⟨that⟩ also, of his farther intentions, had proposed to him that if he were writing a book (as he made show) of inquiry into religion, as to be a guide to others, that he should put himself forth of the communion of the Catholic Church till this were done, and that so by his more unpartial proceeding, it would be of more weight and authority towards all, as being writ by one that was disengaged on either side; and that to this end he had offered him an oath, to forbear for the space of two year (for so long would this book, he thought, be writing) the communion of both churches; and that if he should refuse this, he would suspect his sincerity, and proceed with him as he should think fit. He farther told them that, the night before not being able to resolve to do it and

---

[129] William Laud (1573–1645), soon after appointed archbishop of Canterbury. He was the chief architect of ecclesiastical policy under Charles I, and his arrogance, as well as his high-church doctrines, invited the animosity of Puritans.

doubting what would follow should he refuse it (which he was also loath to do, being in his mind so reasonable a proposition, and so much indeed to the advantage of the credit of his intended work), he was sad, but that now having resolved, through the hope of the great fruit that would follow, he had taken it.

The unlawfulness of this oath, and consequently the not obliging of it,[130] being objected to him by Father Cuthbert and Mʳ Clayton, he to stop their so sudden condemnation of it alleges Father Leander's approbation of ⟨t⟩his act (who, being that morning early gone out of town, could not answer for himself) but, that not sufficing, after some days' dispute about it, he adds to his already (as he had said) taken oath this clause except in danger of death; yet without pretending so much as to ask my Lord of London's consent, any more than indeed he had for making of it, or did after for the breaking of it, communicating with the Protestant Church within less than a quarter of a year; but his tale hung not well together in many things. He did also for their better satisfaction (at least in the ⟨ob⟩ uprightness of his intention) give them in writing that all he did was only out of the desire of the advancement, and for the glory, of the Catholic Church and faith, setting his name to it; and this he did not above two days before he professed himself openly; and it was not five days after before he writ down this unheard of assertion: Roman Catholics are held for heretics by the Church of England, and that they are so shall be proved by William Chillingworth. And in the time that he sought to conceal himself and made the former profession, disputing ⟨about⟩ in defense of his oath (which was in all at least a week), he did to her daughters now go farther (for all that they ⟨that⟩ had been present at his writing that profession of his intention) and, having retired himself from the Catholic communion, did more freely lay before them the obligation of doing the same; and told them that it was the discovery of the unsoundness of Protestant religion (which he confessed was easily made) that was the cause so many turned Catholics, and not the truth of the Catholic; and that people taking it as granted that they must needs be one, ⟨and⟩ finding the Protestant false (which they that looked into it ⟨would⟩ might soon do) did pass with them as an assurance that the other was true; when, if a third way were opened,

---

[130] That is, therefore, he was not bound by it.

the Catholics would have no less to do to defend themselves than the Protestants. The title he then desired to give his third way (though most unjustly) was Christian, without admitting other addition (others believed, ⟨out of⟩ he ⟨did⟩ was in hope his own name would be imposed on it in time for a distinction and he ⟨pro⟩ himself bragged that thirty did depend on his resolution for the choice of their religion, but sure he saw himself much deceived in his number), and he did propose the Protestant church for their communion (in this very time of his affirming himself to be seeking the promotion of the Catholic), as not being, as he said, so straitlaced. Father Leander comes to town, denies his having said any such thing; affirms the case he [Chillingworth] proposed to him was whether one might, for a great good, forbear the sacraments (not forswear the Church's communion) for some time, which was easily answered; and to take occasion from Father Leander of asking for how long, or other question concerning it, he had a little before told him (which after on good cause was suspected not to be one word true) that a friend of his, inclined to be a Catholic, had desired his company in his house in the country, for a month or three weeks, to assist him in resolving, but that the unwillingness to lose mass or the frequentation of the sacraments for ⟨so short⟩ that (though so short) time made him not know how to consent to go.

And [Elizabeth Cary] having one whole day talked with Father Leander alone, none being by but they two and she herself, Mr Chillingworth that night making a relation of their discourse (such a one as he pleased) to one of her daughters, ending it with an exclamation against Catholics and their religion, as founded on lies, and maintained by them, was in all overheard by her, who walked near. He was somewhat surprised, not being able to stand to all he had said; and she, having convinced[131] this zealous lover of truth of falsehood in his relation and dissimulation in his conclusion (he having continued to seem a Catholic still to her), would have forbidden him her house at that instant; but seeing her children farther engaged in the opinion of him and what he had said than to be content with that, she endured his company four days

---

[131] That is, convicted.

longer, yet with so much difficulty to herself that she was fain to forbear her own table to have him ⟨there,⟩ at it; for she, that a little time before, taking him for a good Catholic and a sincere and holy man, respected and loved him exceeding much; and when he had pretended to be in difficulty (both when he came first from Doway, and now about his oath) had much compassion of him and desire to procure his satisfaction; now seeing him a willful deceiver and seducer, was very hardly able to support his presence.

The two first days were spent in a confused discourse of divers things, with many several persons, as Father Cuthbert, Mʳ Clayton, ⟨Mʳ Chaperlin⟩ & another Catholic gentleman, and herself. All of them were earnest (as much touched with the danger they saw her daughters in), she herself sometimes somewhat bitter and ⟨and Mʳ. . . . Chaperlin⟩ the gentleman[132] (who was a zealous Catholic, and a very good man, but somewhat violent) was so fierce that the uttermost of what he could do was to keep his hands from having their part in the dispute; whilst Mʳ Chillingworth received all that was said with so calm a serenity as if his peace and patience were immovable. Yet, not to lose the least part of his supportation, he did continually call upon her daughters to take notice with what mildness he bore all: and by this his behaviour at the end of those two days, his interest in their esteem was much increased; though he had been far from proving anything, which he excused by the confused manner of their discourse, speaking of several things, passing from one to another disorderly, and that many speaking against him alone did distract him. For the remedy of all this, he was to choose the person with whom and manner how he would dispute. He, who never cared to have to do with Father Cuthbert, either as having experienced his work had been often overthrown by him (when in the perplexities he had put her daughters into, they had had recourse to Father Cuthbert (yet without letting him know from whence all came) and had returned thoroughly satisfied), or else suspicious of the advantage he had over himself in their respect, and being willing himself to have in that kind

---

[132] *Marginal annotation:* Mʳ Chaperlin.

⟨and all other⟩ what odds he could, chooses a stranger to them (yet one very capable, for his own credit), being a father of the Society of Jesus,[133] whom they had never seen before; nor none of his order.

He at first makes ⟨him⟩ this father take an oath on the Bible, not to say anything in the heat of dispute which he was not most certain was true and which he did not in his conscience take to be a full and sound answer to what had been said; and though himself took the same oath, it may well be thought his conscience was not (according to his own phrase) so straitlaced as the other's. He forbid all school terms and method[134] as unproper and not understood by those for whom they spoke, but that in long discourses and plain terms they should object and answer; not interrupting one another, nor removing from one thing to another till it were fully satisfied, and by common consent. This seemed fair, but he soon showed that, by the first, he sought not (as he pretended) their clearer understanding but his own advantage (which the Jesuit would have had in the other manner, as much used to such disputations), by his seeking to dazzle their eyes with his multiplication of words, but the father, stripping his arguments of all his exaggerations and exclamations (with which his discourse was disguised and adorned), easily and clearly answered them, so as he was forced to transgress his last order himself, for, having first been fain to change his person, and instead of proving what he had undertaken (in which he had wholly failed) he put the other to prove the contrary (which being clearly done), he was constrained to run from one thing to another (that upon which he at first seemed to build all (⟨being⟩ which was their first difficulty) being clean confuted), till at length he went so far from the matter as he seemed only to aim at proving something, though it had no way relation to anything that had been said, nor no way concerned those they spoke for, being not any question of religion but matter of fact.

[133] *Marginal annotation:* Mr Holland. [Guy Holland, 1587?–1660, also known as Holt, joined the Society of Jesus in 1615 and was arrested March 1628 at the London residence of the Jesuits; he devoted forty-five years to the English mission, chiefly in London.]

[134] That is, the technical vocabulary and logical procedures associated either with Aristotle and scholastic theologians or with Peter Ramus (1515–72), the Protestant logician whose ideas on "method" offered a well-known Renaissance alternative to various aspects of Aristotelian philosophy.

And, whether it were that God would not permit the mask of his feigned mildness to deceive them any longer, or that his pride, which in the former proceeding had found double satisfaction (whilst their earnestness expressed a fear of him and apprehension of his dangerousness, which made him seem to be something; and his holding so well his temper upon it gained him farther credit with her daughters) found itself here more nearly touched to the quick (his adversary dealing so slightly with him (not otherwise uncivilly, but as if he put not his strength to him but wrestled with a child) ⟨as⟩ that he seemed to make nothing of him), he so lost all his pretended serenity as to be so uncivil as to call the other fool and knave, which being only answered with smiles put him into such a rage and fury that he swelled so with it and looked so terribly that he might well have been suspected to be possessed. And now at the end of two days (which he had spent from morning till night with this father), seeming to have almost lost his senses with anger and having no more to say for all his long preparation (of which her daughters had been witnesses, the father of the Society having been warned but the night before he came, late, after Mr Chillingworth had chosen him), he was fain instead of proofs to thunder out threats, with a confused heap of dreadful words as "hell," "damnation," and "devils," etc., as dreadfully spoken, seeking to frighten them whom he knew enough inclined to fear; when by the consent and good will of all he was forbid the house. He, seeing he had lost all he sought there, strove yet to excuse his fury by that which might make it more strange, saying that of his knowledge the Jesuit had been preadmonished to keep temper in all, and had been told how ⟨they⟩ her daughters had been taken with his show of equality, the days before, and how much they disliked all earnestness; which if it were so, and that he knew it, might have served him for a warning to continue it.

He after came twice to her house more, once to speak with Father Fisher[135] of the Society, in private, who desired it in hope to

---

[135] Father John Fisher, or Thomas Piercy (1569–1641), was the Jesuit to whom Chillingworth's conversion at Oxford was generally attributed. In the 1590s he was particularly active as a missionary in the north of England, where he had been born. He was frequently imprisoned (and several times under sentence of death) in the course of his career.

do some good on him, but without effect; and the other time to meet Father Francis de S[anc]ta Clara the Recollect[136] before her daughter at court, where they were to dispute writing instead of speaking, by a new prescription of M[r] Chillingworth's; where having got as little as before, he retired to her eldest son's house,[137] whither also there was lately gone her two younger sons[138] from school, who had been at her house not long before their going to their brother's, and had there received great inclinations to Catholic religion (though they were very young), which made her have some design from that time to steal them away; with both which M[r] Chillingworth (who was now to be their tutor) was acquainted, ⟨being⟩ having been then present at her house (which sure had been enough, had not God blessed them extraordinarily, to have hindered the accomplishment of ⟨it⟩?⟩ either), but he had always laughed at their talking to the children of religion. Yet that inclination left them not wholly till it was accomplished; though her eldest son did use to the elder of them to show his writings against Catholics (he then writing much in the matter, but privately, and always as pretending to be rather an inquirer than an absolute defender of anything; and ever confessing there were few truths so clear that ⟨were⟩ it was not more hard to ⟨be⟩ prove⟨d⟩ them than to find something to object against them; and that to one that would deny more than he, he should not be able to prove plainly (in such a degree as he seemed to require to have things proved to him) what he did yet think to be so) and ⟨to⟩ did treat with that brother as capable of the matter then, though so young; a practice which was apt to lay a strong hold on his nature, had not God preserved him; and Mr Chillingworth did not fail to deal with the younger, giving him for a first principle that there was not any certainty in matter of religion.

---

[136] Franciscus à Sancta Clara, or Christopher Davenport (1598–1680), was born at Coventry and joined the English Recollects of the Franciscan Order at Douay. He was appointed one of Henrietta Maria's chaplains and, arguing that there was no essential or fundamental difference between the doctrines of the Anglican and Roman churches, tried to reconcile the Church of England to Roman obedience.

[137] Great Tew in Oxfordshire.

[138] *Marginal annotation:* Patrick & Placide [Placid was the name Henry Cary, the youngest son, received when he joined the Benedictine order.]

She, now being free from her fear and all things settled in quiet, had yet enough to do to maintain her children, whom she had so earnestly laboured to keep with her, for though the charge of them was somewhat lessened, yet one of them[139] continued to go much abroad and to court, for whom she was not to diminish her solicitude to procure all things (which ⟨were⟩ was the more being now out of mourning), not daring to venture so far on her as to withdraw from her anything she had a will to, till it pleased God to do it. And the longer she kept them, it still grew harder to her to procure wherewith; besides her family's[140] daily increasing, to which she was always subject, being ever ready to charge herself with all those that knew not how to bestow themselves, especially if she had but known (or seen) them before never so little; filling her house by that means with many unuseful servants; for she was always most glad to find those (whose want being reduced to a less compass than hers) she was capable to help; being joyed, when she was not able to do much, to meet those a little would succour, never in her greatest scarcity being able to refuse a little (when she had it) to those that it would relieve, but saying with saint Paula that should she refuse that body, it may be they would not find any that would give them;[141] and that she was confident, if she should want so little she should never fail of somebody that would give it her. But as this confidence was in part human (built on her many friends and much acquaintance), God did permit her in some sort to see herself deceived in it (in as much as it was so) before she died.

Nor did she reckon how often the same body came, if they came when she had it and but for so much as she could spare at the present (never being much given to provide for the future), which did plainly appear in this occasion: that, at a time when she had herself little plenty enough, one[142] that did (amongst many others) frequently resort to her in his need (whom she had known when he had a very great estate and who, being a

---

[139] *Marginal annotation*: Mo[ther]: Clem[entia]. [Anne Cary].

[140] That is, her household's.

[141] See St. Jerome, Letter 108 (para. 15), which commemorates her life. After she was widowed at the age of thirty-three, the Roman patrician known as St. Paula (347–404) came under the influence of St. Marcella and St. Jerome. She traveled extensively to sacred places, spent generously on charities, and devoted herself to the personal welfare of St. Jerome.

[142] *Marginal annotation*: Sr Wil[liam]: Essex.

lone man, that would now at times be something to him which did not seem anything to her to give, when she could come by it) did receive from her in about a year 30 pound by crowns and half crowns at a time, as his occasion required or her store permitted, of which as a grateful acknowledgement he brought her a note at the year's end, which did much encourage her to continue, seeing what she had never perceived the want of, had ⟨had⟩ been considerable to him in his present case. And indeed it may be thought that whatsoever she had had in the morning, she would have had nothing left at night, unless she should have found none that did need or would ask, ⟨and⟩ for she was almost as certain to go to bed without money, whatsoever she might have received ⟨that⟩ in the day, as if she had been obliged to reserve nothing for the morrow, unless some friend of hers had got it out of her hands to keep it for her. Yet she was careful (in such a degree as she could be) not to give frequently nor any considerable matter but to such as would use it well.

Having now continued for two years since her lord's death and having used all means possible for the maintaining of her family, she was brought to the last extremity, not being able to find any way to hold out longer; having so concealed this from her children that they were the last that knew it; and having disfurnished her own chamber wholly (even of her very bed, being fain to sleep in a chair), she kept the door of it locked, that they (who yet were not disaccommodated in anything) might not perceive it; but now there being no more any means possible for her to avoid it, she was fain (the grief and apprehension of it having first cast her into the greatest sickness she ever had) to send to her eldest son, to come and discharge her house and fetch away his sisters; which yet she much feared to tell them. He, who ever showed himself a more than ordinarily good son to her, and her daughter-in-law ever rather furthering than hindering his being so, made what haste he could to provide himself for the purpose; which whilst he was doing, she and all her family were sustained by their charities who knew in what case she was; about which time she was much beholding to Sir William Spencer, a cousin of hers, both for the discharging of a part of the debt she was in for what was past and for his help in her present necessity. What he then did for her in both, may it please God to restore to him, with a plentiful increase, in the next world when he shall come thither.

She here seemed more overcome ⟨with⟩ by grief and distrust than ever, and here God seemed to teach her to have a greater and stronger confidence than ever in what he ordained, by the good success of this which she so much apprehended, in which God Almighty's providence greatly showed itself, the absence of each one of her children continuing no longer than seemed absolutely necessary for some good that came by it. Three of them[143] then went with their brother to be again ⟨to be⟩ tormented, but, by the grace of God, not hurt, by Mr Chillingworth.

She seeing the beginning to have succeeded better than she feared (having much apprehended how her children would take it, particularly how harsh it might seem to her that still loved the court, their brother (who was their only friend that would bid them welcome remaining Catholics) being not like to come to London), she was not long before she recovered her health and new courage, hoping much in God's disposition; and being recovered, she made haste to visit them where they were, with a promise to procure their return to her the soonest it should be possible: but that was not yet done for which Almighty God had brought them thither; for here where the loss of their faith was feared by all, the eldest[144] was to find her vocation to religion; and their little brothers were (after having their dispositions to religion renewed and confirmed by their being with them) to be delivered from thence and Mr Chillingworth's hands; and God did by their being there make Mr Chillingworth known (after they had discovered more of him themselves) to a young Catholic gentleman,[145] who his dissimulation had like to have put in much danger; but God did never permit him to have

[143] *Marginal annotation*: Mo[ther]: Clem[entia]: [Anne Cary]. D[ame]. Magdel[ena]. [Lucy Cary]. S[is]t[e]r Maria. [Mary Cary].

[144] *Marginal annotation*: Mo[ther]: Clem[entia]: [Anne Cary].

[145] *Marginal annotation*: M^r. Harry Slingsby [Henry Slingsby was the second son of Sir Francis Slingsby, a Yorkshire gentleman who settled in Ireland at the beginning of the seventeenth century. His conversion to Roman Catholicism was influenced by the example of his older brother Francis, who entered the Jesuit novitiate in 1639. Under pressure from his father, Harry took up residence at Great Tew, presumably so that Chillingworth might persuade him to recant his conversion. When Francis Slingsby became a Jesuit, he renounced his rights to paternal inheritance in favor of his brother, but his father dissipated most of the property during the Civil War. (Richard Simpson's 1861 edition of Lady Falkland's *Life* appends a memoir of Father Francis Slingsby.)]

power to make one reconciled Catholic fall, though it may be he has concurred to the hindering too many from being so.

Her household having been discharged by her son, her family was now reduced to a very small compass. She from this time gave over clean all those entangling businesses in which she had dealt and by which she had always been a loser, perceiving now plainly her having been deceived in them; and those occasions of going abroad being taken away, she from this time lived always more retired, either in the country or seldom going abroad when she was in London, but when she did, (to avoid occasion of farther debt, by keeping or hiring a coach) she almost always went afoot (which in her lord's time she did not use for respect of him; ⟨nor⟩ and when her children lived with her, and that any of them went amongst company, she forbore it for their sakes, being not willing to put upon any of them that which they could not support, and for this cause she did after give over to do so as long as one of her elder sons was in England, at his request, who was not able to endure her doing it), and the better to go on foot, as also for their being more chargeable every way beyond necessity, she from hence left off chopines,[146] which she had ever worn, being very low,[147] and a long time very fat; and upon the same freedom (from the regard of her children) she now left to observe the custom of going in black as a widow, wearing anything that was cheapest and would last longest; and out of the great detestation of going in debt (which she never did farther from this time) she was more willing to seek the relief of her necessities (when she had occasion) from the charity and assistance of her friends and acquaintance than by borrowing.

Her house was for some time wholly unfrequented; and from hence it was for much the most part only visited by priests and her private Catholic friends; nor did any priests frequently resort thither but such as did every way deserve much esteem; yet if others whose lives might be something less so did by some occasion, or their want of conveniencies, chance to come ⟨thither⟩, though they were not with such importune and earnest solicitation invited thither, she entertained them willingly and civilly. She now also spent her own time almost wholly in reading.

[146] Shoes with high cork soles.
[147] Short.

She was no sooner able to breathe again, but she was desirous to find means to have her daughters back to her; and one of them[148] soon returned, my Lady Duchess of Buckingham's Grace[149] (who was always a great and constant friend to her, to whom she had had the honor to be very much known from my Lady Duchess's infancy) being pleased to undertake to provide for that daughter of hers; and being informed by her daughters of the extraordinary desire her little sons had to see themselves Catholics, and how they were desirous to refuse to go to church, though they should be never so much whipped for it, if it would not make them be taken away from their sisters, and from having ever means to be so; and of what diligence and art they used to observe fasting days without being perceived, enduring for it (especially one of them) extremity of hunger, they not being let to eat most fasting meats as unwholesome for children; she was no less solicitous to contrive how to get them away (though she had but what would barely keep her present little family, which was also paid her by weeks, to prevent such inconvenience as she had formerly run into), and to facilitate this she urged her son to send her little sons abroad to some school (of which she named some) that they might not be under Mʳ Chillingworth's gover[n]ment, which she would not endure to have them, and therefore, if he would not do it, she did assure him, she would steal them away. But her son, not ignorant of her intention (having been informed by Mʳ Chillingworth of what he had been privy to heretofore, as well as of his daily new discoveries, who was so skilfully inquisitive and did so watch over her daughters that he ever knew all they said or writ, how secretly soever) and knowing well his house was less apt for her effecting her design than the places she named, he would not be brought to it; but contrarily (though he judged it not likely to be done from his own house) to take away all possibility of her bringing it to pass, he resolved to send them farther off, amongst Puritans, where they should be more narrowly looked to. This she sought to hinder him from, neither giving over her hope nor her design.

And the whilest, being but only able to live herself, she did expect some good occasion to have her other two daughters home to her again

---

[148] *Marginal annotation:* D[ame]. Magd[alena]. [Lucy Cary].
[149] Katherine Manners Villiers; see note 80.

(knowing that without some just pretense her son would ⟨not consent to⟩ be troubled at it), they most earnestly desiring to come to her on any condition; thinking that, so they might return, they could be contented with anything. Yet this ⟨for⟩ was not for any other cause but the more free exercise of their religion (for which they ⟨their religion/ had there⟩ had there very little commodity) and to be freed from Mʳ Chillingworth's insupportable importunity, which yet was, by God's mercy, ⟨was⟩ now more troublesome than dangerous to them; they ⟨hearing⟩ (as knowing him better) hearing him (for heard he would be) no more as a saint but as a procurator for the devil: for he, in the time of their being there, had made himself very well known to them; so as if, at their coming thither, there was yet remaining in them any suspicion of there being any truth in him, he quickly confuted it. For now declaring his opinions to them in their ⟨true⟩ own colours (which before he had not done absolutely, for though he had opened to them a pit into which they might if they pleased fall, in ⟨to persuading⟩ laying before them what would be most reasonable to be believed, were the Church's authority void, and endeavouring after to destroy that; yet he had never so put these things together as to ⟨make⟩ profess to any one of them his actual misbelief of the Trinity) and importunely pressing them upon them as much as he durst; and to a young Catholic[150] that served one of them (and had been reconciled with them) daring to do more, he would make her hear him by force, holding her aspite of her teeth[151] when she offered to go, and keeping down her hands when she would stop her ears, into which he would bawl his blasphemies (yet though she since fell (may it please God mercifully to raise her again) he had not the content to have any hand in it), and when after all that he had said to them, they saw him pretend to be a Puritan to those that were so, and that their sister-in-law and her mother seemed to esteem him for a kind of saint (though it is like they did not so really, having too much cause to the contrary, but were rather desirous to maintain his credit to the Catholics, in hope he might work something upon them; and to that end they caused to be kept very secret from them some proceedings of his,

---

[150] *Marginal annotation*: Camilla [no other information about this young woman is available].

[151] That is, despite her resistance or defiance.

which they judged would appear in their eyes as unsaintlike as ridiculous; as also they sought to conceal some passages in a sickness he had had upon his first coming down amongst them, which they seemed to impute to a kind of frenzy; yet they did rather appear to be so in their manner than matter), and that the esteem they showed of him made them think his words were of more authority with ⟨their sister and the others⟩ them, when he falsely laid some things to the charge of Catholics, than they deserved to be, they would declare what he had said to them; which he could not doubt but they would do, when he said it; but had no need to fear their doing so, being so good at denying his own words; which he would do to the Protestants before their faces to whom he had spoke it, with such horrible oaths and execrations as would make them tremble to hear, and at the first seemed so strange to them (till use made it familiar) that they were ready sometimes to doubt whether they had heard any such thing or no, and other times to think certainly he had forgot his own words; till that by accusing him of them immediately as he was speaking them, when he would as immediately forswear them, those doubts were solved; as all others that they might have in the matter were, when he, returning to them, would repeat the same things he had ⟨heard⟩ said before, making strange equivocations for his oaths to the Protestants, all which they would tell again and he forswear at the instant with an unheard of impudence (to be in reality), and after would tell them new equivocations, reproving them for discrediting him; and for his own excuse alleging the ⟨example⟩ words of St Paul[152] and our Lord's example for seeming to do one thing when he meant another ⟨in setting his gaze to go to Jerusalem when he passed through Samaria[153] and . . . ⟩, feigning to go farther when he met the two disciples at Emmaus.[154] Nor was it possible for them to find words to question him with before the Protestants, for which he would not make some ⟨strange⟩ strained equivocation, yet such as served his turn; though sometimes no better than one he made use of after disputing with Father Dunstan, who by occasion charged him with his denial of the Trinity ⟨which⟩, but he (it being before Protestants and such as knew him not),

---

[152] See note 126.
[153] Luke 9:51.
[154] Luke 24:28.

fearing to lose his credit, professes the contrary. Father Dunstan, knowing his practice, asked him more precisely, did he believe the Trinity three persons and one God? He affirmed he did. Then the other, who knew he did not ⟨but saw⟩ (as it was then generally well enough known) but saw he cared not what he said to satisfy the present company, desired he would write it down, thinking he durst not have done that for disgracing himself with so many that knew it to be false. Yet he did so; and after said to those that questioned him, that it was true he believed that there was one God and three persons, as there was three hundred thousand thousand persons (men or angels), ⟨but⟩ and thus he meant what he had said; but that he had ⟨not⟩ never said he believed one God in three persons, nor that the three persons were one God, nor that they had anything to do with one another.

Yet for all these denials and forswearings, after ⟨they⟩ her daughters were gone from their brother's, he professed himself openly before those to whom he had forsworn it most ⟨to⟩ (God not permitting there to remain any question on whose side the lie had been, theirs or his), bidding the Protestants (at the table, before all) to take transubstantiation or deny the Trinity, he having as good and the same arguments against one as they against the other. And to hear those that (if they would not acknowledge the name of Puritans) were at least rigid Calvinists dispute with him was no less than admirable. None that had heard it could have doubted but that each was endeavouring to make the other a Catholic; they objecting to him his most high and intolerable pride in thinking the whole world in error and that he alone was able to discern the truth, which nobody else had been able to discover. Had there been none in so long time of a capacity equal to his to find it, or as much in God's favour ⟨as⟩ to be helped by his grace to see the right? had God had no care of ⟨the world⟩ all Christians (to permit them all to err) till he came? and to his saying there had been and were many of the same opinion, though they had not made profession of it (which he would not have done nor thought himself obliged to, had he not been constrained to it by the urgings of some), they would ask him how he knew ⟨they were⟩ there had been such if they had not professed it? and ⟨to⟩ when he affirmed there were many in Poland and Transylvania of his religion, and had been ever since the breach with Rome, they would continue to wonder that God should so neglect the rest of Christendom as to confine the truth so, to that remote corner of the world, that it should never have been heard of in other places. All which arguments, with many more the like, would he turn back on the heads of ⟨Cal⟩ Luther and Calvin and their followers; and the whilest he would highly exalt to them the authority of the Church of Rome and ⟨affirming⟩ affirm that whosoever would make any account of authority in matter of religion must necessarily submit to it; and that its authority and the belief of the Trinity were so unseparable that none that had reason could divide them; and all this hath been before ⟨Catholics⟩ her Catholic daughters, in whose presence to see themselves constrained to make use of arguments for the Church's advantage did seem to torment either side. And another of those that had the like opinions in religion[155] was wont to say that the great conveniency there seemed to be (according to human understanding) of an infallible guide, and the great aptness everyone had to wish there were such a thing, did make them so readily assent ⟨in?⟩ to believe it; and that indeed it ⟨were⟩ would be most reasonable to believe that if God have any care or providence over mankind, he has provided such a guide; did not that church that only pretends to this authority teach things so contrary to reason (of which he counted the Trinity ⟨on⟩ chiefly so) as to oversway; ⟨it being? more⟩ the believing them being more against reason than the other was according to it. Yet, abstracting from all *truth* and *religion*, Mr Chillingworth seemed to be a kind of an honest man and good-natured, never seeking to do anybody any temporal hurt and ready to do courtesies; which, it may be, might be much to his own purpose.

Less than a year after her children went from her, there happened a just occasion for her elder daughter's coming up for some time, about some business to his Majesty concerning ⟨that⟩ herself; and her daughter-in-law being then to come near or to London on her own affairs, she urged her to bring both her daughters with her to town (who, when she once had again, she meant not to part with), but her son, staying himself in the country, the rather that his sisters might the less expect to go (judging it likely they would come thither no more, when his mother had once got them), was at least desirous to stop the younger (of whose going there was

---

[155] *Marginal annotation*: My Br[other]. Falkl[and]: [Lucius Cary].

not any such pretense of necessity), knowing well this would (if anything) make the other come back again, not to leave her sister all alone amongst Protestants, and therefore made many excuses; but her daughters, undertaking the removal of all pretended difficulties, did hope to prevail; writing in this meantime to her that now, if ever, she must contrive how to get her little sons away, for if it were not done whilst they were there, who hoped to come from thence on such a day (some week after), it would be impossible.

She, who had not money to have brought them up the plainest way nor to have paid for their being at London, much less for the sending them over (which would be necessary, being sure their friends would never have permitted her to have kept them else, when she had got them), did not for all that despair; though she found nobody that would encourage her to the undertaking so difficult an enterprise as stealing them out of their brother's house and watchful Mr Chillingworth's hands, her designs being already known to them and they not slack to prevent her. Nor had she any to employ in it any way capable of being trusted with such a matter. Yet she made use of such as she could, procuring two horses to be hired. ⟨and⟩ She sent down two men with them, one being a poor fellow that got his living by going on errands and then no Catholic; the other (who served her) a counterfeit one, who at his best was taken for a simple gross fellow, but known after to have as little honesty as wit. This last was only known to one man in her son's house, the other to all; this, therefore, was to go to the house (the other not appearing in sight) with a letter from her to her elder daughter, with a strange hand on the superscription as coming from a lady her friend, he seeming to be that lady's man. In this letter she directed her daughters the best she could how to deliver their little brothers into these men's hands (but the most she could do was to lay such a plot that, if everybody in the house would stand still in the place she supposed them till all was done, it might succeed, the uttermost she could reach to being to contrive a possibility without all manner of appearance of any probability).

These men were to carry them to Abington[156] (being fifteen mile from her son's and five from Oxford) on the horses they came down on, the

---

[156] Abingdon is a town on the Thames, to the south of Oxford.

men going on foot by then, who [Patrick and Henry] were therefore to ride no faster than those men could ⟨go⟩ walk, which was but a slow pace for such an occasion, ten or twelve mile of it being the plain road to London, which they were sure (as soon as missed) to be pursued in, but she was not possibly able to procure the hiring of more horses. At Abington they were to be met, at an appointed day, by a gentleman that had served her[157] (who was very young) with a pair of oars to be brought from thence to London by water, a thing unusual enough. The money which she could possibly get for to furnish these two companies was ⟨sho⟩ so short that, did they not happen to dispatch their business at the day appointed, they would want money to bring them up again; besides the hired horses were to come back at a set time. Her man then delivered her letter to her daughter, he of the house that knew him[158] (and would, had he been there, have discovered him) being abroad; and in all other things the providence of God seemed so extraordinarily to guide the matter that there was not the least accident which did not concur to advance it; the excuses that had been made for her younger daughters' stay there and their undertakings upon it giving them now more means to whisper much, without suspicion, and to walk out often only with their little brothers (where they would meet their mother's man, whom they charged to come no more in sight of the house, lest that servant of their brother's returning (as he was hourly expected) should meet and know him; as they walked abroad several times, they showed the men to their brothers, and they to them, that they might know one another, and they led them to the place where they should meet (at the time they would appoint when they had resolved on it themselves), which was about a mile from the house; so far were the children to come alone and afoot).

And they, not being able (for many reasons) to execute their design so well on any day as on that of their own departure (when some bustle in the house would better hide it), stayed the men two or three days longer than they were appointed for that purpose, who not being able to stay one day more (because of the word that had been given for the return of the horses), that ⟨servant that had been⟩ gentleman of their

---

[157] *Marginal annotation:* Mr Alexander.
[158] *Marginal annotation:* My Cousin Thom[as]: Hinton.

brother's, that had been absent when his being so was necessary, came that very night when his coming was no less so, it being for his return that their sister-in-law only stayed her journey. And the delay of the delivery of money sent to one of her daughters (by an accident for a quarter of a year), which was now lately brought her, was many ways for the advantage of their business (which, had it come before, would also have been gone), helping to further it in other things, as well as to give the men both for their own charges the time they had stayed them and for his with the boat, who would, by this delay, be like to have none left him to bring them to London. And their eyes seemed here to be blinded (that they suspected nothing) who at other times were most watchful, for Mr Chillingworth (who always pried very narrowly) was just behind her that had the letter and looked over her shoulder when she opened it, yet knew not the hand (for it was her mother's own within), which he was so well acquainted with and was so easy to be known; and though the children themselves kept all very secret, yet their packing up their things and giving many away in the house might have been enough to have made one less suspicious than he suspect. ⟨someth⟩ Nor did their sister-in-law nor any other miss them that morning to take their leaves of them till the coach was gone so far that it was too late, when she, remembering them, lamented their having been forgotten.

Her daughters then, the night before they were to go away (having first conveyed their brothers' cloaks to the men and advertised them to meet them in the place they had appointed next morning by four or five of the clock; and having procured their brothers a play day of the next, that it might be the longer before they were missed) seeming to have much business to do next day before their going, did show a desire to be called very early, which one of their little brothers (by agreement) undertook to do at three a clock, that ⟨they⟩ the boys might have occasion⟨s⟩ to do that avowedly which, considering the wakefulness of Mr Chillingworth (which was well known to them), within whose chamber they lay, could not possibly be done by stealth; and the children's desire to go was so great that it gave them not leave to oversleep, but rising at 3 with as much noise as they could, went to call their sisters; and having run about the house an hour and showed themselves to all that were up, they were by one of their sisters carried down and seen safe out of all the courts of the house, without being descried by any; they running all alone that mile, it being not yet light, to meet men that were entirely strangers to them, whose persons were no way promising nor apt to encourage the children to have any confidence in them. Before they met the men, passing through a little village near their brother's house, they were fain to hide themselves behind bushes,[159] the barking of the dogs having made the people come forth. After they met them, they were fain to leave the highway at the sight of every coach or horse, being much afraid to be overtaken by their sister-in-law's coach or company, which was to follow them in the same way, at least as far as Oxford, whither when they came (it being far in the day), knowing they ⟨should⟩ might be like to be followed thither with a hue and cry, that nothing might have been seen in the town like any description that could be made of them, they took the boys off of their horses, one of the men passing first through the town leading one horse, the boys following on foot (some space after) without hats or cloaks (to look the less like strangers), and last the other man on horseback.

They came to Abington after noon, where they found that gentleman and his pair of oars, without money, as they expected, but, which they did not expect, so drunk (the watermen) that there was no removing for them from thence that night,[160] and those that brought them, not to leave them so, stayed too; when after supper they that came with them and he that was to take them here fell out and made a shift to have it known in the house that they were stolen children, at which the town was raised and the constable came to seize on them, who, happening to be an old acquaintance and the gossip of the poor Protestant fellow's, was by him satisfied, he assuring him they were his mistress's children; and that they were going to their mother, who had sent for them; but having so scaped, they durst not venture to stay till next day, lest some noise of an inquiry coming to this town (one that resorted much to their brother's house living near it) might renew the suspicion, but were fain to take water ⟨that⟩ at ten a clock, at dark night, with watermen not

[159] At this point in the MS traces of a note in Patrick Cary's handwriting are apparent, but the note has been both lined through and cropped.
[160] *Marginal annotation in Patrick Cary's hand*: true.

only not able to row but ready every minute to overturn the boat with reeling and nodding. Yet she (having first heard this news of the danger the two men had left them in) did receive them safe and most ⟨gla⟩ joyedly. ⟨her daughters being come home to her too Her sons⟩ She was fain to put them in some private places in London, often removing them; and for to be able to pay for their diet and lodging, as also through the enlarging of her family (her daughters being come home to her too), she and her household were constrained, for the time she stayed in town, to keep more Fridays in a week than one.

Her sons having been missed at their brother's, at dinner that day they went, and after having been sought all about without being found, they did at last conclude what was become of them, the rather seeing in their chamber, no book nor other thing left that was theirs. ⟨they⟩ Some of them affirmed since that they did not suspect that day, but meant to have sent away the children before their sister's coming back and from that very day to have had them so watched that they should have been no more spoke to by any from their mother. Her eldest son sent instantly all about after them, but soon judging that was to no purpose, it being too late and they like to be too far out of his reach, he made the more speed to inform his wife, there being more hope she might recover them at London; who ⟨as⟩ soon after she heard it acquainted my Lord Newburgh, he the ⟨Councillor⟩ Council Table (whereof himself was one). Their lordships presently called her before them (and whilst she was there with them, ⟨the lords⟩ they sent to search her house for her sons) and examined her; who acknowledged that she had sent for her children and had disposed of them as she thought good; and, though she had been forced to fetch them away from their brother's secretly, she had in that done nothing contrary to the law, since she could not be said to have stolen that which was her own, her son having no pretense to right to keep his brothers from her against her will and theirs, having never been committed to him neither by the state, nor their father; that she had often warned him she would do thus, if he would not remove them from under Mr Chillingworth, whom she would not have have the guidance of her children, and why, she would give my Lord of Canterbury a farther account, when he should please to demand it; that for those that did it, they were her servants, who upon her command went to fetch her children, who came alone to meet them a mile, ⟨as⟩ which plainly showed they were not brought away by force.

The lords telling her it was against the law to send them to seminaries, she desired them to prove they were sent to any such place (they being indeed in London, but she was willing they should think, if they pleased, that they were already over, that they might the easilier pass when they should go) and said that to send⟨ing⟩ them to be bre⟨e⟩d in France was no way against it. They told her to send them out of the land without leave was, showing some orders made to officers of ports to let none pass without licence. She alleged that this concerned not her, nor was she bound to know or take notice of it, being no such officer to whom this was directed; that this was no command to her not to send, but to ⟨them⟩ those officers not to let pass, which if they had done, ⟨they⟩ their lordships might please to question them, not her; at which one of them asked her if she meant to teach them law? She answered, she did but desire them to remember what she made no question they knew before, and that she, being a lawyer's daughter, was not wholly ignorant of. They demanded his name that carried her children over; she assured them she knew it not herself. They told her it was not likely she would trust her sons in the hands of one she knew not; then they referred her to my Lord Chief Justice Bramston[161] by their warrant, and in case she gave him not satisfaction, she was by the same warrant committed to the Tower [of London]. Having presented herself and been (with very much civility) examined by his lordship, and answered as before, she was (after he had spoken very civilly to her) dismissed by him, yet without in express terms [ac]quitting her. She desired to know how she was to be conveyed to the Tower, to which she stood committed if he were not satisfied. He acknowledged he knew not what more to say to her (unless she would be persuaded to bring her sons back) and confessed himself satisfied with her answers and offered her his coach home.

---

[161] Sir John Bramston (1577–1654), created chief justice of the King's Bench in 1635. Cromwell and the Parliament considered his integrity a sufficient asset that they wooed him, unsuccessfully, to accept appointment under their government as well.

He after, being importuned to it, called her two daughters that had ⟨had a hand⟩ done it before him; but when they came, spoke not with them, for, being said to be busy at their coming and they ⟨not⟩ showing little mind to wait, having no business on their side, one of his gentlemen desired them if they pleased to go home, and if his lord had farther business with them, he would send his coach for them some other time, but they never heard more from him. He also sent for and examined those two men that fetched her sons from their brother's, who answered as their lady had done for them, and farther that they had delivered them into the hands of such a one, and knew no more what was become of them, but the seeming Catholic (who was her own man) did, after they were out of his hands, seek by all means to betray them; and was the cause the other to whom he had delivered them was taken; who having also answered as the rest, that he had obeyed his lady in that that was every way lawful, and that he had by her appointment left them in the hands of such a gentlewoman,[162] not knowing now where they were. This gentle-woman was then inquired after. Therefore, to end these examinations, it was contrived that she should give them into the hands of one she had never seen before, nor knew not his name, but this was not needed; for the last man (that had once served her), after having been examined before my Lord Newburgh, and after by my Lord Chief Justice, was at last carried to prison and there detained two days, when she sends to my Lord Newburgh (by whose warrant she supposed it was done) and threatens ⟨him⟩ to sue him in a praemunire[163] for the false imprisonment of her servant. He denies the doing it and puts it off to my Lord Chief Justice, who likewise denies it to have been done by his command. Then the officers, fearing to be charged with doing it on their own heads, both the others having denied it, made haste to rid themselves of him, and the search stopped.

[162] *Marginal annotation:* Mrs Mullens.
[163] That is, she threatens him with a suit which could result in the forfeiture of goods and liberty (the penalties imposed for violating the statute of *Praemunire*, which forbade prosecuting suits in foreign courts, or recognizing their jurisdiction, in matters to which the laws of England applied); for this extension of the original sense of *praemunire*, see *OED* 2b.

In this time there was no house to which she or any of her children went that was not searched. Yet her sons were all the while in London (being about 3 weeks), she neither having money to send them over nor being able to find any that would carry them, though she offered to venture on any (and some that were thought not to deserve much trust), but none durst venture on it; which was at last ⟨undertaken⟩ (when no other means could be found) undertaken and performed by the great charity of a father of the Order of Saint Benet[164] (to whom on all occasions she was ever to be beholding), the money for it being brought, unthought on and unexpectedly, by that same father of the Society [of Jesus] that had disputed with Mr Chillingworth, which same money he desired ⟨might⟩ one to deliver into the hands of whomsoever should carry them over for that purpose, which was done according to his desire; and of that charity of his may it please God to be the rewarder and the reward.

God Almighty showed no less his providence over them in their journey to Paris, for having lighted on a very ill post to Roan [Rouen], of whose being much suspected for a rogue the father was advertised (upon the way, when it was too late to change him) by a merchant, that seemed to fear their ever coming safe to their journey's end, being in such hands. And the post (who had provided them horses as was most for his purpose, giving to the elder brother and himself exceeding good ones, and to the father one as bad) ⟨he⟩ did entice the eldest to outride with him the father and his brother, and did at last get him to light in a by-house afore the others came; and having him already in the house, he did the easilier persuade, or rather constrain, the monk to light too, though much against his will,[165] had he known how to have got the boy again on horseback, whom the post had made to be earnest to stay there and eat; ⟨by⟩ but they were scarce in the house when two soldiers came in, who were soon seen to be

---

[164] *Marginal annotation*: F[ather] · Francis Tressham · whom God reward. [Francis Tresham held the titles of Definitor of the Congregation and Cathedral Prior of Gloucester. Later, at Douay, he became an English Recollect (that is, a Franciscan) without the permission of his superiors and was ordered to reassume the Benedictine habit until he obtained leave for the change from the fathers in General Chapter assembled in 1649.]

[165] Here begins a long marginal note in Patrick's handwriting. It is lined through and was also severely cropped when the MS was bound. Only the final phrase, ⟨. . . the morning that we entered Roan⟩, is partially legible.

acquaintan[c]e and friends of the post's, and by his whispering with them and loiteringly delaying their going again to horse, and at last absolutely refusing to go out from thence (being to have carried them to Roan that night), he more confirmed the suspicion; at which time there arrived, by God's providence, to the same house a travelling gentleman with two men, each of them having a case of pistols, going that night likewise to Roan; with whose help the father made the post to let them at least pass on with this company, who, now not so stout in his denial, was fain to let them go, and he himself (who had, it seems, no business at that house without them) went along too (the soldiers going forth before them, as soon as they had seen what was concluded, pretending to be going to Roan also), and being come to a great wood not far from Roan, and it being near enough night, the post again sought earnestly to ⟨part⟩ make them part from the gentleman's company and to lead them a byway through the wood (which the gentleman would not go, as being dangerous), but by no means being able to bring them to it, he himself went that way alone; and they being come to the end of ⟨it⟩ the wood, where the ways joined, saw the same soldiers standing; who, by their turning back with discontented looks, as soon as they perceived them safely arrived by the other way, ⟨and⟩ it being so near Roan and night, did plainly show their business lay not at Roan, but on the way thither.[166]

Her sons were placed in the Convent of the Benedictine Fathers at Paris, where they found so much care and kindness towards them from R[everen]d Father Gabriel,[167] then Prior, that he did much oblige both ⟨her⟩ their mother and them to him for it; and the younger of them, being since religious in that convent, hath had much reason to acknowledge the fatherly affection of the present father prior towards him; and the elder going after to Rome, and being young and a stranger there, found in Father Willfrid[168] (who was entreated to have a care of him) so true and

---

[166] *Marginal annotation in Patrick Cary's hand*: These were all visions.

[167] *Marginal annotation in Patrick Cary's hand*: Bret [Robert Brett, son of Alexander le Bret of White Stanton and Somersetshire, became a monk at St. Malo, under his uncle Gabriel Gifford, from whom he received the religious name of Gabriel. He died in 1665, at the age of sixty-six.]

[168] Father John Wilfride of St. Michael, Procurator at Rome, whose secular name was Richard Selby.

great a friend in all things that he hath laid upon him and his friends a perpetual obligation. For the maintenance of her sons where they were, she did allot something which she received from the charity of her most Excellent Majesty, who was graciously pleased to continue it to them after her death, till the extremity of these times; in which occasion she was in a very great degree obliged to the very R[everen]d Father Philips,[169] as also in very many other, and likewise to R[everen]d Father Wat.[170]

After having by God's assistance taken order for her sons (yet before they were gone out of London, for she left them ⟨yet⟩ in town in the care of some friends when she went out of town herself), she was, by the plague which began then, forced to think with speed ⟨to⟩ of removing herself and family into the country, having neither money to carry her nor place to go to; but the first was lent, very unexpectedly, by a young Catholic gentleman;[171] and for the second she was fain to content herself with what she could find in a little village far from London, making a shift to dispose of her company in two poor thatched houses, remaining there about half a year; when, her son, having sometime before redeemed that part of his father's estate which was to have been her jointure, in which he had only made use of the right of redemption, to buy it without asking anybody's consent for what was over of the value of it (beyond the debts laid on it, which was not much), he (not to have anything from his father, having displeased him in his marriage) did desire to have divided, half of it for his mother, in some consideration of her jointure, the other half for any of her children ⟨as⟩ that should have most occasion for it, as he and she should agree. For the perfecting this agreement it was very convenient both for her and him that ⟨her son⟩ he and she should meet. She therefore went to his house, without other ceremony than sending to him for his coach (though they were yet at much difference about the stealing away her little sons, which had also been much increased on both sides by

---

[169] Robert Philips, of Scottish origin, became Henrietta Maria's confessor in 1626 after the expulsion of her French priests and attendants. (Henrietta Maria also had a priest named Francis Phillips among her attendants, but Robert Philips seems more likely to have exerted the influence the narrative indicates.)

[170] Father Wat is probably Walter Montagu; see note 179.

[171] *Marginal annotation:* M[r]. Harry Slingsby.

letters), but he took this so well that upon her coming they were soon good friends, he bringing her back and seeing her settled in a better place. At which time she finished the rest of Cardinal Perone's works, which she left unprinted.

From this time, till two year before her death (which was ⟨not⟩ little above one year), she employed herself in setting poor folks on work with yarn and wool for the entertainment of her thoughts and time; when, coming to London again, a cough which she had had almost continually for two-and-twenty year (always, through the much neglect of herself, catching one cold on another), was found to be turned to a cough of the lungs;[172] from which time her whole employment was writing and reading; renewing somewhat her Hebrew, and her Latin by the translation of part of Blosius[173] upon which she was set by Father ⟨Francis⟩.

And not long after, her children beginning to retire from her for the last, either being gone (or removed from her towards going) over, she more ⟨than⟩ frequently and generally than ever (as being more free) sought supply in her occasions from others; which, though by degrees and some use it might be made the more easy to her, and more so by the experience and knowledge she had how much human condition is subject to the humiliation of obligations; there being few so free, amongst the greatest, that have not many times occasion to see themselves in some sort to have much need of others, and to find themselves constrained to seek courtesies from some, ⟨or other?⟩ by which they remain obliged to them, and sometimes farther than they would willingly have known; and that most of those who have pretenses in the world are not without this cause of humiliation, but do rather seek to conceal it than to be really free from it; though the experience she might have had ⟨in⟩ of this in others (as well as herself, who had yet passed through some changes) did allay that inclination of pride that would abhor the contempt of such a proceeding, yet no doubt she could never have given herself leave to have done it, had she not directed it towards God, as in regard of the much greater quiet and justice there is in begging than borrowing (when there is not moral certainty of paying) and as a willing

[172] That is, tuberculosis.
[173] See note 10.

submission to his dispositions. And she could always (when she once, conceiving a thing fit, did give herself to do it) well do anything without difficulty, scar[c]e ever being known to do anything unwillingly, but when she had once resolved anything (how contrary so ever to her) must be done, she could do it with a good will. And as her own experience of the torture and slavery of debt had made her loathe it, so she was apprehensive of occasioning it to her son, whose estate she saw to be not well able to bear more than it was already charged withal. And though this kind of asking, where some civility scarce leaves a liberty of refusing, might be a kind of robbery, yet she was freed from that apprehension by imagining all others to be of her own humour, who would sincerely much rejoice (as has been said already) to find that what she could spare at the present, would be acceptable and beneficial to others (taking it always for the greatest delight in the world to be able to do a pleasure to any), ⟨and⟩ but though this did for some time not wholly deceive her expectation, yet she soon saw the willingness as well as proportion decrease; and that, though those she first sought to in this kind were by the novelty and unusedness of it drawn to show a glad readiness (as some did with much civility), yet to the others, after, it being (by their hearing what she had done) less new and strange, was less welcomely entertained, and so was not long before it brought no other thing but contempt with it (as her inward friends who had persuaded her from it had told her it would), which she received contentedly, though not gladly, ⟨And⟩ and half a year before her death (being then far in a consumption) she was so wholly neglected that she was not looked after nor succoured in any kind, by no one from whom she might have expected it by any title or relation of the world. Yet God so provided that nothing was wanting to her, she being faithfully assisted in all to her last by her inward private Catholic friends; and very near her death, her eldest son, then newly informed how it was (she having forborne herself to let him know her extremity for fear to oppress him; and, for that she had by her former doing (which was not like to be very pleasing to him, could he have helped it) seemed more to take herself out of his care), came to town with his wife on purpose to remedy it; which he did for what appeared at the present, but she (out of the much sense she had of his decreasing estate and great charge) did not make known to him what was farther necessary, so as he left her much as he found her till, being farther advertised by others, he took order with his mother-in-law, then in London, entreating her to see all provided for her that she should need; which she did, being most kindly careful of her.

She lived to see six of her children (by God's great mercy) Catholics and out of the danger ⟨being⟩ living amongst their Protestant friends might have put them into, being all out of England, four of them clothed with the habit of St Benett[174] (she much rejoicing to leave them in the number of the children of such a father), a fifth[175] having desired and hoping for the same happiness amongst the Benedictines at Paris, whom she recommended to the care of her Benedictine friends, in particular to Father ⟨John⟩, Prior of Doway[176] that now is, (who often visited her on her deathbed, she not being ignorant how much a great friend he was to hers; whose great care and charity (towards him) that son of hers has experienced in a very extraordinary degree in these times of so much necessity; ⟨as⟩ and her soul has found no less from his hands, since her death, by his prayers and masses, which he has most freely and liberally afforded to it, saying for her more than a hundred masses) and by ⟨father John/ him ... for her father⟩ and by the same Fa[ther] Prior she did humbly recommend him to Father Clement,[177] then President, who showed much care of him (he being, in the time of his office, clothed and professed) and no less was he pleased to show in a great degree of ⟨the elder⟩ her elder son at

---

[174] St. Benedict; that is, her daughters Lucy, Mary, and Elizabeth, who became nuns in 1638, and Anne, who followed in 1639.

[175] Henry (or Placid). The register of admissions to Lincoln's Inn contains the following entry for 28 September 1654: "Henry Cary, 4th [surviving] son of Henry Lord Viscount Falkland, dec'd," so it appears that Henry abandoned his religious vocation and followed his brother Patrick back to England and the study of law. (See [Fairfax Harrison], *The Devon Carys*, 464n.)

[176] *Marginal annotation in Patrick Cary's hand*: Meutisse [John Meutisse, alias Northall, who died in 1666, is recorded to have aided the nunnery at Cambray in its beginnings. He was elected prior of St. Gregory's at Douay in 1641.]

[177] *Marginal annotation in Patrick Cary's hand*: Reyner [Clement Reyner, who came from an ancient Yorkshire family, studied and subsequently taught at Douay. He served as Procurator of the Congregation in Germany and twice as its president; he became the first abbot of Lambspring, which he founded, and died at Hildesheim in 1651.]

Rome; whom she had sent thither, being recommended to Cardinal Barbarin[178] by the Queen's most Excellent Majesty; whose Eminency incited by so powerful a recommendation, and his own charity, showed him much favour. And in this occasion she was very highly obliged to Mr Mountague,[179] both for the persuading her to the sending him thither (or at least much encouraging her in it) and for his most free and willing offering himself to be employed by the Queen to make the recommendations, as also for his performing it so efficaciously and advantageously; which her Majesty has been graciously pleased (since her [Elizabeth Cary's] death) to renew and reinforce on several occasions in his favour.[180]

She died about the beginning of these troubles of England, in which (had she lived) she would have received the most insupportable affliction she had ever had in the death of her two sons (killed in the wars),[181]

---

[178] Cardinal Francesco Barberini (1597–1679), papal vice-chancellor and nephew of Pope Urban VIII.

[179] Walter Montagu (1603–77) was Lettice Morison Cary's second cousin and author of the pastoral play *The Shepherd's Paradise* (1633), in which Henrietta Maria and other ladies of the court acted. When he was sent to France in 1624 to negotiate her marriage to Charles I, he had formed a friendship with Henrietta Maria which proved to be long lasting. Upon converting to Roman Catholicism, he wrote a letter in November 1635 to his father, the first earl of Manchester, justifying his decision. The letter was published, and so was a reply by Lucius Cary, his *Discourse of Infallibility*. (See p. 269, below.) In 1643 he was arrested with letters sealed with the arms of France and addressed to the king and queen of England. He was imprisoned in the Tower of London until 1647 and eventually banished in 1649. In exile he enjoyed the continued patronage of Henrietta Maria and became abbot of St. Martin near Pontoise.

[180] Patrick Cary subsisted on pensions from Henrietta Maria and, later, Pope Urban VIII until 1650, when he returned to England and unsuccessfully sought support from his relatives. In 1651 he was admitted to Lincoln's Inn but does not seem to have pursued his study of law. In the same year he married Susan Uvedale, the niece of his sister Victoria's husband. During the remainder of his brief life he tried his fortunes in the West Indies and Ireland, as well as England. He was also a literary amateur, whose verses were first published in 1771 and again, in 1819, by Sir Walter Scott under the title *Trivial Poems and Triolets . . . by Patrick Carey*. (For a modern edition, see *The Poems of Patrick Cary*, ed. Sister Veronica Delany [Oxford: Clarendon Press, 1978].) He died in 1657, but his grandson, Lucius Henry Cary, eventually succeeded to the family title as sixth Viscount Falkland.

[181] Lucius (d. 1643) and Lorenzo, or Laurence (d. 1642).

without any sign of hope,[182] for otherwise she would have thought their lives could not have been better lost than in the cause of his Majesty, except in the immediate cause of God.

She had read very exceeding much: poetry of all kinds, ancient and modern, in several languages, all that ever she could meet; history very universally, especially all ancient Greek and Roman historians, and chroniclers whatsoever of her own country; and the French histories very thoroughly, of most other countries something, though not so universally; of the ecclesiastical history very much, most especially concerning its chief pastors. Of books treating of moral virtue or wisdom ⟨and natural knowledge as Pliny/(such as Seneca, Plutarch's *Morals*, and natural knowledge as Pliny/ and of late ones, such as French Mountaine [Montaigne], and English Bacon)[183]⟩ she had read very many when she was young, not without making her profit of them. Of the Fathers ⟨ve⟩ she had read much, particularly the works of St Justin Martyr, St Jerome, very much of St Augustin, and of St Gregory,[184] and of very many others some things, as she could meet with them, ⟨yet⟩ most of what she read of them ⟨was⟩ being translations, in Spanish, Italian, or French, at least for many year. Of controversy, it may be said she had read most that has been

[182] *Marginal annotation*: God be thanked, there is great hopes they both died Catholics [This is recopied possibly by Patrick, in the inner margin, from a marginal note which is certainly in Patrick's handwriting. The original note, which was largely cropped when the MS was bound, is not reproduced verbatim, since in what remains of the original "some" appears between "thanked" and "there."]

[183] Seneca (3 B.C.–A.D. 65) wrote not only tragedies but also many moral essays in prose; Plutarch (46–120), the author of *Parallel Lives*, was equally well known in the Renaissance for the essays and treatises gathered under the heading of *Moralia* (or *Opera Moralia*); Michel de Montaigne (1533–92) and Sir Francis Bacon (1561–1626) were the best-known essayists of the Renaissance.

[184] St. Justin Martyr (c. 100–165) was a Christian apologist of whose works significant parts are extant; they vindicate the truth of Christianity and expound its moral values. St. Jerome (342–420), the most distinguished scholar among the early fathers, translated the Bible into Latin (or, in some instances, reworked previous translations); he also wrote notable letters and theological polemics. St. Augustine (354–430) was formidably prolific; his *Confessions* and *The City of God* remain among his most widely read works. The writings of St. Gregory, or Gregory the Great (540–604), elected pope in 590, include the *Regula pastoralis* ("Pastoral Care," which defines the office and duties of a bishop), the *Moralia* (a commentary on the Book of Job), and the *Dialogues* (which records the miracles and visions of the holy in Italy).

written, ⟨of these⟩ having before she was a Catholic read the writings of all kinds of many Protestant authors; as much of the works of Luther and Calvin and more such; of all English writers of name, of past, Latimer, Jewell,[185] and divers others; and of their newer divines of note whatsoever came forth; and much French of the same matter; after she was a Catholic, some Catholic ones (being well read in all the works of Sir Thomas More before), and she did always continue with leave to read Protestant controvertists. She had read something of very many other things, but in these she had fixed most.

She had writ, besides what hath been named (and innumerable slight things in verse), only one paper of controversy. When Mr Mountague defended that faith with his pen for which he hath now the honour to suffer (together with his services to their Majesties, the second glorious cause)[186] in a letter to his father (in answer to one of his, to him), which was much praised by all; her son writing in answer to it, she writ something against his answer, taking notice in the beginning of it of the fulfilling of his prophecy who said he came not to bring peace but the sword;[187] the son being here against his father, and the mother against her son, where his faith was the question; which paper was thought the best thing she ever writ, and by him it was against was ⟨confessed⟩ acknowledged for a sufficient answer to his, though not satisfactory to him; and that it was, certainly, enough to confute a Protestant clearly; and to answer it again it would be necessary to go farther and deny more than he had done in his.

She had conversed ⟨very⟩ much and with those that were very capable of several conditions and qualities, the conversation of her friends being

---

[185] When Henry VIII broke with the Church of Rome, Hugh Latimer (1490–1555) was one of the preachers who most effectively promulgated the principles of the Reformation; during the reign of Queen Mary, he, along with Nicholas Ridley, the Protestant bishop of Rochester, was burned at the stake in Oxford. His writings consist of his *Sermons*. John Jewel (1522–71) was the chief apologist of the Elizabethan settlement; his *Apologia ecclesiae Anglicanae* (1562) defined the position of the Church of England in relation to the Church of Rome and laid the foundation for most subsequent Anglican theology.

[186] See note 179.

[187] *Marginal annotation*: Ma[tthew]: 10 ˙ [34].

the greatest delight of her life; yet she was never much afflicted for the death or absence of any. From which much conversation and reading she seemed to have much experience in some kinds; for, though she were most forgetful and heedless in small ordinary things, yet in passages[188] of note (of which she had been acquainted with very many) she had a certain and clear memory; but in those things which had no relation to one another, she was apt to confound time strangely, that seeming to her ⟨later⟩ to be later (at least on the sudden) which, being of more importance, was more perfect in her memory than smaller things ⟨happing⟩ which had happened long after. And for what she had read, her memory was good and sure.

She spoke very much and earnestly; her heart was very open, and she easily known; nor was it hard, for those near about her, to get some power over her. Her fashion was in nothing graceful; her neglect, through forgetfulness, of all customary civilities was so notable that it was passed into a privilege; ⟨and⟩ but though her heedlessness in this was so gross that she has divers times come to see such as she respected most and, being come into the room where they were, has so wholly forgotten them, and the intention she came for, as never to mark them, but to go forth again without ever speaking to them; and that she ⟨never⟩ rarely heeded whomsoever she met, and scarce knew any (but those she conversed with daily) when she did not see them in the same place she was used to see them; and that a short absence did make her quite forget their faces (not them) whom she knew exceeding well; and though all this seemed not possibly in her power to help, yet such power on her mind had the high duty she owed the King, that she has been observed never to have forgot his presence, though she hath had occasion given her (and by his Majesty) to make her mistake or forget herself, a-purpose to try her. She was one very generally known, and to ⟨her acquainta⟩ those that knew her, much known; and her faults, it may be, did appear first and did seem greater at some distance than to those nearest hand.

But yet she always seemed to have a most hearty good will to God and his service; and she was a most sound sincere Catholic, greatly coveting

[188] Occurrences.

the conversion of others, in order to which she could have felt nothing that she had suffered; and, as she had ever, from her first being so, gladly made profession of it, so at her death she was most careful to avoid making any show to the contrary; for being then often visited by her son's mother-in-law, my Lady Morison (who was a most earnest Protestant), and using to lie in some kind of trances, in which she was not perfectly herself, fearing she might in one of those say or do anything that might appear less Catholic, should my Lady Morison urge her, ⟨she⟩ when she did not know herself what she did; she did earnestly desire a Catholic friend of hers, Mrs Plat (who assisted her painfully and carefully to her last; and who showed herself so faithful and true a friend to her, even to and after her death, that her eldest son found much cause to give her thanks for her care of his mother; and her Protestant daughter no less to acknowledge herself and all her mother's children greatly beholding to her for it) not to leave her at any time alone with my Lady Morison in this regard. She did most highly reverence all the precepts, ordinances, and even ceremonies of the Catholic Church. She made great account and most use of those prayers to which the Church hath given a particular worth by making them hers, which saying she did more hope to be heard as a child of the Church, though, as she always acknowledged herself, a most imperfect one. She was ever ⟨very?⟩ desirous to show a very high respect to priests, making so great account of their blessings that (as forgetful as she was of worldly customs and ceremonies) she never forgot to ask them but often where she was when she did it, asking them sometimes in streets and public places (in England), afore she was aware.

She honoured very much all the orders in God's Church, all being most welcome to her house, which yet the Benedictine Fathers did the honour to frequent most; to which order she always had the most especial devotion, having received from it the highest and greatest obligations; for, besides that (which she ever highly esteemed so) which she had in common with all her country (as being of that nation that hath received its Christianity from the Benedictine apostleship),[189] she had many

---

[189] It was from a monastery organized according to the Benedictine rule that in 596 Gregory the Great sent forth Augustine of Canterbury (d. 605) and forty companions on a mission to evangelize in England.

particular ones, being herself in part satisfied in religion and reconciled by a Benedictine; and to one of the same order owing wholly (under God) the conversion of her children; her ghostly fathers being from the first to the last of this order; and she herself having been, a little more than a year before her death, admitted into the Confraternity of St Benett by Father ⟨John⟩ Prior of Doway, receiving from his hands the little scapular; and, though she were far from taking upon her to give her children a vocation to religion (knowing well that only belonged to God, nor was she a mother that desired to be rid of them, how much care soever their being with her might cost her) or ⟨from?⟩ seeking to oversway theirs in the choice of the order, yet as she did most willingly give them her consent for the first, so it cannot be denied but she did give it them more gladly to the Order of St Benett, taking a particular joy to see them called to that.

But so well did she esteem a vocation to religion was to be the work of God that she never went about to incline that daughter[190] to it (whom she had offered to our Blessed Lady, with a promise to further her being a nun), esteeming the discharge of her promise to be in performing her part, which (besides doing all that lay in her to have her a Catholic, which she had done with effect) she conceived to consist only in procuring her all means for it and removing impediments, if God should please to give her a vocation, which she believed to be his part and not hers; but, as it may be our Lady's accepting her vow ⟨did⟩ might have obtained her daughter the grace of vocation, so it was certain that vow did much in inclining her to consent to it, which at that time she would else have had difficulty enough to have been brought to: for that, [Mary] being the last of her daughters that had a desire to be a nun, and she [Elizabeth Cary], not apprehending she had any such intention, had set herself to place her where she might be most to her own content (which she judged would be less at home with her, when all the rest of them should be gone) and where she might have the ⟨more⟩ most free exercise of her religion, under the greatest and most powerful protection in the kingdom; and, as it was always more hard to divert her from any design she had once conceived, though never so unlikely (which yet this was not), than to make her quit

---

[190] Mary Cary.

the possession of anything she had in present; so having here already
proposed this to all it concerned, or that were to concur to the effecting
it, (her daughter having then a desire to let her know her intention, which
she had deliberated with herself for some time) it was supposed it would
be the harder to bring her to be content at first; though they knew well
that, when she saw anything resolved on, and that there was no remedy
for it, how contrary soever it were to her, she generally ⟨was⟩ soon made
herself no less content with it than if she had chosen it: but those that
were to propose this to her were scarce entered her chamber for that purpose (not knowing well how to bring it out, as much apprehending her
first receiving it) when she happened (without their giving any occasion
for it) to speak of this vow and oblation to our Blessed Lady, ending it
with saying that therefore she should have had most scruple to have
opposed this daughter, had she had a desire to be religious, of all the rest;
not dreaming of her having any such thought, when they made use of this
opportunity and let her know what they came for; she, though it came
very unexpected to her, yet being taken in the instant when the memory
and fervour of her vow were fresh, consented without saying one word
against it, yet not without signs of strife; and after confessed, had she not
been caught with those words in her mouth, she should have found many
reasons against it and have had much difficulty to have been drawn from
a design she liked so well (being so far forwards and disposed to effecting) to that which was so contrary to it, and which at most was but
a trial (neither knew she how sudden the resolution might have been, and
so subject to change before begun to be put in execution) and for which
she saw no appearance of means to bring it to pass, it sounding but
strangely to propose to Protestants to furnish her (with what was necessary) for religion. Yet having consented and resolved on it (though she
saw what she should otherwise have thought) without making any
objections (but contrarily, having much ⟨resen⟩ hearty resentment of the
little reluctancy which she had had at the instant of hearing it first, as a
most great ingratitude for so high a benefit, to receive with (though never
so small) resistance so great a mercy of God as the ⟨accomplishment⟩ ac-
ceptation of her vow in the accomplishment of it, so beyond her hopes
or expectation), she set herself, after her ordinary manner, with confidence and diligence to bring it about, and beyond all expectation she

found her son (being first assured it was his sister's own desire only, as indeed he could have no cause to doubt other) ready to do all she asked (though he had many ways many reasons to the contrary), which he effected much the more speedily and willingly, the Queen being pleased to do him the honour and his sister the charity to lay her powerful command upon him in that behalf. And her Majesty did also speak so earnestly in the favour of another of them to the King that she procured her what was desired, in a time when the paying of a debt might deserve to be accounted no less (if not more) a benefit than a gift would have been in another former time.

God Almighty did also mercifully grant her a large time with all means and commodity to prepare herself well for death, to which she did most seriously apply herself the last half year of her life; our Lord having discharged her of the care of her children (all which, by his providence, were in the way to be settled out of England and the occasion of danger of heresy), she took better order for her debts which yet remained than could have been expected; and disposed herself for death by much exercise of contrition, resignation, and confidence, ⟨with?⟩ which she expected and received willingly, and with much hope and great acknowledgement of God's great mercy in all, and particularly in her last sickness, in which she was very quiet, pliable and easily ruled, which were not very natural to her; and though all her life before she had a most dreadful apprehension of death, yet now, being on her deathbed questioned by ⟨Father John⟩ Father Prior of Doway,[191] what disposition she was in as to resigned receiving it, she affirmed she was desirous of it. When, being told by him she ought to be content to remain as she was as long as it should please God, leaving herself in his hands, with a perfect indifferency, she answered, that if it were best and that ⟨if⟩ it were God's will she should continue as she was, she resigned herself entirely to it, and that she was indifferent to live or die as it should best please him. In which preparation to death, it is very like she was much helped by her being conversant in the works of Blosius, which it may well be believed the providence of our Lord did for that end put into her hand. ⟨as it is no doubt it was that father's chief design who set her upon the translation, who,

---

[191] *Marginal annotation in Patrick Cary's hand*: John Meutisse.

being a most true friend to her and hers, hath ever showed himself a most earnest seeker of their goods in all things.)

She, having received all the sacraments of the Church from Father Placid's[192] hands, then her ghostly father, and been assisted in this last occasion by the prayers and visits of her Catholic and Benedictine friends, died without any agony quietly as a child, being wholly spent by her disease the   day of October, the year of our Lord 1639, being three- or four-and-fifty year old.

She was buried by her Majesty's permission in her chapel, where the office was performed for her by the charity of the Capuchin Fathers (who were in her life ever ready to do her any courtesy, and she was in particular much beholding to Father John Maria and Father Angell[193] for a great favour which with much pains they procured for her and offered her), and though she had not any Catholic child capable of giving to have her prayed for, yet she found those that freely of their own accord were mindful of her; and besides what many monks, her friends, did privately, the Convents of Doway and Cambray did of their charities sing mass solemnly for her. And for what may yet be wanting to her to suffer in purgatory, may it please God to inspire his servants to assist her with their prayers and sacrifices, and of his mercy give rest to her soul.

---

[192] *Marginal annotation*: Placid Gascoign [John Placid Gascoigne, 1599–1681, a Benedictine from a Yorkshire Catholic family, ultimately became abbot of Lambspring in Germany].

[193] Possibly Angelus à Sancto Francisco (otherwise Richard Mason), 1601–78, a learned Franciscan of the Strict Observance.

APPENDIX A

PASSAGES FROM LODGE'S
TRANSLATION OF JOSEPHUS (1602)

CHAP. XI. *HERODE* BEING INCENSED BY FALSE ACCUSATIONS,
PUTTETH HIS WIFE *MARIAMME* TO DEATH.

[*In the margin:*] *The yeare of the world 3935, before Christs birth 29.*

[XV. vii. 1] But as soone as he [Herod] returned unto his kingdome, he found all his houshold troubled, and both his wife *Mariamme* and her mother *Alexandra* grievously displeased with him. For they supposing (and not without cause) that they were not shut uppe in that Castle for their securities sake, but as it were in a prison; so that in as much as they neither might make use of other mens, nor enjoy their own goods, they were highly discontented. *Mariamme* also supposed that her husband did but dissemble his love, rather for his owne profit and com-moditie, th[a]n for any intire affection he bare towards her. But nothing more grieved her, but that she had not any hope to live after him, if so be he should happen to die, especially for the order he had left as concerning her: neither could she ever forget what commandement before that time he had left with *Joseph*; so that by all meanes possible, she laboured to winne the affections of those that had the charge of her, and especially *Sohemus*, knowing verie well that her safetie depended wholy on his hands. Who in the beginning behaved him-self verie wisely and faithfully, containing himselfe verie circumspectly within the bounds of his commission; but after these Ladies had with prettie presents and feminine flatteries mollified and wrought him by little and little, at last he blabbed out all that which the king had commanded him; especially, for that he hoped not that he should returne with the same power and authoritie, which be-fore he had: and for that cause he thought thus in himselfe, that without incur-ring any danger in regard of *Herod*, he might greatly gratifie the Ladies; who in all likelihood should not be deprived of that dignitie, wherein they were at that time; but would returne him the like kindnes when *Mariamme* should be Queene, or next unto the king. Furthermore, he hoped that if *Herode* also should return with all things answerable to his desires, that he would performe nothing without his wives consent; or upbraid him with the act, if she contradicted: for he knew too well that the king loved her in such sort, as it was impossible to equall or expresse his affections; and for these causes he disclosed the trust that was committed unto him. But *Mariamme* was verie sore displeased to heare that there was no end of her miseries, but they were altogither united and tied to the dangers of *Herode*; and she oftentimes wished that he might never more returne againe in safetie, supposing that her life with him should be verie intollerable, all which she afterwards dissembled not, but openly confessed that which afflicted her with discontent. [2] For when as *Herode* beyond all expectation arrived in his countrey, being adorned with mightie fortune, he first of all, as it became him, certified his wife of his good tidings and happy successe, whom onely amongst all other his friends and wives, he embraced and saluted, for the pleasing conversation and affection that was in her. But she, whilest he repeated unto her these fortunate events of his affaires, rather enter[tai]ned the same with a displeasant attention, th[a]n applauding joy: and these affections [i.e., emotions] of hers likewise she could not conceale. For at such time as he folded his armes about her necke, she unfolded her sorrow in her sighes; so simple and unfained were her affections; and seemed rather to be displeased th[a]n appeased by his narrations. Whereupon *Herode* was sore troubled, perceiving these things not onely suspected, but also fully manifest: but above all things he was distracted, when he considered the incredible and apparant hatred that his wife had conceived against him, which in such sort incensed him that he could not resist the love that had attainted him; so that he neither could continue in wrath, nor listen long to peace; and being unresolved in himselfe, he now was attempted by this; straight distracted by a contrarie affection: so much was his mind travailed between love & hatred, that when as oftentimes he desired to punish the womans pride, his heart by loves mediation failed him in the enterprise. For nothing did more torment him th[a]n this feare, least executing his displeasure against her, he should by this meanes more grievously wound himselfe, thorow the desire he bare unto his deceased delight. [3] Whilest thus he was sweltered and devoured in his passions, and conceived sinister opinions against *Mariamme* his wife; *Salome* his sister and his mother having an inckling of his discontents, thought that they had gotten a fit opportunitie to expresse and execute their hatred towards *Mariamme*: for which cause they conferred with *Herode*, and whetted his spleene and displeasure with varietie of slanders, sufficient at one assault to engender hatred, and kindle his jealousie against her. To these reproches of theirs, he lent no unwilling eares: yet had he not the heart to attempt any thing against his wife, or to give free credit to their report, notwithstanding his displeasure increased, and was inflamed more and more against her, for that neither she could colour her care and discontents, nor he containe himselfe from exchanging his love into hatred: and perhaps at that time he had published some fatall doome against her, had not a happy messenger brought him word, that *Anthony* and *Cleopatra* being dead, *Cæsar* was become Lord of Ægypt: for which cause hasting forward to meete and entertaine him, he left his family in that present estate. Upon his departure he recommended *Mariamme* to *Sohemus*, giving him great thanks for the care he had had of her, and granted him in way of gratuitie a part of Jewry to governe.

When *Herode* was arrived in Ægypt, and had friendly and familiarly conferred with *Cæsar*, he was highly honoured by him: for *Cæsar* gave him those foure hundreth frenchmen that were of *Cleopatras* guard, and restored that part of his countrey unto him againe, which was taken away and spoiled by her. He annexed also unto his kingdome Gadara, Hippon, and Samaria, and on the sea coasts the Cities of Gaza, Anthedon, Joppe, with the tower of Straton: [4] which when he had obtained, he grew more mightie th[a]n before: And after he had accompanied *Cæsar* as far as Antioch, he returned into his owne countrey. Upon his arrivall, he found that fortune which was favourable unto him abroad, too froward at home, especially in regard of his wife, in whose affection before time he seemed to be most happy. For he was as inwardly touched with lawfull love of *Mariamme*, as any other of whom the Histories make report: and as touching her, she was both chast and faithfull unto him; yet had she a certaine womanly imperfection and naturall frowardnesse, which was the cause that shee presumed too much upon the intire affection wherewith her husband was intangled; so that without regard of his person, who had power and authoritie over others, she entertained him oftentimes very outragiously: All which he endured patiently, without any shew of discontent. But *Mariamme* upbraided and publikely reproched both the kings mother and sister, telling them that they were but abjectly and basely borne. Whereupon there grew a great enmitie and unrecoverable hatred betweene the Ladies; and from thence also there arose an occasion of greater accusations and calumniations th[a]n before. These suspitions were nourished amongst them, for the space of one whole yeere after *Herodes* returne from *Cæsar*; and finally this long contrived, and fore-imagined hatred at last brake out violently upon this occasion that ensueth. When as about midday the king had withdrawne himselfe into his chamber to take his rest, he called *Mariamme* unto him to sport with her, being incited thereunto by the great affection that he bare unto her. Upon this his commaund she came in unto him; yet would she not lie with him, nor entertaine his courtings with friendly acceptance, but upbraided him bitterly with her fathers and brothers death. The king tooke these reprochfull words in verie evil part, & was almost ready to strike her, but his sister hearing a greater stir and noise within th[a]n was usuall, sent in the butler, who long before that time was suborned by her, whom she commanded to tell the king, that *Mariamme* had prepared a drinke for him to incite and quicken him unto love, willing him that if the king should be mooved thereat, and should

demaund what he meant, he should certifie him, that *Mariamme* having prepared
a poison for his grace, had dealt with him to deliver it to his majestie. Charging
him moreover, that if the king in hearing him speake of this potion, should
seeme to be mooved therewith, that then he should proceede no further in his
discourse. He therefore (being in this manner before hand instructed what he
ought to doe) at that very instant was sent in to discover his treacherie unto the
king; for which cause with a sober and staied countenance he entred in unto him,
being seriously and well prepared to discourse, and told him that *Mariamme* had
bribed him to present his Majestie with an amorous cup of drinke. Now when
he perceived that the king was troubled with these words, he prosecuted his discourse, alleaging that the potion was a certaine medicine which *Mariamme* had
given him, the vertue whereof he knew not, which he had received according as
he had told him, knowing that it concerned both his owne securitie, and the
kings safetie.

[*In the margin:*] *The yeare of the world 3936, before Christs birth 28.*

Herode, who before this was highly displeased, hearing these words, was so
much the more incensed: for which cause he presently commanded *Mariammes*
most faithfull servant to be examined by torments, as concerning the poison,
supposing that it was impossible for her to undertake any thing whatsoever,
without his privitie. He being tired and tormented after this cruell manner, confessed nothing of that for which he was tortured, but declared unto the king that
the hatred which his wife had conceived against him, proceeded from certaine
words that *Sohemus* had told her. Scarcely had he finished these words, but that
the king cried out with a loud voice, saying, that *Sohemus,* who before time had
beene most faithfull both to him and his kingdome, would not have declared
these his privie commands, except there had been some more inward familiari-
tie and secrecie betwixt him and *Mariamme:* for which cause he presently commanded his ministers to lay hands on *Sohemus,* and to put him to death. As for
his wife, he drew her to her triall, and to this effect he assembled his most familiar friends, before whom he began to accuse her with great spight and
spleene, as touching these potions and poisons aforesaid; wherin he used intemperate and unseemly speeches, and such as for their bitternesse did ill become him in cause of justice; so that in the end the assistants [i.e., those present],
seeing the butte and bent of his desire, pronounced sentence of death against
her: which being past, both he, and all other the assistants were of this opinion,
that she should not so speedily be executed, but that she should be kept close
prisoner in some sure place of the pallace. But by *Salomes* sollicitations *Herode* was
incited to hasten her death, for that she alleaged that the king ought to feare,
least some sedition should be raised amongst the people, if he should keepe her
alive in prison. And by this meanes *Mariamme* was led unto her death.

[5] *Alexandra* her mother considering the estate of the time, and fearing no lesse mischiefe from *Herodes* hands, th[a]n her daughter was assured of; she undecently changed her minde, and abjectedly laid aside her former courage, and magnanimitie. For intending to make it knowne, that she was neither partie nor privie to those crimes, wherewith *Mariamme* was charged, she went out to meete her daughter, and entertained her injuriously, protesting publikely that she was a wicked woman, & ungrateful towards her husband; and that she wel deserved the punishment that was adjudged her, for that she durst be so bold to attempt so hainous a fact, neglecting to requite her husbands intire love, with her unfained loyaltie. Whilest thus dishonestly she counterfaited her displeasure, and was readie to pull *Mariamme* by the haire, the assistants, according to her desert, condemned her generally for her shamefull hypocrisie: but she that was led to be punished, convicted her by her mild behaviour. For first of all, she gave her no answere; neither was any waies altered by her reproches, neither would so much as cast her eie upon her; making it appeare, that she discreetly concealed and covered her mothers imperfections, & was agrieved that she had so openly shewed so great indignitie: expressing for her owne part a constant beha[v]iour; and going to her death without chaunge of colour, so that those that beheld her, perceived in her a kind of manifest courage and nobilitie, even in her utmost extremitie. [6] Thus died *Mariamme*, having beene a woman that excelled both in continence and courage: notwithstanding that she defaulted somewhat in affabilitie and impatience of nature: for the rest of her parts, she was of an admirable and pleasing beautie, and of such a cariage in those companies wherein she was intertained, that it was impossible to expresse the same, in that she surpassed all those of her time; which was the principall cause that she lived not graciously and contentedly with the king. For being entertained by him, who intirely loved her, and from whom she received nothing that might discontent her, she presumed upon a great and intemperate libertie in her discourse. She disgested also the losse of her friends [i.e., relatives] verie hardly, according as in open termes she made it known unto the king: whereby also it came to passe, that both *Herodes* mother, and sister, and himselfe likewise grew at ods with her, and in especiall her husband, from whom onely she expected no hard measure.

[7] After her death the king began more powerfully to be inflamed in his affections, who before times, as we have declared, was alreadie miserably distracted. For neither did he love after the common manner of maried folke, but whereas almost even unto madnes he nourished this his desire, he could not be induced by the too unbridled manners of his wife to alay the heat of his affection, but that daily more and more by doting on her, he increased the same. And all that time especially he supposed that God was displeased with him, for the death of *Mariamme* his wife. Oftentimes did he invocate her name, and more often undecently lamented he her. And notwithstanding he devised all kinds of delights and sports that might be imagined, by preparing banquets, and inviting guests

with princely hospitalitie, to passe away the time, yet all those profited him nothing. For which cause he gave over the charge and administration of his kingdome. And in such sort was he overwhelmed with griefe, that oftentimes he commaunded his ministers to call his wife *Mariamme*, as if as yet she had beene alive. Whilest thus he was affected, there befell a pestilence within the citie, that consumed a great sort of the people, and the better part of the nobilitie, and each man interpreted that this punishment was inflicted by God upon men, for the unjust death of the Queene. Thus the kings discontents being by these meanes increased, he at last hid himselfe in a solitarie wildernesse, under pretext of hunting; where afflicting himselfe incessantly, at last he fell into a most grievous sicknes. This disease of his was an inflammation or paine in the necke: he seemed also in some sort to rave and waxe mad; neither could any remedies relieve him of his agony; but when as the sicknes seemed rather to increase, all men at last grewe almost desperate of his recovery. For which cause his phisition, partly in respect of the contumacy of his disease, partly, because in so great daunger there was not any free election of diet, they gave him leave to taste whatsoever best pleased his appetite, committing the uncertaine event of his health to the hands of fortune.

Appendix B

―――

TEXTUAL COLLATION FOR *MARIAM*

The collation records both substantive emendations adopted by this edition and its departures from the spelling and punctuation of the 1613 text. It does not routinely record the substitution of *j* for *i* or of *v* for *u*, as required by modern orthography, variations between roman and italic type (or in the forms of the letter *s*), or differences in capitalization. However, when the 1613 text is cited for other reasons, the original form of the spelling and type is reproduced. The insertion of apostrophes to mark elisions is noted, except in the case of terminal *d*'s (so, for example, the change from *wandring* to *wand'ring* is recorded, but that from *murderd* to *murder'd* is not), and all apostrophes that have been added to indicate a possessive form are recorded. On the other hand, the addition of apostrophes that normalize the form (for example, of *tis* to *'tis*) without affecting either sense or pronunciation has not been noted. Accents that have been added to aid scansion do not appear in the textual collation; since no such accents appear in the 1613 edition, all markings of this kind are editorial. Abbreviations of speechheadings in the original text (for example, *Alex.* for *Alexandra* or *Nun.* for *Nuntio*) have been silently expanded.

Textual changes are keyed to line numbers wherever possible. However, editorial emendations that are not within a numbered line appear in sequence between the appropriate lines and are identified by abbreviations: sc. head. (scene heading), sp. name (speaker's name), and s.d. (stage direction).

TITLE

Tragedy] Tragedie
Fair Queen] Faire Queene
lady] Ladie

DRAMATIS PERSONAE
missing from all copies except Hu and Ho

Salome, Herod's] *Salome, Herods*
Antipater, his son by [Doris]] *Antipater his sonne by Salome*
Alexandra, Mariam's] *Alexandra, Mariams*
[Silleus]] *Sillius*
[Pheroras], Herod's] *Pharoras, Herods*
[Babas'] first Son] *Babus first Sonne*
[Babas'] second Son] *Babus second Sonne*
[Ananell]] *Annanell*
Bu[tler],] *Bu.*
Company of Jews] *Companie of Iewes*

DEDICATORY SONNET
missing from all copies except Hu and Ho

Dedication Diana's Earthly Deputess] Dianaes Earthlie Deputesse
Mistress] Mistris
Cary] Carye
2 sister's] sisters
hearts] harts
cheer] cheere
3 fair] faire
me the sun] mee the Sunne
4 moon appear] Moone appeere
6 Phoebus'] *Phoebus*
7 beams] beames
8 you,] you
9 He] Hee
Sol, clear-sighted] *SOL*, cleare-sighted
10 Luna-like] *LVNA*-like
chaste] chast
11 He] Hee
be] bee,
12 obscurèd] obscurde

ARGUMENT

PAR. 1 Herod, the son] *Herod* the sonne
Idumean),] *Idumean,*)
favour] fauor
Romans] *Romanes*

Mariam,] *Mariam*
monarchy] Monarchie
[granddaughter]] daughrer
rightful] rightfull
beauty] beautie
he] hee
repudiated] reputia-/ted
whom he] whome hee
PAR. 2 Aristobulus] *Aristobolus*
Hircanus, his grandfather] *Hircanus* his Graund-father
wife's] Wiues
remove] remooue
[second]] first
[first]] second
PAR. 3 he] hee
forced to go answer] forc'te to goe answere
custody] custodie
Josephus,] *Iosephus*
he] hee
commandment] commaundement
he] hee
slain, she] slaine, shee
extremely] extreamely
Josephus] *Iosophus*
PAR. 4 Salome's] *Salomes*
he] hee
PAR. 5 meantime] meane time
again] againe
revisit] reuisite
overthrown Anthony,] ouerthrowne *Anthony*
PAR. 6 news] newes
death;] death,
willingness] willingnes
likelihood] likelyhood
rumour] Rumor
Sohemus,] *Sohemus*
succeeded Josephus'] suceeded *Iosephus*
Herod's return,] *Herods* returne
far from joy] farre from ioye
showed apparent signs] shewed apparant signes
He] Hee
win] winne
she,] she

conceal] conceale
brother's] Brothers
cup] Cuppe
who,] who
said] saide
poison] poyson
told] tolde
PAR. 7 jealousy] Iealousie
than] then
poison] poyson
away] a-/way
rashness] rashnes
intolerable] intollerable
frantic] Frantike
passion] passi-/on

ACT I, SCENE I
Sc. head. *Scena*] Scoena
1 public voice run on] publike voyce
  runne on?
2 Rome's] *Romes*
3 Pompey's] *Pompeis*
4 he] hee
5 do] doe
and,] and
lord,] Lord
7 sex] Sexe
8 us] us,
9 do I find, by self-experience] doe I
  finde by selfe Experience
10 yields] yeelds
grief] griefe
12 joy'd] ioyd
13 drops did rain] droppes did raine
14 again] againe
16 wish'd] wisht
17 wish'd] wisht
18 wish'd his carcass] wisht his Carkas
19 scorn] Scorne
20 firmly] firmely
23 Herod's jealousy] *Herods* Iealousie
24 constancy itself] constancie it selfe
25 he,] hee
liberty] libertie
26 shun] shunne
27 chaste a scholar] chast a Scholler
heart] hart

28 learn] learne
than] then
29 lesson's] lessons
30 abhorr'd] abhord
31 memory] memorie
call] call,
32 love] loue,
33 him;] him,
34 another] an other
unmoisten'd] vnmoistned
35 Aristobulus, the [loveliest]] *Aristobolus*
  the lowlyest
36 angel's] Angels
appear,] appeare:
37 cruel] cruell
ruth;] ruth,
38 Herod's] *Herods*
hear] heare
39 speak] speake
40 yielded] yeelded
brother's] brothers
doom] dome
41 beauty] beautie
fury break] furie breake
42 tomb] Tombe
43 And,] And
grandsire,] Grandsire
requite] requite,
44 ascent,] Assent
45 murder'd] murdred
sprite] spright
47 happy] happie
Sohemus' [mind]] *Sohemus* maide
48 pity my distress'd estate!] pittie my
  distrest estate?
49 Herod's] *Herods*
trusty] trustie
find] finde
50 been] bene
51 bear] beare
52 news] newes
firmly] firmely
53 tear] teare
54 grief] griefe
56 seen] seene
57 milkmaid be] milke-maide bee
58 Than] Then

monarch of Judea's queen] Monarke of
  Iudeas Queene
59 love he wish'd] loue, he wisht
60 death] death,
vaunt-courier] vaunt-currier
61 than] then
63 discontent] discontent,
64 floods of tears] flouds of teares
drench'd] drencht
face!] face?
65 lament] lament,
66 lover's] louers
death's] deaths
67 Ay, now, mine eyes,] I now mine eyes
68 admirer and] admirer. And
lord.] Lord,
71 Why,] Why
methinks] me thinkes
72 freedom] freedome
unrestrain'd,] vnrestraind:
73 creep again] creepe agen
74 feign'd] faind
75 But, tears, fly back] But teares flie
  backe
banks] bankes
76 seen] seene
77 moan be spied] mone be spide
thanks] thankes
78 queen] Queene

ACT I, SCENE 2

Sc. head. *Scena*] Scoena
79 means] meanes
tears] teares
80 news] newes
tyrant's] *Tyrants*
81 brother's [murd'rer's] sake?] brothers
  murthers sake,
82 tear] teare
83 breathless trunk] breathles trunke
84 Edomite,] *Edomite*
Esau's heir] *Esaus* heire
85 Jacob's] *Iacobs*
crown] crowne
86 he,] he
wretch,] wretch
David's chair] *Dauids* chaire

87 No, David's soul,] No *Dauids* soule
bosom plac'd] bosome plac'te,
88 Abram,] *Abram*
89 toad disgrac'd] toade disgrac'te
90 Judah's] *Iudas*
been [fam'd]] bene faind
91 fatal enemy to royal] fatall enemie to
  royall
92 murder] murther
93 cruel] cruell
stood,] stood?
94 mild Hircanus'] milde *Hercanus*
95 gracious] gratious
ready] readie
97 he, ungrateful caitiff,] he vngratefull
  catiffe
withstand] withstand,
99 kingdom's] kingdomes
cruel] cruell
claim] claime
100 Esau's] *Esaus*
heir] heyre
103 Oh] O
Edom's] *Edoms*
derive,] deriue
104 cruel] cruell
105 son] sonne
107 bent,] bent?
108 characters] caracters
109 work thy heart's] worke thy hearts
111 sake] sake,
112 Aristobulus, yet doom'd] *Aristobolus.*
  Yet doomde
113 back] backe
warm] warme
114 miter settled] *Myter* setled
115 Oh,] Oh
less than] lesse then
116 oil] oyle
bring] bring:
117 bright;] bright,
118 anointed] annoynted
119 father] father,
son he slew] sonne he slewe,
120 prince-born] Prince borne
121 deem] deeme
123 fits he show'd] fits, he shewd

signs] signes
124 lunacy] lunacie
126 Hircanus' family] *Hercanus* familie
127 knows if he,] knowes if he
128 again] againe
130 wish'd] wisht
slain] slaine
Sp. name [*Mariam*]] Nun:
131 Doris! Alas,] *Doris,* Alas
132 coals] coales
rak'd] rakte
ago] agoe:
133 [Of] Mariam's love,] If *Mariams* loue
disgrac'd] disgrast
134 glory] glorie
overthrow] ouerthrowe
135 first-born son] first borne sonne
137 only] onely
own] owne
138 boys] boyes
royal] royall
139 style his heirs] stile his heyres
David's throne;] *Dauids* throne,
140 Alexander,] *Alexander*
141 majestic] Maiesticke
Solomon;] *Salamon,*
142 think] thinke
143 Why,] Why?
claim] claime
Alexander's] *Alexanders*
144 gold-adornèd lion-guarded chair]
   Gold adorned Lyon-guarded Chaire
145 David's] *Dauids*
146 Alexander's heir] *Alexanders* heire
147 than] then
148 think] thinke
than right] then right,
150 born to wear the crown] borne to
   weare the Crowne
despite] despight
151 tears] teares
152 passion's] passions
153 cheer] cheere
cheeks] cheekes
154 entertain] entertaine
hour] houre
155 Felicity] Felicitie

when she] when shee
finds] findes
156 habit] habite
cheerless look] cheerlesse looke
157 think] thinke
mind] minde
158 brook] brooke
159 Oh, keep] Oh keepe
whilst] whilest
her;] her,
go,] goe
160 return again] returne againe
161 year] yeere
endur'd] indur'd
162 su'd] sude
obtain] obtaine
164 beautify,] beautifie
166 woo] woe
Anthony?] *Anthony:*
167 prince's] Princes
do] doe
168 minions'] Mynions
seek to win] seeke to winne
169 Felicity] Felicitie
170 minion] Mynion
begin.] beginne,
171 sleight] slight
173 half] halfe
174 been overtaken] bene ouer-taken
176 festival] festiuall
gone;] gone,
177 he] hee
eat] eate
179 boy's] boyes
fairest seem] fayrest seeme
180 glanc'd] glaunst
Mariam's cheek] *Mariams* cheeke
181 deem] deeme
182 either] eyther
like] leeke
183 And,] And
either's beauty's] eythers beauties
184 other's] others
186 either's love] eithers loue,
other's] others
187 only] onely
190 brown] browne

clean forsaken,] cleane forsaken.
191 seek] seeke
been] bene,
192 firm] firme
wanèd] wayned
193 Anthonius'] *Anthonius*
seen] seene
194 hold] holde
195 Roman's] *Romans*
196 shown] showne
198 own] owne
199 empress] Emprise
201 press my tomb] presse my Toome
204 deal] deale
205 th'affairs] th'affaires
206 affairs] affaires

ACT I, SCENE 3

Sc. head. *Scena*] Scoena
207 Why,] Why?
208 suppliant] supliant
209 king.] King,
210 do] doe
Herod's] *Herods*
212 Herod's] *Herods*
213 than] then
crave] craue,
214 crown] Crowne
215 think] thinke
than] then
217 weep] weepe
discontent?] discontent,
218 causeless] causelesse
219 rein] raine
221 daughter's] daughters
far,] farre
maintain] maintaine
222 rejoic'd] reioyc'd
brother's] brothers
223 far!] farre,
woman, 'tis] woman t'is
224 seen] seene
225 Mariam's] *Mariams*
226 Judea's queen] *Iudeas* Queene
228 than] then
choler] collor

229 said than] sayd then
230 Salome's] *Salomes*
only scorn] onely scorne
231 Scorn] Scorne
held.] held,
232 brother's] brothers
seen] seene
233 birth] birth,
far excell'd] farre exceld
234 princess been] Princesse bene
235 parti-Jew] party Iew
parti-Edomite] party Edomite
236 mongrel] Mongrell
240 odds] ods
241 born] borne
242 Abraham's] *Abrahams*
244 black] blacke
I'll] ile
246 shameful] shamefull
husband's] husbands
247 reveal] reueale
248 pass'd] past
favourites] fauorites
249 meant not, I, a traitor to conceal]
ment not I, a traytor to conceale
250 minion] Mynion
slew] slue
251 mean] meane
252 slander'd] slandred
ear] eare
253 Self-guilt] Selfe-guilt
been [suspicion's]] bene suspitious
254 bear] beare
255 Salome's unsteadfast heart] *Salomes*
vnstedfast heart,
256 Josephus'] *Iosephus*
plac'd] plast
257 herself] her selfe,
us'd] vsde
art] art,
258 hapless] haplesse
unchaste] vnchast
259 Come,] Come
go] goe
boot] boote
260 foot] foote

ACT I, SCENE 4

Sc. head. *Scena*] Scoena
261 Salome] *Salome,*
style] stile
262 "foot"] foote,
Mariam? Herod's spirit] *Mariam Herods*
  spirit:
264 live,] liue
miss] misse
267 coals] Coales
269 plac'd] plast
271 vain] vaine,
272 be] bee
273 been] bene
275 been] beene
276 looks] lookes
[all eyes]] allyes
277 now, ill-fated] now ill Fated
278 itself is tied] it selfe is tide
279 now,] now
do] doe
Hebrew wrong,] Ebrew wrong
280 fair] faire
282 ago] agoe
284 certain] certaine
honour's] honours
287 Josephus' veins] *Iosephus* vaines
been stuff'd] bene stuft
289 love] loue,
290 Constabarus'] *Constabarus*
292 blush'd] blusht
293 wip'd] wipt
294 Impudency] Impudencie
295 work] worke
296 employ] imploy
297 cause] cause,
298 Keeps me [from]] Keepes me for
Arabian's] *Arabians*
299 Moses' laws] *Moses* lawes
300 Constabarus] *Contabarus*
remains] remaines
life.] life,
301 bear] beare
302 ease;] ease,
303 fate] fate:
305 privilege] priuiledge

306 barr'd] bard
307 than] then
309 I'll] Ile
custom-breaker] custome-breaker
begin] beginne
310 show my sex] shew my Sexe
freedom's door] freedomes doore
311 off'ring] offring
sin;] sinne,
312 law] lawe
poor] poore
314 future's] futures
316 sons of Babas] sonnes of *Baba*
317 divorce] diuorse
318 possess his room] possesse his
  roome
319 begg'd] begd
life,] life
been] bene
320 tongue, the hind'rer] tongue the
  hindrer
doom,] doome.
321 wand'ring] wandring
322 dream] dreame
change] chaunge
323 see, he] see he
last.] last,
324 him,] him
stay'd] staid

ACT I, SCENE 5

Sc. head. *Scena*] Soena
325 found, fair Salome, Judea's pride!]
  found faire *Salome Iudæas* pride,
326 wisdom] wisedome
327 deem] deeme
328 thee,] thee
than] then
prey] pray
329 devis'd] deuisde
devise;] deuise,
330 means] meanes
331 Salome?] *Salome,*
332 endeavours] indeuours
334 law-giver's] law-giuers
337 custom] custome

338 it;] it,
339 do] doe
do's] do'es
Sp. name Silleus] *Solleus*
341 Thinks] Thinkes
342 fair actions?] faire actions:
345 Arabia, joy] *Arabia* ioy
green] greene
346 happy] happie
347 beauty's queen] beauties Queene
348 foot] foote
depress] depresse
349 shalt, fair Salome, command] shalt
faire *Salome* commaund
350 royal] royall
351 weakness] weaknes
Arabia's] *Arabias*
352 kingdom] kingdome
353 Obodas'] *Obodas*
354 thinks not aught] thinkes not
ought
will.] will?
355 thou, rare creature, Asia's] thou rare
creature. *Asias*
356 it: Obodas'] It: *Obodas*
358 yields] yeelds
359 bosom] bosome
361 whom I go] home I goe
362 Palestine] *Palastine*
363 less] lesse
show] shew,
364 Go] Goe
tomb] toome
365 think] thinke
367 shrink] shrinke
368 do] doe
earth's] earths
369 methinks] me thinkes
wolf] wolfe
talk.] talke,
370 Begone, Silleus. Who] Be gone
Silleus, who
371 walk;] walke,
372 I'll] Ile
quarrel] quarrell
373 command] commaund
374 despite] despight

ACT I, SCENE 6

Sc. head. *Primus. Scena*] primus: Soena
376 most!] most?
377 stranger's] straungers
379 grief] griefe
380 here] heere
381 knows] knowes
been] bin
chief] chiefe
382 do] doe
appear] appeare
384 fair] faire
386 than] then
thyself dost] thy selfe doest
388 Judea's] *Iudeas*
390 me] mee
392 virtuous] vertuous
394 seek] seeke
chaste] chast
chastely] chastly
396 virtuous] vertuous
crowns] crownes
husband's] husbands
397 this uprear thy low] this, vpreare
thy lowe
398 requital beg] requitall begge
399 hapless fate,] haples fate?
400 thankless] thankles
wife?] wife.
402 ago] agoe
fall'n] falne
low] lowe
403 sons of Babas] sonnes of *Baba*
dead;] dead,
404 dost] doest
405 exercis'd] exercisde
406 choler keep] choller keepe
banks] bankes
407 advis'd] advisde
408 upbraided] vpbraided,
thanks] thankes
409 prithee, Salome, dismiss] prethy *Sa-*
lome dismisse
410 dost] doest
413 me] mee
414 Nay,] Nay
416 defy] defie

417 hour] hower
418 jealousy] Iealousie
deep] deepe
419 do mean] doe meane
420 sleep] sleepe
421 transformed] trãsform'd
422 battles] battels
423 wear] weare
424 topsy-turvèd] topsie turued
425 beasts [swim]] beastes, swine
426 burn downwards] burne
downewards
427 winter's] Winters
summer's] Summers
428 thistles grow] Thistels growe
briars] Briers
429 spin or sew] Spinne or Sowe
430 water-bearing] Waters-bearing
433 talk] talke
436 last,] last
437 witness] witnesse
sins] sinnes
438 witness] witnesse
dark] darke
439 witness] witnesse
witness] witnesse
440 Ark] Arke
441 witness] witnesse
witness] witnesse
442 witness David's city] witnesse
Dauids Citie
444 part.] part,
445 Moses,] *Moses*
446 work] worke
447 firstborn] first-borne
448 sign] signe
eat] eate
lamb] Lambe
449 fourteen] foureteene
years] yeeres
450 been] beene
451 will,] will
453 mean] meane
precedent] president
454 instead] in stead
455 fear] feare
457 Silleus'] *Silleus*

459 discuss] discusse
460 gains] gaines
bliss;] blisse,
461 ago] agoe
464 break] breake
vow] vowd
466 certain] certaine
467 soon] soone
469 ill,] ill
470 than now abhorr'd] then now
abhord
472 Farewell,] Farewell
sin] sinne
473 prophesying] prophecying
474 do] doe
begin] beginne
475 than] then
476 Herod's] *Herods*
been] bene
478 been] bene
them,] them
479 hour] houre
480 fatal] fatall
482 Anthonius'] *Anthonius*
die] dye
484 been] beene
485 peril] perill
486 all—] all.
487 sweet-fac'd Mariam,] sweet fac'd
Mariam
488 back,] backe
489 been] bene
spilt,] spilt.
490 work] worke
wrack] wracke
491 yield] yeeld
492 been near] bene neere
s.d. *[Exit.] added to 1613 text*
493 minds] mindes
wholly] wholy
494 only] onely
good,] good:
496 leap] leape
497–9 *indentation added*
497 find] finde
498 mind] minde
stanza break added after 498

499 do] doe
attain] attaine
500 fain] faine
honour leap] honor lep
501 [If] mean] Of meane
do in honour gain] doe in honor gaine
503 add] ad
506 cheerful] chreefull
508 vain] vaine
509 mind] minde
bind] binde
510 Th'other] T'hother
mind] minde
511 variety] varietie
sign] signe
grief] griefe
513 relief] reliefe
514 Nay,] Nay
loss of bliss] losse of blis
515 only] onely
516 settled] setled
517 wish'd] wisht
518 variety] varietie
519 be] bee
520 soon] soone
521 feed] feede
522 property] propertie,
breed] breede
523 again] againe
524 again] againe
525 disdain] disdaine
526 knows] knowes
527 looks] lookes
honour sour] honor sower

ACT 2, SCENE 1
Sc. head. *Scena*] Scoena
1 true,] true
draws nigh] drawes nye
2 Wherein] Wherin
3 long-desired] long desired
6 hour] houre
vain] vaine
7 liberty] libertie
8 self my own again] selfe my owne
againe
9 love, fair maid,] loue faire Mayd

10 moisture] moysture
12 [monarchal] brother's] monachall
Brothers
13 pluck'd] pluckt
14 fair Graphina's palm] faire *Graphinas*
Palme
tied] tide
15 hateful] hatefull
17 easy] easie
18 another's ear] anothers eare
19 choice,] choise
20 solemnly] solembly
swear] sweare
22 What] What?
niece] Neece
princess born?] Princesse borne:
23 Near blood's] Neere bloods
toy,] toy.
24 [us] *inserted*
kindred's scorn] kindreds scorne
26 realm's] Realms
kingdom's mate?] Kingdomes mate,
27 Withal] Withall
28 wish'd] wisht
than] then
Judea's] *Iudeas*
29 skilful] skilfull
30 Mariam's] *Mariams*
31 remove;] remoue.
32 lawful] lawfull
displace.] displace,
34 kingdom's] Kingdomes
35 well-known happiness] well knowne
happinesse
36 meant] ment
37 been] bene
equal] equall
love's host] loues hoast
38 Mariam's] *Mariams*
39 judgments] iudgements
40 Graphina's] *Graphinas*
cheeks] cheekes
41 not, fair] not faire
42 sign] signe
44 hour] hower
45 not,] not
46 feet] feete

47 enrapt] inwrapt
grief] griefe
nigh.] nie,
48 meet] meete
49 fear] feare
50 speak] speake
51 bear] beare
52 spite] spight
break] breake
54 Pheroras' mind.] *Pheroras* minde,
56 find] finde
58 eminency] eminencie
59 handmaid] hand-maid
60 do] doe
62 weak a vassal] weake a vassaile
constrain] constraine
63 yield] yeeld
will;] will,
best,] best
64 princess] Princesse
disdain;] disdaine,
65 study] studie
66 maid?] maide:
67 study still,] studie still
know,] know
have.] haue,
68 weighed] waide
69 study] studie
boot] boote
70 handmaid's] hand-maides
72 than] then
73 study] studie
74 recompense] recompence
75 style] stile
76 show] shew
far-fetch'd] far-fetcht
77 believe] beleeve
Herod's] *Herods*
78 prince-born beauty-famèd] Prince-
borne beautie famed
79 nearer] neerer
than thou, fair virgin,] then thou faire
virgin
81 Herod's] *Herods*
sepulchre] sepulcher
82 And entertain] And entertaine
again,] againe:

83 nuptial] nuptiall
84 hinder'd] hindred
pain] paine
85 Come, fair] Come faire
go] goe
86 wish-endearèd] wish-indeered

ACT 2, SCENE 2

Sc. head. *Scena*] *Soena*
Sc. head. *Babas' Sons*] *Babus Sonnes.*
Sp. name Babas' First Son] *Babus.* 1.
Sonne.
87 Now,] Now
friend,] friend
88 lives,] liues
89 yourself] your selfe
91 six years,] sixe yeares
92 tyrant's] tyrants
93 cruel Herod's] cruell *Herods*
94 scorn] scorne
fear] feare
95 recompense] recompence
96 poor] poore
thanks] thankes
97 feet] feete
98 requital] requitall
99 Oh,] Oh
friendship,] friendship
youth!] youth,
100 "debt"] det
101 amity is tied] amitie is tide
104 banish'd] banisht
109 bounteous] bountious
111 pattern] patterne
112 Jesse's son] *Iesses* Sonne
113 sovereign's nor father's hate]
Soueraignes nor fathers hate,
114 fix'd] fixt
virtue] vertue
116 [needs]] need
117 tomb] tombe
118 Herod's] *Herods*
overlong] ouer long
119 mind] minde
120 quick buried;] quicke buried,
purchas'd] purchast
121 years ago] yeares a goe

confin'd,] confinde.
123 life,] life
years] yeares
125 overpass'd in fears] operpast in
 feares
128 sons of Babas] sonnes of *Babus*
129 excel] excell
Sp. name Babas' Second Son] *Babus* 2.
 Sonne.
131 hateful cuckoo been] hatefull cuckoe
 beene
133 ourselves unseen] our selues vnseene
134 cross'd] crost
135 fix'd] fixt
cruel eye] cruell eye,
136 faces,] faces
sway'd] swaide
137 forc'd] forst
138 than] then
139 you,] you
friend,] friend
fall'n] falne
140 we,] we
pillars] pillers
141 clean depress'd] cleane deprest
142 ready] readie
concealment] concealement
143 you, fair lord,] you faire Lord
dangerless] daungerlesse
144 sons of Babas] Sonnes of *Baba*
rigour] rigor
145 baseness] basenes
oppress] oppresse
Sp. name Babas' First Son] *Ba.* 1. *Sonne.*
147 fear] feare
Herod's death] *Herods* death,
149 mind] minde
152 peril to myself] perill to my selfe
[fear]] leare
153 days] daies
154 Herod's] *Herods*
hear] heare
155 What,] What
coward,] coward
156 beginn'st] beginst
doubt] doubt,
Sp. name Babas' First] *Babus.* 1.

157 brother's] brothers
158 heart] hart
out] out:
159 keen falchion] keene fauchion
you,] you
lord,] Lord
161 tied] tide
gratitude.] gratitude
162 ill;] ill,
163 grieve,] grieue
164 dissented] discented
speaker's will.] speakers will,
165 fear] feare
166 me;] me,
167 father's son.] fathers sonne,
168 unnecessary] vnnecessarie
169 think] thinke
Anthonius'] *Anthonius*
170 bosom] bosome
unbruis'd?] vnbrusde:
171 Then, Caesar,] Then *Cæsar*
172 far abus'd] farre abusde
Sp. name Babas' Second Son] *Babus.* 2.
 Sonne.
173 Constabarus,] *Constab:*
175 amiss] amisse
177 years] yeares
I,] I
178 father's] fathers
179 months] monthes
[lie]] liue
180 Hebrews' cruelty] *Hebrewes* crueltie
spare.] spare,
182 mark] marke
ears to hear,] eares to heare.
183 Octavius,] *Octauious*
184 Julius'] *Iulions*
appear] appeare
185 Methought] Me thought
mildness] mildnes
186 sweetness] sweetnes
looks] lookes
187 Withal] Withall
commix'd] commixt
majestic] maiesticke
188 [phys'nomy]] Phismony
190 ear] eare

192 choler] choller
dispense] dispence
193 than] then
194 been] bin
195 false] false,
198 Concealment] Concealement
avail] auaile
199 certain 'tis] certaine t'is
200 fail] faile
202 ourselves] our selues
cowardice] cowardise:
203 pitiful] pittifull
204 pity] pittie
Sp. name Babas' First Son] *Babus first*
sonne.
205 yield] yeeld
necessity I yield;] necessitie I yeeld,
206 engage] ingage
arm] arme
207 again] againe
kingdom wield] kingdome weeld
208 alarm] alarme
Sp. name Babas' Second Son] *Babus*
second sonne.
211 soul] soule
212 soul] soule
than] then
213 fear go seek a dastard's] feare goe
seeke a dastards
214 undaunted] vndanted
breast] brest
s.d. *[Exeunt.]] added to 1613 text*

ACT 2, SCENE 3
Sc. head. *Secundus*] 2.
Sc. head. *Scena Tertia.*] Scoena 3.
215 [You] royal buildings,] Your royall
buildings
lofty] loftie
216 [stoop]] scope
217 humility] humilitie
218 seen] seene
219 trumpets' haughty] Trumpets
haughtie
220 sour] sow'r
taste,] taste:
222 I, fair city,] I faire Citie

223 Mariam's] *Mariams*
cheek] cheeke
224 glory, and] glory. And
225 town to seek] Towne to seeke
226 sense] sence
wrong,] wrong.
227 thee,] thee
birth,] birth
228 poor] poore
229 born,] borne
fear] feare
230 father's door!] Fathers doore.
231 Herod's] *Herods*
son] Sonne
232 hapless Doris Herod's] haples *Doris,*
Herods
233 kingdom won] kingdome wonne
235 fair] faire
queen] Queene
236 Why,] Why
me,] me
monarch, tied] Monarch tide
237 lack] lake
seen] seene
238 years] yeeres
239 [oaths]] oath
pouring] powring
rain] raine
241 Doris'] *Doris*
obtain] obtaine
243 young] yong
born] borne
244 Herod's] *Herods*
245 ungrateful] vngratefull
scorn] scorne
246 Heaven's] Heauens
247 begg'd] begd
249 enact] inact
250 trophy] Trophee
252 wish'd] wisht
253 wish'd] wisht
254 whilom] whilome
fight.] fight
255 thee,] thee
boy,] Boy
257 Herod's royal] *Herods* royall
dignity] dignitie

258 Mariam's] *Mariams*
only] onely
259 remain] remaine
260 return] returne
Herod's] *Herods*
261 confirm'd. Perchance] confirmd,
  perchance
slain;] slaine.
262 attend.] attend,
263 he'll think] hee'll thinke
264 cruelty] crueltie
265 despise] dispise
266 do] doe
267 natural] naturall
268 cruel] cruell
269 cruelty] crueltie
be] bee
271 city] Citie
272 Herod's] *Herods*
certain] certaine
we] wee
273 subtle] subtill
274 Mariam's] *Mariams*
be] bee
275 poison's drink] poisons drinke
murderous] murtherous
276 skills] skils
277 Herod's] *Herods*
278 foul] foule
Mariam's] *Mariams*
280 revenge's] reuenges
face] face:
282 weakness] weakenesse
284 solitariness] solitarines
moan] mone
s.d. *[Exeunt] added to 1613 text*

ACT 2, SCENE 4
Sc. head. *Scena Quarta*] Scoena 4
285 met,] met
only] onely
286 wish'd] wisht
287 despite] despight
288 hear] heare
answer] answere
289 guess] gesse
291 profess] professe

292 vows] vowes
293 [exception]] expectation
294 Why, aught] Why? ought
[Salome];] *Salom,*
295 wielded] welded
296 arm] arme
scorn] scorne
298 vow's despite] vowes despight
299 Suck] Sucke
mistress] Mistris
300 again to do] againe to doe
301 prithee] prethee
quarrel] quarrell
302 find beginning; rail] finde beginning, raile
name,] name:
304 shame;] shame,
305 Do] Doe
Moses'] *Moses*
laws] Lawes
306 do] doe
despite] despight
309 aught] ought
310 name,] name:
313 pity] pitty
315 unsteady] vnsteady,
316 herself] her selfe
be] bee
317 gain;] gaine,
318 mind] minde
unconstancy] vnconstancie
run] runne
319 obtain] obtaine
320 won] wonne
322 known] knowne
323 go] goe
wind] winde
324 She] Shee
loves] loues,
own] owne
325 merely] meerly
sepulchre] sepulcher
326 fair] faire
foul] foule
327 outside] out-side
328 fill'd] fild
than] then

329 ready] readie
330 aim] aime
husband's] husbands
331 proofs] proofes
myself] my selfe
332 us] vs,
dote] doat
333 mouth,] mouth
334 poisons] poysons
335 Well, Hebrew,] Well *Hebrew*
337 then,] then
338 thanks] thankes
coward's hateful name] cowards hatefull
    name,
339 minds] mindes
342 battle] battaile
day,] day:
346 enamelèd] inameled
347 thee;] thee
348 fight,] fight:
coward's style] cowards stile
350 soul] soule
endure] indure
s.d. *[They fight.] added to 1613 text*
351 windows] windowes
352 show a horrid] shew a horred
phys'nomy] phisnomie
353 breathe] breath
methinks] me thinkes
355 heart] hart
356 list, a twelvemonth;] list a twelue
    month,
357 cheeks] cheekes
paleness climb] palenes clime
358 thyself] thy selfe
359 fight?] fight,
360 keep] keepe
361 resign] resigne
362 soul] soule
abhor] abhorre
364 fear] feare
365 loss] losse
blood] blood,
367 remains] remaines
369 blood's stead] bloods stead,
entertains] entertaines
370 Salome's] *Salomes*

fear] feare
371 Oh,] Oh
soul] soule
prophesy] prophesie
373 Salome,] *Salome*
divine,] diuine
374 than] then
misery] miserie
375 I'll breathe] Ile breath
will;] will,
376 hateless] hateles
Ay, ay] I, I
377 Pity thyself,] Pittie thy selfe
378 Intrude] Intru'd
heart] hart
379 Alas,] Alas
fear] feare
381 thou,] thou
382 leg] legge
383 only] onely
soon] soone
384 fair Salom's] faire *Saloms*
385 less than mortal] lesse then mortall
fear] feare
386 quick recovery find] quicke re-
    couerie finde
387 bear] beare
388 mind] minde
389 Thanks,] Thankes
courteous] courtious
390 Stern enmity] Sterne enmitie
391 engag'd] engagde
393 tied [too] fast] tide so fast,
395 employ'd] imploy'd
397 bosom] bosome
398 in] in,
399 do] doe
400 loss] losse
fear] feare
s.d. *[Exeunt.] added to 1613 text*
401 hear] heare
ears] eares
402 spoils] spoiles
sense] sence
403 human error,] humane error
404 enemy] enemie
405 heady] heddy

408 sense] sence
409 Besides,] Besides
410 weigh] way
ear] eare
413 ears] eares
good] good,
414 ourselves do] our selues doe
be] bee
415 drown] drowne
416 partiality] partialitie
417 pass'd] past
419 us,] vs
420 Herod's] *Herods*
421 bate] bate,
423 not,] not
multitude] multitude,
424 Do carry] Doe carrie
425 weak uncertain] weake vncertaine
426 Herod's] *Herods*
429 think] thinke
peril] perill
432 pawn] pawne
lives] liues,
433 news] newes
Herod's death] *Herods* death,
435 do] doe

ACT 3, SCENE 1
Sc. head. *Tertius. Scena*] tertius: Scoena
Sc. head. *Pheroras.*] *Pheroras:*
2 hours] howers
3 do] doe
think a sister's] thinke a sisters
can make] cane mak
4 decree] decree,
soon] soone
5 Poor] Poore
6 honour happiness] honour, hap-
pines
7 been] bene
felicity] felicitie,
8 equal] equall
seiz'd] seasde
10 happy or displeas'd] happie or dis-
pleasde
11 beauty] beautie
12 mean] meane

mind] minde
13 natural defects—] naturall defects,
14 find] finde
15 loveliness] louelines
ear] eare
18 looks] lookes
wisdom's] wisedomes
19 fair] faire
20 Knows] Knowes
beauty] beautie
21 today] to day
22 than] then
23 beauty.] beautie,
24 ill] ill,
good,] good
25 wisdom] wisedome
26 bars] bares
30 hasty steps] hastie steppes
31 sacrificer,] sacrificer
32 news] newes

ACT 3, SCENE 2
Sc. head. *Scena Secunda*] Scoena 2
33 lips] lippes
son] sonne
peaceful] peacefull
bless'd] blest
34 ear] eare
35 breast] brest
36 speak] speake
fear] feare
37 news] newes
38 thankful] thankfull
40 rejoice] reioyce
41 certain] certaine
42 brothers] brother's
44 royal] royall
45 he,] he
style than] stile then
46 hour] houre
47 back] backe
49 death] death,
rack] racke
50 conceal it] conceale it,
s.d. *[Exit.]* added to *1613* text
51 appear] appeare
52 ear] eare

53 happiness] happinesse
56 lose it, losing] loose it, loosing
57 Joy,] Ioy
Constabarus] *Constan:*
slain] slaine
58 Grieve, soul] Grieue soule
ta'en] tane
59 Smile, cheeks] Smile cheekes
fair] faire
60 Weep,] Weepe
61 Well,] Well
moans. On] mones, on
62 I'll] Ile
win] winne
King's] Kings
64 ne'er the less] nere the lesse
67 herbs] Hearbs
68 sack'd] sackt
69 [not]] no
task] taske
more] more,
70 Constabarus] *Consta:*
71 sons of Babas] sonnes of *Baba*
72 than Constabarus] then *Consta:*
73 [we]] he
Herod's] *Herods*
74 [our] brother's foe,] his brothers
foe:
76 loath] loth
Constabarus] *Consta:*
go] goe
77 Believe] Beleeue
I'll go] Ile goe
hence] hence,
78 Herod's ear] *Herods* eare
80 Do mean] Doe meane
81 Constabarus' quick] *Constabarus*
quicke
82 find] finde
84 behind] behinde
85 First, jealousy—] First Iealousie,
avail] auaile
fear—] feare
86 Shall be] Shalbe
work] worke
87 Herod's ear] *Herods* eare
90 Herod's fear] *Herods* feare

91 I'll] Ile
swear] sweare
climb] clime
92 seeks to poison] seekes to poyson
93 scorn] scorne
95 choler] choller
96 watch'd] watcht
sleight] slite
97 scandal] scandall
98 Turn] Turne
fountains, Herod's] fountaines, *Herods*
99 Pheroras' suit] *Pheroras* suite
100 business] businesse
101 keep] keepe
103 Silleus'] *Silleus*
lord,] Lord?
104 do bear] doe beare
Sp. name Silleus'] *Silleus*
105 Constabarus'] *Constabarus*
107 hateful] hatefull
108 hateful arm] hatefull arme
110 again] againe
mortal harm] mortall harme
Sp. name Silleus'] *Silleus*
111 sign] signe
appear] appeare
112 peril seen] perill seene
113 He bids] Hee bides
fear] feare
114 Arabia's queen] *Arabias* Queene
115 Silleus'] *Silleus*
116 him] him,
brother's sudden coming now] brothers
suddaine comming now:
117 foot no room to walk] foote no
roome to walke
118 night,] night

ACT 3, SCENE 3

Sc. head. *Actus Tertius. Scena Tertia.*] Actus
3. Scoena 3.
119 news] newes
120 blue] blew
122 so,] so
hope,] hope
123 Herod—] *Herod.*
Sp. name [*Mariam*]] *added*

124 What,] What
forest] forrest
125 back] backe
126 than e'er] then ere
127 ruin] ruine
128 city] Citie
129 disgraceful] disgracefull
131 impatient,] impatient
mild] milde
132 again] againe
soon] soone
bred.] bred:
133 reconcil'd] reconcilde
134 solemn vows] solemne vowes
forsworn] forsworne
135 break] breake
vows] vowes
I'll] Ile
break] breake
137 speak] speake
vain] vaine
speak] speake
139 queen] Queene
143 Reject] Reiect,
mock] mocke
144 Scorn] Scorne
counsel] counsell
146 speak] speake
147 fear] feare
fair] faire
148 woeful] wofull
herself] her selfe
149 issue's] issues
be] bee
150 affability is won] affabilitie is wonne
151 turn again] turne againe
152 hypocrite] hypcorite
153 complain] complaine
154 do mourn] doe mourne
lives,] liues
155 believ'd] beleeu'd
157 curtain's drawn] Curtaine's drawne
158 appear again] appeare againe
160 horrid] horred
look] looke
161 fear] feare
scorn] scorne

162 scorn] scorne
fear] feare
brook] brooke
163 enchain] inchaine
165 scorn my look] scorne my looke
166 speech than] speech, then
167 vain] vaine
wind] winde
168 vain] vaine
Herod's] *Herods*
169 vain] vaine
combin'd] combinde
171 Oh,] Oh
172 grief] griefe
173 fair] faire
174 sorrows yields] sorrowes yeelds
relief] reliefe
175 commandress] commandresse
176 safety] safetie
179 unpitied be] vnpittied bee
180 me] mee
181 Poor guiltless queen! Oh,] Poore
   guiltles Queene. Oh
183 Mariam's] *Mariams*
184 endanger] indanger
desert] desart
185 O'er] O're
186 fatal] fatall
unsteadily] vnstedily
187 discoverèd] discoured,
188 down] downe
190 been as certain] bene as certaine
191 marks withal] markes withall
192 matchless wife—] matchles wife.
193 Alexander's] *Alexanders*
194 regal dignity;] regall dignitie.
sovereign] soueraigne
195 yielded] yeelded
196 city, David's Tower—] citie, *Dauids*
   Tower.
197 than] then
198 cruelty?] crueltie:
199 death] death,
Herod's to neglect;] *Herods* to neglect,
200 do] doe
contrary] contrarie
201 Yet, life, I quit] Yet life I quite

202 think] thinke
employ'd] imploi'd
204 than] then
destroy'd] destroi'd
205 well, chaste queen] well chast
Queene
206 darkness] darknes
207 sun] sunne
still, nay more,] still. Nay more
be] bee
209 eyes'] eyes
majesty keeps] maiestie keepes
210 wings] winges
211 law;] lawe,
213 soul] soule
214 Mariam's] *Mariams*
216 keep] keepe
spotless] spotles
217 suspicion] suspition
218 herself] her selfe
220 self] selfe
be] bee
221 spacious] spatious
walk] walke
222 go] goe
223 forbear alone] forbeare alone,
224 overthrow] ouerthrowe
225 thankworthy] thanke-worthy,
226 lawful] lawfull
honour's] honours
227 rear] reare
228 than] then
229 ear] eare
230 live,] liue.
231 chaste] chast
232 kills] killes
233 do] doe
234 Do] Doe
wholly] wholy
235 body,] body
236 that,] that
others' prey] others pray
237 own] owne
238 known] knowne
239 usurps] vsurpes
another's] anothers
240 seeks] seekes

public] publike
grac'd] grac't
242 chaste] chast
243 find] finde
244 body than] body, then
mind] minde
245 mind,] mind
246 seeks] seekes
show,] show:
247 ears] eares
248 pureness] purenes
249 had] had,
250 Been] Beene
fear] feare

ACT 4, SCENE I
Sc. head. *Quartus. Scena*] quartus: Scoena
1 Hail, happy city, happy] Haile happie
citie, happie
3 happy] happie
4 s.d. [*Enter Nuntio.*] *displaced from end of
line 5 to line 4*
5 [How?] *added to the end of line*
6 well,] well
7 brow,] browe
8 day's dark] daies darke
appear,] appeare.
9 dim] dimme
10 Oh, haste] Oh hast
steps,] steps
12 cheer] cheere
14 Methinks] Me thinkes
David's days] *Dauids* daies
15 hours] houres
increas'd] increast
16 Deep] Deepe
Joshua-like,] *Iosua*like
stays] staies
17 runs] runnes
18 sight] sight,
months] months,
days of weeks] daies of weekes
19 hour] hower
than gone] then gon.
20 seeks] seekes
21 world-commanding city, Europe's]
world commanding citie, *Europes*

22 survey'd] suruai'd
23 seen] seene
statue-fillèd] statue filled
24 grief] griefe
been betray'd] bene betrai'd
26 seen] seene
shows] showes
prepare;] prepare,
27 excell'd] exceld
29 fair] faire
Caesar's] *Caesars*
30 world's commanding mistress]
    worlds commaunding Mistresse
32 Yet, Mariam,] Yet *Mariam* :
33 little while,] little, while
eyes,] eyes
34 compass'd] compast
38 Lest sudden] Least suddaine
sense] sence
40 Who's there?] Whose there,
than happy] then happie
41 Pheroras. Welcome, brother.]
    Pheroras, welcome Brother,
42 while] while,

ACT 4, SCENE 2

Sc. head. *Scena*] Scoena
43 safety wait] safetie waite
45 Rome-commanding Caesar] *Rome*
    commanding *Caesar*;
46 honours] honors
47 heart] hart
48 struck] strooke
Herod's] *Herods*
52 kind] kinde
honourable] honorable
53 hapless hour] haples houre
self-stricken] selfe striken
54 father's] fathers
55 suit] sute
thee,] thee
56 Than] Then
harlot's] harlots
58 womb] wombe
59 Herod's] *Herods*
60 burial time] buriall time,
bridal hour] bridall houre

61 joyful] ioyfull
62 news] newes
sour] soure
63 Phasaelus'] *Phasaelus*
stain] staine
64 Pheroras'] *Pheroras*
65 yourself] your selfe
maintain] maintaine,
66 honour] honor
than I,] then I.
67 love's] loues
68 Mariam's] *Mariams*
70 fair] faire
71 than] then
72 Constabarus,] *Constabarus*
your] you
73 sons of Babas] sonnes of *Baba*
bliss] blisse
75 Go] Goe
76 traitors feel] traytors feele
fears] feares
77 beg] begge
78 I'll be deaf] Ile be deafe
tears] teares
79 is,] is
lord,] Lord
Salome divorc'd] *Salom* diuorst
81 enforc'd] inforst,
83 s.d. *[Exit Pheroras.]* added
84 Thee,] Thee
Mariam—Salom, I mean.] *Mariam.*
    Salom. I meane
85 steal] steale
86 wean] weane
s.d. *Exit.*, omitted

ACT 4, SCENE 3

Sc. head. *Quartus. Scena Tertia.*] 4.
    Scoena 3.
87 here] heere
met,] met
88 best] best,
dearest half] deerest halfe
ails my dear] ailes my deare
89 dost] doest
90 dusky habits] Duskey habits,
clear] cleare

91 mind] minde
92 cheerful] cheerfull
find] finde
96 speak] speake
97 Jewry's queen] *Iuries* Queene
Herod's] *Herods*
98 commandress] Commandres
sovereign] Soueraigne
101 think Judea's] thinke *Iudæas*
bound] bound,
103 empress] Empresse
104 win] winne
105 I'll rob] Ile robbe
David's sepulchre] *Dauids* sepulcher
107 all] all,
110 do] doe
112 brother's] brothers
113 wish'd] wisht
114 been] bene
tied] tide
116 grandsire] Grandsyre
died] dide
117 believe no oaths to clear] beleeue no
oathes to cleere
118 sworn] sworne
120 scorn] scorne
121 Hircanus] *Hercanus*
122 long-settled honour] long setled
honor
wear] weare
123 doom] doome
124 realm] Realme
peril] perill
fear] feare
125 Mariam's] *Mariams*
do] doe
126 one] one:
127 kingdom's] Kingdomes
128 ne'er expell'd Hircanus'] nere expeld
Hercanus
129 *missing line*
131 infamy] infamie
enroll] inrole:
132 hearty] heartie
133 show] shew
134 restore,] restore?
136 been] bene

before?] before.
137 that,] that
importunity] importunitie
139 speak, unless] speake, vnles
believ'd] beleeu'd
140 humour] humor
do] doe
142 think] thinke
terms] termes
143 smile,] smile
do] doe
146 look] looke
147 heav'n,] heau'n
vex] vexe
148 will] wil
149 fix'd] fixt
peevishness] peeuishnes
150 slightest] sleightest
than] then
151 yourself] your selfe
152 find] finde
153 look] looke
154 again] againe
bind] binde
157 belied;] belide,
158 signs] signes

ACT 4, SCENE 4
Sc. head. *Quartus. Scena Quarta.*]
4. Scoena 4.
159 drink] drinke
160 queen] Queene
161 I? Some hateful practice] I: some
hatefull practise
162 than] then
163 s.d. *[to the Butler] added to 1613 text*
Confess] Confesse
truth,] truth
instrument] instrument,
164 outrageous] outragious
[poison]] passion
166 Which,] Which
do conceal,] doe conceale
167 less] lesse
168 seize] cease
169 lord, I guess] Lord I gesse,
171 Go,] Goe

172 speak] speake
173 villain] villaine
falsify] falsifie
174 own] owne
175 do] doe
falsehood] falshood
devil,] Diuill
176 enchantress] Inchantres
Oh,] Oh
foul] foule
177 hyssop] Ysop
cleanse thee,] clense thee
evil] euill
178 beauteous] beautious
soul.] soule,
179 Sohemus,] *Sohemus*
180 been true,] bene true:
183 black] blacke
184 add a murder] adde a murther
185 'twere] t'were
186 I'll] Ile
realm] Realme
187 I] *missing except in copy D*
beggar poor] begger poore
188 know—] know.
189 Foul] Foule
rind] rinde,
190 cedar] Caedar
Oh,] Oh
191 mind] minde
192 impurity] impuritie
194 says] saies
195 Oh,] Oh
coals expel] coales expell
196 Herod's bosom] *Herods* bosome
glow?] glowe:
197 plain] plaine
denial] deniall
198 trial] triall
199 thyself] thy selfe
stain] staine
200 perfection?] perfection:
201 do] doe
plain] plaine
202 be] bee
203 oh,] oh
itself] it selfe

204 chaste] chast
205 down] downe
206 wheel] wheele
plac'd] plast
207 Herod's] *Herods*
208 son] sonne
styl'd] stilde
209 half] halfe
210 think] thinke
defiled] defilde
211 o'er] ore
212 darkness] darknes
be] bee
213 live, fair fiend,] liue faire fiend
214 [heav'nly]] heauy
cozen'dst me] cousnedst mee
215 despite] despight
216 despite] dispight
218 loss] losse
219 seen] seene
face;] face,
220 could'st] coul'dst
stars] stares
eyes] eyes?
221 foul disgrace?] foule disgrace:
222 before,] before
223 I'm] I'me
224 wisdom] wisedome
ago a-wand'ring] agoe a wandring
225 face, encount'ring] face incountring
226 freedom] freedome
227 heart,] heart
228 guiltless] guliltles
slain] slaine
229 [lock]] looke
230 usurper's] vsurpers
stain] staine
232 have,] haue
royal] royall
233 do] doe
Mariam. [*Exit Butler.*] They] *Mariam,* they
234 s.d. [*Enter Soldiers.*] added
235 Here,] Here
back, come back] backe, come backe
236 meant] ment
237 Jewry] *Iury*

black] blacke
238 white?] white.
239 Why,] Why
carry her?] carrie her:
Sp. name Soldier] *Sould:*
bade] bad
240 death,] death
241 Why,] Wie
mad.] mad,
242 feel the fury] feele the furie
243 Oh,] Oh
grief returns] griefe returnes
244 pulls me piecemeal] pulles me
   peecemeale
do] doe
245 love] boue
246 hate] hate,
247 bear] beare
and, Hebrew,] and *Hebrew*
248 Seize] Seaze
lion's paws] Lyons pawes
lamb] lam
249 flock] flocke
die.] die,
250 am,] am.
251 than most. Away] then most, away
252 bear] beare
prison,] prison
253 gone indeed? Stay, villains,] gon indeed, stay villaines
254 looks] lookes
sovereign's] Soueraignes
255 Well,] Well
go] goe
die;] die,
256 think] thinke
meant] ment
257 certain] certaine
258 s.d. *[Exeunt.]* added

ACT 4, SCENE 5
Sc. head. *Quartus. Scena Quinta.*]
   4. Scoena 5.
259 Foul villain] Foule villaine
pitchy-coloured soul] pitchie coloured
   soule
260 ear to hear] eare to heare

causeless doom,] caules doome?
261 enforce] inforce
control] controule
262 tomb?] toome.
263 Oh, Salome,] Oh *Salome*
thyself repaid] thy selfe repaid,
265 queen betray'd] queene betraid
266 heart] hart
falsehood won] false-hood wonne
269 hateful] hatefull
271 sin] sinne
cry] crie
273 angel notary] Angell notarie
274 down] downe
brass] brasse
275 Oh,] Oh
276 means thyself] meanes thy selfe
277 soul] soule
well;] well,

ACT 4, SCENE 6
Sc. head. *Quartus. Scena Sexta.*]
   4. Scoena 6.
Sc. head. *Babas' Sons*] Babus Sonnes
279 death;] death,
281 yield] yeeld
282 only] onely
climb] clime
Sp. name Babas' First Son] *Babus 1.*
   Sonne
283 myself resign] my selfe resigne
284 grief] griefe
286 dearly] dearely
288 style] stile
289 mechanic traffic] mechanicke
   traffique
291 needless compliment return] need-
   lesse complement returne
292 [This]] Tis
ceremony] ceremonie
293 burn] burne
296 been] bene
297 hateful mind] hatefull minde
298 [her] nuptial] your nuptiall
299 Therefore, fair] Therefore faire
unborn] vnborne
300 subtlety devis'd] subtiltie deuisde

be] bee
301 Whereby] Were by
guiltless,] guiltles
torn.] torne,
302 me,] mee.
303 weakly] weakely
304 duties;] duties,
die] die:
305 friends'] friends
306 compell'd] compeld
necessity] necessitie
307 farewell, fair city] farewell faire citie
308 beauty] beautie
309 Farewell,] Farewell
311 crew] crue
313 yourselves] your selues
Mariam's] Mariams
bereave;] bereaue,
314 commonwealth] common-wealth
innocency] innocencie
315 human] humane
316 tigers, lionesses] Tygers, Lyonesses
bears] Beares
317 Tear-massacring hyenas] Teare mas-
sacring *Hienas*
nay,] nay
318 prey do] pray doe
feignèd tears] fained teares
319 weep] weepe,
cross] crosse
320 human] humane
321 heav'n] heaue'n
322 do keep] doe keepe
angels'] Angels
323 beautified] beautifide
324 heav'n-depriving] heau'n depriuing
325 sins of [man]] sinnes of many
326 been] bene
328 stay'd] staid
330 today] to day
cause] cause,
331 deeply hate;] deply hate,
332 wreck] wreake
laws] lawes
333 [Your] best] You best,
vain] vaine
335 train] traine

336 [she]] he
337 sottishness] sottishnesse
bewail] bewaile
338 do] doe
enhance] inhance
339 'Twere] T'were
human] humane
fail] faile
340 Than] Then
mischief multiplied] mischiefe
multiplide
341 Cham's] *Chams*
sex] sexe
343 do] doe
344 wills] willes
346 wickedness indued] wickednesse
indude
350 than] then
than devils] then diuels
Sp. name Babas' Second Son] *Babus
second sonne*
351 Come,] come
bless'd] blest
352 freedom] freedome
353 trouble-quiet] trouble quiet
354 vow,] vow
355 forever lead] for ever leade
356 venture] venter
devilish] diuellish

ACT 4, SCENE 7

Sc. head. *Quartus. Scena Septima.*]
4. Scoena 7.
357 Die,] Die
you? That] you, that
358 means. The means! Methinks]
meanes. The meanes! Me thinks
359 find a means to murder] finde a
meanes to murther
withal] withall
361 Why,] Why?
362 Think] Thinke
you?] you:
363 skin] skinne
365 take] take,
366 weaponless] weaponlesse
367 answer,] answere

368 Mariam's skin] *Mariams* skinne
falchions] fanchions
370 do] doe
371 Why, drown] Why drowne
Indeed,] Indeed
device.] deuice,
372 Why,] Why?
turn] turne
373 than do] then doe
beauty prejudice,] beautie preiudice?
374 source?] sourse.
376 Judea's] Iudeas
fertile] firtill
377 devour] deuoure
'Twill] T'will
be] bee
379 murder] murther
383 I'm] I'me
cannot;] cannot,
try] trie
385 Why,] Why
slain] slaine
387 You'll find] Youle finde
means] meanes
again] againe
389 ay] I
s.d. *[Exit.] added to 1613 text*
What,] What
gone,] gone?
390 overthrown?] ouerthrowne:
391 What,] What?
heart's] hearts
392 pass] passe
cruel] cruell
grown!] growne?
s.d. *[Re-enter Salome.] added*
394 soon] soone?
395 creature's] creatures
sun] Sunne
396 sky] skie
moon?] Moone.
397 sun and moon] Sunne and Moone
399 seen] seene
400 mark] marke
Ay,] I
402 soul] soule
excel] excell

403 die] dye
bush—] bush,
404 mark'd] markt
405 fair] faire
406 foul dishonours] foule dishonors
409 fault,] fault
ask,] aske:
410 none.] none,
411 back] backe
task] taske
412 known] knowne
414 bind] binde
415 kings;] Kings,
416 Troy-flaming Helen's] *Troy* flaming
        Helens
fairly shin'd] fairely shinde
417 lays] layes
418 do] doe
shun a bait] shune a baite
419 speak] speake
420 Mariam's] *Mariams*
421 Oh, do] Oh doe
do] doe
422 In sooth] Insooth
been hair] beene haire
423 do excel] doe excell
424 fair] faire
425 speak] speake
427 'twas] t'was
heard;] heard,
I'll] Ile
428 world-amazing] world amazing
429 beauteous] beautious
431 sin] sinne
432 do] doe
433 she's] shee's
434 stranger's ear] strangers eare
436 enchant] inchant
hear] heare
437 deaf] deafe
438 assign'd] assignde
439 deafness] deafenes
eyes?] eyes,
440 murderer] murtherer
deaf and blind] deafe and blinde
441 stars] starres
442 either] eyther

Mariam's] *Mariams*
443 wars] warres
444 soul] soule
445 speak] speake
move;] moue,
447 world's] worlds
448 human] humane
449 heaven's model die,] heauens mod-
ell dye?
450 self-portraiture] selfe-portraiture
drew?] drewe:
451 stars] starres
sky] skie
453 doting] doating
queen.] Queen,
454 ebon-hued] ebon hewde
confess] confesse
455 star] starre
been] beene
seldom seen.] seldome seene,
456 speak] speake
less] lesse
457 Yourself] Your selfe
here] heere
458 shape] shape:
459 near] neere
460 Myself] My selfe
ta'en] tane
461 beauty: go] beautie: goe
ways] waies
462 blackamoor] Blackamore
463 equal Mariam's] equall *Mariams*
464 poor] poore
465 stay'd] staide
467 buy;] buy,
468 countermand] countermaund
469 you'll] youle
pass'd] past
470 Sohemus' love] *Sohemus* loue,
forgot?] forgot:
473 Sohemus—] *Sohemus*:
474 curs'd] curst
475 coz'ning] cousning
shows and proofs] showes, and proofes
477 king,] king
478 Mariam's beauty seen,] *Mariams*
beautie seene:

479 Hittite] *Hittits*
480 been a queen] bene a Queene
481 son,] sonne
482 change,] change:
483 been stay'd again;] bene staid agen,
485 seen my Mariam's] seene my
Mariams
486 Jew] *Iewe*
walk'd] walkt
487 beauteous virtue] beautious vertue
stay'd] staid
489 avails it all?] auailes it all:
weight] waight
490 deceitful] deceitfull
vanity] vanitie
491 Oh,] Oh
492 train] traine
hapless] haples
misery] miserie
493 hapless] haples
been train'd] bene trainde,
494 endless] endles
495 Methinks] Me thinkes
discern] discerne
feign'd;] fainde,
496 human] humane
daz'd by woman's] dazde by womans
498 do] doe
499 forever] for ever
thee,] thee
sweet,] sweet?
500 leave?] leaue.
502 I'll] Ile
death;] death,
503 break] breake
505 face;] face,
506 long-heal'd wound] long heal'd
wound,
508 A shameful] A shamefull
a shameful] a shamefull
509 Oh,] Oh
call'd to mind] cald to minde
anew] anew, *B, C, E, F, G, M, Dyce, Wo,
Eton, NY, EC, Ho, N, Hu, Fo*
a new, *A, D, Y, BP*
510 Mariam's] *Mariams*
heart] hart

511 foul-mouth'd] foule mouth'd
513 black tormentor,] blacke tormenter
514 unsecure,] vnsecure:
515 Mariam's] *Mariams*
517 I'll] Ile
518 guiltless] guiltles
519 heart] hart
520 heavy as revenge;] heauie as reuenge,
521 Methinks] Me thinkes
522 hideous] hiddious
bosom] bosome
523 weighs] waies
go] goe
524 sleep] sleepe
s.d. *[Exit.] added to 1613 text*

ACT 4, SCENE 8
Sc. head. *Quartus. Scena Octaua.*]
  4. Scoena 8.
526 needs] needes
527 Ay] I
beauty] beautie
528 countermand] countermaund
529 as well] aswell
530 cheek] cheeke
roses] roses,
cheek less bright,] cheeke lesse bright:
531 excel] excell
532 As soon] Assoone
533 myself] my selfe
myself conspir'd] my selfe conspirde
534 plot, no adversary] plot: no
  aduersarie
535 Herod's] *Herods*
retir'd] retirde
537 queen] Queene
538 gain,] gaine:
539 sleights] slights
prove,] proue:
540 obtain] obtaine
542 deceit] deceit:
543 Herod's mind] *Herods* minde
544 less than] lesse then
546 beauty's goddess, Paphos' queen,]
  beauties Goddesse *Paphos* Queene
ta'en] tane
547 Julius'] *Iulius*

548 Anthonius' bane,] *Anthonius* bane.
549 Egypt's] *Egipts*
born] borne
551 scorn] scorne
552 Mariam's] *Mariams*
554 pawn] pawne
556 Herod's] *Herods*
drawn] drawne
557 now,] now
558 drawn] drawne
drawn from me,] drawne from me:
559 humility been grac'd] humilitie bene
  grac'te
560 fair] faire
561 think] thinke
562 virtue] vertue
woman] woman,
563 sex] sexe
564 humility and chastity] humilitie and
  chastitie
565 equal] equall
hand.] hand,
566 one,] one
seen] seene
568 sour] sower
570 soul] Soule
adversary's power.] aduersaries power.)
573 dust,] dust:
earth;] earth,
574 Sara's] *Saraes*
575 Ay, heav'n—] I heau'n,
beauty] beautie
576 soul is black] soule is blacke
sin] sinne
577 year] yeare
579 poor] poore
pursue,] pursue?
580 despair?] dispaire:
581 untrue?] vntrue,
582 fair] faire
fair.] faire.
584 Herod, Herod's lawful] *Herod:*
  Herods lawfull
586 robb'd] rob'd
587 adult'ry?] adultry:
588 match'd] matcht
592 beauteous babes,] beautious babes

him?] him:
593 riches,] riches:
youth?] youth,
594 stain] staine
Doris'] *Doris*
595 Oh,] Oh
me,] me
know] knowe
596 Doris' foe?] *Doris* foe.
597 years] yeares
598 ground,] ground:
599 dregs] dreggs
601 drink it: Doris' curse] drinke it:
    Doris curse,
602 thyself] thy selfe
604 Oh, Doris,] Oh Doris
605 heart] hart
608 guiltless] guiltles
610 poison's] poisons
steep'd] steept
611 answer] answere
612 employ'd] imployd
613 Hear] Heare
[Gerizim]] *Gerarim*
615 arm,] arme:
617 baseborn] baseborne
618 unlawful] vnlawfull
619 sense] sence
621 nearest] neerest
622 suspicious] suspitious
623 And,] And
do] doe
627 Now, earth,] Now earth
young] yong
628 methinks] me thinks
known] knowne
629 human] humane
life] life,
630 scorning] scorniug
injury] iniurie
632 adversary's] aduersaries
633 truly said] truely sed
634 win] winne
heart than] heart, then
635 enemy do find] enemie doe finde
636 yield] yeeld

637 metal] mettall
mind] minde
638 honour won] honor wonne
640 wrestle] wrastle
worthless] worthles
641 yield;] yeeld,
642 yield] yeeld
poor] poore
643 task'd] task't
power] power,
seld,] seld
644 lion] Lyon
loudest roar] lowdest roare
645 Truth's school] Truths schoole
certain] certaine
646 High-heartedness] High hartednes
647 virtuous scorn:] vertuous scorne,
648 scorn] scorne
duty overlong] dutie ouer-long
649 scorn] scorne
650 scorn] scorne
scorn to do a wrong,] scorne to doe a
    wrong.
651 scorn to bear an injury in mind]
    scorne to beare an iniurie in minde
652 scorn a freeborn] scorne a free-
    borne
slavelike] slaue-like
bind] binde
654 kind] kinde
655 Do] Doe
fury] furie
656 prevail] preuaile
mind] minde
657 be] bee
658 Then] Than
far than he] farre then hee
659 unpaid] vnpaide
660 She] Shee
661 been] bene
sway'd.] swaide
662 fix] fixe
injury] iniurie
663 virtuous] vertuous
been] bene
664 been] bene

ACT 5, SCENE 1

Sc. head. *Scena*] Scoena
1 far] farre
2 self,] selfe:
3 [your]] her
4 beauty, chastity] beautie? Chastitie
wit?] wit,
5 hapless] haples
fatal place] fatall place,
6 queen t' choose?] Queene t'chuse,
7 certain] certaine
ill-boding] ill boding
8 cull'd] culd
luckless news] luckles newes
9 new] new,
10 him,] him
't had] t'had
been] bene
11 do] doe
view] vew
12 guiltless] guiltles
13 here] heere
14 joy!] ioy.
15 repel] repell
16 Oh, do] Oh doe
17 prithee] prethy
19 tongue's] tongues
20 welcome] welcome,
grief] griefe
21 troop] troope
23 heart] hart
stoop] stoope
24 sun-admiring phoenix'] Sunne admiring *Phœnix*
26 fear] feare
27 look] looke
seem to keep] seeme to keepe
28 bear] beare
29 usurp] vsurpe
30 Mariam's] *Mariams*
31 speak] speake
34 queen] Queene
bewail] bewaile
36 rail] raile
37 stopp'd] stopt
38 [darken]] darke

39 epithet affords] *Epithite* affords,
40 than] then
world's] worlds
41 She] Shee
45 pickthank devil!] picke-thanke
Diuell.
47 story—] storie
48 infamy, I'll] infamy ile
49 answer] answere
50 answer] answere
look'd] lookt
52 smil'd, a dutiful] smilde, a dutifull
scornful,] scornefull
53 look] looke
do call;] doe call,
54 been] bene
withal] withall
55 [Go on. [*sp. name*] Nuntio]] *Nun.*
Go on,
unmov'd,] vnmou'd
56 arrival] arriuall
57 habit] habite
cheerful] cheefull
58 moist] moyst,
Mariam's] *Mariams*
60 pick'd] pickt
crew] crue
61 beckon'd] beckned
call'd] cald
63 What,] What
65 fair] faire
66 ear?] eare:
67 "Tell] Tell
lord,"] Lord,
she—] she.
Me, meant she me?] Mee, ment she mee?
69 mad,] made
lord] Lord,
be] bee
71 she said] she sed
73 "Tell] Tell
breath."] breath.
74 Oh] Oh,
control] controule
75 "If guiltily, eternal] If guiltily
eternall

death"—] death,
76 chaste] chast
soul] soule
77 "By] By
days hence,] daies hence
78 himself] himselfe
alive."] aliue.
79 days] daies
hours] houres
80 divided;] diuided,
81 penitency] penitencie
82 wish'd] wisht
83 Why,] Why
84 prayer had said,] praier had sed:
86 soul] soule
87 remain] remaine
88 dead?] dead,
89 trick] tricke
again] againe
91 Why,] Why
methinks] me thinkes
art] art,
92 ways of cure;] waies of cure,
done] don:
94 not, my lord,] not my Lord
idly] idlely
95 seen] seene
97 entomb'd] intomb'd
years] yeares
been] bene
98 again to slaughter'd] againe to
  slaughtred
99 ears—] eares,
100 moan] mone
101 fears] feares
102 fear] feare
Mariam's] Mariams
104 Mariam's death,] Mariams death
tree] tree,
105 neck] necke
106 be] bee
108 fearful voice [he] cried aloud] fear-
  full voyce she cride alowd
109 "Go] Goe
tried] tride
110 causeless died."] causeles dide.
112 meant] ment

poison's] poisons
113 crown] Crowne
114 herself] her selfe
115 Oh,] Oh
me,] me
116 needs] needes
be] bee
119 jewel] Iewell
121 myself as cruel] my selfe as cruell
122 blow myself] blowe my selfe
123 bless'd] blest
124 dazzl'd] dazled
rest,] rest:
125 precious] pretious
wondrous] wonderous
126 than my crown] then my Crowne
127 laid] laide
folded] foulded
128 sudden] suddaine
down,] downe.
129 pash'd] pasht
pieces] peeces
foe] foe,
130 robb'd] robd
131 us'd] usde
132 Herod's] *Herods*
self] selfe
cross'd] crost
133 graceful moiety;] gracefull moytie,
accurs'd] accurst
134 half] halfe
135 dead,] dead
136 perplexity a while;] perplexitie a
  while,
137 dress'd] drest
138 methinks] me thinkes
139 be] bee
140 certain] certaine
he] hee
141 Why,] Why
go] goe
142 habit] habite
143 frown o'ershade] frowne oreshade
145 She'll] Sheel
weeds] weedes
sense] sence
146 attir'd] attirde

147 Remember,] Remember
yourself] your selfe
149 She's] Shee's
fair] faire
150 Oh,] Oh
151 whiteness] whitenes
snow impair] snowe impaire
154 beauty] beautie
155 pair as here] paire as heere
157 been] bene
158 been] bene
159 Oh,] Oh
I,] I:
160 died] dide
161 But, Salome,] But *Salome*
vex] vexe
162 thyself outmatchèd] thy selfe out-
matched
sex] sexe
163 sex's] sexes
164 imperial crown] imperiall crowne
165 you,] you
fool,] foole
push'd] pusht
166 pull'd] puld
down] downe
167 hers—nay] hers: Nay
much—a look] much a : looke
168 you.] you,
169 Judea,] *Iudea*
brook] brooke
170 robb'd] robd
172 matchless] matchles
173 grasp] graspe
174 aim] ayme
cruel sovereign's head?] cruell
Soueraignes head.
175 Oh,] Oh
think] thinke
176 Palestine,] *Palestine:*
177 bring:] bring,
178 overthrown] ouerthrowne
royal] royall
179 veins] vaines
181 won;] wonne,
182 Oh,] Oh
been liv'd] bene li'ud

184 think] thinke
185 Foul sacrilege] Foule sacriledge
187 villain] Villaine
188 cruel] cruell
another's hand;] anothers hand,
189 word,] word
sword,] sword
190 Hircanus'] *Hircanus*
[died]] did
command—] command.
191 dear] deare
192 bed.] bed,
193 you, sun,] you sun
clear] cleare
194 again] againe
Mariam's] *Mariams*
195 Egyptian blowse] Egiptian blows
196 dowdy] doudy
197 was—] was,
brows?—] brows,
198 Jewry's fair and spotless] *Iuries* faire
and spotles
199 Deny] Denie
beams, and, moon,] beames, and *Moone*
200 stars be dark] starres be darke
Jewry's] *Iuries*
202 bosom] bosome
203 idolaters,] Idolaters
204 Maintain] Maintaine
orbs] orbes
205 apiece] a peece
206 steadfast] stedfast
207 be] bee
209 yield] yeeld
me] mee
210 Mariam's gone] *Mariams* gon
211 feign] faine *A, D, F, G, Dyce, Wo, Y,
Ho, N*
          fame *B, C, E, M, Eton, NY, EC,
BP, Hu, Fo*
Saturn] Saturne
212 sour] sowre
mood] moode
213 feign] faine *A, D, F, G, Dyce, Wo, Y,
Ho, N*
          fame *B, C, E, M, Eton, NY, EC,
BP, Hu, Fo*

214 needs] needes
seek] seeke
216 fair a lass] faire a lasse
217 Leda's beauty] *Lædaes* beautie
218 half so fair] halfe so faire
219 deem] deeme
been slain;] bene slaine,
220 stick] sticke
221 gain] gaine
222 physic's] Physicks
empiric;] Empericke.
223 queen] Queene
storm] storme
beauty's sake;] beauties sake,
224 wit;] wit,
225 night's] nights
angry grief] angrie griefe
226 chaste] chast
227 But, oh,] But oh
pass'd] past
228 property] propertie
229 timeless] timeles
230 rejoic'd] reioyc'd
griev'd,] grieu'd
231 goddess] Goddesse
waste] wast
232 beauty] beautie
233 surpass'd] surpast
234 Mariam's] *Mariams*
235 void of sense;] voyd of sence,
236 Greeks] Greekes
dream] dreame
239 been] bene
Egyptian black] Egiptian blacke
240 fair] faire
been] bene
liv'd] liude
241 beauty] beautie
back] backe
242 drown'd] drownde
deriv'd] deriude
243 beauty] beautie
think] thinke
244 chastity] chastitie
245 link] linke,
246 excel] excell
247 I'll] Ile

myself in endless] my selfe in endles
249 thyself,] thy selfe
than he] then hee
250 brother's blood.] brothers blood,
251 den enclosèd be] denne inclosed bee
252 tears] teares
may'st] maist
253 drown] drowne
happy] happie
254 find] finde
grave;] graue,
255 vault someone] vault, some one
256 have,] haue.
257 contain:] containe,
258 *Here*] *Heere*
slain] *slaine*
s.d. *[Exit.]* added to *1613 text*
259 Whoever] Who ever
260 only] onely
261 deceiv'd,] deceiu'd?
262 today] to day
safety lay!] safetie lay?
263 certainty bereave] certaintie bereue
264 six hours] sixe houres
266 Jews] *Iewes*
267 Salom's] *Saloms*
270 Babas' sons for safety] *Babus* sonnes
for safetie
271 Tonight] To night
remain] remaine
272 guiltless] guiltles
273 divorc'd and slain] diuorst and
slaine
274 sons of Babas] sonnes of *Baba*
death,] death.
276 suit] sute
278 Mariam's] *Mariams*
281 again,] againe
humours] humors
282 knows her chaste] knowes her chast
283 wisdom] wisedome
delay'd] delaide
285 betray'd] betraide
287 strangely, lunaticly] strangely lu-
natickly
288 Mariam's] *Mariams*
289 day's] daies

ordain'd] ordainde

290 posterity] posteritie

291 contain'd] containde

292 admirably] admirablie

variety] varietie

293 Hebrews] *Hebrewes*

294 school of wisdom] schoole of
wisedome

SELECTED BIBLIOGRAPHY

WORKS BY, OR POSSIBLY BY, ELIZABETH CARY (FALKLAND)

Du Perron, Jacques Davy. *The Reply of the Most Illustrious Cardinall of Perron, to the Answeare of the Most Excellent King of Great Britaine.* Translated by Elizabeth Cary Falkland. Douay: Martin Bogard, 1630.

[Falkland, Elizabeth Cary?]. *The History of the Life, Reign, and Death of Edward II. King of England, and Lord of Ireland. With the Rise and Fall of his Great Favourites, Gaveston and the Spencers. Written by E.F. in the year 1627. And printed verbatim from the Original.* London: J.C. for Charles Harper, Samuel Crouch, and Thomas Fox, 1680. (We have consulted copies of this folio in the British Library and Yale's Beinecke Library.)

—————. *The History of the Most Unfortunate Prince King Edward II. With Choice Political Observations on Him and his Unhappy Favourites, Gaveston & Spencer. Containing some rare passages of those Times, not found in other historians. Found among the papers of, and (supposed to be) Writ by the Right Honourable Henry Viscount Faulkland, Sometime Lord Deputy of Ireland.* London: A.G. and J.P. for J. Playford, 1680. This shorter octavo version was included in *The Harleian Miscellany: or a Collection of Scarce, Curious, and Entertaining Pamphlets and Tracts.* Vol. 1. London: Printed for T. Osborne, 1744, 66–91. It was reprinted and edited in 1808 by J. Malham and reprinted yet again by AMS Press, New York, 1965.

—————. *The Tragedie of Mariam, the Faire Queene of Jewry.* London: Thomas Creede for Richard Hawkins, 1613.

—————. *The Tragedy of Mariam.* Facsimile of the original 1613 edition, with introduction and list of textual variants, by A. C. Dunstan and W. W. Greg. Malone Society Reprints. London: printed for the Malone Society by Horace Hart at the Oxford University Press, 1914. (The first issue of this reprint was later supplemented by an unbound six-page pamphlet. References to Dunstan and Greg include this supplementary material.) The 1992 reprint of this edition contains "A Supplement to the Introduction," by Marta Straznicky and Richard Rowland; it provides details of the six pages Dunstan and Greg added to the first issue of 1914.

BIOGRAPHICAL MATERIAL ON THE CARY-FALKLAND FAMILY
(ASTERISKS INDICATE TEXTS THAT FOCUS CHIEFLY ON ELIZABETH CARY)

Aubrey, John. "Lucius Cary: Viscount Falkland." In Aubrey's *Brief Lives*, edited by Oliver Lawson Dick. London: Secker and Warburg, 1949. Reprint. Ann Arbor: Univ. of Michigan Press, 1957, 55–57.

Blain, Virginia, Patricia Clements, and Isobel Grundy, eds. *The Feminist Companion to Literature in English: Women Writers from the Middle Ages to the Present.* New Haven: Yale Univ. Press, 1990, 186 and 354.

Calendar of State Papers, Domestic Series . . . Preserved in the State Paper Department of the Public Record Office (various dates and editors); and *Calendar of State Papers Relating to Ireland . . . in the Public Record Office* (various dates and editors; copies consulted are in the British Library, London).

Clarendon, Edward Hyde, earl of. Sections on Lucius Cary in *The History of the Rebellion and Civil Wars in England Begun in the Year 1641* (edited by W. Dunn Macray, Oxford, 1888) and *The Life of Edward Earl of Clarendon, Lord High Chancellor of England . . . in Which is Included A Continuation of his History of the Grand Rebellion. Written by Himself* (Oxford, 1827). Both biographies of Cary (which are quite hostile to his mother, Elizabeth Cary Falkland) are usefully reprinted in *Clarendon: Selections from The History of the Rebellion and The Life by Himself.* Edited by G. Huehns. Oxford: Oxford Univ. Press, 1978.

C., G. E. [George E. Cokayne]. *The Complete Peerage of England, Scotland, Ireland, Great Britain and the United Kingdom Extant, Extinct or Dormant.* New ed., revised and enlarged. Edited by Vicary Gibbs and H. A. Doubleday. London: The St. Catherine Press, 1910–59.

Dictionary of National Biography. Founded by George Smith. Edited by Sir Leslie Stephen and Sir Sidney Lee. Reissue. New York: Oxford Univ. Press, 1917. (Articles on Lawrence Tanfield, Henry Cary, Viscount of Falkland, and Lucius Cary.)

Duncon, John, ed. *A Letter Conteining Many Remarkable Passages in the Most Holy Life & Death of the Late Lady, Letice, Vi-Countess Falkland.* Written to the Lady Morison at Great Tew in Oxfordshire. London: Rich. Royston, 1648.

*Fullerton, Lady Georgiana Charlotte. *The Life of Elisabeth Lady Falkland 1585–1639.* Quarterly Series, vol. 43. London: Burns & Oates, 1883. Relies heavily on the daughter's *Life*, but usefully reprints letters by and about Elizabeth Cary.

[Harrison, Fairfax]. *The Devon Carys.* 2 vols. New York: privately printed by the De Vinne Press, 1920.

*The Lady Falkland: Her Life. Edited by Richard Simpson. London: Catholic Publishing and Bookselling Co., 1861. (The Appendix reprints a number of important letters by and about Elizabeth Cary.)

Longueville, T. Falklands. London: Longmans, Green and Co., 1897.

Marriott, John Arthur Ransome. The Life and Times of Lucius Cary, Viscount Falkland. New York: G. P. Putnam's Sons, 1907.

*Murdock, Kenneth. The Sun at Noon: Three Biographical Sketches. New York: Macmillan, 1939. The sketches are of Elizabeth Cary (relies heavily on the Life), her son Lucius Cary, and John Wilmot, the earl of Rochester.

Nichols, John G., ed. The Herald and Genealogist. 8 vols. London: John Bowyer Nichols and Sons, 1863–74.

Weber, Kurt. Lucius Cary, Second Viscount Falkland. New York: Columbia Univ. Press, 1940. Reprint. New York: AMS Press, 1967. Discusses Lucius's life with particular emphasis on his intellectual and theological leanings, is generally unfriendly toward his mother, and includes an appendix on Patrick Cary.

CRITICAL DISCUSSIONS OF THE LADY FALKLAND: HER LIFE, BY ONE OF CARY'S DAUGHTERS

Beilin, Elaine. "Elizabeth Cary and The Tragedie of Mariam." Papers on Language and Literature 16, no. 1 (Winter 1980): 45–64.

————. Redeeming Eve: Women Writers of the English Renaissance. Princeton: Princeton Univ. Press, 1987, 157–58.

Foster, Donald. "Resurrecting the Author: Elizabeth Tanfield Cary." Forthcoming in Privileging Gender in Early Modern England, edited by Jean Brink. In Sixteenth-Century Essays and Studies. Kirksville, Mo.: Sixteenth-Century Journal Publishers.

Stauffer, Donald. English Biography before 1700. Cambridge: Harvard Univ. Press, 1930, 148–50.

Weller, Barry. "The Narrated and Narrating Subject of Biography: The Life of Elizabeth Cary, Lady Falkland." Paper presented at the 1992 Modern Language Association Convention.

REFERENCES TO ELIZABETH CARY AS A WOMAN OF LETTERS IN CONTEMPORARY TEXTS

Dedications in: Richard Belling, Arcadia, Book 6, London, 1624; Michael Drayton, Englands Heroicall Epistles, London, 1597, and in 2d ed. of Englands Helicon, London, 1614; also Sir John Davies, The Muses Sacrifice, London, 1612, in The Complete Works of John Davies of Hereford, edited by Alexander B. Grosart, vol. 2. London: Chatto and Windus, 1876. Reprint. New York: AMS Press, Inc., 1967. In addition, the prefatory material to William Basse's Polyhymnia— a collection which was unpublished during Basse's lifetime and which included poems written between 1613 and 1653—contains two sonnets "to the Lady

Viscountess Falkland, upon her going into Ireland" (hence ca. 1620); one sonnet is reprinted in *Poetical Works*, edited by R. W. Bond, 155–56. London: Ellis
and Elvey (Chiswick Press), 1893.
Hierarchomachia, or The Anti-Bishop (ca. 1629–30). Edited by Suzanne Gossett.
Bucknell, Pa.: Bucknell Univ. Press, 1982. In this Catholic play, Cary is
evidently referred to admiringly as a writer under the name "Falconia"; see
lines 2010–13.
Hogrefe, Pearl. *Tudor Women: Commoners and Queens*. Ames: Iowa State Univ. Press,
1975, 135. Brief discussion of poets who wrote dedicatory verses to Cary both
before and after her marriage.

MODERN CRITICAL WORKS
TREATING CARY'S LIFE AND WRITINGS

Barish, Jonas. "Language for the Study; Language for the Stage." Chapter of a
forthcoming book on closet drama.
Beilin, Elaine. "Elizabeth Cary and *The Tragedie of Mariam*" (cited above).
————. *Redeeming Eve: Women Writers of the English Renaissance* (cited above). Ch. 6,
"The Making of a Female Hero: Joanna Lumley and Elizabeth Cary."
Berry, Boyd M. "'Move thy tongue, / For silence is a signe of discontent'; or,
What's Comic in *The Tragedy of Mariam?*" Paper presented in Oct. 1990 at the
Washington, D.C., Society for the Study of Women in the Renaissance.
Abstract published in *Women in the Renaissance: Newsletter Published by the New York
Society for the Study of Women in the Renaissance*. No. 1 (Winter 1992): 2.
Brashear, Lucy. "A Case for the Influence of Lady Cary's *Tragedy of Mariam* on
Shakespeare's *Othello*." *Shakespeare Newsletter* 26 (1976): 31.
Callaghan, Dympna. "Re-reading *The Tragedie of Mariam, the Faire Queene of Jewry*."
In *Woman, 'Race,' Writing in the Early Modern Period*, edited by Margo Hendricks and
Patricia Parker. Forthcoming from Routledge.
Ferguson, Margaret. "Running on With Almost Public Voice: The Case of
'E.C.'" In *Tradition and the Talents of Women*, edited by Florence Howe, 37–67.
Urbana: Univ. of Illinois Press, 1991.
————. "The Spectre of Resistance." In *Staging the Renaissance: Reinterpretations of
Elizabethan and Jacobean Drama*, edited by David Kastan and Peter Stallybrass,
235–50. New York: Routledge, 1991.
Fischer, Sandra K. "Elizabeth Cary and Tyranny, Domestic and Religious." In
*Silent But for the Word: Tudor Women as Patrons, Translators, and Writers of Religious
Works*, edited by Margaret P. Hannay, 225–37. Kent, Ohio: Kent State Univ.
Press, 1985.
Fitzmaurice, James. "Elizabeth Cary's *Mariam* and Jacobean Marriage."
Unpublished paper.
Foster, Donald. "Resurrecting the Author: Elizabeth Tanfield Cary"
(cited above).

Grundy, Isobel. "Falkland's *History of . . . King Edward II*," *Bodleian Library Record* 13, no. 1 (1988): 82–83.

Gutierrez, Nancy. "Valuing *Mariam*: Genre Study and Feminist Analysis." *Tulsa Studies in Women's Literature* 10 (Fall 1991): 233–51.

Holdsworth, R. V. "Middleton and *The Tragedy of Mariam*." *Notes and Queries* 231 (1986): 379–80.

Howard, Skiles. "The Nervy Limbs of Elizabeth Cary." Paper presented at the special session on "Renaissance Women" at the 1990 Shakespeare Association of America (SAA) meeting.

Kennedy, Gwynne. "In 'the Margent of Such a Story': Elizabeth Cary's Queen Isabel." Unpublished paper.

Krontiris, Tina. *Oppositional Voices: Women as Writers and Translators of Literature in the English Renaissance.* New York: Routledge, 1992. (Ch. 3 discusses Elizabeth Cary.)

————. "Style and Gender in Elizabeth Cary's *Edward II.*" In *The Renaissance Englishwoman in Print: Counterbalancing the Canon,* edited by Anne M. Haselkorn and Betty S. Travitsky, 137–56. Amherst: Univ. of Massachusetts Press, 1990.

Mahl, Mary R., and Helene Koon, eds. *The Female Spectator: English Women Writers Before 1800.* Bloomington: Indiana Univ. Press, 1977, 99–102.

Nelson, Karen Lynn. "Elizabeth Cary's *Edward II* and the Court of Charles I." Master's thesis, Univ. of Maryland, 1992.

Pearse, Nancy Cotton. "Elizabeth Cary, Renaissance Playwright." *Texas Studies in Literature and Language* 18 (1977): 601–8.

Slowe, Martha. "Speech Crimes in *The Tragedy of Mariam*." Paper presented at the special session on "Renaissance Women" at the 1990 SAA meeting.

Stauffer, Donald A. "A Deep and Sad Passion" (on *The History of the Life, Reign, and Death of Edward II*). In *Essays in Dramatic Literature: The Parrott Presentation Volume,* edited by Hardin Craig, 289–314. Princeton: Princeton Univ. Press, 1935.

Straznicky, Marta. "Re-writing the Source: The Work of Elizabeth Cary and Authoritative Female Discourse in the Renaissance." Paper presented at the special session on "Renaissance Women" at the 1990 SAA meeting.

Travitsky, Betty. "*The Feme Covert* in Elizabeth Cary's *Mariam*." In *Ambiguous Realities: Women in the Middle Ages and Renaissance,* edited by Carole Levin and Jeanie Watson, 184–96. Detroit: Wayne State Univ. Press, 1987.

————. "Husband-Murder and Petty Treason in English Renaissance Tragedy." *Renaissance Drama,* n.s. 21 (1990): 171–98.

————, ed. *The Paradise of Women.* Westport, Conn.: Greenwood Press, 1981, 209–12.

Weidemann, Heather. "Politics and the Subject in Elizabeth Cary's *Mariam*." Unpublished paper.

Woolf, D. R. "The True Date and Authorship of Henry, Viscount Falkland's *History of the Life, Reign and Death of King Edward II.*" *Bodleian Library Record* 12, no. 6 (1988): 440–53.

SELECTED CRITICISM ON RENAISSANCE WOMEN WRITERS
AND ON IDEOLOGIES OF GENDER

Arnold, Margaret. "Jane Lumley's *Iphigeneia:* Self-Revelation of a Renaissance Noblewoman to Her Audience." Paper presented at the special session on "Renaissance Women" at the 1990 SAA meeting.

Belsey, Catherine. *The Subject of Tragedy: Identity and Difference in Renaissance Drama.* London: Methuen, 1985.

Benson, Pamela. *The Invention of the Renaissance Woman: The Challenge of Female Independence in the Literature and Thought of Italy and England.* University Park, Pa.: Penn State Univ. Press, 1992.

Callaghan, Dympna. *Women and Gender in Renaissance Tragedy: A Study of "King Lear," "Othello," "The Duchess of Malfi" and "The White Devil."* Atlantic Highlands, N.J.: Humanities Press International, 1989.

Dolan, Frances E. *Dangerous Familiars: Representations of Domestic Crime in England, 1550–1700.* Ithaca: Cornell Univ. Press, forthcoming.

———. "'Gentlemen, I have one more thing to say': Women on scaffolds in England, 1563–1680." Forthcoming in *Modern Philology.*

Farrell, Kirby, Elizabeth H. Hageman, and Arthur F. Kinney, eds. *Women in the Renaissance: Essays Reprinted from "English Literary Renaissance."* Amherst: Univ. of Massachusetts Press, 1988. Elizabeth A. Hageman reviews recent studies of Cary and supplies a bibliography on 277–78, 294, and 301.

Ferguson, Margaret. "A Room Not Their Own: Renaissance Women as Readers and Writers." In *The Comparative Perspective on Literature,* edited by Clayton Koelb and Susan Noakes, 93–116. Ithaca: Cornell Univ. Press, 1988.

Fraser, Antonia. *The Weaker Vessel: Woman's Lot in Seventeenth-Century England.* New York: Knopf, 1984.

Goreau, Angeline, ed. *The Whole Duty of a Woman: Female Writers in Seventeenth Century England.* Garden City: Doubleday, 1985.

Hannay, Margaret P., ed. *Silent But for the Word: Tudor Women as Patrons, Translators, and Writers of Religious Works.* Kent, Ohio: Kent State Univ. Press, 1985.

Haselkorn, Anne M., and Betty S. Travitsky, eds. *The Renaissance Englishwoman in Print: Counterbalancing the Canon.* Amherst: Univ. of Massachusetts Press, 1990. Includes a bibliography by Elaine Beilin on Renaissance women writers.

Henderson, Katherine, and Barbara McManus, eds. *Half Humankind: Contexts and Texts of the Controversy about Women in England, 1540–1640.* Urbana: Univ. of Illinois Press, 1985.

Hull, Suzanne. *Chaste, Silent & Obedient: English Books for Women, 1475–1640.* San Marino: Huntington Library, 1984.

Jardine, Lisa. *Still Harping on Daughters: Women and Drama in the Age of Shakespeare.* Totowa, N.J.: Barnes and Noble, 1983.

Jones, Ann Rosalind. *The Currency of Eros: Women's Love Lyric in Europe, 1540–1620.* Bloomington: Indiana Univ. Press, 1990.

————. "Nets and Bridles: Early Modern Conduct Books and Sixteenth-Century Women's Lyrics." In *The Ideology of Conduct*, edited by Nancy Armstrong and Leonard Tennenhouse, 39–72. New York: Methuen, 1987.

————. "Surprising Fame: Renaissance Gender Ideologies in Women's Lyric." In *The Poetics of Gender*, edited by Nancy Miller. New York: Columbia Univ. Press, 1986.

Jordan, Constance. *Renaissance Feminism: Literary Texts and Political Models*. Ithaca: Cornell Univ. Press, 1990.

Klein, Joan Larson, ed. *Daughters, Wives, and Widows: Writings by Men about Women and Marriage in England, 1500–1640*. Urbana: Univ. of Illinois Press, 1992.

Lamb, Mary Ellen. "The Split Subject: Lady Anne Clifford as Seventeenth-Century Reader." Paper presented at the special session on "Renaissance Women" at the 1990 SAA meeting.

Lewalski, Barbara Kiefer. "Writing Women and Reading the Renaissance." *Renaissance Quarterly* 44 (1991).

————. *Writing Women in Jacobean England*. Cambridge: Harvard Univ. Press, 1993.

Mack, Phyllis. *A Fire in the Bosom: Gender and Spirituality in Seventeenth-Century England*. Berkeley: Univ. of California Press, 1991.

Maclean, Ian. *The Renaissance Notion of Woman*. Cambridge: Cambridge Univ. Press, 1980.

Marcus, Leah S. *Puzzling Shakespeare: Local Reading and Its Discontents*. Berkeley: Univ. of California Press, 1988.

Newman, Karen. *Fashioning Femininity and English Renaissance Drama*. Chicago: Univ. of Chicago Press, 1991.

Otton, Charlotte, ed. *English Women's Voices, 1540–1700*. Miami, Fla.: International Univ. Press, 1992.

Pasteur, Gail Kern. "Leaky Vessels: The Incontinent Women of City Comedy." *Renaissance Drama*, n.s. 18 (1987): 43–65.

Rogers, Katharine. *The Troublesome Helpmate: A History of Misogyny in Literature*. Seattle: Univ. of Washington Press, 1966.

Rose, Mary Beth. *The Expense of Spirit: Love and Sexuality in English Renaissance Drama*. Ithaca: Cornell Univ. Press, 1988.

————, ed. *Women in the Middle Ages and the Renaissance: Literary and Historical Perspectives*. Syracuse: Syracuse Univ. Press, 1986.

Smith, Hilda. *Reason's Disciples: Seventeenth-Century English Feminists*. Urbana: Univ. of Illinois Press, 1982.

Stallybrass, Peter. "Patriarchal Territories: The Body Enclosed." In *Rewriting the Renaissance*, edited by Margaret W. Ferguson, Maureen Quilligan, and Nancy Vickers, 123–42. Chicago: Univ. of Chicago Press, 1986.

Suzuki, Mihoko. "Transgression, Masquerade and Desire: Representing the Female Subject in Seventeenth-Century England." Paper presented at the special session on "Renaissance Women" at the 1990 SAA meeting.

Waller, Gary. "Struggling into Discourse: The Emergence of Renaissance Women's Writing." In *Silent But for the Word*, ed. Hannay (cited above), 225–37.

Warnicke, Retha. *Women of the English Renaissance and Reformation*. Westport, Conn.: Greenwood Press, 1983.

Wayne, Valerie, ed. *The Matter of Difference: Materialist Feminist Criticism of Shakespeare.* New York: Harvester Wheatsheaf, 1991.

Wilson, Katharina M., ed. *Women Writers of the Renaissance and Reformation.* Athens: Univ. of Georgia Press, 1987.

Woodbridge, Linda. *Women and the English Renaissance: Literature and the Nature of Womankind, 1540–1620.* Urbana: Univ. of Illinois Press, 1984.

JEWS IN TUDOR-STUART ENGLAND

Ben Gorion, Joseph [pseud.]. *A Compendious and Most Marveilous History of the Latter Tymes of the Jewes Commune Weale.* Trans. Peter Morwyn. 1575. London: J. Daye for R. Jugge, 1558. (Contains a narrative about Herod and Mariam.)

Cardozo, Jacob Lopes. *The Contemporary Jew in the Elizabethan Drama.* Amsterdam: H. J. Paris, 1925.

Fines, J. "'Judaising' in the Period of the English Reformation—the case of Robt. Bruern." *Transactions of the Jewish Historical Society of England* 21 (1968): 323–26.

Israel, Jonathan I. *European Jewry in the Age of Mercantilism. 1550–1750.* Oxford: Clarendon Press, 1985.

Katz, David S. *Philo-semitism and the Readmission of the Jews to England, 1603–1655.* Oxford: Clarendon Press, 1982.

Sisson, C. J. "A Colony of Jews in Shakespeare's London." *Essays and Studies* 22 (1937): 38–51.

Wolf, Lucien. "Jews in Elizabethan England." *Transactions of the Jewish Historical Society of England* 11 (1928): 1–91.

CATHOLICS IN TUDOR-STUART ENGLAND

Allison, Antony Francis, and D. M. Rogers. *A Catalogue of Catholic Books in English printed abroad or secretly in England, 1558–1640.* Bognor Regis, England: Arundel Press, 1956. Reprint. London: Dawson, 1964.

Bossy, John. "The Character of English Catholicism." *Past and Present* 21 (1962): 39–59.

———. *The English Catholic Community, 1570–1850.* London: Darton, Longman and Todd, 1975.

Clancy, Thomas H. *Papist Pamphleteers.* Chicago: Loyola Univ. Press, 1964.

Corns, Thomas N., ed. *The Literature of Controversy.* A special issue of *Prose Studies* 9 (1986). Reprint. London: F. Cass, 1987.

Corthell, Ronald J. "'The secrecy of man': Recusant Discourse and the Elizabethan Subject." *English Literary Renaissance* 19 (Autumn 1989): 272–90.

Edwards, Francis. *The Marvellous Chance: Thomas Howard, Fourth Duke of Norfolk, and the Ridolphi Plot.* London: Hart-Davis, 1968.

Flynn, Dennis. "Donne and the Ancient Catholic Nobility." *ELR* 19 (Autumn 1989): 305–23.

Haigh, Christopher. "From Monopoly to Minority: Catholicism in Early Modern England." *Transactions of the Royal Historical Society*, 5th series, 31 (1981): 129–47.

Hanson, Elizabeth. "Torture and Truth in Renaissance England." *Representations* 34 (Spring 1991): 53–84.

Harpsfield, Nicholas. *A Treatise on the Pretended Divorce between Henry VIII and Catharine of Aragon.* Camden Society, New Series 21. London: Nicholas Pocock, 1828. Reprint. New York: Johnson Reprint Corp., 1965.

Latz, Dorothy. *"Glow-Worm Light": Writings of Seventeenth-Century English Recusant Women from Original Manuscripts.* Salzburg Studies in English Literature. Salzburg: Institut für Anglistik und Amerikanistik, Universität Salzburg, 1989.

Milward, Peter. *Religious Controversies of the Elizabethan Age: A Survey of Printed Sources.* Lincoln: Univ. of Nebraska Press, 1977.

Pritchard, Arnold. *Catholic Loyalism in Elizabethan England.* Chapel Hill: Univ. of North Carolina Press, 1979.

Rowlands, Marie B. "Recusant Women 1560–1640." In *Women in English Society, 1500–1800*, edited by Mary Prior, 149–80. London: Methuen, 1985.

Sander[s], Nicolas. *De origine et progressu schismatis Anglicani* (1585). Translated by David Lewis as *The Rise and Growth of the Anglican Schism.* London: Burns & Oates, 1877.

Trevor-Roper, Hugh. *Catholics, Anglicans, and Puritans.* Chicago: Univ. of Chicago Press, 1987.

Warnicke, Retha M. *The Rise and Fall of Anne Boleyn: Family Politics at the Court of Henry VIII.* New York: Cambridge Univ. Press, 1989.

Willen, Diane. "Women and Religion in Early Modern England." In *Women in Reformation and Counter-Reformation Europe*, edited by Sherrin Marshall, 140–65. Bloomington: Indiana Univ. Press, 1989.

MATERIAL ON HISTORICAL AND BIBLICAL VERSIONS OF HEROD

Grant, Michael. *Herod the Great.* New York: American Heritage Press, 1971.

"Herod." In *The Interpreter's Bible*, edited by George Arthur Buttrick, 2:586–94. New York: Abingdon-Cokesbury Press, 1951–57.

Hoehner, Harold W. *Herod Antipas.* Cambridge: Cambridge Univ. Press, 1972.

Sandmel, Samuel. *Herod: Profile of a Tyrant.* Philadelphia: Lippincott, 1967.

CRITICAL WORKS ON SENECAN DRAMA
IN THE RENAISSANCE, LADY PEMBROKE'S CIRCLE,
AND THE HEROD AND MARIAM PLAYS

Barish, Jonas. "Language for the Study; Language for the Stage." Unpublished paper (cited above).

Braden, Gordon. *Renaissance Tragedy and the Senecan Tradition: Anger's Privilege.* New Haven: Yale Univ. Press, 1985.

Bushnell, Rebecca. *Tragedies of Tyrants: Political Thought and Theater in the English Renaissance.* Ithaca: Cornell Univ. Press, 1990.

Dunstan, Arthur Cyril. *Examination of Two English Dramas: "The Tragedy of Mariam" by Elizabeth Carew; and "The True Tragedy of Herod and Antipater: with the Death of Fair Mariam,"* by Gervase Markham, and William Sampson. Königsberg: Hartungsche Buchdruckerei, 1908.

Freer, Coburn. "Mary Sidney: Countess of Pembroke." In *Women Writers of the Renaissance and Reformation,* edited by Katharina M. Wilson, 481–90. Athens: Univ. of Georgia Press, 1987.

Jondorf, Gillian. *Robert Garnier and the Themes of Political Tragedy in the Sixteenth Century.* Cambridge: Cambridge Univ. Press, 1969, 29.

Lamb, Mary Ellen. *Gender and Authorship in the Sidney Circle.* Madison: Univ. of Wisconsin Press, 1990.

———. "The Myth of the Countess of Pembroke." *Yearbook of English Studies* 11 (1981): 194–202.

Landau, Marcus. *Die Dramen von Herodes und Mariamne.* Weimar: *Zeitschrift für Vergleichende Literaturgeschichte* 8 (1895–96): 175ff.

Valency, Maurice Jacques. *The Tragedies of Herod and Mariamne.* New York: Columbia Univ. Press, 1940.

Witherspoon, Alexander Maclaren. *The Influence of Robert Garnier on Elizabethan Drama.* New Haven: Yale Univ. Press, 1924. Reprint. Hamden, Conn.: Greenwood Press, 1968. See, especially, the last chapter, "The Failure of Lady Pembroke's Movement."

SOURCES OF, AND WORKS RELATED TO, *MARIAM*

Buchanan, George. *Baptistes, sive calumnia.* London: Thomas Vautrolleriles, 1577.

———. *Baptistes, sive calumnia.* In George Buchanan, *Tragedies,* edited and translated by P. Sharratt and P. G. Walsh. Edinburgh: Scottish Academic Press, 1983.

Daniel, Samuel. *The Tragedie of Cleopatra.* In *The Complete Works in Verse and Prose,* edited by Alexander B. Grosart, vol. 3. New York: Russell and Russell, 1963.

———. "A Letter from Octavia to Marcus Antonius" (1599). In Grosart, vol. 1.

Deimling, Hermann, ed. *The Chester Plays.* Early English Text Society, Extra Series, no. 62. London: Oxford Univ. Press, 1892. Reprint. 1926. See, especially, No. 10, "The Slaying of the Innocents," Part 1, 186–205.

Dolce, Lodovico. *Marianna, Tragedia.* Venice: Paulo Ugolino, 1593.

Garnier, Robert. *Marc Antoine.* Paris: R. Estienne, 1578.

Hardy, Alexandre. *Mariamne* in *Théâtre*, edited by Edmund Stengel, 2: 185–229. Paris and Marburg, 1884. Geneva: Slatkine Reprints, 1967. 2 vols. (An English translation is available in *More Plays by Rivals of Corneille and Racine*, translated and edited by Lacy Lockert. Nashville: Vanderbilt Univ. Press, 1968.)

Herod the Great: A Fourteenth Century Play. Translated from the Middle English and Adapted for Modern Performance by Cynthia Bourgeault. New York: The Seabury Press, 1974. (Combines the N-Town *The Magi* and the Chester *The Slaying of the Innocents.*)

Josephus. *The Jewish War* and *Antiquities of the Jews.* Translated by Thomas Lodge in *The Famous and Memorable Works of Josephus.* London: Peter Short, 1602. For a modern edition of Josephus's works, see the Loeb Classical Library's bilingual text. The source narratives for Mariam, from *Antiquities of the Jews*, book 15, are in vol. 8 of the Loeb *Josephus*, trans. Ralph Marcus; completed and edited by Allen Wikgren. Cambridge: Harvard Univ. Press, 1963.

Kolve, V. A. *The Play Called Corpus Christi.* Stanford: Stanford Univ. Press, 1966.

Lumley, Joanna [Jane], trans. *Iphigenia at Aulis* [by Euripides]. Edited by Harold H. Child. London: printed for the Malone Society by C. Whittingham and Co. at the Chiswick Press, 1909.

Sachs, Hans. *Tragedia mit 15 personen zu agirn, der Wütrich König Herodes, wie der sein drey sön und sein gmahel umbbracht. . . . In Bibliothek des Literrarischen Vereins* 136: 132–61. Stuttgart: 1878.

The Second Maiden's Tragedy. Edited by W. W. Greg. London: printed for the Malone Society by H. Hart at Oxford Univ. Press, 1909.

Sidney, Mary, countess of Pembroke. *The Countess of Pembroke's Antonie* (1592). Edited, and with introduction, by Alice Luce. "Literarhistorische Forschungen" series, vol. 3. Weimar: Emil Felber, 1897.

———. *Discourse of Life and Death. Written in French by Ph. Mornay. Antonius. A Tragedie written also in French by Ro. Garnier. Both done into English by the Countess of Pembroke.* London: printed for William Ponsonby, 1592.

BIBLIOGRAPHIC REFERENCES

Greg, W. W. *A Bibliography of the English Printed Drama to the Restoration.* London: printed for the Bibliographical Society at the Oxford University Press, 1939–59.

McKerrow, R. B. *An Introduction to Bibliography for Literary Students.* Oxford: at the Clarendon Press, 1927.

———. *A Dictionary of Printers and Booksellers in England, Scotland and Ireland, and of Foreign Printers of English Books 1557–1640.* London: printed for the Bibliographical Society by Blades, East & Blades, 1910.

Pollard, A. W., and G. R. Redgrave. *A Short-Title Catalogue of Books Printed in England, Scotland and Ireland and of English Books Printed Abroad, 1475–1640.* 2d edition revised and enlarged by W. A. Jackson, F. S. Ferguson, and Katharine F. Pantzer. London: The Bibliographical Society, 1986.

Wing, Donald. *A Short-Title Catalogue of Books Printed in England, Scotland, Ireland, Wales and British America and of English Books Printed in Other Countries, 1641–1700*. 3 vols. 2d ed. New York: Modern Language Association of America, 1982.

Designer:	Nola Burger
Compositor:	BookMasters, Inc.
Printer:	BookCrafters, Inc.
Binder:	BookCrafters, Inc.
Text:	12/14.5 Centaur
Display:	Centaur